THE ARMY

THE ARMY

Brigadier General Harold W. Nelson, USA (Ret)
Editor-in-Chief

Major General Bruce Jacobs, AUS (Ret)
Editor

Colonel Raymond K. Bluhm, Jr., USA (Ret)
Graphics Editor

THE ARMY HISTORICAL FOUNDATION
HUGH LAUTER LEVIN ASSOCIATES, INC.

The Army Historical Foundation

The Army Historical Foundation, a 501(c)(3) nonprofit charitable organization, was founded in 1983 by Generals Lyman Lemnitzer, Bruce Palmer, and Orwin Talbott, with the support of Secretary of the Army John Marsh and Army Chief of Staff Edward Meyer. The foundation's goal is to promote greater appreciation for the contributions that America's Army—Active, Reserve, and National Guard—has made to the nation in over 225 years of service. The motto of the Army Historical Foundation—"Preserve the Heritage, Educate the Future"—summarizes its mission. The foundation's top priority is the building of a national museum for the United States Army, America's oldest military service and the only branch of the American armed forces without its own national museum. The foundation also supports Army history by presenting annual Distinguished Writing Awards for outstanding books and articles on Army history; awarding small grants to museums within the Army museum to assist them with exhibits and programs; providing funds for acquisition and preservation of artifacts, books, and documents for the Army's collections; and sponsoring public historical education and research assistance programs.

Photo of actual 20th Maine battle flag as used at the Battle of Gettysburg, 2 July 1863. Discovered in the attic of the Maine statehouse, it was restored with funds raised by the Army Historical Foundation. (Maine State Museum)

The Army Historical Foundation
2425 Wilson Boulevard
Arlington, Virginia 22201
(703) 522-7901; fax (703) 522-7929
ArmyHstFnd@aol.com
http://www.ArmyHistoryFnd.org

Published by Hugh Lauter Levin Associates, Inc.
© 2001 The Army Historical Foundation
Design: Lori S. Malkin
Project Editor: James O. Muschett
ISBN 0-88363-101-6
Printed in Hong Kong
Distributed by Publishers Group West
http://www.HLLA. com

Contents

No Substitute for Victory
America's Army—Yesterday, Today, and Tomorrow

General Eric K. Shinseki, Chief of Staff, United States Army

Top: *Soldiers who walk in the lead of an advance are "on point" for their units. For more than 200 years the American soldier has been "on point" in this country's evolution from a loose confederation of thirteen colonies to a strong nation. ("This We'll Defend," Mort Künstler)*

Above: *The militia and the Continental Army constituted the first all-American Army. By the time the British army withdrew, the American Revolution had been won because of courage and doggedness of citizens-turned-soldier in the cause of independence. ("Charleston, 28 June 1776," H. Charles McBarron, Soldiers of the American Revolution series, Army Art Collection)*

The Army Vision is entitled, "Soldiers on Point for the Nation: Persuasive in Peace, Invincible in War." When we think about our Army's role in fulfilling the expectations of the American people, that Vision can be used to give us important perspectives on a large, complex organization. The first word is **soldiers**—a reminder that people must always come first if our Army is to succeed. Every day in the Army we do two things. We train soldiers and we grow them into leaders. During most of our history, those soldiers have all been volunteers, as they are today. Soldiers are the center-piece of our formations, and our nation has always honored those who serve. This book is about soldiers and their contributions to the nation. It reminds us that those who serve today carry on a proud tradition.

This book also reminds us that our soldiers have always been **on point for the nation**. "On point" has special meaning for soldiers. Soldiers who walk in the lead position as platoons advance are "on point." They must be well trained and attuned to everything in their environment if they are to act appropriately. They must be fully aware of the intent and needs of their leaders if they are to process information correctly. Just as the individual walking point must demonstrate those qualities if the platoon is to be successful, the entire Army must act collectively to perform the same function for our country in the national security environment. This book reminds us that our nation—and its Army—have faced many challenges together, from surprise attacks to maintaining readiness in peacetime, to ensuring unimpaired communication between the Army and its political leaders. Yet in spite of those difficulties, the Army always rose to the occasion. The first battles in many of our wars may have been bloody reverses, but the soldiers kept the faith and persevered to overcome adversity. As we shape the Army for tomorrow, everyone—policymakers, citizens, and soldiers—must learn from that history and work together to ensure that the Army can truly perform its mission "on point for the nation."

In spite of instances of unreadiness in opening battles, the soldiers' indomitable will to win made the U.S. Army **invincible in war** throughout our nation's history. Several chapters in this book tell that story, and it is an important part of the Army's tradition. We build on it every day. We are reminded of it every time we look at the Army flag with its battle streamers. We can never lose sight of the fact that the ultimate test of any Army is its ability to fight and win the nation's wars.

But other parts of this book remind us that the U.S. Army has been **persuasive in peace** at many times and places in its history. The Army on the frontier spent far more time and effort keeping the peace than fighting. The Army that helped win World War I and World War II spent years in occupation duty while political and economic frameworks were restored. The Army that restored democracy to the Republic of Korea still helps preserve peaceful conditions on the Korean peninsula. The Army that fought in Vietnam simultaneously assisted civil authorities at home and maintained readiness along contested borders overseas. While peacekeeping functions may be ancillary to war fighting, they cannot be ignored, regardless of whether the nation is at war or at peace. Since the end of the Cold War, the U.S. Army has been heavily engaged in peacekeeping operations. Those efforts will surely continue for years to come, meaning tomorrow's Army will need to continue the tradition of being "persuasive in peace."

As the final chapter of this book notes, the technological advances that characterize our times are helping the Army transform itself. The Army must maintain readiness so that it can be invincible in war, and it must continue to meet global commitments to keep the peace. But the U.S. Army is simultaneously making itself more versatile, more deployable, and more responsive. It is improving the lethality and survivability of its formations while making them easier to sustain. As Army transformation proceeds, new capabilities are emerging. Just as smokeless powder, electricity, and the internal combustion engine changed our Army in earlier centuries, the new technology of the twenty-first century will help us transform our Army. In earlier centuries the U.S. Army was often far behind its potential competitors in modernization because funding was not available. Since 1950, we seem to have learned the risks associated with that approach, and we can never forget the cost of such unpreparedness—a cost that is measured in lives and national treasure. This book is another reminder that the real story is in the soldiers, not in the technology. Soldiering always has been and will continue to be, an affair of the heart. Our soldiers are the finest men and women the nation has to offer, and the Army leadership is committed to providing them with the best weapons, equipment, training, and leadership in the world.

Top: *Training time was short for soldiers rapidly deployed to France during World War I. With America's allies in dire need of reinforcement and support, U.S. divisions boarded overseas-bound transports with little preparation for what they would encounter in the front lines. In many instances the training for trench and gas warfare was conducted within hearing range of the sounds of battle. (National Archives)*

Above: *The infantryman of tomorrow's Army must hone the same skills as all of those who came before him and fought in the nation's wars. The soldier of the Army of the future will need to maintain the same high standards of physical conditioning as in the past. The skills that lead to development of a mission-ready soldier continue to be important in today's Army basic training. (Greg Mathieson, MAI)*

Left: *The Army that helped to win World War II was jump-started by the important decision to initiate a peacetime mobilization during 1940–1941. Increases were authorized in active Army strength and the nation's first peacetime draft was set into motion. Reserve officers were called up and the addition of eighteen National Guard divisions doubled the Army's size quickly. ("Goodbye Dear, I'll Be Back in a Year," Mort Künstler, National Guard Heritage series)*

Selected Milestones in the History of America's Army

Colonel Raymond K. Bluhm, Jr., USA (Ret)

"When we were needed, we were there."

EDITOR'S NOTE: The early colonial period in North America was one of surprisingly frequent conflict. The European settlements were not only involved in many conflicts with Indians and pirates, but they also were the secondary battlefields for the frequent dynastic struggles for power in Europe. With little help from their mother countries, the colonies were left to their own resources for self-defense, and had to protect themselves or perish, thus forming the strong tradition of the American citizen soldier.

THE NATIONAL GUARD OF THE U.S.
IN WAR   IN PEACE
THE OLDEST MILITARY ORGANIZATION IN THE U.S.

1636

October 7—

Massachusetts Bay Colony creates three militia regiments, one is the ancestor of the 182d Infantry Regiment, oldest unit in the Army National Guard. The other American colonies soon formalize their own militia units, many creating quick reaction "minute companies" for protection and emergencies.

1636-1637

PEQUOT WAR—

Massachusetts Bay Colony militia, at times allied with various Indian tribes, destroy the powerful Narragansett tribe in a war of raids and reprisals by both sides.

1639-1664

DUTCH-INDIAN WARS—

Colonial militia with Mohawk and Seneca allies conduct a series of raids and battles against a number of Indian tribes in New York and Canada.

1644-1646

March–October—POWHATAN WAR—

Following a surprise morning attack by Indians on settlements along the James River, Virginia militia defeat the coalition of tribes under Chief Powhatan.

1675-1676

KING PHILIP'S WAR—

New England colonial militia engage and finally defeat an Indian alliance led by Wampanoag chief King Philip.

VIRGINIA'S INDIAN WAR—

A dispute between a Virginia farmer and Nanticoke Indians leads to raids and reprisals. Virginia militia under Colonel John Washington defends the colony.

1688-1699

ABNAKI/KING WILLIAM'S WAR—

In response to provocations by New York militia, the Abnaki tribe retaliates against settlements in Maine, and the conflict quickly becomes part of the French-English struggle for domination of North America. Colonial militia and Iroquois battle French and their Indian allies throughout the frontier.

Opposite: *The American soldier through the years—different eras, different challenges, same results. ("To Make Men Free," Norman Rockwell, Army Art Collection)*

Note: *As the history of the U.S. Army parallels that of America, all of the illustrations in this chronology are United States postage stamps commemorating Army achievements. (National Postal Museum, Smithsonian Institution)*

1702-1710

QUEEN ANNE'S WAR—
Colonial militia and Chickasaws attack the Spanish settlement of St. Augustine, again as a part of another European conflict, starting an eight-year war that ranges from Canada to Florida.

1711-1713

TUSCARORA WAR—
A surprise Indian raid against New Bern, NC, begins a series of attacks against settlements in that colony. Assistance from South Carolina militia helps the North Carolinians to finally defeat the hostile tribes.

1715-1716

YAMASEE WAR—
Led by Yamasee warriors, Indians attack settlements near Savannah, GA. Colonial militia, with help from the Cherokee tribe, destroy the Yamasee towns and drive out the survivors.

1739-1743

WAR OF JENKIN'S EAR—
Georgia militia are joined by Indian tribes in the area in a war against Spanish settlements in Florida.

1740-1748

KING GEORGE'S WAR—
New England militia bear the brunt of conflict against the Canadian French and Indian allies. A high point is the militia capture of the French fortress at Louisbourg, Nova Scotia.

1754-1763

FRENCH AND INDIAN WAR—
American militia provide support to the British efforts to expel the French from Canada, and eliminate the threat of attacks from the French Indian allies. A number of Americans who later become senior leaders in the American revolutionary army gain invaluable combat experience in this conflict.

1763-1766

PONTIAC'S REBELLION—
The Ottawa chief Pontiac leads a large alliance of Indian tribes in a major

effort to eliminate white presence in the Ohio Valley. Militia from several colonies respond to the emergency and several battles are waged until a treaty is arranged.

1773-1774

LORD DUNMORE'S WAR—
Indians and colonists are killed when Virginian surveying parties begin work in the Ohio Valley. Virginia militia move against Chief Cornstalk, destroy his villages, and force him to terms.

1775

April 19—
LEXINGTON AND CONCORD, MA—Massachusetts "minutemen" engage British troops seeking to capture militia munitions and colony leaders. They drive the British back and beseige them in Boston.

May 10—
FT. TICONDEROGA, NY—In a surprise attack, Vermont "Green Mountain Boys" under Colonels Benedict Arnold and Ethan Allen capture the fort from the small British garrison.

June 14—
The 1st Continental Congress places the militia at Boston under its control and authorizes ten additional companies of riflemen to be raised. (U.S. Army and Infantry Branch Birthday.)

June 15—
Congress offers Virginia militia colonel George Washington a commission as "General and Commander-in-Chief of the Continental Army." He accepts the next day, but refuses a salary, asking only that his expenses be paid.

June 16—
Congress organizes the Continental Army, establishing engineer, adjutant general, paymaster, commissary general, and quartermaster positions, and sets down the first disciplinary code, the Articles of War. (Birthday of Adjutant General Corps, Corps of Engineers, Finance Corps, and Quartermaster Corps.)

June 17—
CHARLESTOWN, MA—Militia forces under Major General Artemus Ward, and Colonels William Prescott and John Stark defend fortifications on Breeds Hill. They throw back two British attacks, then are forced to retreat after running out of ammunition in what later became known as the Battle of Bunker Hill.

July 3—
CAMBRIDGE, MA—George Washington assumes command. He issues General Order No. 1 the next day, announcing the authority of Congress over the Army.

July 27—
Congress establishes a wartime hospital for the Army headed by Chief Physician, Dr. Benjamin Church. (Birthday of the Army Medical Corps and the Medical Department.)

July 29—
Congress authorizes a chaplain for each regiment and appoints Colonel William Tudor as the first Judge Advocate. (Birthday of the Chaplain Corps and the Judge Advocate General Corps.)

November 2—
MONTREAL, CANADA—An Army expeditionary force led by Brigadier General Richard Montgomery occupies the city after the British flee.

November 17—
Colonel Henry Knox is appointed commander of the Continental Army's Regiment of Artillery. (Birthday of the Field Artillery and Air Defense Artillery.)

December 31—
QUEBEC, CANADA—A night attack on the city fails when Montgomery is killed, Colonel Benedict Arnold wounded, and Colonel Daniel Morgan captured. The American forces lay siege to the city, but receive no reinforcements and eventually must retreat from Canada

1776

January 1—
CAMBRIDGE, MA—At his headquarters, Washington raises the new "Union" or "Cambridge" flag of the United Colonies. It is the first American flag with red and white stripes and it remains the national flag until 1777.

January 6—
Alexander Hamilton's artillery company is authorized. Now designated Battery D, 1st Battalion, 5th Field Artillery, it is the oldest regular Army unit.

January 24—
CAMBRIDGE, MA—Colonel Henry Knox, Chief of Artillery, delivers over fifty cannon transported on sleds more than 300 miles from Ft. Ticonderoga.

July 4—
Second Continental Congress approves the Declaration of Independence.

August 30—
LONG ISLAND, NY—The Continental Army is almost trapped when it is surprised and forced to abandon its defensive positions.

September 7—
Sergeant Ezra Lee, Continental Army, takes a one-man submarine, the *American Turtle*, to attack a British ship off Staten Island, NY. The attack fails because the copper bottom of the ship prevents attachment of a mine.

October 11–14—
LAKE CHAMPLAIN, NY—Brigadier General Benedict Arnold leads a small fleet of army gunboats in delaying actions near Valcour Island that cause the British to halt their advance until spring.

December 12—
Congress approves the first cavalry unit, a regiment of light dragoons under Colonel Elisha Sheldon. (Birthday of the Cavalry/Armor Branch.)

December 13—
Congress appoints Colonel Mottin De La Balme as the first Army Inspector General.

December 25–26—
TRENTON, NJ—Washington leads the Army in a surprise night attack across the Delaware River during a snow storm to defeat the Hessian force garrisoning the town.

1777

January 3—
PRINCETON, NJ—The Continental Army defeats the British in another surprise attack.

February—
Rhode Island authorizes the enlistment of free blacks and slaves to form the First Rhode Island Regiment. It is the first black American regiment.

June 14—
Congress approves the official flag of the United States with thirteen stars

in a blue field and thirteen red and white stripes.

July 31—
Congress commissions nineteen-year-old Marquis de Lafayette a Major General. He is the youngest general ever made in the American Army.

August 6—
ORISKANY, NY—Brigadier General Nicholas Herkimer is mortally wounded leading a militia force into an ambush by British, Loyalists, and Indians.

August 16—
BENNINGTON, VT—Vermont militia led by Colonel John Stark defeat a large Hessian foraging party from Major General John Burgoyne's British column.

September 11—
BRANDYWINE, PA—Washington's Continental Army gives a hard day's fight, but is finally forced to withdraw.

September 16—
Congress commissions Baron De Kalb and Count Pulaski as generals. Pulaski becomes Commander of the Horse, chief of all American cavalry.

October 7—
FREEMAN'S FARM, NY—Major General Benedict Arnold and Colonel Daniel Morgan surprise the British and force them to retreat, leading to the surrender of Burgoyne's army ten days later at Saratoga.

December 19—
VALLEY FORGE, PA—The Army goes into winter encampment. Lack of food and other supplies cause major problems and more than 2,000 soldiers die of cold and disease by spring.

1778

January 25—
Washington orders fortifications built at West Point, NY. Now the home of the U.S. Military Academy, it is the oldest American military post in continuous occupation by U.S. soldiers.

March 19—
VALLEY FORGE, PA—Baron von Steuben conducts the first formal drill training for the Continental Army. His drill regulations are adopted by Congress.

June 28—
MONMOUTH COURTHOUSE, NJ—"Molly Pitcher" works an artillery piece with her

husband as Continental troops fight the British regulars to a draw.

July 4—
KASKASKIA, IL—Colonel George Rogers Clark marches 175 men overland 120 miles to surprise and capture the key British fort.

September 7—
BOONESBORO, KY—Militia under Major Daniel Boone successfully defend the fort for several days against a Shawnee attack.

1779

February 26—
FT. VINCENNES, IL—After a 180-mile march over icy, flooded prairies, Colonel George Rogers Clark's small force takes the fort by bluffing the British commander.

July 16—
STONY POINT, NY—Major General "Mad" Anthony Wayne leads his light infantry in a night bayonet attack to seize the British fort.

August 22—
Major General John Sullivan begins a campaign of destruction against the Iroquois in response to attacks on the New York frontier.

Casimir Pulaski, Savannah, 1779

October 2—
Congress adopts blue as the official basic color of the Continental Army uniform. Except for short periods, there has been an Army Blue uniform ever since. It is now a formal dress uniform.

October 9—
SAVANNAH, GA—Count Casimir Pulaski is killed in an unsuccessful American attack to raise the British siege of the city.

December 5—
MORRISTOWN, NJ—The Continental Army enters winter quarters, and begins its worst and most trying winter. More die than at Valley Forge.

1780

August 16—
CAMDEN, SC—In the worst defeat of the war, the American southern army led by Major General Horatio Gates surrenders to Lord Cornwallis.

September 24—
Three militiamen capture British Major John Andre, exposing Benedict

Arnold's plan to turn over West Point to the British. Arnold escapes, but Andre is hanged.

October 7—
KING'S MOUNTAIN, NC—Carolina militiamen destroy a force of Loyalists in a bitter battle, eliminating British support in that area.

October 26—
TEARCOAT SWAMP, SC—Colonel Francis Marion, the "Swamp Fox," leads a successful attack on Loyalist militia.

1781

January 1—
MORRISTOWN, NJ—Several regiments of the Pennsylvania Line mutiny in protest to living conditions, no pay, and their terms of service. After a week of negotiation the men are released from service; many immediately reenlist.

January 17—
COWPENS, SC—Continental and militia troops under Brigadier General Daniel Morgan soundly defeat a force of British regulars and Loyalists.

March 1—
The Articles of Confederation are ratified. The Continental Army continues as the national army of the confederated states.

March 15—
GUILFORD COURTHOUSE, NC—American regular and militia units commanded by Major General Nathanael Greene battle a British force under Lord Cornwallis, then withdraw.

October 9–19—
YORKTOWN, VA—An American and French army with the help of a French fleet trap Cornwallis and his troops, bombarding them into surrender within ten days.

1782

July 20—
Congress adopts the Great Seal of the United States. The eagle from the seal becomes a common part of the Army insignia.

August 7—
The first American military decoration, the Badge of Military Merit, later renamed the Purple Heart, is established by Washington for meritorious service.

"Swamp Fox" Francis Marion, 1782

November 4—
JOHN'S ISLAND, SC—Captain William Wilmont is killed in a skirmish, making him the last American soldier to die in an official action of the Revolution.

1783

March 12—
NEWBURGH, NY—An army mutiny is avoided when Washington persuades the Army's officers, disgruntled with failure to receive many months' pay, to continue to support Congress.

May 3—
NEWBURGH, NY—Washington awards the first Badges of Military Merit to three noncommissioned officers of the Continental Army, Sergeants Elijah Churchill, William Brown, and Daniel Bissell, Jr.

December 23—
NEW YORK, NY—Washington returns to Congress his commission as General and Commander in Chief of the American Forces. He is succeeded by Major General Henry Knox.

1784

January 14—
Continental Congress ratifies Treaty of Paris ending the Revolution.

June 3—
The 1st American Regiment is established, replacing the wartime Continental Army as the first unit of the American Regular Army.

1787

January 24—
MASSACHUSETTS—Major General Benjamin Lincoln leads militia to restore civil order in the state's western regions and disperse insurgents led by Daniel Shay.

1789

March—
The Constitution is adopted and President George Washington becomes the Commander in Chief of the Army and Navy.

August 7—
The Department of War is established under Secretary Henry Knox.

1790

October 19—

EEL RIVER, OH—Army regulars and Kentucky militia on a punitive campaign against the Miami Indian tribe are ambushed and defeated.

1791

November 4—

WABASH RIVER, IN—Major General Arthur St. Clair leads a second punitive expedition against the Miami tribe into disaster. Almost half of the small U.S. Army is killed.

1794

August 20—

FALLEN TIMBERS, OH—A bayonet charge by Major General "Mad" Anthony Wayne's well-trained Legion routs Little Turtle's Indian coalition from their positions among a huge tangle of tree fall.

October 20—

PENNSYLVANIA—Militia under Colonel "Light Horse Harry" Lee successfully put down the anti-tax "Whiskey Rebellion."

1798

July 3—

George Washington accepts a commission as the first Lieutenant General and is made General in Chief of the Army in the Quasi-war crisis with France. Alexander Hamilton is commissioned as his deputy.

1799

December 14—

MT. VERNON, VA—Washington dies still on "active" Army service. His title and the rank of Lieutenant General are abolished.

1801

June 10—

Two batteries of U.S. Army artillery serve at sea with the fleet during the war with Tripoli, which lasts until 1805.

1802

March 16—

Congress establishes the United States Military Academy at West Point, NY.

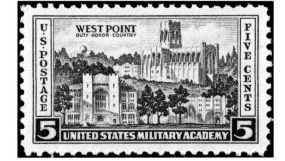

1803

December 20—

Brigadier General James Wilkinson, Army General in Chief, is appointed governor of the new Louisiana Territory. The Army is given responsibility to explore, map, and secure the new territory for settlement.

1804

May 14—

WOOD RIVER, IL—Captain Meriwether Lewis and Lieutenant William Clark with forty soldiers, begin the first exploration of the Louisiana Territory to the Pacific Ocean. Their Corps of Discovery is gone two years.

October 14—

A second Army expedition conducts the first exploration of the Red and Ouachita Rivers, the southern boundary of the new territory.

1805

April 27—

EGYPT—Army Captain William Eaton, the American Envoy, leads a small force of Arabs and U.S. Marines across the desert from Egypt to "the shores of Tripoli" to capture the city of Derna.

August 9—

An Army exploration party under Lieutenant M. Zebulon Pike is sent on an unsuccessful effort to discover the source of the Mississippi River.

November—

Lewis and Clark, with a party of twenty-seven soldiers and three civilians, reach the Pacific Ocean.

1806

April 19—

An Army party heads up the Red River to explore the southwest.

July 15—

Lieutenant Pike leads an exploration of the Rocky Mountains during which he discovers Pike's Peak.

1808

February 7—

Lieutenant Pike's party reaches and explores the Rio Grande River area.

1811

November 7—

TIPPECANOE, IN—Major General Henry Harrison's 4th Infantry and Kentucky militia defeat a surprise attack by Shawnees led by the Prophet.

1812

May 14—

Congress authorizes an Ordnance Department to be established. (Birthday of the Ordnance Corps.)

June 18—

War is declared against Great Britain.

August 15—

FT. DEARBORN, IL—A column of soldiers and families abandoning the fort under a truce is massacred by British-led Indians.

August 16—

FT. DETROIT, MI—Brigadier General William Hull surrenders the fort to the British without a fight. He is later court-martialed.

October 13—

QUEENSTON HEIGHTS, CANADA—Initially successful, the American attackers are forced to withdraw after heavy losses.

1813

January 21—

RAISIN RIVER, OH—A detachment under Brigadier General James Winchester is defeated and captured; Indians kill many of the prisoners.

April 15—

MOBILE, AL—Soldiers under Major General James Wilkinson seize Mobile from the Spanish, securing the U.S. claim to the disputed West Florida territory.

April 27—

YORK, CANADA—An Army amphibious assault across Lake Ontario surprises the British defenders. Brigadier General Zebulon Pike is killed by a magazine explosion as the British retreat.

May 27—

SACKETT'S HARBOR, NY—Brigadier General Jacob Brown turns back a British invasion force from Canada.

October 5—

THAMES RIVER, CANADA—Major General William H. Harrison's 27th Infantry and mounted Kentucky militia defeat a British and Indian force, killing the Indian leader Tecumseh.

November 11—

CHRYSLER'S FARM, CANADA—After a series of brave, but unsuccessful assaults against the British, American forces withdraw. Major General Wilkinson is relieved as senior Army general and court-martialed.

1814

March 27—

HORSESHOE BEND, AL—Militia general Andrew Jackson's force of Regulars, militia, and Indians destroy the stronghold of the Creek "Red Stick" faction. Jackson is appointed a brigadier general in the Regular Army, and promoted to major general in May.

July 5—

CHIPPEWA, CANADA—Brigadier General Winfield Scott's brigade breaks the British line for an American victory. Misled by the American's militia grey uniforms, the British are shocked to discover they are Regulars.

July 25—

LUNDY'S LANE, CANADA—American and British regulars fight past midnight, but end in a draw.

August 24–25—

WASHINGTON, D.C.—British troops occupy and burn the city after defeating an American force at Bladensburg, MD. President James Madison is in the field, the last time an American president personally commands soldiers in combat.

September 12–13—

FT. MCHENRY, MD—Major George Armistead commands the fort garrison of Regular Army artillery, infantry, and Maryland militia in blocking the British naval attack on Baltimore. Their defense inspires the writing of "The Star Spangled Banner."

December 24—

Signing of the Treaty of Ghent ends the war with Great Britain.

1815

January 8—

NEW ORLEANS, LA—A defensive army of Regulars, militia, and volunteers under Major General Andrew Jackson inflicts a bloody defeat on the British attackers. Neither side knew a peace treaty had been signed.

1816

September—

WEST POINT, NY—Cadets receive the first grey cadet uniforms in honor of the grey uniforms worn by soldiers at Chippewa and Lundy's Lane.

1817

November 20—

Encouraged by Spanish and British agents, Creek and Seminole Indians attack army supply transports in Georgia and northern Florida, beginning the First Seminole War. The war lasts until November 1818.

1818

April 7—

ST. MARKS, FL—Troops under Major General Andrew Jackson take the town from the Spanish to use as a supply base against the Seminoles. Agents supplying the Indians are arrested and executed.

May 27—

PENSACOLA, FL—Jackson occupies the town while other U.S. units attack nearby Seminole villages.

August 30—

FT. BELLE FONTAINE, MISSOURI TERRITORY—Companies of the Rifle Regiment board keelboats and move up the Missouri as the advance party of the Army's Yellowstone River Expedition.

1819

NORTHFIELD, VT—The first military training of college students begins at what will become Norwich University. It is the beginning of the Army Reserve Officer Training Corps (ROTC), which today provides the majority of Army officers.

June 21—

ST. LOUIS, MISSOURI TERRITORY—The scientific group of the Army Yellowstone Expedition departs up the Missouri River on a steamboat, the first use of such a boat on the river. The main body of the expedition, the 6th Infantry under Major Stephen Long, follows on 5 July.

1821

March 2—

Congress directs a major reorganization and reduction of the Army. Jacob Brown remains the Army's only major general and is stationed in Washington as Commanding General of the Army.

1823

June 23—

COUNCIL BLUFFS, MO—In response to Arkaree attacks against traders, Colonel Henry Leavenworth leads the 6th Infantry in a campaign against the tribe. It is the Army's first action against Indians west of the Mississippi River.

1824

May 24—

FT. MONROE, VA—The first Army's first professional school, the Coast Artillery School of Practice, is established.

May 31—

Army engineers begin the land survey for the Chesapeake and Ohio Canal. The canal is completed in 1850.

1826

July 10—

Jefferson Barracks, MO, is founded as the first Army post west of the Mississippi. It is deactivated in 1946.

1827

May 26—

Edgar Allan Poe enlists in the Army as Edgar A. Perry. He is discharged in 1829 as a sergeant major, but later attends West Point for a year.

1828

July 7—

Army engineers begin the survey for the Baltimore and Ohio Railroad, the first passenger rail service in the country.

1830

December 8—

The U.S. Army stops issuing soldiers a daily whiskey ration, replacing it with a sugar and coffee ration.

1832

April 26—

ILLINOIS—In response to Sac-Fox Indian attacks on Illinois settlers, a force of Regulars and Illinois militia pursue the Indians under Black Hawk. The Indians are defeated at Bad Axe River, WI, in August. Abraham Lincoln serves for a short time in the Illinois militia.

May 1—

Captain Benjamin L. E. Bonneville, disguised as a fur trader, leads a secret Army expedition into Spanish and Indian territory to explore and gather information.

1833

March 2—

1st Regiment of Dragoons is organized for duty in the West. Later redesignated 1st Cavalry Regiment, its units are the oldest continuously serving cavalry in the Army.

1834

January 29—
For the first time, Army troops are used to help settle a labor dispute when violence occurs during a strike by workers on the Chesapeake and Ohio Canal.

1835

December 28—
FLORIDA—The Second Seminole War begins when Major Francis L. Dade and a column of 110 men from the 2d and 3d Artillery Regiments are ambushed by Seminole Indians. Only two soldiers survive.

December 31—
WITHLACOOCHEE RIVER, FL—Army troops defeat a band of Seminoles, who retreat into the swamps. Hampered by poor logistics and bad leadership, the Army fights dozens of battles against the Indians until a truce in May 1842.

1836

May 23—
Congress approves formation of the 2d Regiment of Dragoons.

June 9—
FT. DEFIANCE, FL—A counterattack by the outnumbered garrison breaks a siege by 250 Seminole Indians.

1838

May 8—
Under Presidential order, troops of Major General Winfield Scott begin gathering the last Cherokee Indians for removal to reservations west of the Mississippi River. During the 1,200-mile winter march later known as the "Trail of Tears," many Indians perish.

July 5—
Army Corps of Topographical Engineers is created by Congress to lead exploration and mapping of the nation.

1842

June 10—
Lieutenant John C. Fremont leads an Army expedition with Army Scout Kit Carson to explore and map routes for emigration through the Rocky Mountains.

1843

May—
ST. LOUIS, MO—A second Army expedition by Fremont departs for Oregon. Later he makes a winter crossing of the Sierra Mountains into California. The expedition takes 14 months.

1845

May 18—
FT. LEAVENWORTH, KANSAS TERRITORY—Colonel Stephen W. Kearny leads five companies of 1st Dragoons on a show of force through Indian country. They travel 2,200 miles in 99 days.

June 20—
Lieutenant Fremont leads a third Army expedition into Mexican territory. Possibly on secret orders, he ends up in California in time to help capture it in 1846.

August 12—
Lieutenant James W. Abert leads an Army scientific expedition for three months into the Kiowa and Commanche territory.

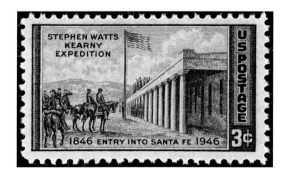

1846

April 25—
TEXAS—Mexican cavalry attack a patrol of 2d U.S. Dragoons, initiating open hostilities.

May 8—
PALO ALTO, TX—Army troops under Brigadier General Zachary Taylor attack and force the Mexicans to withdraw.

May 9—
RESACA DE LA PALMA, MEXICO—Taylor's army attacks a larger Mexican force and with skillful use of artillery defeats them. Taylor is made major general and field commander of the U.S. Army in Mexico.

May 13—
War is officially declared with Mexico.

August 18—
SANTA FE, NEW MEXICO TERRITORY—Newly promoted Brigadier General Kearny and his "Army of the West" enter Santa Fe without a fight, ending a two-month march.

September 24—
MONTERREY, MEXICO—After a hard siege of four days, the Mexicans surrender the town to Taylor's army.

September 25—
SANTA FE, NEW MEXICO TERRITORY—After setting up a local government, Kearny receives orders to capture California. He heads west with 300 1st Dragoon Regulars mounted on mules.

1847

January 9—
SAN GABRIEL, CA—A joint Army-Navy force inflicts final defeat on Californians resisting American occupation.

February 22–23—
BUENA VISTA, MEXICO—American artillery again plays a major part in Taylor's soldiers defeating a much larger Mexican force in a two-day battle.

February 28—
SACRAMENTO RIVER, MEXICO—Missouri volunteers under Colonel Alexander W. Doniphan win their second victory against Mexican forces, then continue a heroic march into Mexico from Santa Fe to join Taylor's army.

March 9—
VERA CRUZ, MEXICO—Major General Winfield Scott conducts the Army's first major amphibious landing and lays siege to the city. It surrenders two weeks later.

April 18—
CERRO GORDO, MEXICO—Captain Robert E. Lee finds a way for Scott's army to out-flank and defeat the Mexican defensive position.

September 8–13—
CONTRERAS AND CHURUBUSCO, MEXICO—Scott's army fights through two heavily fortified villages and finally captures Chapultepec, the main fortified position overlooking Mexico City.

September 14—
MEXICO CITY, MEXICO—Scott's victorious American army marches into the city and begins occupation duty.

1848

February 2—
Treaty of Guadalupe-Hidalgo ends the war with Mexico.

NOTE: FROM 1848 TO 1861 THE U.S. ARMY FIGHTS TWENTY-TWO INDIAN WARS AND OVER 206 SEPARATE ENGAGEMENTS. ONLY A SELECTION CAN BE LISTED HERE.

1849

April 4—
FT. SMITH, AK—Captain Randolph B. Marcy begins three-month Army expedition with dragoons and infantry to survey a southern wagon and potential rail route to Sante Fe.

August 15—
SANTA FE, NEW MEXICO TERRITORY—Lieutenant Colonel John Washington leads a punitive Army expedition against the Navaho tribe, penetrating into the Indian stronghold of Chelly Canyon for the first time.
September—
The Army initiates operations against Indians in northern California after an Army exploration party is attacked and a captain killed.

1850

June 27—
UTAH TERRITORY—Army explorers Captain Stansbury and Lieutenant Gunnison complete the first survey of the Great Salt Lake area. They map a key route that will be used by stage coaches, pony express, and the Union Pacific railroad.

1853

March 29—
WASHINGTON, D.C.—The Army Corps of Engineers under Brigadier General Montgomery Meigs begins construction of the north and south wings of the U.S. Capitol building.
October 26—
SEVIER, UTAH TERRITORY—Ute Indians massacre a detachment of the Mounted Rifle Regiment surveying a railroad route nearby.

1854

March 30—
A patrol of 1st Dragoons is ambushed by Apaches near Taos, NM. Only thirty-eight troopers survive. The Army begins year-long campaign against the Apaches.

1855

January 16—
After a three-day chase, 1st Dragoons overtake and rout a band of Apache raiders using sabers since the soldiers' hands are too cold to operate firearms.
February 15—
Congress restores the rank of Lieutenant General for Winfield Scott.
March 3—
Money is approved to buy 33 camels for an experimental U.S. Army Camel Corps for use in the southwest. Congress also

authorizes the 1st and 2d Cavalry Regiments, the U.S. first units called "cavalry."
December 15—
FLORIDA—The Third Seminole War begins and Army troops fight the final campaign against the few remaining bands of Seminoles, concluding it in 1858.

1857

May 28—
FT. LEAVENWORTH, KANSAS TERRITORY—An Army punitive expedition departs against Mormon settlers in Utah who are resisting federal authority. The Army occupies Salt Lake City in June 1858 and conflict is settled without a major battle.
October 5—
Soldiers are employed to supervise elections and protect voters throughout Kansas Territory, permitting election of an anti-slavery state legislature.

1858

May 17—
FT. WALLA WALLA, WA—A surrounded detachment of 164 soldiers holds off a much larger Indian force in a day-long battle, then escapes after nightfall.

1859

October 5—
HARPER'S FERRY, VA—Army Lieutenant Colonel Robert E. Lee, assisted by Lieutenant J. E. B. Stuart, directs a detachment of Marines in the capture of radical abolitionist John Brown and his men.

1860

April 30—
FT. DEFIANCE, NEW MEXICO TERRITORY—Over 1,000 Navajo Indians attack the fort, but are driven off by the small garrison of 3d Infantry.
June 21—
Congress selects Assistant Surgeon Albert J. Myer to be the Army's first Signal Officer. A separate Signal Corps is authorized in March 1863. (Birthday of the Signal Corps.)
December 17—
South Carolina secedes and the Civil War begins. Almost one-third of the Regular Army officers resign to join the Confederate Army.

SUMTER 1861

1861

April 12—
CHARLESTON, SC—After a 34-hour bombardment by Confederate artillery, Major Robert Anderson surrenders Fort Sumter.
July 21—
MANASSAS, VA—Federal forces under Brigadier General Irvin McDowell are

defeated along Bull Run in an attempt to seize the rail town of Manassas. The Army accepts delivery of its first hot air balloon, but the balloon does not reach the battle.
August 5—
Congress abolishes flogging in the Army. It had been abolished in 1812 but reinstated.
August 10—
WILSON'S CREEK, MO—A surprise attack gives Union forces early success that could not be sustained against a strong Confederate counterattack, and the Union withdraws.
September 24—
VIRGINIA—The Union Army first uses an observer in a hot air balloon to observe and adjust artillery fire by telegraph to the ground.
October 1—
The Army establishes its first Balloon Corps under civilian Thaddeus Lowe. The Corps is disbanded in June 1863 and there are no further balloon operations until 1890.

1862

February 6–16—
FORTS HENRY AND DONELSON, TN—Major General Ulysses S. Grant conducts a successful joint Army-Navy campaign to capture the Confederate forts, opening the Tennessee River as a route deep into the South.

April 6—
SHILOH, TN—Confederate forces under Major General Albert S. Johnston surprise a Union army under Major General U.S. Grant. Grant holds his force together and, reinforced, counterattacks the next day driving the Confederates back. Army field hospitals are used for the first time.

April 12—

Big Shanty, GA—A team of Union raiders steal the Confederate locomotive *General* and attempt to destroy the rail tracks. They are captured after a chase by another locomotive, and eight are hanged. Survivors are later presented with the first Medals of Honor.

May 24—

The Army uses a mobile wagon-mounted field telegraph for military operations for the first time.

May 31–June 1—

Fair Oaks and Seven Pines, VA—Confederates under General Joseph E. Johnston conduct a disorganized attack on Union forces. Johnston, badly wounded, is replaced by General Robert E. Lee.

June 7—

Major General Benjamin Butler, Union military governor of New Orleans, issues General Order No. 28, stating southern women who show disrespect to Union soldiers will be treated as prostitutes.

June 8—

Cross Keys and Port Republic, VA—Dividing his Confederate force, Major General Thomas "Stonewall" Jackson holds one Union army at bay while turning on another and defeating it.

July 2—

Congress passes the Morrill Act granting public lands to establish colleges that will include military tactics in their curriculum, taking another step toward the Reserve Officer Training Program (ROTC).

July 12—

President Lincoln approves the act of Congress to create the Medal of Honor. Initially proposed for Army enlisted soldiers, officers were also included. A medal for the Navy had been approved in December 1861.

August 19–23—

Ft. Ridgely, MN—Sioux under Little Crow attack settlers and the undermanned fort before artillery drives them away. Fighting continues in the upper midwest throughout the year.

August 25—

The War Department authorizes the enlistment of black soldiers for the first time. Over 178,000 will serve.

August 29–30—

Manassas, VA—The newly formed Union army of Major General John Pope is defeated near Bull Run after a two-day battle.

September 17—

Sharpsburg, MD—Culminating a two-week campaign, Major General George McClellan engages Lee's army along Antietam Creek. McClellan does not follow up an apparent victory and is soon replaced.

October 29—

Island Mount, MO—A regiment of black soldiers, the 1st Kansas Colored Volunteers, fights in combat for the first time in the war.

December 13—

Fredericksburg, VA—Frontal assaults against Confederate positions end in a major defeat for the Union army of Major General Ambrose Burnside.

1863

April 17–May 2—

Brigadier General Benjamin Grierson leads three Union cavalry regiments on a 600-mile raid through Georgia, Mississippi, and Louisiana.

April 22—

The Bureau of Colored Troops is established to oversee the recruiting and organization of black soldiers into the Union Army.

May 1–4—

Chancellorsville, VA—A brilliant flanking maneuver by Major General Thomas "Stonewall" Jackson's corps catches the Union army by surprise. Jackson is wounded by his own troops at nightfall, and dies a week later of pneumonia.

June 9—

Brandy Station, VA—Union cavalry surprise Major General J. E. B. Stuart's Confederate cavalry in the largest cavalry battle fought in America.

July 1–3—

Gettysburg, PA—The Army of the Potomac, under Major General George Meade, defeats Lee's Army of Northern Virginia. Lee withdraws, ending the last Southern hopes for a military victory in the war.

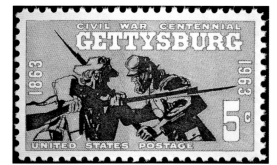

July 4—

Vicksburg, MS—The year-long joint Army-Navy campaign to open the Mississippi River ends when Union forces under Major General U. S. Grant capture this last Confederate bastion.

July 13–16—

Army troops are sent to New York to quell anti-draft riots.

September 16—

Twelve-year-old drummer boy Willie Johnson, 3d Vermont Infantry, is pre-

sented the Medal of Honor, the youngest person ever to receive it.

November 24–25—

Chattanooga, TN—Union forces capture Lookout Mountain and rout the Confederates from Missionary Ridge, opening the way into Georgia.

1864

January 6—

Canyon de Chelly, New Mexico Territory—Militia Colonel Kit Carson begins an winter campaign against the Navahos that will bring an end to the war with that tribe.

February 9—

Richmond, VA—109 Union soldiers tunnel out of the Confederate Libby prison in the largest escape of the war. Half reach Union lines.

March 11—

The U.S. Army Ambulance Corps is established.

March 12—

General Order No. 98 appoints U. S. Grant as Lieutenant General and the first General in Chief of Armies of the United States, with overall command of all the Union armies.

May 5–6—

The Wilderness, VA—Lee's army attacks Meade's Army of the Potomac as it moves through a heavily wooded area. The confused fighting is inconclusive with heavy losses. Grant orders Meade to continue to advance south.

May 7–12—

Spotsylvania Court House, VA—Grant's efforts to outflank Lee result in a series of costly battles against the entrenched Confederates without a conclusive result.

May 13—

Arlington, VA—PVT William Christman, 67th Pennsylvania Infantry, is the first soldier buried in the newly opened Arlington National Cemetery.

June 14—

Union Army engineers complete a 2,200-foot pontoon bridge over the James River in eight hours, the longest ever constructed in the war.

June 15—

Petersburg, VA—After failing in direct assaults against Confederate defenses, the Union army begins a siege of 11 months.

July 20–September 1—
ATLANTA, GA—Confederate defenders under Major General John B. Hood strike out against the approaching Union army of Major General William Tecumseh Sherman. Hood finally evacuates the city. Major General James B. McPherson, Commander, Army of the Tennessee, is killed, the only commander of a Union Army to die in action.

October 19—
CEDAR CREEK, VA—Major General Jubal Early's Confederates attack Major General Phil Sheridan's army, almost routing it. Sheridan rallies his men and counterattacks, defeating Early and securing the Shenandoah Valley for the Union.

November 16—
ATLANTA, GA—Major General William T. Sherman and his army begin a march to the sea that will end December 13th with the capture of Ft. McAllister, GA.

December 15–16—
NASHVILLE, TN—A Union army under Major General George H. Thomas attacks Confederates led by Hood, defeating them decisively.

1865
January 13—
FT. FISHER, NC—In a major joint operation, army and naval forces successfully seize the last major Confederate port on the Atlantic.

April 1—
FIVE FORKS, VA—Union infantry and dismounted cavalry overwhelm Confederate defenders, and threaten to block Lee's retreat.

April 2—
PETERSBURG, VA—Union troops burst through weakened Confederate lines and take the town. Lee leads his army west to escape.

April 3—
Richmond surrenders and the first Union flag, a cavalry guidon, is raised over the city.

April 6—
The first Medals of Honor presented to black soldiers are given to twelve members of five U.S. Colored volunteer regiments for bravery in battle at New Market Heights, VA, September 1864.

April 9—
APPOMATTOX COURT HOUSE, VA—With Union forces behind and ahead of his army, Lee surrenders the Army of Northern Virginia to Grant.

April 28—
MISSISSIPPI RIVER—In the worst ship disaster in U.S. history, the steamboat Sultana explodes, killing 1,700 Union soldiers, most just released from Confederate prisons.

May 26—
The last major Confederate army is surrendered by Major General Kirby Smith at Shreveport, LA.

NOTE: IN THE THIRTY-YEAR PERIOD 1865–1895, THE U.S. ARMY IS CONSTANTLY DEALING WITH INDIAN UPRISINGS AND CROSS-BORDER RAIDS BY MEXICAN BANDITS. HUNDREDS OF ENGAGEMENTS WERE FOUGHT IN ALMOST EVERY STATE WEST OF THE MISSISSIPPI AGAINST APACHES, COMMANCHES, SIOUX, UTES, KIWOAS, CHEYENNES, NEZ PERCES, SNAKES, MODOCS, AND OTHERS. A SELECTION OF MAJOR CONFRONTATIONS IS LISTED.

1866
January 24—
Dr. Mary E. Walker, a nurse with the Union Army, becomes the first woman to receive the Medal of Honor.

July 28—
President Andrew Johnson signs the law establishing black Regular Army regiments for the first time, four infantry (38th, 39th, 40th, and 41st) and two cavalry (9th and 10th). These replace the volunteer U.S. Colored regiments disbanded after the Civil War.

August 20—
President Johnson declares the Civil War officially over.

December 21—
FT. PHIL KEARNY, WYOMING TERRITORY—Captain William Fetterman disobeys orders and leads a detachment of eighty soldiers and civilians into a trap. They are wiped out by Sioux Indians under Crazy Horse.

1867
March 30—
SITKA, ALASKA TERRITORY—Army troops arrive to establish U.S. control over the newly purchased Alaska Territory. A detachment of the 9th Infantry under Major Charles O. Wood receives the official transfer from Russia to the U.S. on 29 October.

August 2—
FT. PHIL KEARNY, WYOMING TERRITORY—A small work-detail of soldiers and civilians armed with new breech-loading rifles hold off 1,500 Sioux Indians by using their wagons as a fort. It becomes known as the Wagon Box Fight.

1868
May 30—
Former Union Major General John A. Logan establishes the first Memorial Day.

September 17–25—
BEECHER'S ISLAND, COLORADO TERRITORY—A group of fifty Army scouts under MAJ George Forsyth hold off a large Cheyenne war party from a sandy island in the Arikaree River. After seven days of fighting, troopers of the 10th Cavalry come to their rescue.

November 27—
WASHITA RIVER, OKLAHOMA TERRITORY—As part of a winter campaign, Lieutenant Colonel George Custer leads the 7th Cavalry in a successful attack on a Cheyenne camp, but a small cavalry detachment chasing retreating Indians is wiped out.

1869
March 3—
The Army forms two black American infantry regiments, the 24th and 25th Infantry, by combining four understrength infantry units. The two cavalry regiments, 9th and 10th, remain unchanged.

May 10—
PROMONTORY POINT, UTAH TERRITORY—A battalion of the 21st Infantry commanded by Major Milton Cogswell serves as the honor guard for the ceremony linking the Central and Union Pacific Railroads. On its way to Presidio of San Francisco, the battalion is the first military unit to cross the continent by rail.

July—
YUKON RIVER, ALASKA TERRITORY—Captain Charles Raymond explores the river area.

July 11—
SUMMIT SPRINGS, COLORADO TERRITORY—The 5th Cavalry, guided by Army Scout William "Buffalo Bill" Cody, defeats a force of Cheyenne Dog Soldiers.

1870

February 9—
The Army Signal Corps establishes the first Weather Service. A group of twenty-two Signal Corps observer-sergeants is used to report observations daily to Washington, D.C., by telegraph.

June 20—
FT. MCKAVETT, TX—Sergeant Emanuel Stance, 9th U.S. Cavalry, receives the first Medal of Honor awarded to a black Regular Army soldier for actions in skirmishes with Indians.

August—
FT. DUNCAN, TX—The first Seminole Negro Scouts are enlisted. The scouts serve along the southwest border until disbanded in 1914.

1872

November 29—
LAVA BEDS, CA—Modoc Indians under Captain Jack resist removal to a reservation, resulting in the Modoc War. The Indians withdraw into a rough area of volcanic rocks and hold out despite repeated Army efforts to capture them.

1873

April 11—
Major General Edward R. S. Canby is killed by the Modoc leader Captain Jack during truce negotiations. The Army resumes attacks without success and suffers heavy losses. Canby is the only Regular Army general officer killed in the Indian wars.

June 3—
After continued pursuit, Captain Jack and his band surrender. He and the other four assailants of Canby are tried and hanged.

1874

August 30—
In the Red River War, Colonel Nelson A. Miles leads a force of 6th Cavalry and 5th Infantry in a five-hour running battle over 12 miles in pursuit of a Cheyenne war party.

1875

June 2—
A 4th Infantry detachment under Lieutenant Adolphus W. Greely completes the first telegraph line into the Oklahoma Indian Territory.

1876

June 17—
ROSEBUD RIVER, MONTANA TERRITORY—As a part of a larger plan to trap the Sioux and their Indian allies, an Army column under Major General George Crook moves up the river, but is attacked and turned back.

June 25—
LITTLE BIG HORN RIVER, MONTANA TERRITORY—Unaware of Crook's retreat, Lieutenant Colonel George Custer leads the 7th Cavalry against a large Indian village. Custer and five companies are wiped out. The remaining seven companies hold out until rescued two days later.

September 9—
SLIM BUTTES, MONTANA TERRITORY—Captain Anson Mills and some 3d Cavalry surprise and attack a hostile Sioux village, causing the Indians to surrender or flee.

November 25—
POWDER RIVER, MONTANA TERRITORY—In below zero weather, companies of the 2d, 4th, and 5th Cavalry under Colonel Ranald Mackenzie surprise the Cheyenne village of Dull Knife, and after fierce fighting destroy it.

1877

January 8—
WOLF MOUNTAIN, MONTANA TERRITORY—Over 500 Sioux and Cheyenne attack Colonel Nelson Miles's camp during a heavy snow storm. Alerted ahead of time, Miles's men defeat the attack.

June 13—
WALLOWA VALLEY, WASHINGTON TERRITORY—Angry at mistreatment, Nez Perce warriors kill some settlers, and the band under Chief Joseph flees west. The Army follows, suffering several defeats, but refuses to cease pursuit.

June 14—
WEST POINT, NY—Lieutenant Henry O. Flipper becomes the first black American to graduate from the Military Academy. He is assigned to the 10th Cavalry.

October 4—
BEAR PAW MOUNTAINS, MONTANA TERRITORY—Chief Joseph surrenders his trapped Nez Perce band after a six-day battle. Troops

under Colonel Nelson A. Miles caught the Nez Perce following a long and bloody pursuit over 1,700 miles.

1879

May 30—
IDAHO TERRITORY—A group of Bannock and Piute Indians leave their reservation and conduct raids on settlers. Troops under Major General O. O. Howard pursue them through the summer, fighting several engagements until the Indians surrender in September.

June 14—
FT. MISSOULA, MT—The experimental 25th Infantry Bicycle Corps, commanded by Lieutenant James A. Moss, begins a 900-mile ride to St. Louis, MO. They complete the trip in forty days.

September 4—
OJO CALIENTE, ARIZONA TERRITORY—Apaches under Victorio attack a camp of the 9th Cavalry, then disappear into Mexico. The 9th fights Victorio's Apaches back and forth over the border until he is killed by Mexican troops in 1880.

1881

February 8—
Army Surgeon Major George N. Sternberg discovers the germ causing pneumonia. He also does research on cholera, yellow fever, and other diseases, becoming known as the "father of American bacteriology."

May 7—
An Army scientific expedition under Lieutenant Adolphus W. Greely departs for an Arctic exploration. The group becomes stranded there for three years.

August 30—
FT. APACHE, AZ—Conflict begins when Apaches resist the arrest of an anti-white prophet by the post commander, Colonel Eugene Carr. Geronimo leads a band away and others join, beginning a four year war with numerous raids, ambushes, and pursuits across the border.

1882

July 17—
BIG DRY WASH, ARIZONA TERRITORY—Troops of 3d and 6th Cavalry led by Captain Adna R. Chaffee outflank and surprise an

ambush planned by White Mountain Apaches, inflicting such heavy losses on them that the Indian survivors return to the reservation.

1885

February 21—
WASHINGTON, D.C.—The Washington Monument, recently completed by the Army Corps of Engineers, is dedicated.

November 9—
CAJON PASS, CA—The last spike is driven for the California Southern Railway. The Army surveyed the railway and protected its crews during construction.

1886

January 11—
Mexican militia attack the camp of Captain Emmet Crawford, who has been leading the pursuit of Geronimo with a select force of Indian Scouts. Crawford is killed.

September 4—APACHE WARS—
Lieutenant Charles Gatewood volunteers to ride into Geronimo's camp to discuss the Apache's surrender. An Army pursuit force under Captain Henry W. Lawton tracked Geronimo for eight months over 2000 miles, and he is finally ready to talk.

1887

March 1—
The Army Hospital Corps is established.

1890

December 28–29—
WOUNDED KNEE CREEK, MONTANA TERRITORY—When a mystical Indian religious cult called "Ghost Dancers" promises supernatural powers against white man's weapons, there is unrest among the northern Sioux. The 7th Cavalry under Colonel James Forsyth is sent to disarm one group. Fighting erupts and over 150 Indians and 25 soldiers are killed.

December 30—
WHITE CLAY CREEK, MONTANA TERRITORY—Sioux ambush a patrol of the 7th Cavalry and the 9th Cavalry comes to its relief. Major General Nelson Miles concentrates his forces around the reservation and the Sioux surrender within a week.

1891

March 9—
Congress authorizes additional Indian Scout units—eight troops of cavalry and 19 companies of infantry—formed around tribal groups.

1894

May 11—
The Army is called out to restore order in five states when violence erupts over a labor strike by Pullman rail car workers.

SANTIAGO 1898

1898

April 25—
War is declared against Spain.

June 22—
The Army V Corps under Major General William Shafter lands at Daiquiri, Cuba, and moves against Santiago.

June 23—
LAS GUASIMAS RIDGE, CUBA—Dismounted cavalrymen of the 1st and 10th Cavalry, and 1st Volunteer Cavalry (Rough Riders), attack and seize Spanish positions.

June 30—
CAVITE, PHILIPPINE ISLANDS—The first Army soldiers of 2d Division, VIII Corps, land south of Manila. In cooperation with Philippine insurgents, the city is soon surrounded.

July 1—
EL CANEY AND SAN JUAN HILL, CUBA—Simultaneously attacking the two main Spanish positions, Army regulars and volunteers charge and capture the hilltop forts after hard fighting. Santiago is placed under siege.

July 14—
CUBA—Black soldiers of the 24th Infantry volunteer to nurse soldiers suffering from yellow fever and malaria. Over half of the sixty volunteers die of the diseases.

July 17—
Santiago, Cuba, surrenders and Army troops enter the city.

July 25—
GUANICA, PUERTO RICO—An Army expeditionary force under Lieutenant General Nelson A. Miles lands. It is the last time the senior general of the Army leads troops in the field.

August 9—
COAMO, PUERTO RICO—An Army column under Major General James H. Wilson breaks through a Spanish fortified gorge. Other Army columns are also on the move to seize towns.

August 13—
MANILA, PHILIPPINE ISLANDS—The Spanish sign an armistice, but not knowing this, Brigadier General Arthur MacArthur leads an attack into the city.

December 10—
Treaty of Peace signed with Spain.

MANILA 1899

1899

February 4—
MANILA, PHILIPPINE ISLANDS—War begins between U.S. Army troops and the

Philippine Republican Army encamped around the city.

March 31—
U.S. Army troops capture the Philippine Republic's capital of Malolos.

April 27—
RIO GRANDE DEL PAMPANGA, PHILIPPINE ISLANDS—Under heavy fire, Colonel Frederick Funston leads a small raiding party across the river in canoes to outflank the Philippine position. He and two other soldiers receive the Medal of Honor.

November 11—
SAN JACINTO, PHILIPPINE ISLANDS—The 33d U.S. Volunteers defeat a large Philippine Republican unit.

November 13—
TARLAC, PHILIPPINE ISLANDS —U.S. Army soldiers occupy the last capital of the Philippine Republicans. Philippine leaders switch to a guerrilla war.

December 9—
LUZON, PHILIPPINE ISLANDS—A battalion of the 34th U.S. Volunteers under Lieutenant Colonel Robert L. Howze destroys a Philippine guerrilla brigade in a three-hour battle.

TIENTSIN 1900

1900

May 26—
The War Department issues General Order No. 155, creating the Army War College.

July 8—
CHINA—The American Expeditionary Force commanded by Major General Adna R. Chaffee arrives in China to join an international relief force battling the Boxer Rebellion.

July 13—
TIENTSIN, CHINA—While leading the 9th Infantry in the capture of the city, Colonel Emerson H. Liscum, regimental commander, is mortally wounded after taking the colors from a fallen color bearer.

August 14—
PEKING, CHINA—Musician Calvin P. Titus, 14th Infantry, climbs the wall to help open the main outer gate into the city. He later receives the Medal of Honor.

August 15—
PEKING, CHINA—Battery F, 5th Artillery, blasts through the inner gates of the Forbidden City after Lieutenant Charles P. Summerall calmly walks up and chalks an "X" on them as an aiming point. Soldiers of the 14th Infantry penetrate the city, but are ordered back.

September 17—
LUZON, PHILIPPINE ISLANDS—Soldiers of the 37th Volunteer Infantry and 15th

Infantry seize a fortified guerrilla village, but suffer heavy losses.

September—
Major Walter Reed, Army Medical Corps, discovers yellow fever virus is transmitted by mosquitoes.

1901

February 2—
The Army Nurse Corps is established by Congress with 202 members. In addition, Congress authorizes the Philippine Scouts to be formed under American Army officers to assist in establishing order in the Philippine Islands.

March 23—
LUZON, PHILIPPINE ISLANDS—Posing as prisoners, Colonel Frederick Funston leads a raiding party into the camp of Philippine leader Emilio Aguinaldo and captures him.

September 28—
BALANGIGA, SAMAR, PHILIPPINE ISLANDS—Guerrillas surprise C Company, 9th Infantry, at Sunday breakfast, killing forty-eight soldiers.

November 17—
CADUCAN RIVER, PHILIPPINE ISLANDS—Soldiers under Major Littleton Waller scale cliffs to destroy a guerrilla headquarters dug in above the river.

1902

January 1—
The Army officially changes the color of its uniform from blue to olive drab. The olive drab had been worn as the field uniform for some time.

May 20—
CUBA—Major General Leonard Wood ends his term as military governor, turning power over to an elected Cuban president. The Army begins its withdrawal.

July 4—
President Theodore Roosevelt declares the Philippine insurrection over.

1903

January 21—
Congress revises the 1792 Militia Act.

February 14—
The Army General Staff is established and the office of Chief of Staff of the Army is created as a result of reforms by Secretary of War Elihu Root.

June 23—
The Model 1903 Springfield rifle is adopted by the Army. It will remain in use more than fifty years.

August 16—
Lieutenant General Samuel B. M.Young becomes the first Army Chief of Staff.

1904

September–November—
SAMAR, PHILIPPINE ISLANDS—Members of the fanatical Pulahane religious sect wipe out two Philippine Scout units and their American Army officers.

1905

May 1–24—
JOLO ISLAND, PHILIPPINE ISLANDS—The Army conducts the first of three campaigns to quell radical Muslim Moro tribesmen. The Moros are angry at American efforts to curtail slavery and tribal fueding.

1906

March 6–8—
JOLO ISLAND, PHILIPPINE ISLANDS—The Army wages the second Jolo campaign in response to attacks by Muslim tribes.

April 18—
SAN FRANCISCO, CA—Army troops, under Major General Adolphus W. Greely, assume control and direct relief operations when the city is struck by a massive earthquake.

July 25—
SAMAR, PHILIPPINE ISLANDS—Soldiers of the 24th Infantry and Philippine Constabulary beat off a series of assaults by hundreds of Pulahane religious fanatics armed with bolo knives.

December—
The Army begins the use of metal "dog tags" for identification.

1907

January 25—
The Coast Artillery and Field Artillery are established as separate branches of the Army.

March 4—
President Theodore Roosevelt gives the Army Corps of Engineers the mission of building the Panama Canal after three years of unsuccessful civilian efforts. Lieutenant Colonel George W. Goethals is appointed as director of the project.

July 1—
The Army Signal Corps forms an Aeronautical Division to oversee hot air balloon activities. Ten balloons are in service by the end of the year.

December 23—
Army Chief Signal Officer, Brigadier General James Allen issues bids specifications for the Army's first airplane.

1908

March 8—
The Army receives three contract bids to build an aircraft. The Wright brothers win and promise to deliver in 200 days.

April 23—
The Army Reserve is created by Congress.

September 9—
Army Signal Corps Lieutenant Frank P. Lahm becomes the first military passenger in an airplane with a 6.5-minute flight at Ft. Myer, VA.

September 17—
Army Lieutenant Thomas Selfridge becomes the first military airplane fatality when the plane in which he is riding with Orville Wright crashes at Ft. Myer, VA.

1909

May 26—
Army pilots make their first flight in Dirigible No. 1.

August 2—
The Army accepts the Wright Flyer as its first aircraft. The Wright brothers receive a $5,000 bonus for exceeding the specified speed of 42.5 mph.

1910

June—
The Army begins using the first aluminum canteen and cup with a folding handle, and introduces branch collar insignia for enlisted personnel.

July 11—
SHEEPSHEAD BAY, NY—Lieutenant Jacob E. Fickel fires a military firearm, a Springfield rifle, from a military plane for the first time.

1911

January 15—
Army Lieutenant Myron S. Crissy drops a live bomb for the first time from a military airplane from a height of 1,500 feet.

March—
The Army adopts the M1911 .45-caliber automatic pistol.

April 11—
COLLEGE PARK, MD—The Army establishes the first Army pilot school.

June 11—
FT. SILL, OK—The Army establishes the School of Fire, which is redesignated the Field Artillery School in 1919.

December 22—
JOLO, PHILIPPINE ISLANDS—Captain John J. Pershing surrounds Bud Dajo, a major stronghold of rebellious Moros, and forces it to surrender.

1912

January—
The Army begins the first use of the "smokey bear" campaign hat.

February 23—
The Army establishes the new rating of "Military Aviator."

June 5—
Lieutenant Colonel Charles B. Winder, Ohio Army National Guardsman, becomes the first Guard pilot.

July 5—
Three Army officers, including Lieutenant Henry E. "Hap" Arnold, become the first to qualify as "Military Aviators."

August 12—
Aircraft are used for the first time in maneuvers with ground forces.

August 24—
The Army Reserve Corps is established by Congress.

November 12—
The Army Signal Corps obtains its first "flying boat," a two-seat Curtiss-F airplane.

1913

March 5—
In anticipation of possible border problems with Mexico, the Army forms the 1st Provisional Aero Squadron.

March 26—
The Army is called to assist when massive floods hit the midwest. The Army Corps of Engineers is given national responsibility for flood control.

June 9—
FT. SILL, OK—The Army opens the School of Musketry, forerunner of the Infantry School.

June 13–15—
JOLO, PHILIPPINE ISLANDS—Captain John J. Pershing leads an assault on Bud Bagsak, the last Moro insurgent stronghold, ending the uprising and the third Jolo campaign.

1914

April 28—
VERA CRUZ, MEXICO—Army troops land to assist sailors and Marines in establishing order.

May 2—
VERA CRUZ, MEXICO—Major General Frederick Funston is placed in command of all American forces and made military governor until U.S. forces depart in November.

May 5–6—
Captain Douglas MacArthur leads a daring night patrol behind Mexican lines and returns with three railroad locomotives.

July 18—
The Aviation Section is created within the Army Signal Corps with responsibility to supervise all U.S. Army aircraft and balloons.

August 3—
PANAMA CANAL ZONE—The Army Corps of Engineers completes work on the canal six months early and under budget. It is the largest and most difficult canal construction project done to date. The work of Colonel William C. Gorgas in eliminating malaria and yellow fever was key to the success.

August 10—
PLATTSBURG, NY—The Army opens the first Plattsburg Camp for training civilian businessmen in military skills. Previous camps had been limited to students.

November 19–26—
The Army Air Service conducts its first cross-country flight from Ft. Sill, OK, to Ft. Sam Houston, TX, a distance of 429 miles.

MEXICO 1916-1917

1916

March 9—
COLUMBUS, NM—Mexican revolutionaries led by Pancho Villa attack the town and the nearby camp of the 13th Cavalry. The surprised soldiers drive off the attackers, killing many of Villa's men and pursuing the rest across the border.

March 15—
The Army Punitive Expedition of three brigades under Brigadier General John J. Pershing crosses the border into Mexico after Pancho Villa. Lieutenant George S. Patton accompanies Pershing as an aide. Airplanes of the 1st Provisional Aero Squadron are used to scout and deliver messages by air for the first time.

March 29—
GUERRERO, MEXICO—The 7th Cavalry makes a 17-hour forced march, surprising 500 of Villa's men, killing 35–40.

April 12—
SANTA CRUZ DE VILLEGAS, MEXICO—A detachment of the 13th Cavalry is attacked in the town. The troopers fight their way to a ranch and hold off their attackers until a relief force arrives.

May 5—
OJOS AZULES, MEXICO—Six troops of the 11th Cavalry and Apache Scouts under Major Robert Howze attack a larger group of Villa's men, killing sixty without a loss.

June 3—
Congress establishes The Army of the United States (AUS) composed of the Regular Army and Army Reserve plus Army National Guard personnel called to federal service. In addition, the Veterinary Corps is established, one officer and sixteen enlisted men for every 400 animals in the service.

June 21—
CARRIXAL, MEXICO—A force of several hundred Mexicans confront two troops of the 10th Cavalry on a reconnaissance patrol. Two officers and ten "Buffalo Soldiers" are killed, as well as 75 Mexicans.

CAMBRAI 1917

1917

January 9—
The Punitive Expedition of 11,500 soldiers begins its withdrawal from Mexico.

April 6—
The U.S. declares war against Germany.

May 26—
Newly promoted Major General John J. Pershing is selected as Commander in Chief of the American Expeditionary Force.

June 3—
President Wilson signs the Selective Service Act establishing a draft and increasing the size of the military services.

June 13—
After a stop in England, Pershing and members of his AEF staff land in France to begin planning with the Allies.

June 26—
ST. NAZAIRE, FRANCE—Units of the 1st Division under Major General William L. Sibert are the first to land in France.

July 4—
PARIS, FRANCE—Concluding a ceremony with General Pershing at the tomb of Marquis d'Lafayette, Colonel C.E. Stanton remarks, "Lafayette, we are here!"

July 14—
> First Lieutenant Louis J. Genelba, Medical Corps, is the first American wounded in World War I. He is serving with British medics.

August 14—
> The first National Guard division, the 42d, is organized for deployment overseas with Colonel Douglas MacArthur as its Chief of Staff.

October 21—
> LUNEVILLE SECTOR, FRANCE—Soldiers from the 1st Division occupy positions in the front trenches for the first time.

October 23—
> The first American artillery shot is fired into German lines by Battery C, 6th Field Artillery.

October 30—
> YPRES, BELGIUM—The 37th and 91st Divisions are sent to assist the British Army in Belgium. They fight in the Flanders region until the end of the war.

November 2–3—
> BATHELEMONT, FRANCE—German troops raid trenches manned by the 1st Division, killing three soldiers of the 16th Infantry, the first of the 50,510 U.S. battle deaths in the war.

November 20–December 3—
> GOUZEACOURTI, FRANCE—The 11th Engineers, one of three U.S. Army engineer regiments supporting the British, engages in front-line fighting.

1918

January–March—
> U.S. divisions replace French units and assume responsibility for sections of the front line.

January 2—
> The Army authorizes the wound chevron for wear on the left uniform sleeve by soldiers wounded in action.

January 9—
> ARIZONA—Troop E, 10th Cavalry, fights the last skirmish against Indians when it captures a small band of Yaqui Indians who have crossed the border from Mexico.

February 5—
> SAARBRUCKEN, GERMANY—Signal Corps Lieutenant Stephan W. Thompson becomes the first American pilot to shoot down an enemy plane.

February 6—
> The troopship *Tuscania* is sunk by a German submarine with heavy loss of Army National Guardsmen.

February 12—
> The Army begins using service numbers to identify enlisted soldiers in the AEF. When the system is extended to officers in 1921, Pershing receives number O-1.

February 16—
> The Army's 2d Balloon Company is deployed over the front lines. During the war 5,866 U.S. balloon ascents will be made.

February 26—
> American units suffer their first German gas attack. They are unprepared and some units have ninety-five percent casualties.

March 5—
> The U.S. Army Tank Service is formed under Brigadier General Samuel D. Rockenbach.

March 11—
> Army pilot Lieutenant Paul Baer takes on seven German planes, shooting down one. He is the first aviator awarded the Distinguished Service Cross.

March 21–April 6—
> FRANCE—The 6th Engineer Regiment, 3d Division assists the British in stopping the German Somme offensive.

April 28—
> Army Signal Corps pilot Captain Edward V. Rickenbacker downs his first enemy plane. He will be the top American ace with twenty-six confirmed kills.

May 28—
> CANTIGNY, FRANCE—Soldiers of the 1st Division's 18th and 26th Infantry attack and seize the town in America's first offensive action of the war.

May 31–June 5—
> MARNE RIVER, FRANCE—Soldiers of the 2d and 3d Divisions rush to the front to help stop a massive German offensive. The heroic defense by the 3d Division earns it the nickname "Rock of the Marne."

June 16–17—
> JUAREZ, MEXICO—Soldiers of the 24th Infantry and 5th and 7th Cavalry cross into Mexico to drive Pancho Villa from the town. In a major fight, several hundred of Villa's men are killed.

June 28—
> Congress establishes the Chemical Warfare Service, which is redesignated Chemical Corps in 1945. (Birthday of the Chemical Corps.)

July 18–August 7—AISNE-MARNE CAMPAIGN
> FRANCE—The 1st and 2d Divisions spearhead a successful Allied attack, forcing the Germans back to the Vesle River and ending the threat to Paris.

August 10—
> AEF commander General Pershing forms the American First Army, bringing most American divisions together for t he first time.

August 15—
> VLADIVOSTOK, RUSSIA—The 27th Infantry lands as part of an Allied Siberian Expedition under Major General William S. Graves. The 31st Infantry joins a week later.

August 18—OISNE-AISNE OFFENSIVE
> The 32d, 77th, and 28th Divisions participate with the French in breaking through German defenses.

September 4—
> MURMANSK, RUSSIA—The U.S. Army's North Russian Expeditionary Force lands to secure the area for the Allies. It is composed mainly of troops from the 85th Division.

September 11—
> Horse-mounted troops of the U.S. 2d Cavalry penetrate five miles into German lines during the night.

September 12–16—ST. MIHIEL OFFENSIVE
> The new First Army launches the first all-American operation. The 304th Tank Brigade under Lieutenant Colonel George S. Patton, Jr., conducts the first American tank attack.

September 16—
> OBOZERSKAYA, RUSSIA—U.S. soldiers suffer their first casualties in fighting Russian Bolsheviks.

September 26—MEUSE-ARGONNE CAMPAIGN
> Quickly shifting forty miles, the First Army initiates a nine-division offensive, driving deep into the German lines.

October 2—
> ARGONNE FOREST, FRANCE—Elements of the 307th and 308th Infantry Regiments ("The Lost Battalion"), under Major Charles W. Whittlesley, are cut off and hold out for five days under fierce attack. Their last carrier pigeon, "Cher Ami," is used to fly a note redirecting friendly artillery fire landing on them.

October 4–7—
> ARGONNE FOREST, FRANCE—The 28th and 77th Divisions fight hand-to-hand through strong German defenses in the dense forest.

October 8—
> ARGONNE FOREST, FRANCE—Corporal Alvin C. York takes over as leader of a patrol, killing and capturing almost 150 Germans. He is awarded the Medal of Honor and promoted to sergeant.

October 18—
> Headquarters, AEF, approves the first wear of shoulder sleeve insignia (patches) for units, formalizing a trend started with the 81st Division's wildcat insignia.

November 11—
> ***COMPIEGNE, FRANCE—An armistice is signed ending hostilities with Germany.***

December 1—
The U.S. Army of Occupation (Third Army) under Major General Joseph T. Dickman moves into its zone in Germany with eight divisions.

1919

January 19—BATTLE OF SHENKURSH
RUSSIA—U.S. North Russian forces defend against a major Bolshevik offensive.

May 1—
VARGA RIVER, RUSSIA—Soldiers of 339th Infantry fight off a large Bolshevik attack.

July 7—
WASHINGTON, D.C.—The Army's First Transcontinental Motor Convoy departs for San Francisco. It is the first motor vehicle trip across the country and takes nine weeks at an average speed of six mph. Lieutenant Colonel Dwight D. Eisenhower goes along as an observer.

August 5—
U.S. forces are withdrawn from Northern Russia. More than 400 casualties have been suffered.

September 3—
By Public Law 45, Congress appoints John J. Pershing as the first General of the Armies of the United States. Although the title existed previously from 1798 to 1802, he is the only officer to actually hold it.

1920

April 1—
The Army expeditionary force in Siberia is recalled.

July 1—
The Army Chemical Corps and Army Finance Department are established.

1921

November 11—
ARLINGTON NATIONAL CEMETERY, ARLINGTON, VA—The Tomb of the Unknown Soldier is dedicated and the first Unknown is buried. The casket had been selected in Europe from three by Sergeant Edward F. Younger, 2d Battalion, 50th Infantry. Three Army Medal of Honor awardees act as pallbearers—Charles Whittlesley, Alvin York, and Samuel Woodfill.

1922

January 25—
The U.S. Army Band, "Pershing's Own," is established.

1923

January 23—
KOBLENZ, GERMANY—Soldiers of the 8th Infantry, 4th Division, lower the U.S. flag flying over Ft. Ehrenbrietstein, ending the U.S. Army's World War I occupation duties in Germany. The flag will be raised over the fort again 6 April 1945, when the Army begins its second occupation of German soil.

1924

July 22—
Following a tour to the Pacific, Brigadier General William Mitchell predicts a future Japanese attack on Pearl Harbor. He is ignored.

September 24—
Army pilots complete the first successful flight around the world.

1925

October 28—
The court-martial of Colonel William Mitchell (former Brigadier General) begins for "conduct prejudicial to good order and military discipline." He is found guilty in December and resigns two months later.

1926

July 2—
The Army Air Corps is established as a branch separate from the Signal Corps.

1927

June 11—
Colonel Charles A. Lindbergh, Army Air Corps Reserve, receives the first Distinguished Flying Cross for making the first solo trans-Atlantic flight 20-21 May. He also receives the Medal of Honor.

1928

February 23—
Congress approves the rank of general for the position of Army Chief of Staff.

September 28—
BROOKS FIELD, TX—Eighteen soldiers and three containers of equipment are dropped by parachute for the first time in a demonstration.

1932

January 21—
WINSLOW, AZ—Six Army bombers drop five tons of supplies to snowbound Navajo Indians, saving many lives.

February 5—
SHANGHAI, CHINA—Soldiers of the 31st Infantry Regiment land to join an international force trying to restore order in the city and to secure the American section from Chinese attackers. They remain for four months, returning to their home base in the Philippines in July.

February 22—
The Army establishes the Purple Heart medal for combat wounds.

July 28—
WASHINGTON, D.C.—Troops under General Douglas MacArthur, Army Chief of Staff, disperse World War I "bonus march" veterans from the city.

1933-1983
Civilian Conservation Corps USA 20c

1933

April 10—
The newly created Civilian Conservation Corps is placed under Army control.

1934

February 9—
President Franklin D. Roosevelt orders the Army to provide airmail service on twenty-six air routes because of fear of commercial contract fraud.

April—
The Army officially discontinues the cavalry saber as a weapon.

1935

March 1—
A General Headquarters, Air Force, is created within the Army Air Corps. This is seen as the first real step in creating a separate Air Force.

1936

November 11—
Army pilots in the balloon *Explorer* set a new altitude record of fourteen miles.

1939

January 9—
The Army adopts the .30-caliber M-1 Garand as its standard rifle. It will remain in production until the 1950s.

September 1—
General George C. Marshall, the first Army Chief of Staff commissioned from the pre-ROTC college training program, takes office.

1940

January 23—
HAMILTON FIELD, CA—The Army successfully tests the first air movement of units by flying a battalion of the 65th Coast Artillery 500 miles in 38 bombers.

29 USA
America's first peacetime draft, 1940

April 21—
NORWAY—The first American military officer dies in World War II. Captain Robert M. Losey, an Army Air Corps observer, is killed in a German air raid.

July 10—
The Army forms the Armored Force under Brigadier General Adna R. Chaffee.

August 16—
LAWSON FIELD, FT. BENNING, GA—The Army Parachute Test Platoon, established on 18 July, is led by Lieutenant William Ryder in its first parachute jump.

PHILIPPINE ISLANDS 1941-1942

1941

February 1—
The Army Alaskan Defense Force conducts a 600-mile test of the use of dog teams and sleds for cross-country travel.

March 20—
The Air Corps Ferrying Command, later redesignated Air Transport Command, is established.

June—
The Army introduces the "steel pot" helmet to replace the World War I–style helmet.

June 28—
The War Department combines all the Army air elements into the new Army Air Forces under Major General Henry H. "Hap" Arnold.

September 26—
The Military Police Corps is established.

December 7—
HONOLULU, HI—Pearl Harbor, Schofield Barracks, and Wheeler Army Air Field are attacked by Japanese aircraft. Four Army pilots get credit for downing Japanese aircraft.

December 8—
War is declared against Japan, then later Germany and Italy. The Army activates its first mountain unit, the 87th Mountain Infantry Battalion.

December 10—
NORTH LUZON, PHILIPPINE ISLANDS—U.S.-Philippine defense forces unsuccessfully resist the first Japanese landings. Numerous other landings follow throughout the islands.

December 16—
PHILIPPINE ISLANDS—Army pilot Lieutenant Boyd D. Wagner becomes the first American ace of World War II.

December 24—
BINALONAN, PHILIPPINE ISLANDS—The 26th Cavalry makes the last U.S. cavalry horse charge to repulse a Japanese attack. Within days the horses are killed for food.

1942

January 7—
BATAAN, PHILIPPINE ISLANDS—American forces are withdrawn to final defensive positions on the peninsula as the advancing Japanese forces close in. American rations and ammunition are in short supply.

January 12—
BATAAN, PHILIPPINE ISLANDS—Second Lieutenant Alexander R. Ninninger, 57th Infantry, Philippine Scouts, earns the first Army Medal of Honor in World War II for leading a counterattack.

January 14—
The Army Air Force awards a contract to build the first military helicopter.

January 26—
First U.S. Army troop convoy arrives in Northern Ireland.

March 11—
Under Presidential order, General Douglas MacArthur, his family, and some staff, depart the Philippines by PT boat.

March 16—
AUSTRALIA—First U.S. Army troops land. When General MacArthur arrives the next day he states, "I shall return."

March 23—
The Army begins implementing orders to gather and confine Japanese-Americans into relocation camps in western U.S.

March 30—
AUSTRALIA—General MacArthur is named Allied Supreme Commander, Southwest Pacific.

April 9—
BATAAN, PHILIPPINE ISLANDS—Bataan falls after a heroic and desperate defense against overwhelming Japanese forces. With food and ammunition gone, Major General Edward P. King, Jr., surrenders the surviving "Battling Bastards of Bataan." The six-day Bataan Death March begins, and many more die.

April 18—
USS *HORNET*, PACIFIC—Army pilot Lieutenant Colonel James H. Doolittle leads sixteen Army B-25 bombers off an aircraft carrier to make a surprise first retaliatory attack on Japan.

May 6—
CORREGIDOR, PHILIPPINE ISLANDS—Lieutenant General Jonathan M. Wainwright surrenders all U.S. and Philippine Army forces.

Corregidor falls to Japanese   May 6, 1942

Thousands of American and Filipino soldiers are made prisoners, including nineteen U.S. Army generals.

May 14—
The Women's Army Corps, formerly Women's Army Auxiliary Corps, is established.

June 6—
MIDWAY ISLAND, PACIFIC—Major General Clarence L. Tinker, commander of the 7th Air Force, disappears while leading a bombing raid, becoming the first U.S. Army general to die in action in World War II.

June 12—
PLOESTI, ROMANIA—Army Air Force bombers conduct the first raid on major Axis oil fields from a base in Egypt.

June 22—
FT. STEVENS, WA—The coastal Army post is shelled by a Japanese submarine, the first foreign hostile attack on the U.S. coast since the War of 1812.

July 31—
The Army Transportation Corps is established. (Birthday of the Transportation Corps.)

August 19—
DIEPPE, FRANCE—Fifty Army Rangers participate with British Commandos in a raid on the German-held port. They are the first U.S. troops to fight in France in World War II.

September 15—
NEW GUINEA—The first elements from the 32d Division arrive to assist Australian-New Zealand forces.

September 17—
Newly promoted Army Engineer Brigadier General Leslie R. Groves is placed in command of the super-secret "Manhattan Project" to develop an atomic bomb.

September 21—
The Army Air Force makes the first test flight of a B-29.

October 13—
GUADALCANAL—The soldiers of 164th Infantry, Americal Division, land to assist the Marines fighting on the island.

October 22—
ALGERIA, NORTH AFRICA—Major General Mark W. Clark leads a small party ashore at night from a submarine to negotiate with pro-Allied French officials.

Allies land in North Africa November 1942

November 8—

NORTH AFRICA—Three Army invasion task forces conduct Operation Torch, the first amphibious landings against the Axis in North Africa. The 2d Battalion, 503rd Airborne Infantry, makes the first U.S. combat airborne assault.

November 12—

GUADALCANAL—The 182d Regimental Combat Team, American Division, lands to reinforce U.S. forces. Fighting continues until 9 February.

November 16—

BUNA, NEW GUINEA—The 32d Infantry Division joins Australian units to eliminate a Japanese beachhead. Bitter fighting will last two months.

November 20—

SOLDIER'S SUMMIT, CANADA—The 1,422-mile Alaska Military (ALCAN) Highway, built mostly by seven Army Corps of Engineer regiments, opens nine months after the project began. The strategic road connects Alaska with Dawson Creek, Canada.

EGYPT LIBYA 1942 1943

1943

January 15—

The Pentagon, built in sixteen months under the direction of the Army Corps of Engineers, is opened. It is the largest office building in the world.

January 27—

Army Air Force planes conduct the first U.S. air attack against Germany. The 149th Post Headquarters Company, the first WAC unit ever deployed overseas, arrives in Algiers, North Africa.

February 19—

KASSERINE PASS, TUNISIA—U.S. II Corps is hit by a massive German counterattack

V-mail delivers letters from home, 1943

and its lines are penetrated. Heavy losses are suffered. Allies recover the pass five days later.

February 28—

BURMA—Army engineers begin construction of the Ledo Road over the mountains to link Burma and China.

March 17—

TUNISIA—Major General George S. Patton's II Corps, led by the 1st Infantry Division, attacks and seizes El Guettar, but hard fighting continues.

March 26—

Second Lieutenant Elsie S. Ott, an Army nurse, receives the first Air Medal given to a woman for gallantry in escorting patients over 10,000 miles from India to the U.S.

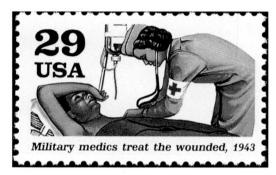

Military medics treat the wounded, 1943

April 18—

SOLOMON ISLANDS, PACIFIC—Using information gained by breaking Japanese codes, Army Air Force P-38s intercept and shoot down Japanese Admiral Yamamoto's plane, killing him.

May 6–13—

TUNISIA—II Corps and British allies capture Tunis and Bizerte. All Axis forces in Tunisia surrender.

May 11—

ATTU ISLAND, AK—The 7th Infantry Division lands against scattered Japanese resistance. After heavy fighting the island is secured on 30 May.

June 13—

Army Brigadier General William "Wild Bill" Donovan activates the Office of Strategic Services (OSS) for special operations behind enemy lines.

June 21—

YUMA, AZ—Nurse Lieutenant Edith Greenwood receives the first Soldiers Medal awarded to a woman for heroism while saving patients in a hospital fire.

June 30–August 25—

SOLOMON ISLANDS—Operation Cartwheel—The 43d and 37th Infantry Divisions begin operations on New Georgia Island. They are joined by the 25th Division in heavy fighting along the Munda Trail.

July 9–August 17—

SICILY—Operation Husky—Elements of the 82d Airborne Division conduct the first major U.S. parachute assault. It is followed by amphibious landings of the

"Willie and Joe" keep spirits high, 1943

U.S. Seventh Army and British forces. The new Army amphibious truck DUKW ("duck") is used for the first time. The battle for Sicily lasts six weeks.

September 9–14—

SALERNO, ITALY—Operation Avalanche—Fifth U.S. Army under Lieutenant Mark Clark lands near Naples. VI Corps units fight inland, but strong German counterattacks almost overwhelm the beachhead.

October—

The Army establishes the Combat Infantryman's Badge.

October 2—

NAPLES, ITALY—The 82d Airborne Division enters the city, while the Fifth Army continues to move north.

October 12—

VOLTURNO RIVER, ITALY—Fifth Army units begin assault crossings over the river on a forty-mile front.

November 5—

THE WINTER LINE, ITALY—Fifth Army units attack the heavily fortified German defensive line with no success.

November 16—

The Army approves a combat boot to replace the service shoe for field wear.

November 20–23—

MAKIN ATOLL, PACIFIC—A 165th Infantry task force lands and fights in support of the Marine assault on the nearby atoll of Tarawa.

December 2–17—

THE WINTER LINE, ITALY—U.S. Fifth Army renews attacks, breaking through in some areas, but German defenders continue to hold key mountain positions.

December 24—

President Roosevelt announces General Dwight D. Eisenhower as Supreme Commander of the Allied Expeditionary Force for the invasion of France.

December 25—

BOUGAINVILLE, SOLOMON ISLANDS—The American Division arrives to relieve Marine units.

1944

January 2—

SAIDOR, NEW GUINEA—Using a surprise landing under cover of smoke, the 126th Infantry, 32d Infantry Division, captures the important port and airfield.

Allied forces retake New Guinea, 1944

January 6—
BURMA—Brigadier General Frank D. Merrill assumes command of the 5307th Provisional Unit, later known as "Merrill's Maurauders."

January 15—
WINTER LINE, ITALY—Fifth Army breaks through and continues toward the next German defenses on the Gustav Line.

January 20–22—
RAPIDO RIVER, ITALY—Strong German defenses turn back a river crossing by the 36th Infantry Division with heavy U.S. casualties.

January 22—
ANZIO, ITALY—U.S. VI Corps lands in Operation Shingle, surprising the Germans. The Germans soon rally and bitter fighting begins.

January 29–30—
ANZIO, ITALY—1st and 3d Ranger Battalions are surprised by waiting German armor units and virtually wiped out while leading a night attack to capture Cisterna and break out of the beachhead.

January 31–February 7—
KWAJALEIN ATOLL, PACIFIC—7th Infantry Division lands and battles for a week to secure the small atoll.

February 29—
ADMIRALTY ISLANDS—After a reconnaissance by Sixth Army Alamo Scouts, the 1st Cavalry Division makes an amphibious landing and begins clearing the Japanese.

March 4—
BERLIN, GERMANY—U.S. Army Eighth Air Force planes make their first raid on the German capital.

March 5—
BURMA—U.S. Army engineers parachute in to assist British forces.

March 15—
MONTE CASSINO, ITALY—U.S. Army Air Force bombers join other Allied planes to destroy the hilltop monastery held by the Germans.

April 9—
NHPUM GA, BURMA—The 1st and 3d Battalions, "Merrill's Marauders," break through to relieve the 2d Battalion, which had been holding out against Japanese attacks for ten days.

April 23—
BURMA—A U.S. Army YR-4 helicopter of the 1st Air Commando Squadron is used to evacuate wounded from a combat area for the first time.

April 28—
ENGLISH CHANNEL—German E-boats attack a convoy of Army troops practicing for D-Day. Almost 750 soldiers and sailors die.

May 11—
ANZIO, ITALY—The reinforced Fifth Army breaks out of the beachhead and attacks the German Gustav Line.

May 27—
BURMA—The 209th Engineer (Combat) Battalion joins Task Force Galahad to fight as infantry, the first of several engineer battalions sent as reinforcements for the attack on Myitkyina.

May 29—
BIAK, NEW GUINEA—First tank battle in Southwest Pacific occurs when Japanese defenders attack 162nd Infantry, 41st Infantry Division.

June 4—
ROME, ITALY—The soldiers of 88th Recon Troop, 88th Infantry Division, are the first troops to enter the city. More units race to follow.

Allies in Normandy, D-Day, June 6, 1944

June 6—
NORMANDY, FRANCE—Operation Overlord (D-Day), the Allied invasion of France, begins with airborne landings followed by a seaborne assault. German resistance is heaviest on Omaha Beach where units of 1st and 29th Infantry Divisions land. The 2d Ranger Battalion scales cliffs at Point-du-Hoc to seize German guns. On Utah Beach, the soldiers of the 4th Division are led by Brigadier Theodore Roosevelt, Jr., son of the former president. A World War I veteran, he is the only general officer in the initial assault waves. He will receive the Medal of Honor.

June 15—
B-29s of the Army Air Force based in China make the first raid on Japanese main home islands since the Doolittle attack in 1942.

June 17—
COTENTIN PENINSULA, FRANCE—The 9th Infantry Division seals off the area, trapping the German defenders. Other Allied units continue to press north and east out of the beachhead.

June 22—
WASHINGTON, D.C.—President Franklin D. Roosevelt signs the GI Bill giving broad

benefits to veterans. It will have a major long term impact on soldiers and American society.

June 23—
CHERBOURG, FRANCE—The 9th Infantry Division breaks into the town's defenses, but it will take another three days of fighting to clear the city.

July 3—
NORMANDY, FRANCE—U.S. First Army begins its fight through the hedgerows, capturing St. Lo on the 18th.

July 22—
GUAM—The 77th Infantry Division lands with Marines to seize the island.

July 25—
NORMANDY, FRANCE—First Army initiates Operation Cobra, a breakout using a concentrated bombing strike. Bombs land on U.S. positions, killing Lieutenant General Lesley J. McNair. He is the highest ranking American officer to die by "friendly" fire.

August 3—
MYITKINA, BURMA—The soldiers of Galahad Force capture the important town after a hard three-month struggle. Casualties and illness during the campaign end the Marauders as an effective fighting force.

August 14–15—
SOUTHERN FRANCE—Operation Dragoon—VI Corps lands a three-division force against moderate resistance and quickly expands the beachhead for Seventh Army.

Allies free Rome, June 4; Paris, Aug. 25, 1944

August 25—
PARIS, FRANCE—Paris is liberated. French units are permitted to enter the city first, followed by the soldiers of the 4th Infantry Division.

—
FRANCE—The Army initiates the "Red Ball Express," a unique fast delivery system using over 6,000 Quartermaster and Transportation Corps trucks and one-way

road traffic to speed supplies to the advancing U.S. forces. Other "express" routes are soon in operation.

September 10–11—
Linkup is made by the two Allied invasion forces in France. Luxembourg City is liberated and the first U.S. patrols move into Germany.

September 17—
THE NETHERLANDS—The U.S. 82d and 101st Airborne Divisions conduct a daylight parachute assault as part of Operation Market-Garden. The plan is to seize bridges as a part of a larger Allied operation to secure a route of advance for British armored forces.

September 22—
HEURTGEN FOREST, GERMANY—The 9th Infantry Division begins its fight into the dense forest, meeting stiff resistance. The bitter forest fighting will last months and involve five U.S. divisions.

U.S. troops clear Saipan bunkers, 1944

October 17—
LEYTE GULF, PHILIPPINE ISLANDS—The U.S. Army returns to the Philippines. The 6th Ranger Battalion secures several small islands in preparation for the larger invasion.

October 20—
LEYTE, PHILIPPINE ISLANDS—Liberation of the Philippines begins. Sixth Army lands the 7th, 24th, and 96th Infantry, and 1st Cavalry Divisions at two beaches. Wading ashore, MacArthur proclaims, "I have returned."

October 21—
AACHEN, GERMANY—The Germans surrender the badly damaged city to VII Corps after weeks of resistance.

October 30—
FRANCE—The 442d Infantry breaks through German lines to reach the "lost" battalion of the 141st Infantry that had been surrounded for a week.

November 15—
MAPIA ISLAND, PACIFIC—Eighth Army begins its first offensive operation with a landing by the 31st Infantry Division.

December 6—
BURG-BERG, GERMANY—The 2d Ranger Battalion captures the critical Castle Hill and holds it for two days against German counterattacks, suffering over 25 percent casualties.

P-51s escort B-17s on bombing raids, 1944

December 10—
BURMA—The U.S. 475th Infantry joins Chinese troops to defeat a strong Japanese attack. This regiment, the 124th Cavalry, and Chinese troops form the Mars Task Force.

December 15—
Army Air Force Major Glenn Miller, Director of the Air Force Band, disappears on a flight between England and France. The plane is never found.

—
Congress reactivates the rank of General of the Army and appoints four soldiers to it: George C. Marshall, Douglas MacArthur, Dwight D. Eisenhower, and Henry H. Arnold.

December 16—
ARDENNES, BELGIUM—The Battle of the Bulge begins. Two German Panzer Armies attack U.S. First Army front line units, shattering the 28th Infantry Division and 14th Cavalry Group, surrounding the 106th Infantry Division, and forcing back 4th Infantry and 9th Armored Divisions. The battle will be the largest in the history of the U.S. Army.

Bastogne and Battle of the Bulge, Dec. 1944

December 19—
BASTOGNE, BELGIUM—The 101st Airborne Division, with elements of the 9th and 10th Armored Divisions and other units, establishes a defensive perimeter around the vital crossroads town. Efforts to reach the 28th and 106th Divisions are abandoned as the Germans advance.

December 20—
ARDENNES, BELGIUM—Army engineers frustrate the Germans by destroying bridges and creating roadblocks, while U.S. reinforcements move to block the German penetration.

December 22—
BASTOGNE, BELGIUM—Brigadier General Anthony McAuliffe, acting commander of

the 101st Airborne Division, replies to a German demand to surrender with "Nuts!" The defender's supplies are scarce and bad weather prevents aerial resupply.

December 26—
ARDENNES, BELGIUM—Lieutenant Colonel Creighton Abrams's 37th Tank Battalion, 4th Armored Division, breaks through German lines to relieve the Bastogne defenders.

December 31—
Private Eddie Slovik is shot by a firing squad for desertion in the face of the enemy. He is the only soldier so punished and is the first soldier executed for desertion since the Civil War.

ANTISUBMARINE   1941–1945

1945

January 9—
LUZON, PHILIPPINE ISLANDS—The 40th, 37th, 6th, and 43d Divisions land in Lingayen Gulf and press inland. Army Air Force B-29s lend support.

January 15—
MYITKYINA, BURMA—The first convoy to use the Ledo road arrives. The convoy crosses into China on the 28th. Chiang Kai-shek renames the road the "Stilwell Road."

January 22—
GERMANY—The U.S. 3d Division initiates the offensive to trap and destroy German forces in the Colmar pocket.

January 28–29—
BELGIUM/LUXEMBOURG—First and Third U.S. Armies launch offensives to breach the German West Wall defenses.

January 31—
LUZON, PHILIPPINE ISLANDS—The 1st Cavalry Division launches its 5th and 8th Cavalry as motorized "flying columns" to reach Manila. At the same time the 187th and 188th Glider Infantry, 11th Airborne Division, come ashore on the west coast.

February 3—
LUZON, PHILIPPINE ISLANDS—The 1st Cavalry Division enters Manila. In the west, the 511th Parachute Infantry jumps in and links with the 188th Glider Infantry.

February 6—
MANILA, PHILIPPINE ISLANDS—The 1st Cavalry and the 37th Infantry Divisions

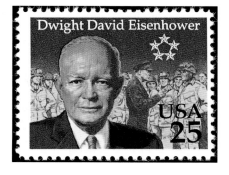
Dwight David Eisenhower
USA 25

begin clearing the city. It is finally declared secure on 3 March after heavy fighting and many casualties.

February 16—
CORREGIDOR, PHILIPPINE ISLANDS —The 3d Battalion, 34th Infantry, assaults by sea, while two battalions of the 503d Parachute Infantry parachute onto "the Rock." On 2 March the American flag is raised over the battered fortress.

February 18—
ITALY—During the night, the 86th Infantry, 10th Mountain Division, scales a steep cliff, surprising and defeating German defenders.

February 21—
BATAAN, PHILIPPINE ISLANDS—Sixth Army units complete the recapture of Bataan.

February 23—
GERMANY—Units of XIII and XIX Corps successfully conduct river crossings over the Roer River, moving deeper into Germany.
—
LOS BANOS, PHILIPPINE ISLANDS—Elements of the 11th Airborne Division use amphibious and parachute landings to liberate the civilians held in a POW camp.

March 7—
REMAGEN, GERMANY—The 9th Armored Division captures the damaged Ludendorf Bridge over the Rhine river. First across is 27th Armored Infantry Battalion, with other units close behind.

March 14—
LUZON, PHILIPPINE ISLANDS—Major General Edwin D. Patrick, commander, 6th Infantry Division, is killed near the Japanese Shimbu defense line. He is the first of two Army division commanders to die from enemy action. The second, Major General Maurice Rose, commander, 3d Armored Division, is killed in Germany on 30 March when his command group encounters German tanks.

March 24—
GERMANY—The 17th Airborne Division and a British parachute division are dropped across the Rhine River in Operation Varsity. Their mission is to secure bridgeheads for other units to cross.

April 1—
LIPPSTADT, GERMANY—The U.S. Ninth and

First Armies join, trapping two German Army Groups in the Rhur pocket.
—
OKINAWA—In Operation Iceberg the Tenth Army lands the 7th and 96th Infantry Divisions and two Marine divisions against initially light Japanese resistance.

April 4—
MERKERS, GERMANY—Soldiers of the 90th Infantry Division discover millions of dollars of Nazi stolen art treasures and gold in a salt mine.

April 11—
GERMANY—Lead elements of the 2d Armored Division are first U.S. units to reach the Elbe River. Meanwhile, units of XX Corps liberate Buchenwald concentration camp and a nearby Allied POW camp. Other camps are liberated as soldiers advance deeper into Germany.

April 18—
IE SHIMA, RYUKYU ISLANDS—War correspondent Ernie Pyle, beloved by the GIs, is killed by a Japanese sniper while visiting the soldiers of the 77th Division.

April 25—
TORGAU, GERMANY—Patrols from the 69th Infantry Division make first contact along the Elbe River with Soviet forces advancing from the east.

April 29—
Soldiers of the Third Army liberate Dachau concentration camp.

May 7—
REIMS, FRANCE—The German High Command surrenders all land, sea, and air forces unconditionally to the Allies effective 9 May. President Truman declares 8 May as "V-E Day."

May 25—
WASHINGTON, D.C.—The Joint Chiefs of Staff approve Operation Olympic, the invasion of Japan, for 1 November.

June 15—
GERMANY—Third and Seventh Armies are designated as the U.S. occupation forces.

June 16–17—
CHICAGO, IL—Over 16,000 Army troops are called to operate trucks when civilian truck drivers strike.

June 18—
OKINAWA—Lieutenant General Simon B. Buckner, Jr., X Corps commander, is killed by an enemy shell. He is the most senior U.S. Army officer ever killed by enemy action.

June 23—
LUZON, PHILIPPINE ISLANDS—The reinforced 1st Battalion, 511th Airborne Infantry, parachutes behind enemy lines to link with Filipino guerrilla units.

June 30—
LUZON, PHILIPPINE ISLANDS—Soldiers of the 37th Infantry Division capture the last major town. Soldiers of X Corps secure

Mindanao three weeks later. This completes the recapture of the main islands.

July 2—
OKINAWA—X Corps mops up Japanese defenders, ending the Ryukyu campaign.

July 16—
TRINITY SITE, NM—The Manhattan Project successfully detonates the first atomic bomb.

August 6—
HIROSHIMA, JAPAN—The first operational atomic bomb is dropped by the U.S. Army Air Force B-29 *Enola Gay* from the 509th Composite Squadron. The pilot is Colonel Paul W. Tibbits.

August 9—
NAGASAKI, JAPAN—A U.S. Army Air Force B-29, *Bock's Car*, flown by Major Charles W. Sweeney, drops a second atomic bomb.

August 30—
ATSUGI, JAPAN—Japan accepts the Allied terms for unconditional surrender and the 11th Airborne Division is flown in to begin occupation duties. 1st Cavalry Division troops formally occupy Tokyo on 8 September.

September 2—
TOKYO BAY, JAPAN—The official document of surrender is signed on the deck of the USS* Missouri *by Japanese and Allied officials.

September 3—
BAGUIO, PHILIPPINE ISLANDS—Lieutenant General Jonathan M. Wainwright, recently released from Japanese prison, accepts the surrender of the Japanese commander in the Philippines.

September 8—
INCHON, KOREA—Army X Corps troops arrive to begin occupation duty. U.S. Military Government of Korea will last until 15 August 1948, when the Republic of Korea (ROK) is formed.

1946

January 26—
EGLIN FIELD, FL—The Army activates the 1st Experimental Guided Missiles Group to study techniques for future guided missiles.

April 16—
WHITE SANDS, NM—The Army begins experimentation with captured German V-2 rockets. German rocket parts, equipment, and scientists are brought to the base.

May 22—
The Army launches the WAC Corporal missile, its first surface-to-surface ballistic missile.

1947

June 18—
Colonel Florence A. Blanchfield, Army Nurse Corps, receives the first Regular Army commission given to a woman.

July 26—
The National Security Act of 1947 is signed, establishing the Department of Defense, the Department of Army (formerly the War Department), the Joint Chiefs of Staff, and the Air Force as a separate service.

August 4—
The Medical Service Corps is established.

1948

May 10–July 9—
The Army is directed to take over the nation's railroads to prevent a strike.

June 12—
Congress passes the Women's Armed Services Act, establishing the Women's Army Corps.

July 26—
President Harry S. Truman issues Executive Order 9981, desegregating the Army and other military services.

November 20—
The Army Signal Corps sets a new high altitude balloon record of 26.5 miles.

1949

February 24—
The Army launches a Bumper-WAC rocket into the ionosphere. It is the first man-made object to enter space.

July 1—
The Philippine Scouts are disbanded by the Army after 48 years of service.

August 16—
General of the Army Omar N. Bradley is appointed as the first Chairman of the Joint Chiefs of Staff.

UN DEFENSIVE 1950

1950

May 5—
The Uniform Code of Military Justice is enacted by Congress, replacing the Articles of War as the judicial regulations for the U.S. armed forces.

June 25—
North Korean People's Army (NKPA) invades the Republic of Korea (ROK).

July 5—
OSAN, ROK—First U.S. ground combat in Korea. Lieutenant Colonel Brad Smith's Task Force Smith, 24th Infantry Division,

engages advancing NKPA units. The Task Force suffers the first Americans killed in the war and is forced to withdraw after seven hours.

July 6—
ROK—Army's first Mobile Army Surgical Hospital (8055th MASH) arrives.

July 8—
U.S. Far East commander, General of the Army Douglas MacArthur, is named as commander of the U.N. Command. Army Colonel Robert R. Martin, commander, 34th Infantry, becomes the first officer killed in the war.

July 10—
CHONUI, ROK—The first U.S. soldiers are found executed by NKPA. Many others will be found during the war.

July 14–20—
ROK—U.S. units fall back from the Kum River line to the successive delaying positions, finally setting up Pusan Perimeter, where they hold against strong NKPA attacks.

August 4—
ROK—Army helicopters conduct the first medical evacuation of the war.

September 15—
INCHON, ROK—U.S. Army X Corps, led by Major General Edward M. Almond, invades Inchon. While Seoul is cleared, 7th Infantry Division units link up with the Eighth Army units advancing from Pusan.

September 21—
General of the Army George C. Marshall is appointed Secretary of Defense. He is the first professional military figure to serve in that position.

October 8—
38TH PARALLEL, ROK—First U.S. unit, 1st Cavalry Division, crosses into North Korea in pursuit of retreating NKPA.

October 20—
SUKCHON, NORTH KOREA (NK)—The 187th Parachute Infantry make the first parachute assault of the war to trap fleeing NKPA troops.

November 1—
NK—First attacks by Chinese People's Volunteer Army (CPVA) units hit the Eighth Army.

November 2–6—
UNSON, NK—The 8th Cavalry is trapped by CPVA forces and its 3d Battalion is destroyed.

November 21—
NK—7th Infantry Division units reach the Yalu River on the border with China.

November 26–December 1—
NK—The 31st Regimental Combat Team (Task Force MacLean/Faith) from 7th Infantry Division is overwhelmed by large CPVA forces east of Chosin Reservoir.

November 29–December 1—
KUNU-RI, NK—2d Division, acting as rear guard for Eighth Army's withdrawal to Pyongyang, sustains very heavy losses against the CPVA.

December 2–24—
NK—3d Division defends the port of Hungnam and assists X Corps's 1st Marine Division and attached Army elements withdrawing from Hagaru-ri.

December 23—
ROK—Lieutenant General Walton Walker, commander, U.S. Eighth Army, is killed in a jeep accident.

1951

January 25—
ROK—Operation Thunderbolt— Lieutenant General Matthew B. Ridgway orders the first U.N. counteroffensive against the advancing CPVA.

February 13–15—
CHIPYONG-NI, ROK—Colonel Paul F. Freeman's 23d Infantry task force is surrounded, but holds firm, stopping the CPVA advance.

March 7–15—
ROK—Operation Ripper forces the CPVA out of Seoul.

March 23—
MUNSAN-NI, ROK—The 187th Parachute Infantry Regimental Combat Team conducts an airborne assault.

April 5–9—
ROK—Operation Rugged— U.S. Army units lead U.N. forces north to Phase Line Kansas.

April 11—
President Truman relieves General MacArthur.

April 19—
WASHINGTON, D.C.—General of the Army MacArthur delivers his famous "Old Soldiers Never Die" speech to Congress.

October 1—
ROK—Eighth Army orders total racial integration of all units. The all black 24th Infantry and 159th Field Artillery are disbanded.

October 15—
ROK—The 2d Division's 23d Infantry, with the French Battalion, capture Heartbreak Ridge after a month-long battle.

December 5–29—
ROK—The first National Guard division in Korea, the 45th Infantry Division, moves into the front lines. It is followed by the 40th Infantry Division in January.

1952

June 10—
KOJE-DO ISLAND, ROK—Army troops end a CPVA-NKPA prisoner uprising in which Brigadier General Francis T. Dodd was taken captive by the POWs. Later riots at other camps are also quelled.

June 11—
The Army's first Special Forces unit, the 10th Special Forces Group, is activated at Ft. Bragg, NC. A total of eighteen Regular, Reserve, and Army National Guard groups will eventually be formed.

June 26—
ROK—A 2d Division outpost on Old Baldy is assaulted by CPVA, beginning a nine-month battle for the mountain.

October 14—
ROK—31st Infantry, 7th Infantry Division, attacks Triangle Hill, beginning a three-week battle.

1953

March 23—
A major CPVA attack on 7th Infantry Division troops on Pork Chop Hill starts a see-saw four-month battle for that position.

May 25—
FRENCHMAN'S FLAT, NV—The Army fires the first Mk 19 atomic artillery shell from a 280mm cannon named "Atomic Annie."

July 26–27—
ROK—3d Battalion, 31st Infantry, defends outposts Westview and Dale against a CPVA assault in last official battle of the war.

July 27—
Korean armistice agreement takes effect.

August 5—
PANMUNJON—A second POW exchange, Operation Big Switch, begins. A total of 13,444 U.N. POWs are returned. There were 389 known American POWs that were not returned. Twenty-one decide to stay in North Korea.

1954

April 1—
FT. BRAGG, NC—The first Army helicopter battalion is activated.

November 1—
REPUBLIC OF SOUTH VIETNAM (RVN)—Military Assistance Advisory Group (MAAG) Vietnam is established to assist with delivery of equipment and supplies to the South Vietnamese military.

1955

February 12—
The U.S. agrees to send soldiers to train the South Vietnamese Army.

August 17—
The Civil Affairs Branch is established, initially as the Civil Affairs/Military Government Branch in the Army Reserve, then redesignated in 1959.

1956

February 1—
REDSTONE ARSENAL, AL—The Army Ballistic Missile Agency is established.

February 21—
WHITE SANDS PROVING GROUND, NM—The Army successfully fires the first Redstone missile.

June 12—
The Army adopts its official flag.

August 2—
Albert Woolson, former drummer boy with the 1st Minnesota Volunteer Heavy Artillery, dies at age 109. He is the last Union Army veteran.

August 24—
An Army H-21 completes the first transcontinental helicopter flight in 37 hours.

September—
The "brown shoe" Army ends when the Army green uniform with black shoes is introduced.

December 1—
The Army inactivates its last combat mule unit, replacing it with a helicopter unit. Two days later the Army also discontinues the use of carrier pigeons.

1957

April 29—
FT. BELVOIR, VA—The Army's first nuclear power reactor is dedicated.

May—
The Army adopts the M-14 rifle to replace the M-1 rifle, BAR, and M-1 carbine.

September—
The Army creates the Strategic Army Corps, a two-division quick response contingency force. "STRAC" becomes a byword for superior professionalism.

September 24—
President Dwight D. Eisenhower orders troops from the 101st Airborne Division and Arkansas Army National Guard to Little Rock, AK, to enforce federal school desegregation.

1958

January 31—
The Army launches its first satellite, the 30.8-pound *Explorer,* into orbit. A second one is launched 26 March.

May 30—
ARLINGTON CEMETERY, VA—The Unknown Soldiers of World War II and Korea are buried.

July 19—
BEIRUT, LEBANON—Army Task Force 201 composed primarily of the 187th Battle Group, 24th Infantry Division, joins Marines in Operation Bluebat. Army General Paul D. Adams is placed in command of the operation designed to halt a civil war in Lebanon. One American soldier is killed and one wounded before all forces are withdrawn in October.

1959

July 8—
BIEN HOA, RVN—The first U.S. Army casualties occur when Viet Cong raiders kill advisors Major Dale R. Buis and Master Sergeant Chester M. Ovnand during an attack on the base.

December 19—
Former Private Walter Williams, the last surviving Confederate soldier, dies at age 117.

1960

January 25—
An Army Hawk missile hits an Honest John rocket in flight for the first surface-to-air kill of a rocket by an anti-air missile.

February 25—
The Army successfully launches the first solid fuel Pershing ballistic missile from a mobile tactical launcher. The missile can carry a nuclear warhead.

1961

June 9—
SAIGON, RVN—South Vietnamese President Ngo Dinh Diem requests U.S. advisors to train RVN military forces.

October—
FT. BRAGG, NC—President Kennedy approves the green beret for wear by the Special Forces.

December 11—
RVN—The first two Army H-21C Shawnee helicopter companies and crews arrive to provide the first direct airlift support to the RVN army.

December 22—
RVN—Army Specialist James Davis is killed in action. Many consider this the start of what will be the longest war in U.S. history.

NOTE: DURING THE VIETNAM WAR, THE U.S. ARMY CONDUCTS HUNDREDS OF OPERATIONS. ONLY A FEW ARE LISTED TO SHOW THE TYPE OF OPERATIONS AND LOCATIONS.

1962

February 6—

SAIGON, RVN—Military Assistance Command Vietnam (MACV) is established to direct the growing U.S. advisory and assistance program. General Paul D. Harkins is appointed the first commander on 8 February.

February 14—

RVN—U.S. advisors are given permission to return hostile fire in self-defense. During the war 378 Army advisors will be killed and 1,393 wounded in action.

March 15—

The Vietnam Advisory Campaign begins. It is the official military start of the war. In all there will be seventeen campaigns, lasting until 1973.

July 1—

General Orders No. 38 establish an Intelligence and Security Branch, which is renamed in 1967. (Birthday of the Military Intelligence Corps.)

July 25—

The first Army armed helicopter unit, the Utility Tactical Transport Company, is activated.

September 30—

OXFORD, MS—Army troops are sent to quell civil unrest and restore order after racial violence erupts at the University of Mississippi.

October—

Army units are placed on alert and some begin moving to assembly areas along the east coast when Soviet missiles are discovered in Cuba.

1963

February 14—

FT. BENNING, GA—The 11th Air Assault Division (Test) is activated to test and demonstrate the Army's use of aviation and air assault concepts.

October 22—

All soldiers of an armored division are transported by air for the first time in Operation Big Lift. The 2d Armored Division is flown from Ft. Hood to Germany in sixty-five hours.

1964

June 20—

SAIGON, RVN—General William C. Westmoreland replaces General Harkins as Commander, USMACV.

July 1—

RVN—Army medical evacuation helicopter pilot Major James L. Kelly is killed in action. His call sign, "Dustoff," becomes the nickname for all medical evacuation helicopters.

July 6—

CAMP NAM DONG, RVN— Captain Roger H.C. Donlon leads the eleven men of Special Forces Detachment A-726 and their Vietnamese troops in a desperate defense of their camp against a Viet Cong battalion. Donlon is awarded the first Medal of Honor of the war.

October—

FT. BRAGG, NC—The Army deploys the entire 5th Special Forces Group to South Vietnam to oversee all Special Forces operations. Prior to that Special Forces teams were deployed individually.

1965

April—

LONG BINH, RVN—The 1st Logistical Command is activated to supervise the logistics for MACV and Army forces.

April 6—

President Lyndon Johnson authorizes American ground forces to conduct ffensive operations.

April 30—

DOMINICAN REPUBLIC—The 82d Airborne Division lands to establish civil order and stability. Under the command of Army Lieutenant General Bruce Palmer, Jr., the U.S. ground forces remain until 27 September.

May—

RVN—The first major Army combat unit, the 173d Airborne Brigade, arrives in South Vietnam under Brigadier General Ellis W. Williamson.

July—

SAIGON, RVN—The U.S. Army Vietnam (USARV) is created as an administrative and support headquarters for U.S. Army forces in RVN. In addition, the 2d Brigade, 1st Infantry Division, and 1st Brigade, 101st Airborne Division, arrive in country.

July 1—

FT. BENNING, GA—The 11th Air Assault Division (Test) is inactivated and is reflagged as the 1st Cavalry Division (Airmobile), which quickly embarks for RVN, arriving there 11 September. It will be the only division to fight in all four of the RVN corps and to receive the Presidential Unit Citation.

September—

U.S. I Field Force Vietnam is formed to supervise Army combat operations in the central highlands. In addition the 1st Cavalry Division (Airmobile) and the 18th Engineer Brigade are deployed to RVN.

October 24–26—

PLEI ME, RVN—Using its rapid helicopter mobility, the 1st Cavalry Division (Airmobile) breaks the week-long siege of the Special Forces camp.

November 14–15—

IA DRANG VALLEY, RVN—In the first major U.S. combat of the war, the 3rd Brigade, 1st Cavalry Division, lands on Landing Zone X-Ray and destroys three North Vietnamese regiments. On the final day of the fighting 2d Battalion, 7th Cavalry, is surprised on the march to Landing Zone Albany and suffers heavy casualties.

December—

II CORPS, RVN—The 3d Brigade, 25th Division, arrives.

1966

January 24–March 6—

I/II CORPS, RVN—The first major joint combat operation crossing RVN corps boundaries is conducted by the 1st Cavalry Division (Airmobile), U.S. Marines, and South Korean Army units.

March—

U.S. II Field Force is formed to coordinate Army combat operations in RVN III and IV Corps.

April—

The remaining units of the 25th Infantry Division, 1st Signal Brigade, and 44th Medical Brigade deploy to RVN. The 1st Signal Brigade will become the largest combat signal unit ever formed by the Army.

May—

RVN—1st Aviation Brigade is organized to provide aviation support to Army units throughout RVN.

August—

III CORPS, RVN—The 4th Infantry Division and 196th Light Infantry Brigade arrive.

September—

RVN—The 11th Armored Cavalry Regiment and 18th Military Police Brigade arrive. Army military police will serve throughout the country in a variety of roles from convoy protection to security of MACV and the U.S. Embassy.

September 14–November 24—

TAY NINH PROVINCE, RVN—Started by the 196th Light Infantry Brigade, Operation Attleboro uncovers a large enemy base area and develops into the largest operation to date. It eventually includes 1st Infantry Division, 3d Brigade, 4th Infantry Division, 173d Airborne Brigade, and RVN units.

October 18–December 30—

II CORPS, RVN— Operation Paul Revere IV continues operations along the Cambodian border by the 4th Infantry Division and elements of the 25th Infantry Division and 1st Cavalry Division (Airmobile).

America's Army has been the sword and shield of the Republic for over 225 years, never failing to serve the nation with dedication, courage, and loyalty

November—
FT. BENNING, GA—The 199th Light Infantry Brigade is deployed to RVN.

November 2—
DEMILITARIZED ZONE (DMZ), ROK—A patrol of the 23d Infantry, 2d Infantry Division, is ambushed by North Koreans, and six U.S. soldiers are killed.

December—
FT. LEWIS, WA—The 9th Infantry Division deploys to RVN IV Corps where it forms the ground element of a ship based mobile Army-Navy riverine force. It is the first U.S. unit to establish a base and operate in rivers and swamps of that area.

December 27—
BONG SONG, RVN—Occupied by an artillery battery and defended by a company of 1st Battalion, 12th Cavalry, Landing Zone Bird is attacked at night and overrun by a North Vietnamese Army (NVA) regiment.

1967

January 8—
III CORPS, RVN—In Operation Cedar Falls, U.S. forces invade the "Iron Triangle," a longtime enemy stronghold, and conduct major jungle-clearing operations to open the area.

February 11—
BONG SON, RVN—Operation Pershing, the longest 1st Cavalry Division operation, begins to secure this coastal area and destroy the Viet Cong and NVA units operating there.

February 12—
DMZ, ROK—North Koreans ambush a patrol of the 23d Infantry, 2d Infantry Division, killing one soldier.

February 22—
III CORPS, RVN—Operation Junction City—the largest U.S. operation to date, involving 22 battalions of the 1st, 4th, and 25th Infantry Divisions; 196th Light Infantry Brigade; 11th Armored Cavalry Regiment; and four RVN battalions. A battalion of the 173d Airborne Brigade makes the only U.S. parachute assault of the war.

April 5—
PLEIKU PROVINCE, RVN—The 4th Infantry Division begins Operation Francis Marion in the western central highlands.

April 29—
DMZ, ROK—A patrol of the 2d Infantry Division ambushes North Korean infiltrators, killing one.

May—
CAMBODIA—The 5th Special Forces Group initiates Operation Daniel Boone, secret long-range cross-border intelligence patrols and raids into Cambodia.

May 22—
DMZ, ROK—North Korean raiders blow up a U.S. barracks, killing and wounding several U.S. soldiers.

August 10—
DMZ, ROK—A construction team from the 13th Engineers is attacked by North Koreans, resulting in three soldiers killed.

August 20—
FT. BRAGG, NC—The 20th Engineer Brigade deploys to RVN.

September—
RVN—The 23d (American) Division is activated to command the 196th, 198th, and 11th Light Infantry Brigades.

September 13—
RVN—Major General Keith Ware, commander, 1st Infantry Division, is killed when his helicopter is shot down. Awarded the Medal of Honor in World War II, Ware is the first of five Army general officers killed by enemy action in the war.

October 7—
IMJIM RIVER, ROK—A patrol boat from the 2d Infantry Division is ambushed by North Koreans.

November 1–22—
DAK TO, RVN—The 173d Airborne Brigade battles a large North Vietnamese force dug into the mountains, winning the Presidential Unit Citation for its actions. Units of the 1st Cavalry Division (Airmobile) are also involved.

December—
FT. CAMPBELL, KY—The remainder of the 101st Airborne Division deploys to RVN.

1968

During this year the 3d Brigade, 82d Airborne Division, and 1st Brigade, 5th Division (Mechanized), deploy to RVN.

January 22–29—
DMZ, ROK—U.S. 2d Infantry Division o

utposts and defensive positions are hit by a series of North Korean harassing attacks.

January 30–April 1—
RVN—Army units throughout South Vietnam defend themselves against a sudden Tet holiday attack by VC and NVA forces. Counterattacks are quickly launched. By 1 April the Viet Cong are destroyed, and the NVA forces have withdrawn with heavy losses.

February 2–March 2—
HUE, RVN—The 3d Brigade, 1st Cavalry Division (Airmobile), and 1st Battalion, 501st Infantry, 101st Airborne Division, seal off the west and north sides of the city, holding against three NVA regiments. On 21 February the units launch an assault into the city, and liberation by allied forces is complete on 25 February.

March 11—
III CORPS—A major operation is begun to secure the Saigon region and the five nearby provinces using twenty-two U.S. Army battalions from the 1st, 9th, and 25th Infantry Divisions and eleven RVN battalions.

March 16—
MY LAI, RVN—Members of the 11th Infantry Brigade, 23rd (American) Infantry Division, kill a large number of civilians in the small village. The platoon leader, Lieutenant William Calley, is court-martialed and given a life sentence, which is later shortened. Twenty-four other officers and enlisted men are charged with dereliction of duty and/or war crimes.

March 27—
DMZ, ROK—U.S. 2d Division soldiers surprise a group of North Korean infiltrators and kill three.

April 1–7—
KHE SANH, RVN—In Operation Pegasus, the 1st Cavalry Division (Airmobile) breaks the North Vietnamese siege of the U.S. Marines in their Khe Sanh fire base.

April 5—
U.S.—Soldiers are dispatched to several major cities to assist local authorities in restoring order after racial riots occur.

April 19—
A SHAU VALLEY, RVN—Two U.S. airmobile divisions, the 1st Cavalry and 101st Airborne, plus units of the 196th Light Infantry Brigade conduct a large air assault operation into the A Shau valley, a major North Vietnamese fortified area and supply center.

April 21—
DMZ, ROK—A company of the 31st Infantry, 7th Infantry Division, engages a North Korean Army company in a firefight.

July 1—
General Creighton W. Abrams, Jr., takes command of MACV.

July 20—
DMZ, ROK—Patrols from both the 2d and 7th Divisions are attacked by North Koreans.

August 5—
DMZ, ROK—A patrol from the 38th Infantry, 2d Infantry Division, is ambushed.

August 15—
I Corps RVN—The U.S. XXIV Corps is activated to direct military operations in the corps area. It will be the only U.S. corps.

August 28—
Chicago, IL—Army Regulars and National Guard troops are deployed to assist in restoring civil order following anti-war demonstrations and riots at the site of the Democratic Party National Convention.

September 19—
DMZ, ROK—2d Division patrols and quick-reaction forces isolate and destroy a North Korean infiltration squad.

October 11—
DMZ, ROK—A 2d Division patrol engages North Korean infiltrators in a skirmish, killing two.

1969

During this year two brigades of the 9th Infantry Division and 3d Brigade, 82d Airborne Division, become the first U.S. Army combat units to leave RVN.

January 1–August 31—
IV Corps, RVN—Units of the 9th Infantry Division begin Operation Rice Farmer with RVN forces to secure areas of the Mekong Delta.

January 23—
DMZ, ROK—U.S. 2d Division outposts repulse small attacks by North Koreans.

March 1—
Kontum Province, RVN—The 4th Infantry Division conducts Operation Wayne Grey in the highlands.

March 13—
DMZ, ROK—U.S. Army fence repair patrols are attacked and repulse the North Koreans without losses.

April 15—
II Corps, RVN—The 173d Airborne Brigade begins pacification operations in the An Lao valley.

May—
DMZ, ROK—2d Infantry Division patrols and outposts receive sporadic attacks by North Korean infiltrators.

May 11–20—
A Shau Valley, RVN—Following an air assault, 3d Battalion, 187th Infantry, 101st Airborne Division (Airmobile), battles a dug-in NVA regiment on Ap Bia Mountain (Hamburger Hill) and fights unsuccessfully for ten days to dislodge it. On 20 May, reinforced by two more battalions and RVN troops, U.S. troops force the NVA off with heavy losses.

June 8—
Chu Lai, RVN—Army Nurse First Lieutenant A. Sharon Lane dies of wounds suffered in an enemy rocket attack as she was finishing her night shift. She is the only American servicewoman killed by enemy action in the war. Six other Army nurses die during the war from non-hostile causes.

—
President Richard Nixon announces the withdrawal of 25,000 U.S. ground troops.

August 17—
DMZ, ROK—A helicopter from the 59th Aviation Company strays north of the DMZ and is shot down. Three U.S. soldiers are captured.

October 18—
DMZ, ROK—A jeep from the 7th Infantry Division is ambushed, four U.S. soldiers are killed.

November 11–15—
Washington, D.C.—Regular Army and National Guard units are placed on alert for possible riot control duty as two large anti-war demonstrations are held in the city.

December 7—
I Corps, RVN—Operation Randolph Glenn. The 101st Airborne Division (Airmobile) coordinates with RVN units to secure the populated areas of Thua Thien Province.

1970

The 1st Infantry Division; 4th Infantry Division; 25th Infantry Division (less its 2d Brigade); 1st Logistical Command; 44th Medical Brigade; and 3d Brigade, 9th Division, depart RVN.

March 23—
New York, NY—Troops are sent to help settle labor unrest.

April 1—
I Corps, RVN—The 101st Airborne Division (Airmobile) initiates Operation Texas Star in the western provinces of the corps.

May 1–June 29—
Cambodia—American infantry, airmobile, and armored units stage Operation Binh Tay, a three-pronged advance into enemy supply and assembly areas in Cambodia, catching the NVA by surprise.

May 4—
Kent State University, OH—Ohio Army National Guardsmen called out to maintain order during anti-war demonstrations overreact and open fire. Four students are killed.

June 11—
The Army promotes Colonel Anna M. Hayes, Chief of Army Nurse Corps, and Colonel Elizabeth P. Hoisington, Director of WAC, to brigadier general, making them the Army's first female general officers.

September 5—
Thua Thien Provence, RVN—The 101st Airborne Division (Airmobile) joins with the RVN 1st Division to conduct Operation Jefferson Glenn, the last major U.S. operation of the war.

November 21—
Son Tay, North Vietnam—Flown in Air Force helicopters, a team of 56 Special Forces soldiers, led by Colonel Arthur "Bull" Simons, land on top of a suspected prison camp holding American POWs. The camp is empty. Killing numerous enemy, but disappointed, the Operation Kingpin raiders escape without loss.

December 22—
Washington, D.C.—Congress prohibits U.S. combat forces or military advisors to Cambodia or Laos.

1971

The 5th Special Forces Group; 11th Armored Cavalry Regiment less its 2d Squadron; 1st Cavalry Division (Airmobile) less its 3d Brigade; 2d Brigade, 25th Infantry Division; 18th and 20th Engineer Brigades; 23d (Americal) Infantry Division with the 11th and 198th Infantry Brigades; 173d Airborne Brigade; and 1st Brigade, 5th Infantry Division, are all withdrawn from RVN.

February 8—
Laos—Operation Lam Son 719—U.S. Army aviation supports RVN units conducting an attack into Laos.

April 30–May 1—
RVN—U.S. I Field Force and II Field Force are disestablished.

1972

The 101st Airborne Division (Airmobile); last squadron of the 11th Armored Cavalry Regiment; 3d Brigade, 1st Cavalry Division (Airmobile); and 196th Infantry Brigade are withdrawn. U.S. XXIV Corps is inactivated.

May 15—
RVN—Headquarters, U.S. Army Vietnam, is disestablished.

June—
RVN—General Frederick C. Weyand becomes the last Commander, MACV.

August 23—
RVN—The 3d Battalion, 21st Infantry, the last remaining U.S. Army combat unit, is deactivated, ending the Army's ground combat role after seven years, three months.

November 7—
RVN—The 1st Signal Brigade is withdrawn.

1973

January 27—
PARIS, FRANCE—A peace pact is signed by the representatives on 27 January.
—
AN LOC, RVN—Army advisor Lieutenant Colonel William B. Nolde is killed by an enemy artillery shell. He is the last American soldier to die in the war. During the war over 30,800 soldiers died from all causes, more than twice any other U.S. military service.

March 16—
RVN—As a part of the POW release, Army Captain Floyd J. Thompson is freed after nine years as a Viet Cong prisoner. He is the longest-held POW in American history.

March 28—
RVN—The 1st Aviation Brigade departs.

March 29—
TON SON NUT AIR BASE, RVN—U.S. MACV is disestablished, the 18th Military Police Brigade withdraws, and only the Army personnel with the Defense Attache Office remain. During the war the Army was the principal U.S. force, deploying eighty-one infantry battalions, three tank battalions, twelve cavalry squadrons, seventy artillery and air defense artillery battalions, and 142 aviation companies and air cavalry troops.

1974

January—
The Army activates the first of three new Ranger battalions that will comprise the 75th Infantry Regiment (Ranger), later redesignated 75th Ranger Regiment.

June 4—
FT. RUCKER, AL—Second Lieutenant Sally W. Murphy graduates from flight school as the Army's first female helicopter pilot.

September 4—
WASHINGTON, D.C.—General Creighton W. Abrams, Jr., Army Chief of Staff, becomes first Chief to die while serving in the position.

1975

April 29–30—
RVN—Soldiers assigned to the Defense Attache Office play a key role in Operation Frequent Wind, the evacuation of American and Vietnamese personnel as Saigon falls to the North Vietnamese.

October 8—
The United States Military Academy is opened to attendance by women.

1976

July 7—
WEST POINT, NY—The U.S. Military Academy enrolls its first women cadets. Of the 119 who start, sixty-two finish and are commissioned in the Army.

August 18—
PANMUNJOM, DMZ, ROK—Two U.S. Army officers are killed when a U.N. maintenance crew in the truce compound is attacked without warning by North Korean soldiers.

1977

June 10—
The Secretary of the Army restores the Medal of Honor to Dr. Mary E. Walker. During the Civil War she was the first female Army contract surgeon, and was imprisoned by the Confederates for four months in 1864. The medal had been revoked in 1916.

1978

June—
The Army adopts the new "fritz" Kevlar helmet to replace the World War II steel helmet.

October—
The Women's Army Corps is disestablished and women are integrated into the other branches approved for them.

1979

November—
The Army changes from solid green fatigues to the camouflaged Battle Dress Uniform as a field uniform.

1980

April 24—
IRAN—Operation Blue Light, the Army-led effort to rescue U.S. hostages held by Iranian militants, fails. After loss of required helicopters, Colonel Charles Beckwith orders a withdrawal. During the preparations to depart, a helicopter and plane collide on the ground causing loss of U.S. lives and equipment.

May 28—
WEST POINT, NY—Cadet Andrea Hollen becomes the first woman to graduate from the Military Academy.

1981

July—
The M-1 Abrams tank is adopted as the Army's new main battle tank.

November 13—
WASHINGTON, D.C.—The Vietnam Memorial is dedicated on the Washington Mall.

1982

January—
SINAI DESERT—Soldiers from the 82d Airborne Division are deployed as the first U.S. troops of the U.N. Multinational Force and Observers (MFO) to man posts between Egypt and Israel. The mission continues today as the Army's longest-running participation in a peacekeeping force.

1983

April—
The Army introduces the first Bradley Fighting Vehicles into its units.

April 12—
The Army establishes a separate Aviation branch. (Birthday of the Army Aviation Branch.)

April 18—
BEIRUT, LEBANON—Three soldiers are killed in a terrorist truck bombing of the U.S. Embassy.

September 30—
The Army receives its first AH-64 Apache helicopter.

October 25–November 2—
GRENADA—A parachute assault by the 1st and 2d Ranger Battalions, 75th Infantry, initiates Operation Urgent Fury, a U.S. invasion of the island. The Army's Delta Force and the 82d Airborne Division also participate in joint service operations to rescue American medical students and civilians and restore order to the country.

1984

February 3–11—
Lieutenant Colonel Robert L. Stewart becomes the first Army Astronaut in space as a crew member on Space Shuttle *Challenger* flight STS-41B. Over the next sixteen years, thirteen other soldier astronauts serve in the space program.

November—
DMZ, SOUTH KOREA—U.S. soldiers engage North Korean troops in a sharp firefight to protect a defector making a break for freedom.

1985

January—
The Army replaces the M1911 .45-cal pistol with the 9mm Beretta.

September—
The Army discontinues wear of the Army tan/khaki uniforms.

December 12—
GANDER, NEWFOUNDLAND—Over 200 soldiers of the 101st Airborne Division returning from U.N. duty in the Sinai are killed in a plane crash. It is the worst U.S. military air disaster.

1987

April 9—
In recognition of the increased emphasis on special operations, the Army creates a separate Special Forces branch.

1989

October 1—
General Colin L. Powell, the Army's senior black officer, is selected to be Chairman of the Joint Chiefs. He serves in that position until retirement October 1993.

December 20–January 31—
PANAMA. Soldiers from the 7th Infantry Division (Light), 82d Airborne Division, 193d Infantry Brigade, 5th Infantry Division (Mechanized), Special Forces, and 75th Ranger Regiment, together with Marines, conduct Operation Just Cause, a coordinated attack to seize and secure Panama. The goals are to capture dictator Manuel Noriega, and free American hostages held by his forces. Noriega is captured on 3 January and brought to the U.S. for trial. Twenty six U.S. Army soldiers are killed.

DEFENSE OF SAUDI ARABIA 1990–1991

1990

August 6—
The U.N. authorizes sanctions against Iraq for invading Kuwait.

August 9—
SAUDI ARABIA—A brigade from the 82d Airborne Division arrives as the first Army element of Operation Desert Shield, an allied force to deter Iraqi aggression. Eventually two U.S. Army corps and supporting units are in place along with allied units.

1991

January 17—
SAUDI ARABIA/IRAQ—Army AH-64 Apache helicopters fire the first shots against Saddam Hussein's army when they attack ground radars to open a path for Air Force air strikes.

February 23—
SAUDI ARABIA/KUWAIT/IRAQ—Offensive ground action of Operation Desert Storm begins with armed helicopters and Special Forces teams moving into Iraq. The VII and XVIII Corps penetrate Iraqi defenses and attack the Iraqi army. Central Command Commander in Chief, Army General H. Norman Schwarzkopf, directs the 100-hour campaign.

February 26—
IRAQ—VII Corps defeats Iraqi Republican Guard units in the Battle of 72 Easting.

February 27—
IRAQ—The U.S. 1st Armored Division destroys the Iraqi Madinah Division.

February 28—
IRAQ—A unilateral cease fire is called by the Allies.

March 2—
While withdrawing, Iraq's Hammurabi Division fires on the 24th Infantry Division (Mechanized) and is mauled in response, losing over 600 vehicles.

March 3—
SAFWAN, IRAQ—Allied and Iraqi military leaders meet, and the defeated Iraqis accept all U.N. demands.

March 31—
EUROPE—The last of the Army's Pershing II missiles are removed from Europe under the Intermediate-Range Nuclear Forces Treaty.

April 6—
IRAQ—Army units, including aviation and elements of the 3d Division (Mechanized), deploy into Turkey and Iraq for Operation Provide Comfort to protect Kurdish refugees from Iraqi attacks.

1992

August–October—
HOMESTEAD, FL—Soldiers from the 82d Airborne Division, 10th Mountain Division (Light), and other Regular and Army National Guard units, assist with disaster relief following Hurricane Andrew.

October 3–4—
MOGADISHU, SOMALIA—During Operation Restore Hope, Task Force Ranger, composed of U.S. Rangers and Delta Force members, is trapped in the center of the city after successfully capturing Somali leaders. When two U.S. helicopters are shot down, the Rangers are diverted to rescue the survivors. The small force holds off thousands of Somali tribesmen until a column from the 10th Mountain Division (Light) reaches them, and together they fight their way out.

1993

October 1—
Army General John Shalikashvili is named Chairman of the Joint Chiefs of Staff. He is the first foreign-born U.S. soldier to achieve that position.

1994

March 8—
Army Chief of Staff General Gordon R. Sullivan announces the Force XXI project to redesign the Army to incorporate the use of the latest digital electronics in the 21st century.

April 14—
IRAQ—Two U.S. Army Blackhawk helicopters are shot down by U.S. Air Force jets when the helicopters are mistakenly identified as Iraqi intruders. A number of soldiers are among those killed.

September 8—
BERLIN, GE—The U.S. Army Berlin Brigade is inactivated and the last U.S. soldiers depart Berlin for the first time since 1945.

September 19—
HAITI—Units of the 10th Mountain Division (Light) are the first troops airlifted into Port au Prince from the USS *Eisenhower* as part of Operation Restore Democracy to re-establish civil order.

October 10—
KUWAIT—The first companies of the 24th Infantry Division (Mechanized) arrive and deploy to defensive positions along the Iraqi border in Operation Vigilant Warrior, a response to aggressive actions by the Iraqi army.

1995

December 14—

BOSNIA—Soldiers of the 1st Armored Division are ordered to Bosnia as part of Task Force Eagle, the U.S. element of the NATO Operation Joint Endeavor force sent to restore order

December 31—

BOSNIA—Engineers of the 1st Armored Division successfully complete a record-length pontoon bridge over the swollen Sava River, permitting the division to move into its area of responsibility.

1997

April 2—

Lieutenant General Claudia Kennedy becomes the Army's first female officer to reach that rank.

October 1—

The 4th Infantry Division (Mechanized) is selected to be the Army's test unit for conversion of all its electronic equipment to digital format.

1998

February—

KUWAIT—U.S. Army troops are rushed to Kuwait in response to an Iraqi threat.

November 11—

KUWAIT—The 1st Brigade, 3rd Infantry Division (Mechanized), deploys for Operation Desert Thunder to counter threats from Iraqi forces.

1999

February 25—

AUSTRIA—Army helicopters and medical personnel are sent to assist in the rescue of avalanche victims.

March 31—

MACEDONIA—Three Army sergeants patrolling near the border with Kosovo are taken prisoner by Serbian forces. They are beaten and remain prisoners until released 1 May.

April 21—

TIRANA, ALBANIA—Army Apache attack helicopters and support units arrive for possible use against Serbian army forces in Kosovo.

May 5—

ALBANIA—An Army Apache helicopter crashes during training, killing the two crewmen. They are the first U.S. casualties in the operation.

June 13—

KOSOVO, YUGOSLAVIA—Soldiers from the 82d Airborne and 1st Infantry Divisions are the first U.S. troops to enter Kosovo as part of the U.N. operation to bring peace to the area.

July 23—

PUTUMAYO PROVINCE, COLOMBIA—Five soldiers of the 204th Military Intelligence Battalion are killed when their RC-7 DeHavilland airplane crashes into a mountain while on an anti-drug mission.

July 31—

General Eric Shinseki becomes the first Japanese-American soldier to become Chief of Staff of the Army.

October 12—

General Shinseki announces a major phased reorganization and re-equipping of the Army to transform it from a heavy force to a more balanced and responsive strategic ground force. Two brigades at Ft. Lewis are selected for the initial changes.

2000

June 21—

WASHINGTON D.C.—President Clinton awards twenty-two Medals of Honor to former soldiers from WWII. Twenty were members of the 442d Infantry Regimental Combat Team/100th Infantry Battalion.

July–August—

More than 1,000 active and National Guard soldiers assist the Forest Service in fighting forest fires raging in ten states.

October 16—

Army Chief of Staff General Shinseki announces that a black beret will become the standard headwear for soldiers.

October 27—

Congress approves a bill to promote Second Lieutenant William Clark, co-leader of the Lewis and Clark Expedition, to Captain, Regular Army, effective 26 March 1804. Clark left the Army in 1807.

December 16—

Former Army general Colin Powell is named to be the next Secretary of State by President-elect George W. Bush. Powell is the sixth Army officer to serve in that position.

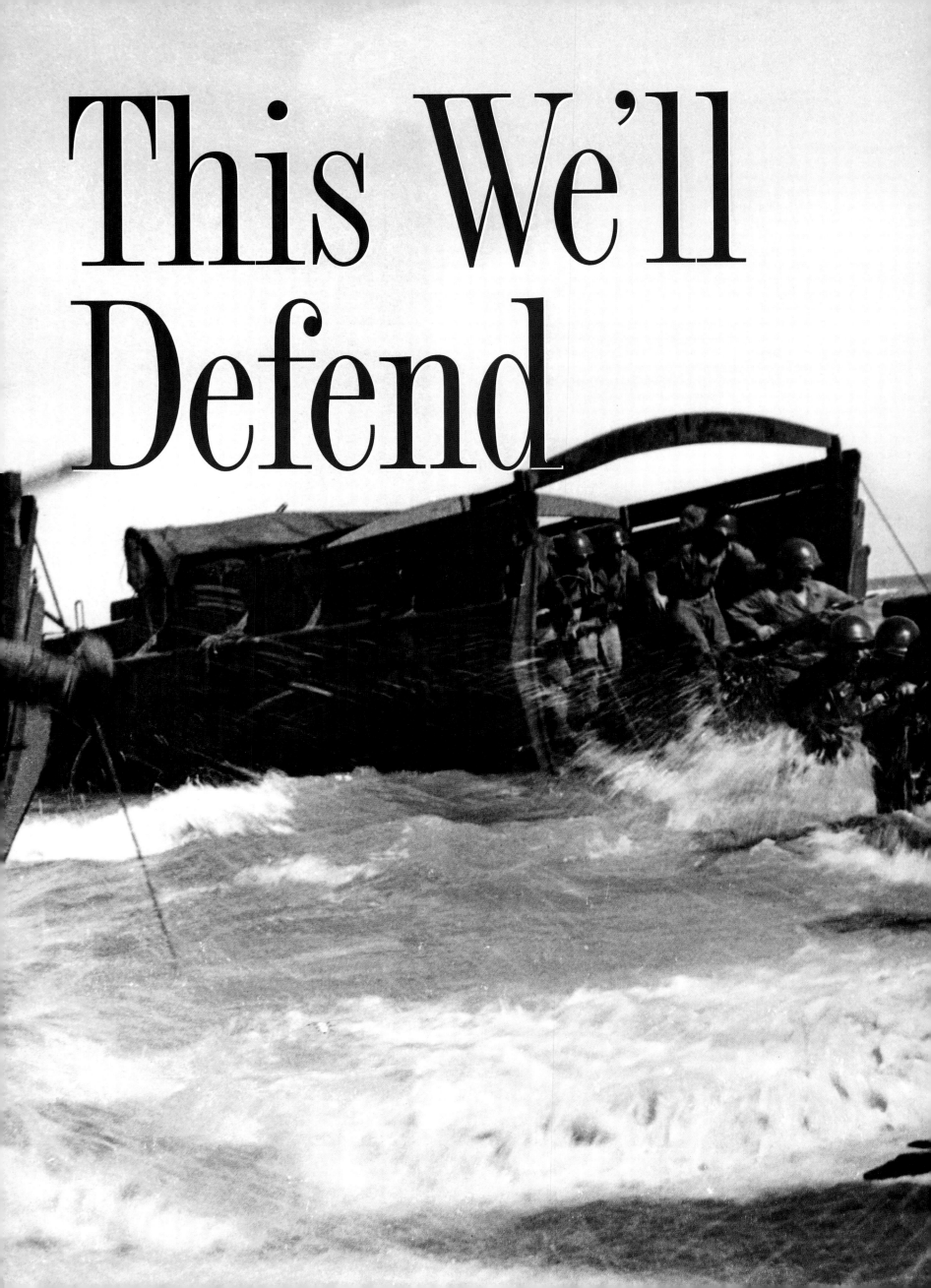

This We'll Defend

This We'll Defend
The Spirit of the United States Army, 1775-2000

Brigadier General Harold W. Nelson, USA (Ret)

Pages 38–39: A classic Pacific amphibious assault in World War II. The photograph captures the confident spirit of American troops who had already turned the tide of the war in favor of the Allied Forces. The 41st Infantry Division hit the beach at Wakde Island, Dutch New Guinea, 18 May 1944. President Roosevelt declared: "There are many roads to Tokyo; we will neglect none of them." (Bruce Jacobs Collection)

Above: A comprehensive collection featuring combat soldiers of the U.S. Army from colonial days through the Gulf war is the basis for a colorful poster in commemoration of the Army's 225th birthday, celebrated in 2000. The Army's heritage reflects its origins in the militia, the Continental Line, and the regular Army brought into being by the Continental Congress in 1775. (Association of the United States Army)

The Army seal bears the motto "This We'll Defend" surmounting a liberty cap thrust aloft on a pike. To some, the motto seems obscure, but the defense of liberty is the enduring thread that connects the selfless service of an American soldier in Bosnia at the end of the twentieth century with similar service of a patriot who came to the defense of the revolution in 1775.

The Army of the United States celebrated in this book was built on traditions of militia service in the British colonies combined with observations, experience, and doctrine associated with the British army as it existed in those colonies before 1775. For 150 years, those traditional relationships had secured liberties for colonial Americans. When political, economic, and social factors led key Americans to declare independence to ensure those liberties in 1775, the new nation's Army reflected its origins: a combination of militia formations and the new Continental Line arrayed to face formations of British regulars supported by mercenaries and loyalist militias.

Above: An early test of arms for the "colonials" occurred when Massachusetts militiamen met the British regulars on 17 June 1775 at the place that would go down in history as Bunker Hill (actually Breed's Hill). It was here that a legend was born when an officer cautioned his men, "Do not fire until you see the whites of their eyes!" ("Bunker Hill," H. Charles McBarron, Army Art Collection)

Below: The official seal of the Department of the Army, the successor to what was known as the War Department prior to World War II. (William B. Folsom)

Left: Ready to take their places in the long line of American soldiers who have dedicated their lives to the nation's defense, new Army men and women in formation behind their drill instructor at ceremonies marking the conclusion of basic training. The most important lesson they have already absorbed is that becoming a soldier means becoming part of a team. (Army Recruiting Command)

From the outset, becoming a soldier meant joining a team. While the modern recruiting slogan, "Be all you can be," stressed individual fulfillment, the context of that fulfillment is the team. Soldiers become part of a unit. They learn to perform certain tasks in specified ways so that the team can achieve effects beyond the capabilities of a single individual. Teams then learn to work together so that effects of various types can be harmonized to achieve even more dramatic results. In essence, the history of the

Below: *Early on in the making of future soldiers the lesson is taught that teamwork training in peacetime produces cohesive units that will perform effectively under wartime pressure. (Army Recruiting Command)*

Right: *It has been noted that "the battle is the pay-off." This truism hits home when soldiers take up their weapons on the front lines. Despite painful wounds, Captain Bobbie E. Brown led his men up a shell-shattered hillside near Aachen, Germany, in WWII— a hill incongruously topped by a Christian cross. Brown would later receive the Medal of Honor. ("Battle of Crucifix Hill," Don Stivers, National Infantry Museum Edition)*

Army is the history of increasingly complex teams working together with continued success.

In the early days, the force was largely infantry, but the infantry teams themselves presented a complicated picture. While the majority sought to assume the weapons and tactics of the standard European army, the American frontier experience resulted in light infantry teams who styled themselves as "rangers" and practiced tactics that later generations of soldiers would

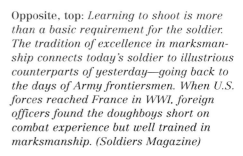

Above: In the series of Virginia battles from Mechanicsville to Malvern Hill—the Seven Days' Battles, in June 1862—Lee's Confederate forces missed the opportunity to drive McClellan's Union troops into the James River when he was forced to retire from the battle in the face of devastating Union artillery fire. Among the Union soldiers who saved the day were gunners of the U.S. 5th Artillery Regiment. ("Malvern Hill," Don Stivers)

Below: Complex WWII amphibious operations required multiple service components to improve their ability to work together. In recent times "joint" activities have become more commonplace. (Soldiers Magazine)

Bottom: Army engineers' training includes acquisition of expertise in the assembly of pontoons to construct bridges—a much-needed art even in peacetime. (Army Recruiting Command)

attribute to "unconventional warfare." Other frontiersmen drew on their experience fighting and hunting with long rifles to bring long-range marksmanship onto battlefields otherwise characterized by musketry emphasizing volume of fire delivered at short ranges. Both variations, coexisting with conventional infantry, make frequent appearances in the U.S. Army.

Infantry could not survive against an eighteenth-century European-style army without artillery and cavalry to round out the battlefield capabilities. The combat arms could not move and subsist without the support of combat engineers, commissariats, ordnance artificers, and quartermasters. Throughout ensuing centuries each of these capabilities became more sophisticated, and the material progress associated with steam power, the internal combustion engine, the telegraph, telephone, and radio, all added new teams to the panoply of capabilities required for success in combat. At the same time, as the United States took a more active role on the world stage, the U.S. Army was being sent farther and farther from its recruiting bases in the defense of liberty. Each generation's "modern Army" included more diverse teams.

The U.S. Army's specific heritage has made this progress appear complex. The militia/regulars dimension of the heritage has always meant that our Army combines a number of state organizations with a grouping of soldiers who were called directly into federal service. Throughout most of our history, this distinction has been important, but it may occasionally receive excessive attention. For most of the nation's history, all formations have used the same drill book and organizational structures, striving to produce effective teams with the resources available. By the twentieth century, the nation was well served by an Army composed of Active, Reserve, and National Guard units sharing common standards and equally committed to the defense of liberties.

The mobilization/demobilization dimension of the heritage surely introduces greater complexity into the training and employment of effective teams. Any nation dedicated to the preservation of liberty can naturally be expected to hope for the peaceful resolution of conflict. A nation blessed by tranquil borders and broad oceans that insulate it from many foreign quarrels can be expected to forget that all conflicts cannot be solved peacefully. For the U.S. Army, these natural tendencies have resulted in a long history of trying to build effective fighting teams while being rushed into the fight. As General George C. Marshall testified so eloquently during the European crisis before U.S. entry into World War II,

Top, left: *Today's Army medics have learned much from the study of moving casualties as practiced in WWII action. Here, a wounded 7th Infantry Division soldier is trundled down a jungle trail in the Pacific theater. (Soldiers Magazine)*

Above: *An artist's tribute to the infantry-man—from the minuteman of colonial days down through history and focusing on the modern Army ground soldier. ("Take a Trip With Me," Peter G. Varisano, Army Art Collection)*

Far left: *Becoming familiar with the workings of a typical Army motor pool, a soldier obtains valuable on-the-job training to prepare for unit maintenance duties. (Soldiers Magazine)*

Left: *There is always the ultimate in "adventure training" for those who take advantage of opportunities such as learning the techniques involved in a free fall from an airborne troop carrier. (Soldiers Magazine)*

Above: *Group physical training (PT) remains an important part of a soldier's conditioning. (Army Recruiting Command)*

Opposite, bottom center: *Training frequently takes Special Forces trainees into swamp-like terrain to prepare them for rigors of future SF missions. (Soldiers Magazine)*

Opposite, bottom right: *Captain Larry Bullock supervises sorting mail for U.S. troops in Saudi Arabia during the Gulf war. As in every war, Army ability to "deliver the mail" to the troops is a major morale factor. (Greg Mathieson, MAI)*

45

Above: *At Chippewa, Upper Canada, on 5 July 1814, a British commander expected the Americans to be untrained troops he would easily defeat. But Winfield Scott's well-trained brigade advanced against heavy fire—and the enemy commander realized his error in judgment. "Those are regulars, by God!" he exclaimed. ("The Battle of Chippewa," H. Charles McBarron, Army Art Collection)*

Above: *An early-morning run on a beachfront toughens muscles and adds to the general fitness of recruits. (Army Recruiting Command)*

Below: *"Full field" road march, an important milestone in turning recruits into soldiers. (Army Recruiting Command)*

"When there was time, there was no money. When there is money, there is no time." This tendency to go from inadequately trained and equipped teams to full-blown commitment to armed conflict was a constant in our history for the Republic's first 175 years. Whether the ensuing forty years of the Cold War were an anomaly or the beginning of a new era remains to be seen.

In every war of our history, our citizens have enthusiastically joined the Army at the start of a crisis. They have just as enthusiastically criticized everything they found there: the discipline was arbitrary, the living conditions were intolerable, the equipment was inadequate, and the leaders were benighted. In most of our wars, many of the complaints were justified, but veterans and recruits worked together to overcome obstacles. They built the teams that forged victories.

In the larger, longer wars, the Army could not rely upon the continued enthusiasm of volunteers. More than any other service, the Army's history has been shaped by the presence of draftees on its teams. One effect of the draft was to encourage volunteering, often thought to be a more honorable expression of a willingness to serve the nation. But in the big wars of the twentieth century and during periods of draft during the Cold War, volunteers filled the Navy and Air Force before they filled the Army. As a result, from the front lines to the highest headquarters and most distant depots, the Army integrated its draftees with its volunteers. The results were gratifying. Talent and commitment were encountered in both categories of new soldiers, and distinguished service to nation has been part of the tradition of the draftee as well as the volunteer soldier.

Though the Army was adept at integrating volunteers and draftees, its record of integrating minorities is not nearly as impressive. African-

American soldiers served in combat formations in the Revolutionary War. They proved their valor and effectiveness more extensively in the Civil War, but they were forced to make that contribution while serving in segregated units under white officers. That separate and unequal opportunity continued through the last years of the Indian Wars and the Spanish-American War. When the United States mobilized for World War I, official policies tried to limit African-Americans to service units. Those policies were still in place when World War II mobilization began twenty-five years later, but shortages of infantrymen in the European theater in 1944 gave many soldiers a much delayed reminder of the effectiveness of racially integrated teams. In several instances, African-American sergeants in support units accepted reductions in rank to take places in hard-pressed infantry units. In spite of their impressive example, integration was not imposed until the 1950s. Yet, within a decade, the Army made great progress toward becoming an equal opportunity organization, although the racial tensions that divided the nation in the late 1960s and early 1970s were reflected in the Army as well. By the start of the new millennium, the Army had achieved the kind of racial integration in its teams that should be expected in an organization dedicated to the defense of liberty.

The integration of women into the Army's teams is another aspect of its complex history. The origins are not as deep; the "Molly Pitchers" of the Revolution never wore a uniform, and their daughters and granddaughters did not seek a place in the combat teams. But succeeding generations of women were welcome in the ranks as the demands of the twentieth

Top: *In the waning years of the nineteenth century when the Army was scattered across the U.S. landscape in dozens of small forts and garrisons, troops frequently were turned out to keep the peace on the frontier. On 11 August 1880 a courageous foray by 10th Cavalry troopers put an end to the raids of the Apache leader known as "Victorio." ("The Chase at Rattlesnake Springs," Don Stivers)*

Above: *Clambering through an obstacle course, traditionally one of the most strenuous aspects of training. (Army Recruiting Command)*

Top, left: *A soldier of the 101st Airborne Division stands ready to go in the Gulf war in 1991. ("101st Ready For It," Peter G. Varisano, Army Art Collection)*

Above: *A training platoon works out to attain the "fine edge" that men and women new to the Army achieve following basic training. (Army Recruiting Command)*

Top, right: *The battle of New Orleans—actually fought at nearby Chalmette in January 1815—earned fame and a nickname ("Cottonbalers") for the U.S. 7th Infantry Regiment in the War of 1812. In the action, the 7th crossed bayonets with British infantry to save an American artillery battery from being overrun. They fought with great distinction, but not from behind cotton bales. ("Cottonbalers, By God," Dale Gallon)*

Below: *Army drill sergeants devote ample time to the basics in basic training. Recruits are taught the meaning of the salute, and how to execute it properly. (Army Recruiting Command)*

century's wars strained the nation's resources. The burgeoning dimensions of administration and the promise of improved medical care were the two main routes of access for women in uniform early in that century. The opportunities for women increased as the Women's Army Corps of World War II included female soldiers who joined a vast array of teams that had once been composed entirely of males. The Women's Army Corps was another "separate but unequal" organization whose days were numbered. As society's attitudes toward women's roles began to change in the 1970s, the Army made a transition back to a volunteer service. By improving opportunities for women to serve, the Army attracted far more quality recruits. Improved opportunity required integration. Political considerations kept certain specialty fields closed to women, but the new millennium saw women serving on all frontiers in the defense of liberty.

Today's soldier may be defending liberty in Kosovo or Korea as part of a team trained and equipped to take direct military action as required. Those teams are integrated in every sense of the word: men and women working together, National Guard, Reserve, and Active soldiers sharing tasks, U.S. units working alongside units of other nations. Other soldiers are on the Green Ramp at Fort Bragg, ready to fly to the defense of liberty whenever or wherever the call may originate. National Guard and Army Reserve soldiers team with active component units to train for future conflicts and often interrupt training to respond to natural disasters. Given the nation's long history of being unprepared when requirements for armed defense of liberty arise, many soldiers spend long hours planning for transition to active combat, training for that eventuality, or developing and maintaining the resources that would be needed if conflict should come. They seldom pause to put their contributions into context. If they did, "This We'll Defend" is still the motto that provides that context, and their selfless service to nation is as valuable today as it has ever been in the proud history of our Army.

Above: *On the "drop zone," troopers of the ready-to-go 82d Airborne Division take part in an XVIII Airborne Corps exercise at Fort Bragg, North Carolina.*

Left: *A U.S. soldier serving with the United Nations' International Peacekeeping Force during Operation Joint Endeavor pauses to provide assistance to a Bosnian woman and her son. Army troops are on duty around the globe on a variety of missions in support of U.S. national interests. (Greg Mathieson, MAI)*

Left: *On duty in one of the most visible assignments in the Army, a soldier of the 3d U.S. Infantry—The Old Guard—stands watch at the Tomb of the Unknowns at Arlington National Cemetery. The Army has maintained this watch since 1921. (Greg Mathieson, MAI)*

Above: *Out on the far frontiers of U.S. national strategy, Army troops must be prepared for any climate or terrain, including the rigors of arctic winter operations.*

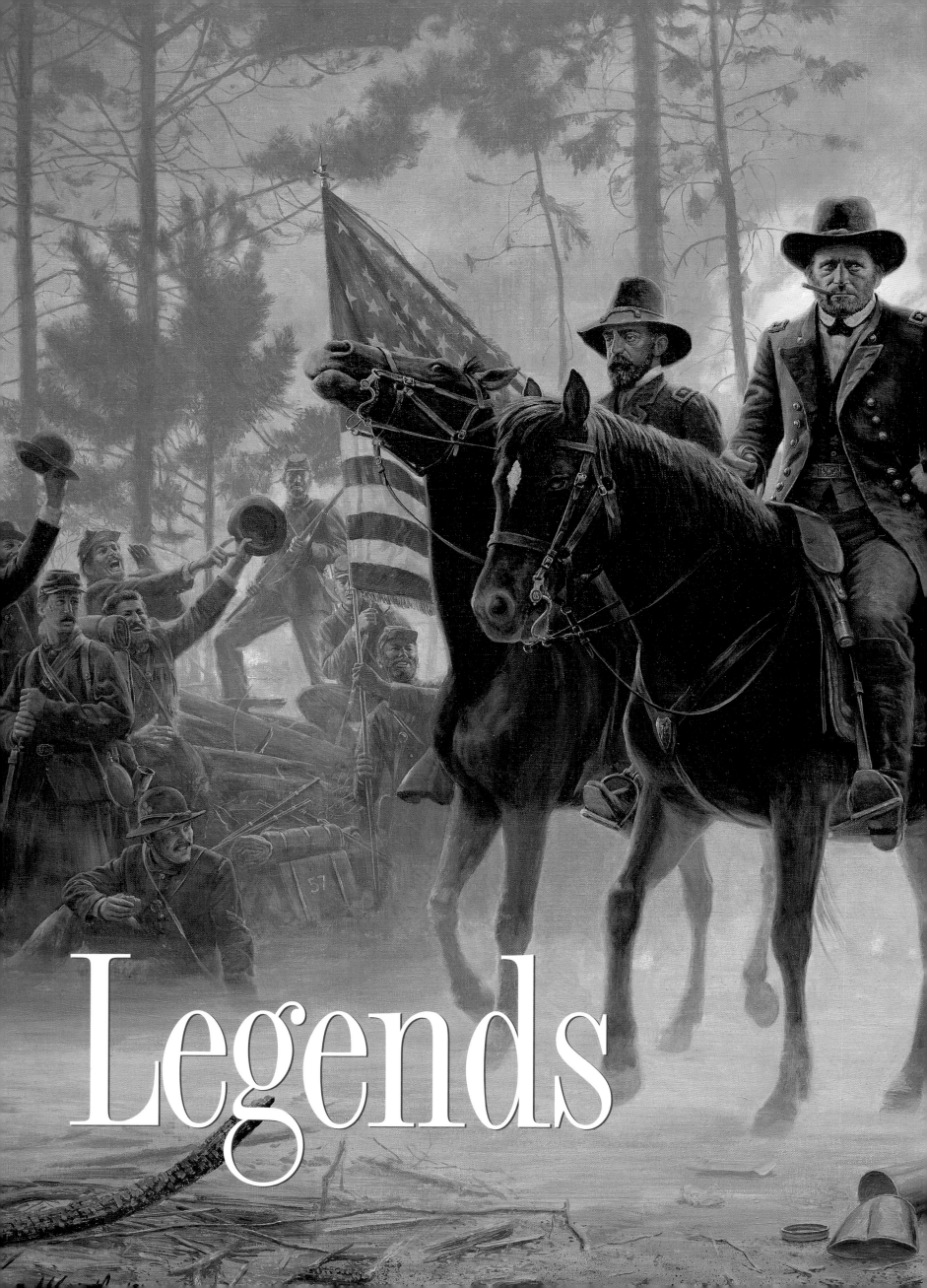

Legends

Legends
The Great Chiefs and Commanders

Lieutenant Colonel Samuel J. Newland, USA (Ret)

In this scene from the American Revolution, Francis Marion and his South Carolina militia, and William Washington and the Continental Dragoons, use flaming arrows to set fire to the Motte house, occupied by British troops, as Mrs. Motte turns away unable to watch its destruction. ("The Capture of Fort Motte," Mort Künstler)

A study of leaders and leadership in the United States Army is as fascinating a study as the history of the American Republic itself. As the American nation has matured and transitioned from a small republic to a world power, so has the American Army and its concepts of leadership. Today a study of American military leaders shows a considerable number of outstanding individuals, despite the fact that we as a nation have often been reluctant warriors. Some of our legendary leaders functioned on the strategic level, others as army commanders, and still others achieved renown as tactical leaders on the battlefield. Leadership is important to our Army on every level—from squad through the highest levels of command

That the American Army even developed strong military leaders in its earliest history is a compliment to the talents and abilities of those early leaders who served to protect the interests of the early Republic. Without question, the classic example of an early American leader who exemplifies the best of the American military tradition is George Washington. He was both the father of our country and, in many respects, the father of the American military establishment. Washington began his military service as a Virginia Militia officer, and first served the British crown in the French and Indian War. Washington serves as a prime example of one of America's first truly professional soldiers. While he was dedicated to and proud of his farming operation at Mount Vernon, to which he repeatedly returned, he was also very well read in military affairs. Washington studied contemporary military literature to improve his knowledge of the military art. He exhibited an advanced knowledge and understanding of leadership and military affairs that was above and beyond many of the militiamen and even Continental officers of the period.

He led the nation as the commander of the Continental Army through the Revolutionary War. Admittedly, he made errors as he matured to the status of a great commander, but his leadership capabilities developed and he successfully led the Army in the field, energizing both the Army and the people. His success was due not only to his ability to develop a professional American Army from provincial militia, but also to his development of a logical strategy for employing this new army. Though by nature an impatient

Above, left: The Battle of Fallen Timbers, fought on 20 August 1794, paved the way for the settlement of the Ohio region. General Anthony Wayne accomplished this task with the use of well-trained Regulars augmented by Kentucky Militia. In many respects, this was a forecast of the way the new republic would fight its future wars. ("Fallen Timbers," H. Charles McBarron, Army Art Collection)

Above: Washington's military service began as a Virginia officer in the service of the British crown during the French and Indian War. This 1772 portrait shows him as a Virginia provincial officer in 1758; the earliest portrait of Washington painted from life.. (Charles Wilson Peale, Washington/Curtis/Lee collection, Washington and Lee University)

Pages 50–51: While General Ulysses S. Grant's ordinary soldier's uniform did not particularly set him apart, his understanding of war—that victory comes through the destruction of the enemy's army—made him one of the great captains of the American Civil War. ("Grant in the Wilderness," Mort Künstler)

An artillery battery during the Revolution is depicted here: enlisted man (behind cannon), mounted artillery field officer, artillery company officer (saluting), and four enlisted artillerymen. ("Artillery, 1777–1783," Henry Alexander Ogden for the U.S. Army Quartermaster General)

Top, left: *The Commander-in-Chief's Guard was a unit within the Continental Army charged with the escort of General Washington from 1777 to 1783. Today's soldier would be struck by the variety of uniforms in Washington's Army, particularly when the multitude of militia units are included. (H. Charles McBarron, "Military Uniforms in America Volume I: The Era of the American Revolution, 1755–1795," Presidio Press, 1974, by permission of the Company of Military Historians)*

Top, center and right: *Two of the distinct regional uniforms of the Colonial militia are illustrated here. ("6th Virginia Regiment, Continental Line, 1776," and "Colonel David Hall's Delaware Regiment, Continental Line, 1777–1783," H. Charles McBarron, "Military Uniforms in America Volume I: The Era of the American Revolution, 1755–1795," Presidio Press, 1974, by permission of the Company of Military Historians)*

Above: *Alexander Hamilton is normally thought of as a political rather than a military leader, but it was Hamilton who chaired the committee at the close of the Revolutionary War that solicited the report, "Sentiments on the Peace Establishment," from General Washington. This report would form the basis of the new republic's military structure. ("Alexander Hamilton," P. T. Weaver, Army Art Collection)*

and combative man, Washington quickly learned that his newly formed Continentals and his militiamen were no match for the main body of the British army. Thus, he avoided direct battles with the main body of the British army and fought when he knew that he had a reasonable chance of winning. He placed primary importance on recruiting and maintaining the existence of the Continental Army in the field. His Continental Army was a force in waiting and, as long as it existed, the British could not declare victory. Washington understood this and employed his Army accordingly, elevating him from the tactical to the strategic level.

Beyond his leadership of the Army in the field, Washington exhibited a key characteristic that has been valued by leaders in today's Army—vision, a plan for defending the nation in the future. In 1783, the new American nation was becoming a reality. Responding to Alexander Hamilton, who served as chairman of the Committee on the Peace Establishment, Washington submitted his ideas on a permanent military policy for the new nation. Washington developed his concepts after appropriately soliciting input from selected military leaders and presented his concepts in a document entitled "Sentiments on a Peace Establishment." Washington's vision for the defense of the nation was an army composed of both a standing military force and a well-organized militia. He proposed this concept to the government while it was in the process of formation. When he was elected the first president, Washington, in conjunction with his Secretary of War Henry Knox, proposed legislation to establish the dual tracked defense establishment that he had proposed.

The defense establishment devised in the 1790s was far weaker than Washington had planned, due more to the mistrust of a national military force than to Washington's lack of leadership. Thus, he was not permitted to establish the type of military establishment that he and his fellow leaders from the Revolution sought to build. Conversely, Washington exhibited his foresight and leadership in 1794 when the Whiskey Rebellion challenged the authority of the federal government of the new nation. Decisively and against the advice of some of the nation's political leaders, President Washington took to the field as commander in chief and suppressed the rebellion. As a military and political leader, Washington, the nation's first

commanding general and first president, rightfully established himself as a legendary leader of the American Republic.

Washington, who led various campaigns and served as a strategic leader both in the military and political arenas, is best remembered as a leader on more senior levels. It is difficult to find examples of leadership of Washington's stature in the decades following his retirement from public service. The U.S. Army for most of that period was small, even miniscule at times. For example, in 1784 the Army's strength was cut to 55 men at West Point and 25 at Fort Pitt. The old revolutionary firebrand Elbridge Gerry attempted to limit the Army through Constitutional language to an average

Like Yorktown at the close of the Revolutionary War, the Battle of Saratoga, fought in 1777, was a military disaster for the British and a boon for the Continental Army's cause. It proved that the American Army was a force that could not simply be dismissed as a bunch of ragtag rebels. ("Saratoga," Army Art Collection)

Far left: Henry Knox was a trusted colleague of George Washington's who had an excellent reputation as a Continental Army officer. After the Constitution was ratified Knox became Washington's Secretary of War and together with the Commander in Chief worked to structure a military force to defend the new nation. ("Henry Knox," Constantino Brumidi, Army Art Collection)

Left: Major General Anthony Wayne served the nation in a number of capacities before his untimely death in 1796. He fought in numerous engagements in the American Revolution, first as a Pennsylvania militia and later as a Continental officer, and was the senior officer in the United States Army during 1792–1796. He achieved fame through his defeat of the Northwestern Indians at the Battle of Fallen Timbers in 1794. ("Anthony Wayne," Peter Frederick Rothermel, Army Art Collection)

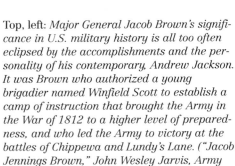

Top, left: *Major General Jacob Brown's significance in U.S. military history is all too often eclipsed by the accomplishments and the personality of his contemporary, Andrew Jackson. It was Brown who authorized a young brigadier named Winfield Scott to establish a camp of instruction that brought the Army in the War of 1812 to a higher level of preparedness, and who led the Army to victory at the battles of Chippewa and Lundy's Lane. ("Jacob Jennings Brown," John Wesley Jarvis, Army Art Collection)*

Top, center: *Major General Winfield Scott, nicknamed "Old Fuss and Feathers," did not begin his military career until 1808, but became brigadier general by 1814. He was the predominant figure in the U.S. Army in the period between 1814 and the beginning of the American Civil War. His greatest accomplishment was the campaign to take Mexico City during the Mexican War. ("Winfield Scott," Giuseppina Vannutelli, Army Art Collection)*

Top, right: *As the nation was in the process of girding itself for the War of 1812, Indian problems on the frontier persisted. On the eve of the war William Henry Harrison won a significant victory over the Indian tribes at Tippecanoe, earning for himself a place in U.S. military history and providing him with the name recognition for a successful run for the presidency in 1840. (Army Art Collection)*

Bottom: *Winfield Scott's greatest campaign was his drive to take Mexico City, regarding it as the key to victory (or in today's parlance, the center of gravity) in the war against Mexico. The painting depicts the assault on Mexico City in 1848. ("South Side of the Castle of Chapultapec," James Walker, Army Art Collection)*

Opposite, bottom left: *Major General George B. McClellan was a ambitious and talented Union general who had the ability to inspire, organize, and train troops. Conversely, in the face of the enemy he proved to be hesitant and lacked the ability to lead on the senior level, although he had shown strong leadership qualities in the Mexican War. He was relieved by President Lincoln after his failures at Antietam in the fall of 1862. ("George Brinton McClellan," Alexander Lawrie, Army Art Collection)*

strength of 2,000 men or a maximum size of 3,000 men. Fortunately, this attempt was defeated. Still, in 1812, shortly before the outbreak of war, the Army had but 3,040 soldiers and 172 officers, which meant that much of the fighting would have to be done by militia and volunteers.

In such an austere environment, one which lasted through the beginning of the Civil War, it should come as no surprise that few military leaders emerged to bolster the kind of military tradition, whether citizen soldier or professional, set by Washington. The predominant leader in the first half of the nineteenth century and one who contributed to the American tradition was Winfield Scott. Scott emerged in the American military tradition shortly before the onset of the War of 1812. Like Washington, Scott was self-educated, having read widely on the wars of the previous century. Scott, originally a lawyer, did not receive his commission until 1808. His effective leadership of an often inept and ill-trained Army began to show in 1814 when the troops he trained and drilled met the British at Chippewa and Lundy's Lane and proved themselves equal on the field.

Even though he owed his military career to the expansion of the Army during the War of 1812, Scott retained his commission as a regular after the conclusion of the war. In the period between the War of 1812 and

the Mexican War, Scott was not consistently successful. The classical tactics from the eighteenth century that he had learned through his self-education did not serve him well during the Seminole War in 1836. Conversely, as major general and commanding general of the U.S. Army during the Mexican War in 1846, Scott led the outnumbered American Army to victory. His effectiveness in Mexico was evident in several ways. First, he staged an amphibious landing near Vera Cruz with landing craft specially constructed for the task, which proved to be one of the first joint Army-Navy amphibious operations. Second, he showed considerable wisdom by avoiding a direct assault on the city of Vera Cruz and capturing it by siege. In many respects, his advance on Mexico City was his finest moment. His willingness to cut his Army loose from its naval and logistical support and advance through extremely inhospitable enemy territory to take Mexico City showed audacity and originality. Targeting the city rather than the Mexican army, which he felt was the key to unraveling the Mexican resolve to resist, saved American lives and at the same time brought the war to a successful conclusion.

Despite his presence as one of the dominant influences in the period, Winfield Scott would not play the same role in the Civil War since he retired in November 1861. The coming war posed a problem for the political leadership because finding suitable leaders to lead the Army to victory was a difficult task for Lincoln in the early stages of the Civil War. In the years 1861–1863 Lincoln was repeatedly disappointed by numerous leaders: Irvin McDowell, Joe Hooker, George McClellan, and even George Meade, the hero of Gettysburg. Ultimately, he came to trust an officer whose name has become synonymous with Union victory in the war, Ulysses S. Grant.

Ulysses Simpson Grant, an Ohio native, was a graduate of the U.S. Military Academy at West Point. The first part of his military career was undistinguished, although he was brevetted first lieutenant and captain for gallantry during the Mexican War. He left the Army in 1854 and was unsuccessful in subsequent civilian careers. When the Civil War broke out, Grant reentered the service with the rank of colonel, and within a few months had been promoted to general officer. While many Americans remember Grant for the heavy casualties suffered during some of his campaigns or the politi-

Top: *An infantry officer and a dragoon clad in the campaign uniforms worn during the Mexican War. ("The American Soldier Series, 1847," Army Art Collection)*

Above: *Major General Zachary Taylor became famous in the Mexican War at the battle of Buena Vista, a tactical triumph over the Mexican Army. Though not a strategist like his contemporary Winfield Scott, Taylor had the ability to inspire and lead troops on the tactical level. (National Archives)*

Left: *General U. S. Grant offers one very important lesson to today's military leaders. Though in some engagements he suffered horrible casualties, most notably Cold Harbor, he consistently focused on his goal of engaging the enemy force and destroying its army. ("Ulysses S. Grant," L. Hart Darragh, West Point Museum)*

Top, left: Grant was distinguished by his time in the field—he was not a desk-bound officer. In this way he could see and feel the flow of the battle and better command his troops. Grant is shown here in the field during the Wilderness Campaign, on 8 May 1864. (Library of Congress)

Top, right: The 72d Indiana Volunteer Mounted Infantry Regiment, Colonel John T. Wilder's Mounted Brigade of 1863–1865, was known as the "Lightning Brigade." ("The Lightning Brigade," Company of Military Historians)

Right: Major General John B. Gordon was an exceptional leader of men. After suffering multiple wounds at Antietam, Gordon recovered to command on the north side of Gettysburg and would fight until the war's end at Appomattox. Following the Civil War he entered politics. (Library of Congress)

Far Right: General John Bell Hood was one of Lee's most dependable tactical leaders on the battlefield. He led spirited attacks on the Antietam battlefield, but during the second campaign in the North, he was seriously wounded on the second day of Gettysburg, robbing Lee of a key asset in his main attack. (Museum of the Confederacy)

Opposite, top: General Phillip H. Sheridan was an outstanding officer who first served on the frontier but who won his greatest laurels during the American Civil War. He served as Commanding General of the U.S Army following General Sherman, and urged support for the National Guard as a way to shore up the nation's defenses. ("Sheridan Rallying the Troops," collection of Mrs. John Nicholas Brown)

cal scandals of his postwar presidency, Grant should be remembered for his true legacy to American military leadership. Grant, though not as well read in military history as Washington or Scott, seemed to sense, almost intuitively, the necessity for closing on the enemy and persistently hammering the rival force until it was defeated. He was not the apostle of the grand Napoleonic battle, the singular, grand engagement that seemed to fixate so many of his contemporaries. Instead, Grant realized that the war would have to be concluded through a series of battles, linked together in a campaign rather than a single or solitary battle. Grant's persistence and determination to engage the enemy and focus on its destruction became his hallmark. He stubbornly pursued his goal, occasionally suffering reverses and taking heavy casualties. Above all, he pursued the logical and strategic goal, the destruction of the Confederate army, which would translate into the defeat of the Confederacy. His understanding of these modern concepts of warfare proved to be his enduring legacy.

Again, there are many types of military leaders who could be highlighted in the American experience, leaders who functioned on different levels of war. Washington is best known for his ability to energize, to lead on the national level whether in the military or political arena. Grant achieved

fame for commanding field armies and for his ability to doggedly engage his enemy until victory was his. On a little knoll in south central Pennsylvania, an officer in Union blue offers another example of leadership, direct leadership of men in battle. This officer, Colonel Joshua Lawrence Chamberlain, has become a legendary example for the Army. As the second day of the Battle of Gettysburg began in the late afternoon of 2 July 1863, Chamberlain was called upon to secure the Union defense at a place called Little Round Top. He began this task at a disadvantage because his regiment was thrown

Above: *On 2 July 1863, Colonel Joshua Chamberlain's 20th Maine was given the task to hold the extreme left of the Union position at Little Round Top. Chamberlain's now famous stand at Gettysburg has caused the Army to use his example in numerous publications on leadership. ("Chamberlain and the 20th Maine," Mort Künstler)*

Left: *Robert Gould Shaw, the "boy colonel" from Massachusetts, is shown reviewing his command, the 54th Massachusetts, whose heroic actions were made famous by the film Glory. The 54th Massachusetts was one of many U.S. Colored Regiments raised by the Union for the American Civil War. ("Colonel Robert Gould Shaw and the 54th Massachusetts," Mort Künstler)*

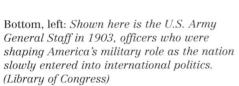

Bottom, left: *Shown here is the U.S. Army General Staff in 1903, officers who were shaping America's military role as the nation slowly entered into international politics. (Library of Congress)*

Bottom, right: *Lieutenant General Nelson Appleton Miles, who was Commanding General of the United States Army from 1895 to 1903, was a bona fide Civil War hero and was wounded numerous times. Miles was extremely influential in postwar operations on the western frontier and commanded during the Spanish-American War. He was also a recipient of the Medal of Honor. ("Nelson Appleton Miles," Caroline Thurber, Army Art Collection)*

in to halt a potential Union disaster and with little preparation. The Union's Army of the Potomac faced Major General John Bell Hood's Confederates, who were under Lieutenant General James Longstreet's command. Hood's soldiers were close to overrunning the extreme left of the Union line and rolling up the Federal flank. The extreme left was held by the 20th Maine Regiment commanded by Chamberlain, formerly a professor of rhetoric at Bowdoin College in Maine. Chamberlain was ordered to hold the extreme left of the Union line at all costs. With great courage and determination, he led his men as they repelled repeated Confederate attacks, and with ammunition gone, he ordered and led the regiment's now famous bayonet charge that broke the Confederate attack.

Chamberlain's spirited defense of the Union at Little Round Top has become legend in Army circles. Yet Chamberlain emerges from this battle as unique because his ability to inspire his men was not limited to his exemplary leadership at the battle at Gettysburg. At Petersburg in 1864, Chamberlain again demonstrated his leadership when, while bearing his regiment's flag in an attempt to rally and redirect his troops, he was struck through the hips by a single minié ball. He refused to fall despite this serious wound. Instead, Chamberlain drove his sword into the ground to maintain his erect posture and retain control of his regiment, only falling when he fainted from loss of blood. Another memorable act, and one that indicated a profound understanding of military leadership, occurred at Appomattox, where then Major General Chamberlain was given the task of accepting the surrender of the Army of Northern Virginia. When Lee surrendered and his troops marched by the victorious Union Army, Chamberlain ordered his troops of the 1st Division, V Corps, to switch to "carry arms," appropriately saluting their brave foes. This act clearly indicates that Chamberlain, though best known for his direct leadership on the field, had an understanding that went beyond the direct leadership waged by a field officer—he understood that there had to be a spirit of reconciliation to start to put the nation back together after a bitter Civil War.

Many other examples of leadership could be found on battlefields of the Civil War. Grant succeeded in transitioning from a significant position of

military leadership to one of political leadership. One of his key lieutenants, William T. Sherman, however, proved that excellence in fighting the nation's enemies on the battlefield did not always translate into senior leadership in the nation's capital. Once Grant was elected president in 1868, he promoted Sherman to full general and appointed him as commanding general of the Army. Sherman had, together with Grant, brought a distinctly modern flair to the Civil War, cutting a path of destruction through the South and being instrumental in bringing the South to its knees. In so doing, he earned a position as one of the military legends of the Civil War. As commanding general of the Army, however, Sherman proved both unwilling and unable to master Washington politics, and weary of infighting, moved his office to St. Louis, Missouri. He voluntarily resigned in 1883. He achieved fame due to his leadership in his now famous "March to the Sea" and his role in leading the Army though its postwar downsizing, when congressional moves threatened its very existence.

Leaders like Sherman, Nelson A. Miles, and George Crook, and reform-minded theorists like Major General Emory Upton provided leadership for the Army during the only military contingency facing the nation during the last years of the nineteenth century, concluding the Indian Wars, a task that lasted until the end of the nineteenth century. When the Span-

ish American War broke out in 1898, a popular leader, Teddy Roosevelt, was added to the Army's tradition of military leadership.

As the nation entered the twentieth century, the American military establishment had to undergo major changes in its structure to successfully defend itself and its interests and allies abroad. Beginning in 1903 and culminating with the National Defense Act of 1916, the Army went through a remarkable transition, essentially adopting the structure it has today—a force composed of the Regular Army, Army Reserve, and National Guard. The first leader to test the validity of this concept was General John J. Pershing, commander of the American Expeditionary Force during World War I. "Black Jack" Pershing, a USMA graduate, had a rich career that prepared him well for the first American entry into a European war. Pershing served in the final Indian War campaign at Wounded Knee and as a military

Above: *One of the famous generals of the Western Indian Campaigns, Major General George Crook, shown here with one of his Apache scouts during the western campaigns in 1885. (National Archives)*

Far left: *General Tasker Howard Bliss, president of the Army War College (1903–1905), was a career Army officer who missed the Indian Campaigns but held a number of significant Army positions in the years preceding the Spanish-American War. He was Chief of Staff of the Army during most of World War I and a delegate to the Paris Peace Conference from 1918 to 1920. ("Tasker Howard Bliss," Frank Ingoglia, Army Art Collection)*

Left: *Major General Wesley Merritt, a cavalry officer during the American Civil War, was commander of the U.S. Expedition to the Philippines in 1898. After the Spanish-American War, Merritt served on the Army General staff. (National Archives)*

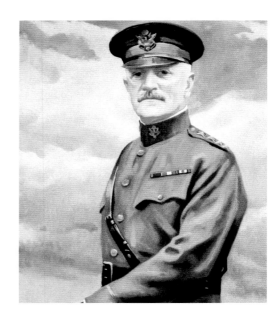

Top, left: *General Peyton Conway March was an artillery officer who served in the Spanish-American War and the Philippine Insurrection. As Chief of Staff (1918–1921), March played a significant role in the buildup and employment of the U.S. Army for WWI and the demobilization of the Army after the war. (Nicodemus David Hufford, Army Art Collection)*

Top, center: *Major General Frederick Funston became well known for his role in suppressing the Philippine Insurrection, and receiving the Medal of Honor for his heroism in the conflict. Funston was also involved in the occupation of Vera Cruz during the 1916 punitive expedition into Mexico. (National Archives)*

Top, right: *General John J. Pershing achieved his greatest recognition as the commanding general of the Punitive Mexican Expedition in 1916 and commander of the AEF in France, in 1917–1919. As Chief of Staff of the Army (1921–1924), Pershing promoted military preparedness with the establishment of the War Plans Board. ("John Joseph Pershing," Richard Leopold Seyffert, Army Art Collection)*

Right: *General Pershing is greeted by French Allies upon arrival in France in 1918. Pershing insisted that American troops would fight as a national unit, rather than being parceled out with the French and British armies. ("General Pershing Arrives in France," Mort Künstler)*

Opposite, top left: *General Charles Pelot Summerall helped suppress the Philippine Insurrection, in the Boxer expedition, and was heavily involved in operations in France during World War I. He was Chief of Staff of the Army from 1926 to 1930, and was instrumental in forming mechanized forces in the Army. (Ray Edward Goodbred, Army Art Collection)*

Opposite, top center: *Major General Omar Bundy was commander of the 2d Division in France during WWI. Though George Marshall seemed to regard him highly, General Pershing relieved Bundy in the field. (National Archives)*

Opposite, top right: *Lieutenant General Robert Lee Bullard was commander of the U.S. Second Army during the Argonne offensive in World War I. He was an aggressive and capable division and corps commander and was the organizer of the AEF's Infantry schools. (National Archives)*

attaché in Japan during the Russo-Japanese War. He served in combat in Cuba in the Spanish-American War, and the Philippine and Moro insurrections. He also commanded the punitive expedition against Mexico in 1916, an operation that served as a dress rehearsal for the mobilization for World War I. Pershing's leadership abilities were recognized earlier by President Theodore Roosevelt, who promoted him from captain to brigadier general, largely due to the qualities he demonstrated in the Philippines and his keen observations forwarded to Washington during the Russo-Japanese War.

The same qualities that caused Roosevelt to promote Pershing ahead of his contemporaries were shown when he commanded the AEF in France. In the campaigns of World War I, the United States participated as a nation working within an alliance, the first time the nation had participated in this type of warfare since the American Revolution. Pershing took

American troops to the continent and insisted that the American Army fight as a cohesive force with its own section of the front, rather than be piecemealed out to the Allies as reinforcing elements. As a consequence, even though the American Army fought under the overall Allied commander, Marshal Ferdinand Foch, the bulk of it fought as an American Army under American commanders.

Pershing's career continued past the Allied victory in France. He became Chief of Staff of the Army in 1921, and much like his predecessor William T. Sherman, had the task of reorganizing and downsizing the Army in the postwar era. Perhaps the greatest contribution that Pershing made in the postwar era was the mentoring of a young officer who would become his successor in commanding coalition warfare, George C. Marshall.

Marshall was the ranking member of a triad of three leaders who became true legends in the Second World War—the other two being Dwight D. Eisenhower and Douglas MacArthur. Marshall, unlike many of his predecessors in the key position of Chief of Staff, was a graduate of Virginia Military Institute. He initially demonstrated his talents and abilities during the World War I campaigns in France, where Marshall served as operations officer of the 1st Division and Chief of Staff of VIII Corps. His leadership skills and meticulous planning brought him to Pershing's

Above: *Major General Fox Conner is regarded as one of the most brilliant students of warfare in the American Army. Conner was an exceptional educator and mentor of junior officers and at the same time was a capable practitioner. (National Archives)*

Far left: *General Douglas MacArthur excelled as both a student and as an officer in the field. As Chief of Staff of the Army from 1930 to 1935 he worked to erase the many deficiencies that plagued the Depression-era Army. He briefly retired from the Army in 1937 but was recalled to active duty in 1941, to become Supreme Commander in the Pacific during WWII and later commander of the U.N. Command Far East during the Korean conflict. (Robert Oliver Skemp, Army Art Collection)*

Left: *General George C Marshall's career was varied, clearly demonstrating his ability to be a leader both in the military and the governmental realm. He had two assignments with National Guard units, in Massachusetts and Illinois, and held both high ranking military and civilian positions. As a military leader who crafted the American strategy for World War II and selected many of the Army's key leaders, his organized and disciplined approach to his duties is legendary in military histories. ("George Catlett Marshall," John Edward Bannon, Army Art Collection)*

A coalition leader who functioned at the highest levels of government, General Dwight D. Eisenhower maintained his ability and willingness to talk with common soldiers. Here Eisenhower talks to a soldier from Company E, 502nd Parachute Infantry Regiment, at the 101st Airborne Division's holding area on the eve of the Normandy invasion. Eisenhower was an infantry officer who spent WWI in the U.S. His career progressed slowly during the interwar years, but during that period he served under Fox Conner and Douglas MacArthur, experiences that greatly affected his professional development. Eisenhower's abilities were recognized by General Marshall, and he was appointed Supreme Commander of the Allied Expeditionary Forces in Western Europe. From 1945 to 1947 he was Chief of Staff of the Army, where he presided over demobilization and retired from active duty in 1948. He was recalled in 1950 to become Supreme Allied Commander, NATO. (National Archives)

Below: General George S. Patton remains one of the most intriguing personalities among the senior U.S. commanders in World War II. Suffering from learning disabilities as a boy, he conquered his problems and became a fierce competitor in everything he tried, from sports to war. While his personality exhibited many quirks and excesses, Patton intuitively understood operational warfare and waged it in his campaigns. (National Archives)

Bottom, right: General Joseph Warren Stillwell, who served during World War II in the China-Burma-India Theater, was one of the American Army's "old China hands." Stillwell, who had been U.S. Military Attache in China before the war, was known for his direct style and his constant pleas for reform in the Nationalist Chinese army. ("Vinegar Joe Stillwell," Mort Künstler)

attention. From 1919 to 1924 Marshall was Pershing's aide, and after infantry commands and instructor duties at both the Army Staff College and the Army War College, he became Chief of Staff of the Army in 1939. Though he had been a capable officer throughout his career, Marshall excelled as Chief of Staff. It was Marshall, in his new appointment, who led the effort to mobilize the nation for World War II. In the process, he earned the respect of both the president and Congress. Marshall deserves credit for being the key U.S. military architect for Allied victory in World War II.

Once he retired from the Army in 1947, Marshall was appointed Secretary of State. In this capacity, he led the nation and its allies in the reconstruction of Europe. The award of the Nobel Peace prize to Marshall, for his development of the Marshall Plan, makes him the only professional American military leader to achieve that high distinction.

While Marshall remains a giant in the American military tradition, few Army officers can match the legendary status of General Douglas MacArthur. He was the son of Civil War hero Arthur MacArthur, and was commissioned in the U.S. Army following his graduation from the U.S. Military Academy in 1903. He was an outstanding student at West Point,

but for the first decade of his career his assignments were fairly routine, other than a stint as aide to President Theodore Roosevelt. After 1915, with his promotion to major, his career literally took off. By June 1918 MacArthur was a brigadier general, and at the war's end, he commanded the 42d "Rainbow" Division. In the interwar years, he served as the superintendent of the U.S. Military Academy, and in November 1930 he reached the highest position in the United States Army with his appointment to Chief of Staff.

As Chief of Staff, MacArthur exhibited great energy, but as he wrestled with manpower and procurement, he exhibited a failing that repeatedly haunted him. In exasperation over the lack of resources for the Army, he made critical comments about the president to the media. He survived with only a severe tongue lashing. When MacArthur retired from the Army in 1937, he was granted permission to accept advisory duties in the Philippines, where he had considerable expertise. As World War II approached, however, MacArthur was called back to active duty as a lieutenant general and first served as commander of U.S. Army Forces Far East and later as Supreme Allied Commander in the Pacific (1941–1945). As Allied Commander, he oversaw the Pacific Campaign that brought about the defeat of Imperial Japan. Once World War II ended, he was first appointed Supreme Allied Commander, Japan, and, in 1947, Commander in Chief, Far East Command. In this postwar command MacArthur was responsible for the reconstruction and reforms of Japan, a task that was executed brilliantly.

In 1950 another challenge faced this seventy-year-old General of the Army—the outbreak of the Korean War. After a string of bitter defeats, General MacArthur achieved a brilliant success with the Inchon invasion, a daring amphibious landing to cut the lines of communication of the North Korean Peoples Army and bring about its destruction. This was MacArthur's finest hour. His plan achieved its goal and sent the remnants of the North Korean Army reeling northward in defeat. While he served the nation brilliantly, MacArthur failed to understand, or ignored, the delicate balance between the honesty and candor officers must demonstrate while refraining from public disagreement with the commander in chief. This failing resulted in his relief and final departure from the Army.

While Marshall was America's war planner, its strategist on the national level, MacArthur was a military strategist who understood well the advantages of joint and combined warfare. Yet another American officer, whom both Marshall and MacArthur noted for his potential, would achieve the greatest acclaim as a theater commander. Dwight D. Eisenhower, like so many other leaders in this chapter, was a USMA graduate. Commissioned shortly before the U.S. entered World War I, Eisenhower did not see action during the conflict. Instead, he served the entire war in the continental United States. His career in the interwar period was not significantly different from other contemporary Army officers, a time when far too many Americans questioned the necessity of any sizeable Army. Ike served most of that period as a major, and did not have a battalion command until 1940, and even that was brief. But despite his lack of command time and combat experience, Eisenhower had two unique experiences that would provide him with the skills he needed to become one of the nation's great captains.

Top: *General Harold K. Johnson entered the Army in the decade preceding WWII. Fighting in the Pacific, he became a prisoner when Bataan fell and survived the Bataan Death March. Following his liberation, he advanced rapidly in the Army, holding many positions of responsibility, culminating in 1964 when he became Chief of Staff of the Army. General Johnson was in this key position during the Army's expansion for Vietnam. (Joseph Richards Essig, Army Art Collection)*

Above: *General Frederick C. Weyand was commissioned as an ROTC graduate in 1938 and was called to active duty in 1940. In this conflict he spent most of his service in the intelligence community, with emphasis on the Pacific. In Korea, he was a battalion commander in the 7th Infantry and was G-3 of the 3d Infantry Division. He is best known for his role as military advisor to the Paris Peace talks during the Vietnam War and as Commander of MACV (1970–1973). General Weyand was Chief of Staff of the Army from 1974–76. (Bjorn Peter Egeli, Army Art Collection)*

Left: *Hand-picked for the task of creating a women's Army auxiliary, Colonel Oveta Culp Hobby built the volunteer force into the Women's Army Corps in WWII. Awarded the Army Distinguished Service Medal, she later was a cabinet member in the Eisenhower administration. (National Archives)*

Right: *A future chairman of the Joint Chiefs of Staff, John W. Vessey began a distinguished Army career when he was mobilized with the 34th Infantry Division in 1941. Vessey enlisted in the Minnesota National Guard while still a high school student. On active duty he rose to first sergeant and served with distinction in North Africa, and received a battlefield commission at Anzio. He made the Army a career and served as JCS chairman during 1982–85. (Department of Defense)*

Far right: *General Creighton W. Abrams was an armor officer who served with distinction in the European Theater, and was commander of 2d Armored Cavalry (1951–1952) and the 3d Armored Division (1960–1962). During the Vietnam War he was commander of MACV from 1967 to 1972, and Chief of Staff of the Army from 1972 to 1974. (Herbert Elmer Abrams, Army Art Collection)*

Bottom, left: *When the Germans launched their Ardennes offensive in December 1944, the determined stand of the 101st Airborne Division and attached elements became the symbol of U.S. resistance to what seemed an overwhelming German tide. Bastogne was relieved by a task force from the 4th Armored Division led by then Lieutenant Colonel Creighton Abrams, the first American unit to carve a corridor to the encircled "Screaming Eagles." ("To Relieve Bastogne," Don Stivers)*

Bottom, right: *William Westmoreland was one of the numerous general officers that emerged as a leader from World War II. During that war he served in Sicily, and was chief of staff of the 9th Infantry Division at the end of World War II. He was then to serve as commander of the 187th Airborne Regimental Combat Team in Korea, but is best remembered for his role as commander of MACV, during the Vietnam conflict. He was Chief of Staff of the U.S. Army from 1968 to 1972. ("William Childs Westmoreland," Herbert Elmer Abrams, Army Art Collection)*

First, he served as Brigadier General Fox Conner's chief of staff in the 20th Infantry Brigade in Panama during the early 1920s. Conner, an outstanding officer and mentor of younger officers, put his chief of staff through a rigorous program of study. This gave Eisenhower a deep understanding of military thought and of military literature from the classical to the contemporary. Eisenhower then served as aide to General Douglas MacArthur from 1933 to 1935 while MacArthur was Chief of Staff of the Army, and from 1935 to 1939, as a military advisor to the Philippine government under MacArthur. While serving under MacArthur could be challenging, which Eisenhower readily admitted, MacArthur was an Army institution and clearly added to Eisenhower's education.

Eisenhower's greatness can best be seen when viewed as a great captain in war waged by an alliance. Pershing commanded American troops in an alliance but was subordinate to an alliance supreme commander who was French. Eisenhower, as Supreme Commander, Allied Expeditionary Force, was the first American to command such an allied force. As commander of the alliance, he was exceptional. From the beginning of the buildup in England in 1943, until the war's end in Europe, Eisenhower

was able to maintain the coherence of the diverse personalities—from French General Charles De Gaulle to British Field Marshal Montgomery—and focus on the destruction of the German Army in the field. His strategies were not innovative or daring, but his consistent focus on the destruction of the adversary through alliance warfare made Dwight Eisenhower this nation's first great alliance commander.

Within the category of legendary great chiefs and commanders, many other U.S. Army leaders can be justifiably added to those previously discussed. General George S. Patton is one example. In spite of the excesses of his personality, Patton was one of the first American leaders to intuitively grasp the operational art, long before it was developed as a doctrinal principle. Patton's campaign in Europe during World War II remains a classic, particularly his ability to reorient elements of his Third Army and respond so rapidly to the German Ardennes offensive. Another to be included is General Matthew B. Ridgway. It was Ridgway who, during the Korean War, took the Eighth U.S. Army, dispirited after the disastrous retreat from North Korea, and forged it into an aggressive force that pushed the Chinese and North Korean forces back across the 38th parallel.

Top, left: *General Bruce Palmer entered military service shortly before World War II and after a tour on the Army Staff spent the remainder of the war in the Pacific Theater. A student of the profession of arms, General Palmer spent time as a student and instructor in the Army school system in the 1950s and was commander of Task Force 20 and U.S. Land Forces in the Dominican Republic. He was deputy commander of the United States Army, Vietnam, Vice Chief of Staff of the Army from 1968 to 1972; and acting Chief of Staff for several months in 1972. ("Bruce Palmer, Jr." Herbert Elmer Abrams, Army Art Collection)*

Top, right: *General Bernard William Rogers was commissioned during World War II after his graduation from West Point, and within a year of his graduation, was appointed a faculty member at the academy. In the years 1947–1950, he attended Oxford as a Rhodes Scholar. He commanded the 3d Battalion, 9th Infantry, in the Korean War and after a series of commands, was Commandant of Cadets at West Point from 1967 to 1969. General Rogers was Chief of Staff of the Army (1976–1979), and was named Supreme Allied Commander, North Atlantic Treaty Organization, in 1979. ("Bernard William Rogers," Robert Clark Templeton, Army Art Collection)*

Bottom, left: *General Edward Charles Meyer was commissioned during the Korean War and by 1951 was in Korea serving as a platoon leader, company commander, and battalion staff officer. General Meyer was associated with airborne units after Korea and when the Vietnam conflict escalated, he became brigade commander of the 3d Brigade, 1st Cavalry Division (Airmobile), and later commander of the 2d Brigade in the same division. As Chief of Staff of the Army (1979–1983) he promoted modernization of the force, which was possible through the Reagan military buildup. ("Edward Charles Meyer," Everett Raymond Kinstler, Army Art Collection)*

Bottom, right: *General John Adams Wickham entered the Army shortly before the Korean War broke out and initially served in Europe. As a young officer he attended Harvard and then returned to West Point to teach from 1956 to 1960. During the Vietnam War he held several commands in the 1st Cavalry Division and was U.S. Representative in the Four Party Military Commission, Vietnam, in 1973. As Chief of Staff of the U.S. Army (1983–1987), he implemented the new light division structure and supervised the increase in numbers of both the Active and Reserve divisions. ("John Adams Wickham," Margaret Holland Sargent, Army Art Collection)*

Top, left: *Carl Edward Vuono was commissioned in the years following the Korean War. An artillery officer, General Vuono commanded the 1st Battalion, 77th Artillery, 1st Cavalry Division, in Vietnam and was commander of the 82d Airborne Division Artillery (1975–1976). He commanded TRADOC (1983–1985), and as Chief of Staff of the Army (1987–1991), he led the Army in the transition from the Cold War and in the campaign to liberate Kuwait. ("Carl Edward Vuono," Ned Bittenger, Army Art Collection)*

Top, right: *Gordon R. Sullivan was commissioned in the Army through the Norwich University ROTC program. He saw early service in Vietnam as an advisor (1962–1963), and returned for a second tour in 1969–1970 with Headquarters, I Field Force. He commanded both armored and infantry units, to include command of the 1st Brigade, 3d Armored Division, and the 1st Infantry Division (Mechanized). He became Vice Chief of Staff of the Army in 1990 and was appointed Chief of Staff of the Army in 1991. As Chief of Staff he promoted the transition of the Army from its Cold War past to the high-tech Army of the future. ("Gordon R. Sullivan," Ned Bittenger, Army Art Collection)*

Right: *General Powell shown with a group of soldiers during the Vietnam War. (Photo Courtesy of General Powell)*

Bottom, left: *General Colin Powell is the sixty-fifth Secretary of State. Prior to this appointment, General Powell served in the Army for thirty-five years. He was commissioned after completing ROTC at the City College of New York, and like many of his generation served in the Vietnam War. During the war, Powell was assigned to the Americal Division. He held a myriad of command and staff positions in the Army, completing his career as the Chairman, Joint Chiefs of Staff in 1993. (Department of Defense)*

Bottom, right: *Born in Poland, three years before the outbreak of WWII, General John M. Shalikashvili reached the U.S. as a youth. His Army career began after graduation from Army Officer Candidate School in 1959. In his lifetime of service he rose to Supreme Allied Commander, Europe, during 1992–93. In 1993 he became Chairman of the Joint Chiefs of Staff, earning the dual distinction of being the only foreign-born Army four-star general and Chairman, JCS. (Department of Defense)*

MacArthur was pessimistic that this could be accomplished but a determined Ridgway accomplished it nonetheless.

Clearly two officers of the modern era also deserve to be mentioned—Generals Colin Powell and Norman Schwarzkopf. Like Marshall, Powell, after rising to the position of Chairman, Joint Chiefs of Staff, was appointed to serve as Secretary of State under President George W. Bush. Schwarzkopf, who trained and commanded the Gulf war forces, successfully managed a most unlikely and often fractious coalition of European and Arab allies to defeat a numerically superior Iraqi army.

From its earliest days the United States Army has produced legendary leaders who shaped the Army, established a solid military tradition, and in the process, helped shape this nation and the politics of the world. As the years pass, this list of great U.S. Army chiefs and commanders can only grow.

Top Soldiers

Top Soldiers

The Noncommissioned Officers of the Army

Command Sergeant Major Scott Garrett, USAR

The United States Army noncommissioned officer (NCO) corps was born in June 1775. However, the roots of the NCO Corps go back to the earliest American colonial experience when each town formed a militia company. Using a system of small squads for guard duty and patrols, the colonists followed the European system of noncommissioned officers to lead these small groups. From its beginning in the American Revolution to the present, American NCOs have served this nation in times of war and peace earning for themselves the designation, "backbone of the Army." No other army in the world places the same level of confidence, responsibility, and independence on its NCO Corps as does the U.S. Army.

Although the U.S. Army has long had Sergeants Major at the regiment and battalion level, the position of Sergeant Major of the Army (SMA) is a fairly recent development in the 225-year history of the Army. Established in 1966 at the beginning of the Vietnam War, the SMA stands first in an unbroken line of NCOs that stretches back to the American War for Independence. Throughout Army history, NCOs have performed crucial tasks as small unit leaders, trainers, and technical experts in addition to serving as guardians of Army standards and traditions.

The Continental Congress authorized establishment of noncommissioned officers in June 1775, when it organized the first units of the Continental Army. In 1779, the duties of the Army's NCOs, sergeants major to corporal, were standardized in *Regulations for the Order and Discipline*

Above: The victory of the Allied—American and French—forces at Yorktown, Virginia, on 19 October 1781 culminated with the surrender of Lord Cornwallis to General George Washington. This blow to the pride and power of Britain's expeditionary forces signaled the victory of the American colonies in their fight for independence and ended the Revolutionary War. ("Yorktown," H. Charles McBarron, Army Art Collection)

Pages 74–75: Baron A.H.F. von Steuben, drillmaster of the Revolution, demonstrates proper drill to men of the Continental Army. ("The Camp of the American Army at Valley Forge, February 1778," Edwin Austin Abbey, Pennsylvania Capitol Preservation Committee)

Opposite: They called him "First Soldier" in his company or troop. Since time immemorial his job has been to turn raw recruits into fighting men. The archetype professional soldier depicted here molded new men into experienced troopers in the hard "school of the soldier," an early-day version of on-the-job training. ("First Sergeant," Don Stivers, International Edition)

Top, left: *Even before there was a United States, there were American soldiers who excelled at unconventional warfare. The French and Indian War of 1754–1763 was part of a series of colonial wars in North America that served to develop basic military traditions in both U.S. and Canadian forces. Here, two of Roger's Rangers make their report in a British fortress in the Lake Champlain area of New York in 1760. ("To Range the Woods," Army Art Collection)*

Top, right: *Sergeants William Brown (left) and Elijah Churchill receiving the first Badges of Military Merit. General George Washington established the first U.S. military decoration on 7 August 1782. Only three soldiers, all NCOs, are known to have received it. In 1932, on the 200th anniversary of Washington's birth, the War Department ordered creation of the Purple Heart medal, the design of which is based on the Badge of Military Merit. ("Newburgh, New York, 3 May 1783," H. Charles McBarron. 1975, Army Art Collection)*

Opposite, top: *In the War of 1812, the British tried to seize Baltimore by combined sea and land assaults. Barely remembered was the Battle of North Point, Maryland, which thwarted the British landward attempt to capture the city. On 12 September 1814, 3d Brigade, Maryland Militia, was ordered to delay the advancing British. Again and again NCOs of the militia helped to steady their troops. A two-hour battle failed to break the Maryland line, and the British withdrew. ("The Battle of North Point," Don Troiani, National Guard Heritage series)*

Right: *Shown is Sergeant Major John Champe, 2d Partisan Corps in 1780. General Washington sought a volunteer to capture the traitor Benedict Arnold and return him to justice. Known for his daring and patriotism, Champe made the attempt. Circumstances thwarted his bold plan and Champe was forced to evade capture. ("The Escape of Sergeant Champe," Currier & Ives, Anne S. K. Brown Collection, Brown University)*

of the Troops of the United States. Commonly called the "Blue Book" after the color of its cover and used well into the next century, it was written by Baron Augustus H. F. von Steuben, a Prussian volunteer commissioned by Congress as a major general in Continental Army service. Steuben put the sergeant major at the head of all NCOs in a unit and made him responsible for their conduct. His various duties included maintaining

discipline, preparing rosters, assigning details, and conducting parades. From that time until after World War I, the number and organizational placement of NCOs varied considerably, but they were usually assigned at battalion level and above.

Very early in the history of the Army it was necessary to set NCOs apart from other soldiers by a distinctive mark or insignia of rank. The militia NCOs who gathered around Boston in April 1775 after Lexington and Concord wore or carried whatever insignia of rank they had, sometimes none at all. Most often they carried a halberd, a small sword, or perhaps wore a sash. There was no uniformity, and men from one unit did not recognize the NCOs from another. While a halberd might be fine in camp or garrison, it was not a true weapon, and was usually left behind on campaign in favor of a sword or musket. In July 1775, General Washington ordered emblems of rank for the uniforms of both officers and NCOs. Corporals were directed to wear a green strip of cloth on the right shoulder, while sergeants one of red. Later, Washington ordered sergeants to wear a pair of red silk epaulettes, but corporals continued to wear only one green epaulette of worsted cloth. For the first time, colors were used to indicate arm-of-service: yellow for artillery; white, infantry; dark blue, cavalry. The sergeant major had no specific rank insignia at this time.

Chevrons, commonly called "stripes," were first worn on uniform sleeves in 1821. They were worn in pairs, point up, with one on each arm.

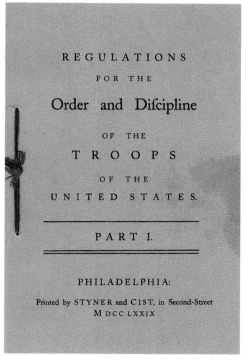

REGULATIONS

FOR THE

Order and Diſcipline

OF THE

TROOPS

OF THE

UNITED STATES.

PART I.

PHILADELPHIA:

Printed by STYNER and CIST, in Second-Street
MDCCLXXIX

Above: *Regulations for the Order and Discipline of the troops of the United States, commonly called the "Blue Book" because of the color of its cover, was written by Baron von Steuben. Published in 1779 and used well into the next century, it standardized the duties of noncommissioned officers. (Vince Hawkins collection)*

79

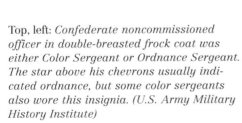

Top, left: *Confederate noncommissioned officer in double-breasted frock coat was either Color Sergeant or Ordnance Sergeant. The star above his chevrons usually indicated ordnance, but some color sergeants also wore this insignia. (U.S. Army Military History Institute)*

Above: *NCO Rank Insignia, 1775–1821. (Center of Military History)*

Top, right: *Ordnance Sergeant (left) and Dragoon Officer in dress uniform with enlisted men of the 1st Dragoons in campaign dress. Pictured at Fort Leavenworth in 1836. ("The American Soldier," H. Charles McBarron, Army Art Collection)*

Right: *Union and Confederate NCOs in mortal combat for possession of the colors. Corporal Francis A. Waller, 6th Wisconsin Volunteer Infantry, earns the Medal of Honor on 1 July 1863, at the Battle of Gettysburg, killing a Confederate color bearer and seizing his battle flag. ("The Fight for the Colors," Don Troiani, Historical Art Prints Ltd.)*

Colors continued to designate arm-of-service. Thereafter, during the 1820s through 1850, there were intermittent periods when chevrons were not worn. When they were, it was usually, but not exclusively, point up. In 1851, the basic design and orientation of chevrons was set and remained so until the major uniform and insignia changes of 1902. During these years, chevrons were worn point down, one on each sleeve above the elbow. As in previous years, chevrons denoted rank while color indicated arm-of-service. In 1902, NCO chevrons were turned point up and greatly reduced in size. Chevron color continued to represent arm-of-service. Just prior to World War I, colored chevrons were eliminated and all were made in the same khaki color on material the same, darker olive drab color as

Top: *"A heavy column of enemy's infantry, about 10,000 strong, is moving from opposite our extreme left toward our right." This message from a Union signalman on Little Round Top, regarding the march of Confederate General James Longstreet's Corps, on 2 July 1863, at Gettysburg helped save the Union left flank. ("Signals From Little Round Top," Don Stivers)*

Above, left: *Color Sergeant and men of the 9th Illinois Volunteer Infantry stand their ground on the left flank of the Union line during the morning of the first day at Shiloh, 6 April 1862. ("Plenty of Fighting Today," Keith Rocco, National Guard Heritage series)*

Above: *The sergeant who became president: Commissary Sergeant William McKinley, 23d Ohio Volunteer Infantry. Enlisted in June 1861, earned a battlefield commission in September 1862, he would muster out at the end of the Civil War with the rank of major. (August Penziger, National Portrait Gallery, Smithsonian Institution)*

Above: *Engineer officer flanked by Infantry Corporal (left) and Infantry First Sergeant (right) with Artillery and Infantry advancing in the Western Theater during 1863. ("The American Soldier," H. Charles McBarron, Army Art Collection)*

Right: *Garrison duty. Wearing Model 1902 full-dress uniforms, the regimental bugler listens while the First Sergeant (seated) of A Company, 6th Infantry Regiment, provides guidance to his subordinate NCOs, circa 1902. (Henry Alexander Ogden for the U.S. Army Quartermaster General)*

NCO Rank Insignia, 1902–1920: (top row, left to right) Sergeant Major Senior Grade, Coast Artillery, 1902; Squadron or Battalion Sergeant Major, 1902; Ordnance Sergeant, 1917; Ordnance Sergeant, 1918. (Bottom row, left to right) Chief Musician, Cavalry, 1902; Color Sergeant, 1902; First Sergeant, Engineers, 1902; Sergeant First Class, 1918. As a war economy measure, only single chevrons were worn from May 1918 to March 1921. Stripes were authorized only for right sleeve in that period.

the uniform. Technical branch symbols were included under the chevron stripes in a dull red color.

In the aftermath of World War I, the NCO Corps was drawn down as the Army itself diminished in size. A great proliferation of enlisted grades and titles had come into being during the war. At the very top level of the NCO Corps, for example, there were no less than eleven different varieties of "top sergeants." In 1920, the Army restructured the NCO Corps to distinguish between "rank" or "pay grade" and "position." All enlisted soldiers were grouped into seven pay grades, from private (grade seven) to Master Sergeant (grade one) without regard to military specialty. Although the top five were NCO grades, conspicuously missing was the rank or title of sergeant major. The highest enlisted rank was now master sergeant. Thereafter, the functional position of sergeant major was filled by the senior master sergeant in the unit followed in rank order by the next senior sergeant.

Thirty-eight years later the situation changed. In June 1958, Congress again fundamentally altered the enlisted rank structure with sweeping changes. Two new pay grades representing three ranks were authorized: E-8, first sergeant or master sergeant; E-9, sergeant major. Also in 1958, the Army adopted the basic chevron design still in use. In April the following year, the first NCOs in over a generation were promoted to sergeant major to serve in duty positions at battalion level and above. The new insignia for this highest enlisted rank was three stripes and three rockers with a five-pointed star in between.

Top, left: *An NCO of the American Expeditionary Force, France 1918, seated with French children. U.S. soldiers abroad have often served as goodwill ambassadors whose actions have an enduring impact on the United States' role in the world. Relationships formed with local civilian populations have proved of lasting value to American foreign policy. (Rock Island Arsenal Museum)*

Top, center: *First Sergeant Samuel Woodfill, 60th Infantry Regiment, 5th Division, was a Regular Army NCO who received the Medal of Honor and a battlefield commission for action in World War I. Discharged from the Army in late October 1919, he reenlisted the following month as a sergeant. Along with Sergeant Alvin York, Woodfill was one of the pallbearers selected by General Pershing for burial of the Unknown Soldier in 1921. (National Archives)*

Top, right: *Cavalry officers, NCOs, and soldiers in 1902 full-dress uniform. (Henry Alexander Ogden for the U.S. Army Quartermaster General)*

By the mid-1960s, the Army leadership realized that a nontraditional solution was necessary. In October 1965, there was a Sergeants Major Personnel Conference. This senior NCO leadership recommended creation of a new position: Sergeant Major, United States Army. General Harold K. Johnson, Chief of Staff of the Army, supported this recommendation saying that if "we were going to talk about the noncommissioned officers being the backbone of the Army, there ought to be established a position that recognizes that this was in fact the case."

Thereafter, events moved rather swiftly. General Orders No. 29, dated 4 July 1966, established the position of Sergeant Major of the Army. The individual would be selected by the Army Chief of Staff and tenure as SMA would correspond with that of the Chief. A week later, General Johnson personally administered the oath of office to the first Sergeant Major of the Army, William O. Wooldridge. As no distinctive rank insignia yet existed, the new SMA continued to wear the standard sergeant major rank insignia. A new SMA collar insignia was approved, and Mrs. Wooldridge helped affix a pair on her husband's uniform.

Left: *Some of the enduring strengths of the NCO Corps are initiative, innovation, and improvisation. Useful not only in war, these skills are also needed in peacetime when the Army usually has to operate with very limited funding. Aptly, this 1922 photograph illustrates an NCO directing hands-on training in the field during one such lean period. (National Archives)*

Above: *Distinctive collar insignia for Sergeant Major of the Army that was adopted in 1966.*

Above, right: *Soldiers in assault boats prior to the landings in North Africa on 8 November 1942. In war and peace, NCOs are crucial to small unit leadership and maintaining unit cohesion. (National Archives)*

Below: *Women volunteers served in the Women's Auxiliary Army Corps (WAAC), which in 1943 was redesignated the WAC (Women's Army Corps) and validated as part of the wartime Army. WAC noncoms operate a small printing press during WWII. During that war over 150,000 women served with or in the Army. (Center of Military History)*

As the first Sergeant Major of the Army, Wooldridge had to define the role of that position, and he well understood that everything he did would set a precedent. In this monumental undertaking he had two advantages: his years of military experience and the unqualified confidence of General Johnson. The only written guidance the Chief of Staff ever gave SMA Wooldridge was a note card with several general tasks typed on it. Wooldridge folded the card and carried it in his wallet.

In order to emphasize that the SMA was more than just for display, the Office of the Sergeant Major of the Army was located just across the hall from the Office of the Chief of Staff, giving the SMA direct access to the Chief.

SMA Wooldridge said that "the single most significant item to evolve from my term" was establishment of the command sergeant major (CSM) program. General Johnson authorized the new position on 13 July 1967.

He directed Headquarters, Department of the Army, to manage CSM selection, assignment, and careers of those select individuals who would hold the most senior enlisted positions from battalion level through HQDA.

Along with creation of the CSM program, the Chief of Staff also directed that a new rank insignia be designed. He suggested adding a wreath to the star on sergeant major stripes. Some months later, in March 1968, General Johnson presented the first CSM rank insignia to SMA Wooldridge: a five-pointed star within a laurel wreath set between three stripes and three rockers. This was worn by both the SMA and command sergeants major until a distinctive SMA rank insignia was later created.

Over the course of years, various methods have been used to select the SMA. However nominations are solicited, it is the Chief of Staff who makes the final determination as to who will be his SMA. When the position was originally created, it was thought that each SMA would serve concurrently with the tenure of the Army Chief of Staff. In practice, the tours of duty did not always coincide. SMAs have served from two to four years, depending upon a variety of circumstances. Moreover, duty as SMA is the capstone of a distinguished career. Afterwards comes retirement. In the beginning this was not so. When the first SMA completed that assignment, he went to another.

The fifth SMA (1975–79), William G. Bainbridge, designed the first distinctive rank insignia worn exclusively by the Sergeants Major of the Army. His design replaced the star and wreath central device of a command

sergeant major with two five-pointed stars of equal size, horizontally aligned. This insignia was used until 1994. On 13 October of that year, General Gordon R. Sullivan, Army Chief of Staff, pinned a newly redesigned rank insignia on his SMA, Richard A. Kidd. The designer, SMA Kidd, reduced the two stars in size and placed an American bald eagle in between. This is the pattern still in use today.

As long ago as 1775, there was concern about NCOs having the necessary skills and experience. However, aside from the specialized training necessary to qualify NCOs in a few technical skills, there was little or no attempt to formally school them. The attitude was that line NCOs would learn everything they needed while serving with their units. Most soldiers spent their entire service within the same regiment. From the Revolutionary War until the eve of World War II, NCOs could not take their rank with them—stripes belonged to the unit. If a soldier transferred or his unit was

Above: *Women's Army Corps (WAC) color party and unit at Fort McClellan, Alabama, performs the Retreat Ceremony in the early 1970s. This was headquarters of the WACs until they ceased to be a separate component in 1976. ("The American Soldier, 1954–1976," H. Charles McBarron, Army Art Collection)*

Right: *Signal Corps Radio Tractor Number 2 and its crew in 1915. Of note is that the crew members are wearing the 1902 full-dress uniform rather than field service. (Center of Military History)*

NCO AND SPECIALIST RANK INSIGNIA,
1902-1920
1. Quartermaster Sergeant Senior Grade, 1916. 2. Master Signal Electrician, 1918. 3. Master Engineer Junior Grade,
1916. 4. Master Gunner, 1908. 5. Engineer, Coast Artillery Corps, 1908. 6. Master Signal Electrician, Air
Service, 1918. 7. Master Engineer Senior Grade, Tank Corps, 1918. 8. Chief Mechanic, 1907.

Left: *Specially trained and qualified non-commissioned officers served as interpreters and interrogators when German prisoners of war were taken. Scene here was captured by a combat artist in Normandy, France, in 1944. ("The Interrogation of a German Prisoner," Manuel Bromberg, Army Art Collection)*

Top: *NCO rank insignia indicating both branch and military specialty from 1873–1902 (top to bottom, left to right): Sergeant First Class of Signal Corps, 1891; Chief Musician, Cavalry, 1899; Color Sergeant, Infantry, 1883; Hospital Steward, 1887; Electrician Sergeant, 1899; Color Sergeant, Infantry, 1901; Drum Major, Cavalry, 1899. Insignia with tan background was for the tropical uniform introduced during the Spanish-American War in 1898. (Center of Military History)*

Above: *Specialist noncom rank insignia from 1902–1920 (top to bottom, left to right): Quartermaster Sergeant Senior Grade, 1916; Master Signal Electrician, 1918; Master Engineer Junior Grade, 1916; Master Gunner, 1908; Engineer, Coast Artillery Corps, 1908; Master Signal Electrician, Air Service, 1918; Master Engineer Senior Grade, Tank Corps, 1918; Chief Mechanic, 1907. (Center of Military History)*

disbanded, he started over as a private in the new command. In 1940, the Army introduced permanent enlisted promotions to individuals. This was a significant step along an uneven path that eventually led to systematic professional training and education for NCOs.

Among the reasons why the Army created the Office of the Sergeant Major of the Army in 1966 were to help enhance the duty performance, responsibility, and professionalism of the NCO Corps. The Chief of Staff approved creation of a Noncommissioned Officer Education System in (NCOES) 1969. When the new program achieved full implementation, there would be a graduated system of progressively more advanced formal military training and education. At the top of this system was a senior NCO course where E-8s were prepared for duty as sergeants major.

The Army further demonstrated its commitment to an enhanced NCOES on 15 July 1972. General Order 98 authorized establishment of the United States Army Sergeants Major Academy. This course was designated the capstone of military education for carefully selected senior NCOs. It

Top, left: *Master Sergeant Nicholas Oresko, 302d Infantry Regiment, 94th Infantry Division, was presented with the Medal of Honor by President Harry S. Truman in 1945. Master Sergeant Oresko earned the nation's highest valor award while leading his platoon in an attack against strong enemy positions near Tettingen, Germany, on 23 January 1945. (National Archives)*

Top, right: *A sergeant issues orders during action on Guadalcanal in 1943. ("Sergeant Gives Orders," Aaron Bohrod, Army Art Collection)*

Above: *Sergeant First Class Webster Anderson, Battery A, 2nd Battalion, 320th Field Artillery, 101st Airborne Division, was awarded the Medal of Honor near Tam Ky, Republic of Vietnam, on 15 October 1967. In addition to directing his battery's defenses against a determined North Vietnamese infantry assault, he personally killed several of the enemy, but above all took care of his soldiers. (National Archives)*

was, unlike the lower levels of NCO courses, military occupation specialty immaterial and similar to the senior service schools for officers.

The first Sergeants Major Academy class of 105 students began its course of instruction on 8 January 1973 at Fort Bliss, Texas. In 1987, a new USASMA complex was built and, ten years later, a major addition was added. Originally, the resident course lasted six months. In 1995, the duration of instruction was lengthened to nine months. Competition for the limited slots is intense and successful completion of the course by E-8s is no guarantee of eventual selection for sergeant major. Attendance is also open to qualified Army Reserve and National Guard personnel. Interestingly, the first CSM of the academy was William G. Bainbridge, who later became the fifth SMA.

Since its establishment in 1966, the first and subsequent SMAs have confronted an unending series of challenges with significant implications for enlisted personnel and their families: the beginning and end of the Vietnam War; major military force reductions and restructuring at the end of the Vietnam and the Cold wars; end of the draft and implementation of an all-volunteer Army; the Gulf war; and numerous missions worldwide in places like Panama, Somalia, and the Balkans.

In addition to responsibility for overseeing NCOES programs in Regular Army major commands, the SMA was given oversight, in 1980,

The U.S. Army Sergeants Major Academy at Fort Bliss, Texas. This part of the Army "school house" system is the capstone of the Noncommissioned Officer Educational System. In order to earn the insignia of a sergeant major an NCO must be a graduate. (Sergeants Major Academy)

Graves Registration specialists learning their difficult trade in training to be prepared for the time when their skills may be needed. (Soldier Magazine)

of those in the Army Reserve and National Guard. As parts of the national defense effort, the Guard and Reserve became correspondingly more significant after the collapse of the Soviet Union in 1991 and resultant military reductions in force. These changes greatly enhanced the roles of the leading CSMs in the Guard and Reserve. Although subordinate to their respective commands, they still work very closely with the SMA. A senior CSM serves in the Office of Chief of the Army Reserve and as the chief enlisted advisor to the Director of the Army National Guard.

Gun drill at the turn of the twentieth century. Sergeants taught their men to master weapons, such as this 10-inch coast defense gun. (Thure de Thulstrup, Anne S. K. Brown Military Collection, Brown University)

In an ever-changing world, the Army cannot be static. Consequently, the duties and responsibilities of the SMA continue to evolve. The SMA is both the principal advisor on enlisted affairs to the Chief of Staff and ombudsman for enlisted personnel. The SMA spends nearly half his time traveling to visit troops worldwide. Frequently, his wife accompanies him to meet with military spouses and hear their concerns.

Symbolically, the importance attached to the top NCO of the Army is confirmed by protocol: the Sergeant Major of the Army ranks just after the Director of the Army Staff and ahead of all other lieutenant generals on that staff. Even so, symbolism is only a minor factor. Of far greater significance is direct access to the Chief of Staff and serving on various senior boards and committees. The SMA is also often called to testify before congressional committees regarding issues related to enlisted soldiers and their families. Thus, the SMA directly influences policies that affect the entire Army.

The history of the Sergeant Major of the Army is ongoing. Since its establishment the position of SMA has developed and evolved along

91

FIRE TEAM MANEUVERS
ERLANGEN, FRG.

"THE NCO"

ADAM GLENDAY '90.

The NCO in the field, as drawn during a 1990 field training exercise in Erlangen, Germany. ("The NCO," Adam Glenday, Army Art Collection)

with the Army. Moreover, those who are privileged to serve as SMA continue to make their mark on both the position and on the Army. Missions change, technologies change, but taking care of soldiers will always remain the single greatest priority of the serving Sergeant Major of the Army.

Troops of the 2d (Indianhead) Infantry Division during a 1991 field training exercise in Korea. ("Ready, Set, GO!" Brian Fairchild, Army Art Collection)

Sergeant Major of the Army flag that was approved on 22 March 1999 by the Chief of Staff of the Army. The SMA is unique in many ways, including being the only enlisted position to have a flag.

Present and accounted for! Current and future noncommissioned officers of the Army.

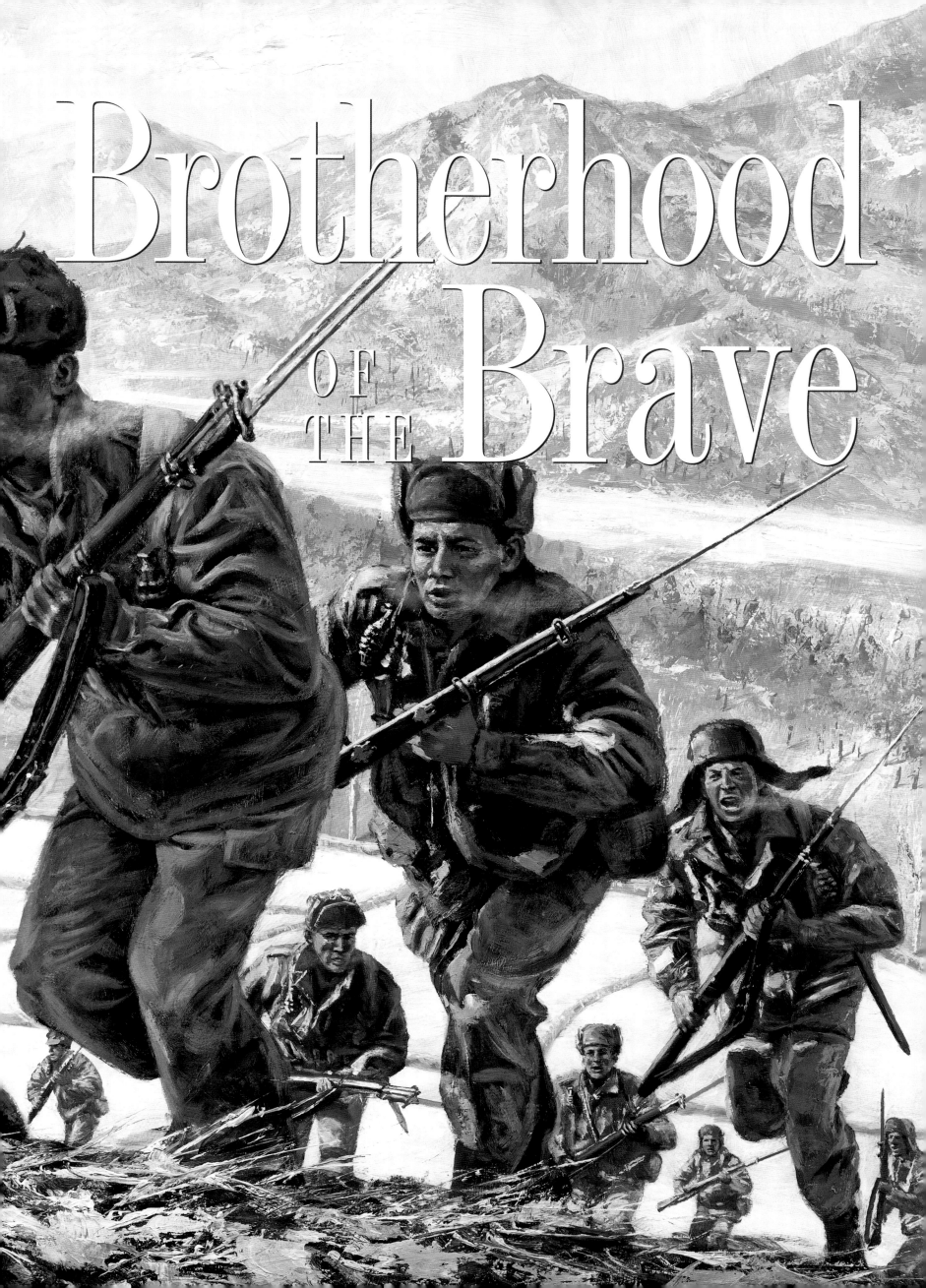

Brotherhood OF THE Brave
The Army's Medal of Honor Heroes

Major General Bruce Jacobs, AUS (Ret)

The date was 23 March 1863. Six gaunt, emaciated, recently released prisoners were being taken to the Judge Advocate General in Washington, D.C., to revise and review evidence concerning their last mission. The remnants of a Union Army scouting detachment known as "Andrews's Raiders," they had just been exchanged for Confederate Army prisoners. The six had been captured after an 1862 exploit that involved the daring theft of a railroad locomotive.

Much to their amazement, and some consternation, they learned that they were also to meet with Secretary of War Edwin M. Stanton. Stanton welcomed them and introduced the others present in his office—Salmon P. Chase, Secretary of the Treasury, and Andrew Johnson, Governor of Tennessee, where their adventure had been launched. He asked for details of their experiences.

Private Jacob Parrott, at nineteen, was the youngest and served as spokesman for the group. Of the original twenty-two in the Raiders' party, six had been executed, eight had successfully escaped, and six had escaped and been recaptured. Now, one year later, the six were back in Union lines.

The Secretary told the six Union soldiers that he and the nation were appreciative of their devotion to duty, handed each one $100, and then turned to James C. Whetmore, State Agent for Ohio. As the six, and their comrades, had come from three Ohio regiments (2d, 21st, and 33d) of the 9th Brigade, Stanton asked Whetmore to see to it that each of the six was appointed by the Governor to be first lieutenants in Ohio regiments.

Then, almost as an afterthought, he opened a desk drawer, took out six small leather cases, and methodically lined them up on the desk. The account that appeared in the *Washington Chronicle* on 26 March 1863 relates that Stanton picked up one of the small boxes and turned directly to Parrott.

"None of these," he told the young man, "has yet been awarded to any soldier. I now present you with the first one to be issued." Stanton then presented medals to the others. They had been awarded the first Medals of Honor in the history of the United States Army. The other Raiders would be awarded the Medal of Honor in subsequent years, including posthumous awards to those who had been executed.

They would forever be linked with soldiers of future generations whose names would be inscribed in the Roll of Honor, commemorating those who gave of themselves "above and beyond the call of duty" in the ranks of the United States Army.

President Lincoln signed the Army Medal of Honor bill into law on 12 July 1862. A contract to produce the medals was given to Wilson Silver Smiths in Philadelphia, and on 14 February 1863, the War Department received the first 500 medals from Wilson.

The idea for a medal recognizing Army heroism got its impetus on 17 February 1862, when Senator Harry Wilson of Massachusetts introduced a resolution to provide "medals of honor" to soldiers of the Army and voluntary forces who should "most distinguish themselves by their gallantry in

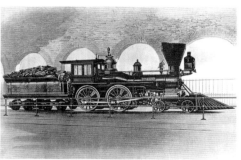

Top: *In what seemed to be an impulsive moment, Secretary of War Edwin M. Stanton presented the first Army Medals of Honor midway through the Civil War. Six Union soldiers had reported to him on their daring scouting mission and subsequent experiences as prisoners. Stanton reached into a desk drawer and presented each man a Medal of Honor. "None of these has yet been awarded," he told them. (National Archives)*

Above: *Union Army scouts known as "Andrews's Raiders" captured "The General" (Western & Atlantic R.R.) at Big Shanty (now Kennesaw), Georgia, 12 April 1862. After a 90-mile chase the train was re-taken by Confederates. The Raiders were captured, and several were executed. The survivors were awarded the Medal of Honor.*

Opposite: *Near Fort Wagner, South Carolina, the commander of the 54th Massachusetts Volunteer Infantry was killed leading his regiment of African-Americans. There were 270 casualties in the attack. Sergeant William Carney planted the flag, fought off all efforts to capture it, and became the regiment's first Medal of Honor hero. ("The Old Flag Never Touched the Ground," Rick Reeves, National Guard Heritage series)*

Pages 94–95: *On the day after Chinese New Year, in the Korean winter of 1951, a powerful U.S. counterattack was launched. Easy Company, 27th Infantry Regiment (Wolfhounds), policed up bayonets discarded by others. Captain Lewis L. Millett, a field artilleryman turned infantryman, called for his men to "fix bayonets." The result was what historians would term the most ferocious bayonet attack since Cold Harbor in the Civil War. ("Cold Steel," Don Stivers, U.S. Army War College Edition)*

Right: *In the second year of the Civil War, a Congressional resolution to create an Army Medal of Honor gained the signature of President Abraham Lincoln on 12 July 1862. In March of the following year the resolution was amended to permit award of the Medal to officers as well as enlisted men. The "father" of the legislation was Massachusetts Senator Harry Wilson.*

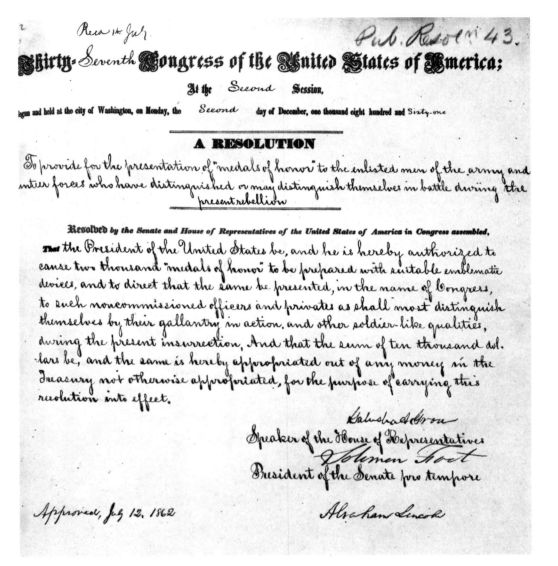

Although approved in 1862, the Army Medal of Honor was not available for award to any U.S. soldiers until 1863. The first 500 Medals were manufactured for the Army by the Wilson Silver Smiths, a distinguished Philadelphia firm. The Medals were delivered to the War Department on 14 February 1863. (National Archives)

The bitter fighting in the Confederate lines at Vicksburg, Mississippi, on 19 May 1863, was but the start of the campaign by the Union Army under General Ulysses S. Grant to seize the river bastion. A memorable assault by the 1st Battalion, 13th Infantry, resulted in heavy losses, but earned its place in history. ("First at Vicksburg," H. Charles McBarron, Army Art Collection)

action, and other soldier-like qualities." A similar measure to recognize naval heroes was already in effect, having been approved on 12 December 1861. Originally the Wilson bill provided only for enlisted men to be eligible for the medal, but this was quickly amended to include officers.

It would take wartime fervor to make the subject of medals agreeable to the public and, perhaps surprisingly, even to the military itself. Winfield Scott, commanding general of the Army, a hero of the War of 1812 and the Mexican War, along with fellow Americans of that era, was opposed to medals, medallions, or decorations reminiscent of the trappings of European armies. In the years between the end of the War for Independence and the date when the Army Medal of Honor was authorized by Congress, the most common way of rewarding combat bravery was the brevet system. This meant promotion to a temporary higher rank, usually without commensurate increase in pay.

Perhaps because the Medal was a Congressional mandate, the Army was slow to define the requirements, including how recommendations would be made, by whom, and time limits. The Medal was soon the sine qua non to recognize bravery above and beyond the call of duty, but the lack of definition would lead to major internal issues for the Army through the years.

Curiously enough, the first exploit to be recognized with the Medal took place a year before Senator Wilson introduced the Army Medal of Honor legislation. The award was to Assistant Surgeon Bernard J. D. Irwin for his valor at Apache Pass, Arizona. In a running battle during 13–14 February 1861, Irwin took command of troops, attacked, and defeated hostile Indians who stood in his way. The Medal, however, was not issued until 24 January 1894, nearly thirty-three years later.

Irwin's case was by no means unique. The Medal, created in 1862 and first issued in 1863, was to be retroactively awarded for dozens of prior Civil War actions. There were, for example, twelve Medals awarded for the action at Bull Run in July 1861. Other winners during the war included Arthur MacArthur, father of Douglas MacArthur, who in turn would be awarded a Medal some eighty years later for his actions in World War II—the first father and son awards.

In the spring of 1863, Major General Ulysses S. Grant was pounding away at Vicksburg. Before settling down to the siege that eventually overcame Confederate Lieutenant General John C. Pemberton, he decided upon one last massive assault. He called for 150 volunteers to storm the heights in advance of the main attack by troops of Major General William T. Sherman's corps. As the volunteers advanced, they met deadly fire. Nevertheless, they pushed up the heights toward the Confederate works. Practically every one of the survivors, some eighty-three in all, received the Medal of Honor for that day's actions.

In the wake of George Armstrong Custer's ill-fated fight at Little Big Horn, Montana, 25 June 1876, the company commanders of a surviving regimental element recommended a great many of their men for the Medal. To Brigadier General Alfred A. Terry, the department commander, it appeared that "company commanders have recommended every man . . .

As a young lieutenant in a Wisconsin regiment in the Civil War, Major General Arthur MacArthur earned the Medal for his daring rescue of regimental colors. His son, General of the Army Douglas MacArthur, would join him on the Roll of Honor when he was named a Medal recipient in World War II for his valor in the defense of the Philippines in 1942. (National Archives)

A breathtaking gallop toward enemy lines to rescue his wounded commander led to the award of the Medal of Honor to First Sergeant Conrad Schmidt, Company K, 2d U.S. Cavalry. The 1864 Civil War action occurred near Winchester, Virginia. Schmidt, who was born in Germany, did not receive the Medal until 1896. ("Sergeant's Valor," Don Stivers, 2d Armored Cavalry Regiment Edition)

Above: *Lieutenant Colonel André C. Lucas earned the Medal of Honor in Vietnam for heroic action as his battalion pulled out of besieged fire support base "Ripcord." (National Archives)*

Above, right: *Captain Thomas Custer would be remembered as one of five Army men twice awarded the Medal before Army regulations decided only one Medal of Honor could be given to any individual. During the Civil War Custer earned the Medal for gallantry in cavalry action in 1863 and again in 1865. He was George Armstrong Custer's younger brother. (National Archives)*

that behaved ordinarily well during the action," and rejected the entire list, asking that only those who clearly indicated outstanding heroism be nominated. A list of twenty-two names was finally submitted and approved, with two additional Medals being awarded in the 1890s. Interestingly, one of the Army's few two-time winners of the Medal, Captain Thomas W. Custer, died next to his brother in the battle.

In 1890, twenty-two Medals of Honor for Civil War actions were added to the roster of heroes. The number actually increased thereafter to forty in 1891, and sixty-six in 1892. In 1894, no less than 127 veterans of the Civil War received their medals. In the forty years following the Civil

War, the Army's almost constant conflict with the American Indian tribes west of the Mississippi River gave occasion for soldiers to be recognized for their heroism and gallantry under fire.

Another question evolved around whether the Medal could be awarded to a soldier for a sustained series of actions extending over several days or even weeks, or if it ought to be confined to an outstanding and climactic moment in the heat of battle. This condition has never been precisely defined. For example, Major Charles W. Whittlesey and Captains George G. McMurtry and Nelson M. Holderman, leaders of the "Lost Battalion" of the 77th Division in World War I, were cited for valor in the Argonne Forest, 2–8 October 1918.

General Douglas MacArthur's WWII citation offered no dates but was awarded "for conspicuous leadership in preparing the Philippine Islands to resist conquest, for gallantry and intrepidity above and beyond the call of duty in action against invading Japanese forces, and for the heroic conduct of defensive and offensive operations on the Bataan Peninsula."

In Vietnam, Lieutenant Colonel André Cavaro Lucas, commander of the 2d Battalion, 506th Airborne Infantry, 101st Airborne Division, was recognized for his extraordinary leadership in the defense of Fire Support Base Ripcord during the battle that raged from 1 July to 23 July 1970. The 39-year-old 1954 graduate of West Point died as he was leading the withdrawal of the battalion from its untenable position.

It had become obvious by the turn of the century that some of the practices that governed the award of the Medal needed to be reconsidered. There was, for example, great dissatisfaction in the long delays in processing paperwork for the Medal; individuals could apply for the Medal, there being no requirement for eyewitness supporting accounts; nor was there any statute of limitations on how long after the battle a claim might be submitted and considered.

At the suggestion of his advisors, President William McKinley directed the Army to revise its somewhat vague regulations relevant to the awarding of the Medal. The result was that, effective 26 June 1897, all applications for the Medal of Honor would have to fit into one of three categories: for military service from the outbreak of the Civil War to 21 December 1889; for services between 1 January 1890 and the date of the new regulation; or cases "that may arise for service performed hereafter."

For the first time eyewitness supporting accounts were required. For actions subsequent to 1 January 1890, there would be no "applications." Instead, recommendations would be made by commanding officers or another individual who had personally witnessed the action. The regulation also stated that, in the future, recommendations would have to be made within one year after "performance of the act for which the award is claimed."

The popularity of the Medal of Honor led to an unanticipated problem. A number of imitations of the Medal were in circulation, some of them issued by respectable patriotic societies and even veterans' organizations. The Army decided to settle upon a new and distinctive design and to take

Opposite, top: A stirring moment during the Battle of Gettysburg, on 3 July 1863. After the regimental standard bearer was killed, Private George C. Platt, 6th Cavalry, engaged in a hand-to-hand fight to retain the flag and keep it from falling into enemy hands. His Medal was awarded thirty-two years later. ("Medal of Honor," Don Stivers, 6th U.S. Cavalry Edition)

Major Charles Whittlesey (right) led the 77th Division's "Lost Battalion" in the Argonne Forest. General John J. Pershing saluted his refusal to surrender when surrounded and cut off from the main body. (National Archives)

On 10 October 1871, at the Brazos River, Texas, 2d Lieutenant Robert G. Carter of the 4th Cavalry held the line against attacking Indians until reinforcements came to the rescue. (National Archives)

9th U.S. Cavalry soldiers, veterans of Indian campaigns, include (wearing Medals) Sergeants George Jordan (seated, lower left) and Henry Johnson (standing, upper right). (Nebraska State Historical Society)

1862   1896   1904   1944

Above: *In a rare moment when the Medal was presented in the field with military flourishes, ten soldiers of the 4th U.S. Cavalry were awarded the Medal for their actions at the Red River, Texas, on 29 September 1872. ("Heroes of the Red River," Don Stivers, 4th Cavalry Edition)*

Top, right: *Photograph shows (left to right) evolution of the Army Medal of Honor design from its inception in 1862 to the 1944 version. The 1896 Medal closely resembles the original. The 1904 design by Brigadier General George L. Gillespie is essentially that of the modern medal except for the ribbon design.*

Below: *Lieutenant Colonel Theodore Roosevelt with his "Rough Riders" (1st U.S. Volunteer Cavalry) in a victory photo after the famed battle in the San Juan hills during the Cuba campaign in July 1898. The ebullient "T. R." was recommended for the Medal but papers gathered dust until the 1990s. Roosevelt's Medal was approved by President Bill Clinton. (National Archives)*

Bottom, right: *Private Augustus Walley, 9th U.S. Cavalry, was recommended for the Medal of Honor after coming to the aid of his wounded commander in the 1898 San Juan battle. This award was not approved, but Walley previously had earned the Medal in an 1881 campaign against Apaches in New Mexico. ("A Day of Honor," Don Stivers, 9th, 10th HCA Edition)*

steps to prevent the use of similar medallions. Brigadier General George L. Gillespie, then chief of Engineers, is credited with creation of a new design. Gillespie had himself earned the nation's highest award as a young officer in the Civil War. Gillespie also provided a means for protecting the Medal against imitations. He was granted a patent on his new Medal design, and on 19 December 1904, he transferred the patent "to W. H. Taft and his successor or successors as Secretary of War of the United States of America."

Action undertaken by Congress on 27 April 1916 provided for the creation of a Medal of Honor Roll. To provide Medal of Honor recipients with "special status," the act stated that when a Medal of Honor recipient reached age 65, he would have his name recorded on the Honor Roll and be entitled to a special pension of $10 a month for the rest of his life. The act also stated that the applicant's Medal of Honor must have been won by an action involving actual conflict with the enemy, distinguished by conspicuous gallantry or intrepidity at the risk of life above and beyond the call of duty.

This resulted in an Army Board being convened to review all awards of the Medal since 1863, to identify any that might have been awarded or issued "for any cause other than distinguished conduct . . . involving actual

During the 1900 Boxer Rebellion in China, an allied force attempted to rescue foreign civilians trapped in the walled city of Peking. Two companies of the 14th U.S. Infantry appeared to be stymied. The call went out for a soldier to scale the wall. Trumpeter Calvin P. Titus replied with words that went down in history. ("I'll Try, Sir!" H. Charles McBarron, Army Art Collection)

conflict with the enemy." Between 16 October 1916 and 17 January 1917, the Board reviewed all of the records pertaining to the 1,615 Medals that had been awarded up to that time, and struck 911 names from the official list. Among those dropped were the names of 864 members of one Civil War regiment.

In general, following the presentation of the first six Medals, the method of presentation gradually became more formal. There were occasional instances during the Civil War and Indian campaigns when recipients of the Medal were honored in full view of their comrades. This rather indifferent procedure came to an end during the administration of President Theodore Roosevelt. The colorful former lieutenant colonel of the "Rough Riders," the 1st Volunteer Cavalry of San Juan Hill fame in the war with Spain, knew well the value of esprit de corps. Roosevelt signed an Executive Order outlining a basic policy still in force. This order stated that awards were to be made with formal and impressive ceremony and that the recipient "will, when practicable, be ordered to Washington, D.C., and the presentation will be made by the President, as Commander-in-Chief, or by such representative as the President may designate." In all, there would be thirty soldiers of the Spanish-American War placed on the Medal of Honor Roll, nine of them troopers of the all-black 10th U.S. Cavalry.

General Pershing summoned seventeen of the AEF's heroes to his headquarters at Chaumont, Haute Marne, France, where, on 19 February 1919, he presented the first increment of Medals of Honor in WWI. In the above photo, Pershing presents the Medal to Sergeant Harold Johnston of the 89th Division. Pershing would later praise Major Whittlesey, First Lieutenant Samuel Woodfill, and Sergeant Alvin York "as typifying the rank and file of our great Army." (National Archives)

By the time the American Expeditionary Force was deployed to Europe in 1917–18, the modern era of the Medal of Honor was well underway. The AEF, under its commander General John J. Pershing, established and enforced stern standards. Ninety-six members of the American force in

Top: *Corporal (later Sergeant) Alvin C. York reported to his brigade commander following the exploit that made the onetime conscientious objector a national hero. "Well, York," said the general, "I hear you captured the whole damned German army." York replied he had taken only 132 prisoners. (National Archives)*

Middle: *Lieutenant Alexander R. Nininger, a 1941 graduate of West Point, served with the 57th Infantry, Philippine Scouts. After the withdrawal to Bataan in January 1942, Nininger fought in hand-to-hand combat, trying to stem the Japanese tide. (National Archives)*

Bottom: *Sergeant Jose B. Calugas, born in Barrio Tagsing, Iloilo Province, typified the tough soldiers of the Philippine Scouts. When the Japanese invaded, he ran 1,000 yards under fire to another battery's position to put a gun back in action after its crew had been killed. (National Archives)*

World War I ultimately were awarded the Medal of Honor. The first actual awards were made by Pershing close to the battlefields where the honors had been earned. Among this group were four Army aviators who were members of the Army Air Service.

With the advent of World War II, General George C. Marshall, as chief of staff, was determined that his soldiers would be recognized on a timely basis. "We cannot do too much in the way of prompt recognition of the men who carry the fight and live under the conditions that exist at the fighting front," he declared. He was equally determined that nothing should tarnish the Medal of Honor's value and high esteem. A hand-picked War Department Decorations Board, which had the final say on every recommendation, was guided by a two-point philosophy: failure to act promptly would defeat the purpose of the decorations system; and awards not fully merited would depreciate the significance of the medal.

Only sixty-four days after Pearl Harbor, War Department General Order No. 9 announced the award of the Army Medal of Honor, the first in World War II, to Second Lieutenant Alexander R. Nininger, Jr., a 1941 West Point graduate. He died 12 January 1942 in hand-to-hand fighting while commanding a counterattacking unit of Philippine Scout infantry during the Japanese invasion of Bataan. Two days later the heroism of Sergeant Jose Calugas, a Philippine Scout, earned him the second Army Medal of the war.

On a number of occasions during World War II, presentation of the Medal was made by field commanders. Second Lieutenant Van T. Barfoot, a 45th Infantry Division soldier who had already earned a battlefield commission, received his Medal of Honor from Lieutenant General Alexander M. Patch, the commander of Seventh Army, with his division commander, Major General William W. Eagles, and his own company witnessing the occasion in an open field that was close enough to hear the guns supporting the front.

President Franklin Delano Roosevelt presented the Medal to (then) Colonel James A. Doolittle at the White House on 20 May 1942 after the Army flier's return from the first air raid on Tokyo. In January 1943, the President, who was attending an Allied summit conference in Casablanca, took advantage of the opportunity to present the Medal to Brigadier General William H. Wilbur. The award recognized Wilbur for a series of actions during his command of a small detachment that went ashore in advance of the main force landings in an effort to negotiate with French defenders to avoid an armed clash with longtime Allies. In the wartime years and prior to his own death in April 1945, President Roosevelt would personally award the highest medal to forty-two soldiers.

President Roosevelt's successor, President Harry Truman, who had served as a captain of field artillery in World War I, carried on the tradition. On one occasion twenty-eight armed services members reported to the White House en masse to receive the coveted award. Mr. Truman often said, "Of my duties as President of the United States, the one from which I derive the greatest satisfaction is the bestowal of this highest decoration in our land in the name of the Congress. As a soldier I know what the Medal means."

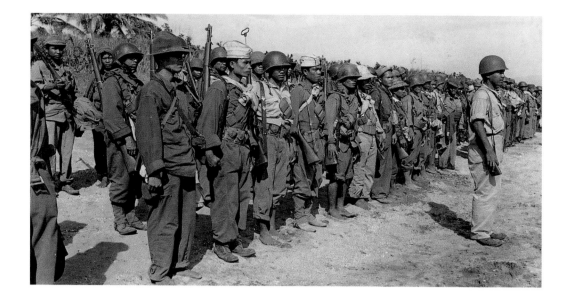

The greatest number of WWII Medal of Honor exploits took place during the battle of France. The citations of sixty-one soldiers, of the total 209 awards in the European Theater of Operations, tell the tale of the bitter campaigns fought on French soil during and after the assault on the Normandy Coast in June 1944. The immortals of this campaign include soldiers of the landings on D-Day and the days that followed: Staff Sergeant Walter D. Ehlers of the 1st (Big Red One) Infantry Division, and Technical Sergeant Frank D. Peregory of the 29th (Blue and Gray) Infantry Division. There was

Top, left: *Philippine Scouts, authorized in 1901 in the U.S. Army, were led by an officer corps of U.S. Regular Army officers and NCOs.Following the Japanese invasion in 1941, they fought bravely in defense of their home islands. (National Archives)*

Above: *Shortly after his return from the Far East where he led the first raid on Japan, James A. ("Jimmy") Doolittle was summoned to the White House by President Roosevelt on 20 May 1942. By then a newly promoted brigadier general, he was among the first of the Army aviators to be awarded the Medal in WWII. (National Archives)*

Middle, left: *Technical Sergeant Charles E. "Commando" Kelly killed forty enemy soldiers in a gully near Altavilla, Italy. And that was only the beginning of his incredible saga in WWII. His Medal was personally bestowed by General Mark Clark. Kelly would never tell what Clark whispered to him during the presentation. (National Archives)*

Middle, right: *With Major General George S. Patton (right) President Franklin D. Roosevelt, during a conference at Casablanca, 24 January 1943, found time to award the first Medal of Honor for action in North Africa to Brigadier General William H. Wilbur. Wilbur, then a colonel, on a special mission behind enemy lines, led an attack against a hostile artillery battery firing on U.S. troops. (National Archives)*

Left: *Twenty-eight WWII soldiers assembled at the White House to receive the Medal of Honor from a WWI field artilleryman, President Harry S. Truman. The date was 23 August 1945, a few days after the atomic bombs were detonated, and within a few weeks of the war's end. President Truman would again greet Medal of Honor heroes in the Korean War. (National Archives)*

Following page, top: *Only five days after D-Day, on the bitterly contested road to Carentan, Lieutenant Colonel Robert G. Cole, leading his battalion of the 101st Airborne Division, encountered four heavily defended bridges. He led a bold bayonet attack that gained a bridgehead across the Douve River and opened the door to Carentan. ("Against All Odds," James Dietz, Army Art Collection)*

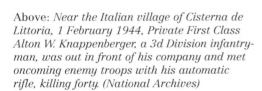

Above: *Near the Italian village of Cisterna de Littoria, 1 February 1944, Private First Class Alton W. Knappenberger, a 3d Division infantry-man, was out in front of his company and met oncoming enemy troops with his automatic rifle, killing forty. (National Archives)*

Above, center: *In tribute to his father's old regiment, Brigadier General Theodore Roosevelt, Jr., named his jeep "Rough Rider" when he was assistant division commander, 1st Infantry Division, in North Africa. "Young Teddy," who had earned the Distinguished Service Cross in WWI, suffered a fatal heart attack after helping to lead the 4th Infantry Division at Utah Beach on D-Day. (National Archives)*

Above, right: *The youthful 2d Lieutenant Audie Murphy came out of WWII as one of the most highly decorated soldiers in the Army. The future motion picture and television star was awarded the Medal for "indomitable courage and refusal to give an inch of ground" in a battle near Holtzwihr, France, on 26 January 1945. (National Archives)*

also the gallant Lieutenant Colonel Robert G. Cole, who led his paratroopers of the 101st Airborne Division in one of the most daring bayonet attacks in U.S. military history on the road to Carentan, 11 June 1944. Also included was Brigadier General Theodore Roosevelt, Jr., who led the assault waves of the 4th Infantry Division ashore on Utah Beach, 6 June 1944.

The ETO contingent of Medal of Honor heroes concludes, fittingly, with the stories of Captain Michael Daly and Private Joseph F. Merrell, who fought their way into the outskirts of the Nazi shrine city of Nuremberg in the vanguard of the 3d Infantry Division, 18 April 1945. The German surrender came just a short time later on 7 May 1945.

A total of seventy Army Medals of Honor commemorate the Army's war in the Asiatic-Pacific theater of operations, including one in the China-Burma-India theater. New Guinea, where Army forces met the Japanese in battle as early as 1942, was destined to be the locale for eight who would be named to the Medal of Honor Roll. Three Army men would earn the

Top, left: *In the area of operations least known to most Americans in WWII—the China-Burma-India theater—U.S. forces concentrated on providing support and training assistance to the Chinese forces of Chiang Kai-shek. An 81mm mortar crew is shown in support of an initiative by the U.S. "Mars Task Force" in 1944 to seize objectives in northern Burma. (National Archives)*

Top, right: *Drawing his pistol after his rifle jammed during action on Guadalcanal, Captain Charles W. Davis, an infantry battalion executive officer, led an attack against the Japanese, who were delaying the advance by the 25th Division. He was a major commanding the battalion when this photograph was taken during the New Georgia campaign in 1943. Seated is Major General J. L. Collins.*

Left: *Japanese tenacity in the New Georgia campaign prolonged the U.S. campaign in the Solomon Islands. Progress was impeded by strong enemy defenses, mud, dense jungle, and inaccurate maps. Seeking to wrest a vital airfield at Munda from the enemy, U.S. infantrymen on a flanking move found themselves fording streams and fighting for high ground. (National Archives)*

Above: *Commonplace in the Pacific island-hopping campaigns commanded by General Douglas MacArthur were operations in deep tropical jungle settings, such as this scene on Bougainville. An infantry patrol follows an M4 medium tank and prepares to meet the enemy during the campaign that cost the U.S. its heaviest casualties since Guadalcanal. (National Archives)*

Medal on Guadalcanal. The bitter battle for New Georgia in 1943 would also result in three Medal of Honor heroes, among them the bespectacled and gentle young man who would be immortalized in song, Private Rodger Young. As the war moved north, ever closer to the home islands of Japan, two more, both posthumous, came out of the smoke and fury of Saipan.

Among the nine Army men awarded the Medal of Honor in the Okinawa campaign was Private First Class Desmond T. Doss. When his company in the 77th Infantry Division was fighting for its life at the Escarpment, Doss, a medic, stepped out of obscurity and into the pages of history. There was also the young replacement Private First Class Clarence B. Craft, a new man in the 96th Infantry Division, on a hilltop where his battalion had been stymied for twelve days. In a daring one-man attack, he led the way in the capture of the hill that was the key to the Japanese defenses.

The Medals awarded for actions in the U.S. return to the Philippines reflect the intensity of combat. In the liberation of the Philippines in

Above: *The promise by General MacArthur that U.S. forces would return to the Philippines was redeemed by U.S. infantrymen during 1944–45. In February 1945, the liberation of Manila was accomplished by the 37th Infantry Division in tandem with the 1st Cavalry Division. But the campaign on Luzon would continue almost until the end of the war. ("We Have Returned," James Dietz)*

Above, right: *The long-awaited liberation of the Philippines, 1944–45, threw U.S. troops against an enemy who would fight to the bitter end. In many close encounters defenders had to be rooted out by infantrymen equipped with flamethrowers. There were thirty-five Army Medal of Honor actions in the campaign, evidence of the enemy's tenacity and determination. (National Archives)*

In command of the 24th Infantry Division, the first U.S. division into Korea in July 1950, Major General William F. Dean, an experienced WWII commander, went into the field to rally his outnumbered and outgunned soldiers. In the photo (opposite, bottom left) *a U.S. soldier looks at the enemy T-34 tank that Dean stalked and halted before he went "missing in action." He eluded capture for thirty-three days before being captured. He would survive the POW camps to wear the Medal awarded by President Truman.*

1944–45, thirty-six men earned the Medal of Honor—twenty-two for action on Luzon, the others for battle action at Leyte, Mindanao, and Negros.

The final Medal of Honor action in World War II, Corporal Melvin Mayfield's one-man assault against Japanese positions in the Cordillera Mountains on 29 July 1945, came 1,327 days after Pearl Harbor.

In the excitement of the decisive U.S. victory in World War II, the suggestion was made that the Medal of Honor should be bestowed upon General of the Army Dwight D. Eisenhower in recognition of his leadership during the campaigns in Europe. He refused, declaring the award "has got to remain a medal for the soldier who comes to grips with the enemy at close quarters." Many years later, the former Supreme Allied Commander in Europe told a young Korean War hero upon whom he had just bestowed the medal, "Son, I would rather have the right to wear this than be President of the United States."

The first week of July 1950 found the 24th Infantry Division, fresh from nearly five years of occupation duty in Japan, assembling to fight in Korea. It was spectacularly understrength as it deployed, piecemeal, to the Korean peninsula to confront the North Koreans who had stormed across the border into the Republic of Korea (South Korea). Near the end of the fourth week of fighting, Sergeant George D. Libby smashed a roadblock south of Taejon, where the division was fighting for its life. Libby, an engineer, pushed a number of wounded men on board an M-5 tractor from an artillery outfit and posted himself to ride "shotgun." Knowing that only this driver could operate the M-5, Libby interposed himself between the driver and the enemy fire being directed at them. They crashed the roadblock and got the wounded men to an aid station. By then it was too late for the fatally wounded Libby, the first Army Medal of Honor man in this new war. In the decades that would follow, many troops, Americans and others, would cross the Han River on the Libby Bridge, named for the courageous Army engineer.

On the following day the division's commander, Major General William F. Dean, disappeared. As he led small groups of his scattered command in a vain effort to stem the enemy tide in the outskirts of Taejon,

he grimly insisted, "We must hold them! I don't want to have to fight for every mile of this ground again." Over a year after his disappearance it was learned he had been taken prisoner. On 9 January 1951 the Medal was presented by President Truman to his wife Mildred in a White House ceremony. General Dean remained a prisoner until the end of the war.

In a thousand days of combat in Korea there would be seventy-eight Army Medal of Honor men, including two more who, like General Dean,

An artist's view of action 24 April 1951, when an overwhelming enemy attack resulted in close combat action in the 3d Infantry Division sector near Taejon, Korea. Corporal Hiroshi Miyamura, in charge of a machine-gun crew, took on the enemy with his bayonet. Although gravely wounded, he insisted upon staying behind to cover the withdrawal and was taken prisoner. Only upon his release from a POW camp in 1953 (below), did he learn that he had been awarded the Medal of Honor. ("Corporal Hiroshi H. Miyamura," George Akimoto, Army Art Collection)

109

Above: *A portrait entitled ". . . and live to wear it" highlighted a photograph of three fighting heroes of the Korean War who survived to receive the Medal in a White House ceremony on 19 May 1951: Sergeant John A. Pittman, Sergeant Ernest R. Kouma, and Second Lieutenant Carl H. Dodd. (New York Sunday News)*

Right: *On 19 October 1950, the United Nations counteroffensive, which would take lead elements to the Yalu River, was well underway. U.S. troops of the U.N. force entered P'yongyang, the capital of North Korea. Having reversed fortunes since the grim days of July and August, jubilant troops began to talk of being home by Christmas. (National Archives)*

As the advent of winter rain and snow slowed the tempo of activity along the "Minnesota Line" in Korea, mud became a predominant enemy. A sand-bagged 45th Division tank of the 180th Infantry, mobilized from Durant, Oklahoma, waits for orders during the November 1952 defensive actions. (National Guard Bureau)

would learn only after leaving POW camps, that they had been awarded the Medal of Honor. They were First Lieutenant James L. Stone and Corporal Hiroshi Miyamura. In a valiant fight near Taejon during 24–25 April 1951, Corporal Miyamura had been taken prisoner after leading his squad of the 7th Infantry, 3d Division. During the battle, Miyamura left his machine gun and seized a rifle to rush the enemy in a one-man bayonet attack. Survivors of his squad recommended him for the Medal of Honor.

During 1950, in six months of combat, twenty-four Army men were named to receive the medal. The pace quickened in 1951 as the U.S. forces counterattacked and engaged in successful offensive operations. However, the advent of static warfare prevailed starting in 1952 and there were twelve Medal of Honor awards presented in contrast to thirty-two in 1951. In June 1953, as peace talks seemed on the verge of a conclusion, offensive action picked up. Between 10 June and 27 July, in the final six weeks of the war, six names were added to the roll of Medal of Honor heroes. In total, there were seventy-eight Medal recipients for Korean War action. Ten years would pass before a U.S. president would again be called upon to present the nation's highest combat medal.

In 1961 President John F. Kennedy approved the Armed Forces Expeditionary Medal for presentation to soldiers, sailors, airmen, and marines committed to Cold War operations. In 1962 he issued an executive order to authorize the awarding of the Purple Heart for wounds received in Cold War situations. Yet another executive order, on 26 August 1962, provided

for the Bronze Star, the Legion of Merit, and lesser awards for U.S. military personnel serving with "friendly foreign troops" in armed conflict. The president and the senior service chiefs believed that service members in Cold War "hot spots" also deserved full recognition for instances of valor. On 25 July 1963, Congress authorized the Medal of Honor as well as lesser awards for "military operations involving conflict with an opposing foreign

Clockwise from top, left:

A soldier moves warily through a bombed-out Korean street. (AP/Wide World Photos)

An Army unit picks its way through the hilly Korean terrain. (AP/Wide World Photos)

1st Cavalry Division infantrymen launch an assault on Korean enemy positions with assistance of tanks from the 24th Infantry Division. (AP/Wide World Photos)

Artillery redlegs keep up a heavy rain of fire directed toward Korean enemy positions in support of infantrymen preparing to attack Triangle Hill. (AP/Wide World Photos)

Left: *Moving in single file, men of an 8th Cavalry Regiment unit plant their company guidon within sight of enemy forces north of the 38th Parallel. The road in the background leads directly to P'yongyang. (AP/Wide World Photos)*

111

Above: *Almost exactly eleven years after the last shots were fired in Korea, Captain Roger H. Donlon was in command of a Special Forces base camp at Nam Dong in the Republic of Vietnam. Donlon led a heroic defense of the camp. Five months later President Lyndon B. Johnson presented him the first Medal of Honor for Vietnam action. (National Archives)*

Opposite, top right: *The drama of Vietnam nighttime action is captured in this work of combat art. ("Night Battle," John Wheat, Army Art Collection)*

Below, left to right:

Then a second lieutenant, Charles Q. Williams, serving as executive officer of a Special Forces camp at Dong Xoai, led the defense of the sprawling position during a 14-hour attack, 9–10 June 1965. He would be the second Army recipient of the Medal of Honor for valor in Vietnam. (National Archives)

Private First Class Milton L. Olive, III, was taking part in a search and destroy mission with his platoon from the 2d Battalion (Airborne), 503d Infantry, on 22 October 1965. He and four buddies were moving together when a grenade was thrown into their midst. Olive grabbed the grenade and fell on it, shielding the others from the blast. (National Archives)

Then Specialist Fifth Grade Lawrence Joel, a medic in the 1st Battalion (Airborne), 503d Infantry, suffered multiple incapacitating wounds in action in Vietnam on 8 November 1965. He continued treating wounded soldiers during the attack. (National Archives)

force." By the end of 1964, the advisor force in South Vietnam had grown to over 20,000 and there had been ten awards of the Distinguished Service Cross and fifty-six Silver Stars.

In 1965, Captain Roger Hugh C. Donlon was a thirty-year-old infantry captain assigned to the 7th Special Forces Group at Fort Bragg, North Carolina, and in May 1964 he was sent to Vietnam. By the mid-point of his deployment Captain Donlon was in command of the Special Forces camp at Nam Dong on the Laos border. Donlon's command consisted of his own twelve-man A-team, officially designated Special Forces Detachment 726, plus a 311-man South Vietnam "strike force" and their families, and sixty ethnic Nung guards of Chinese origin.

During the night and early morning hours of 6 July 1964, Donlon and his men fought tenaciously to ward off a Viet Cong attack. Donlon himself was wounded four times but continued to rally his men. "His dynamic leadership, fortitude, and valiant efforts," the citation would state, "inspired not only the American personnel but the friendly Vietnamese defenders as well and resulted in the successful defense of the camp." He was recommended for the Medal of Honor.

On 5 December 1964 he found himself in the East Room of the White House where he was awarded the Medal by President Lyndon B. Johnson. Johnson said, "This Medal of Honor awarded in the name of the Congress is the first such honor to be bestowed upon an American military

man for conspicuous gallantry above any beyond the call of duty in our present efforts in the Republic of Vietnam."

There would, in time, be a total of 156 Medals of Honor conferred upon Army heroes in Vietnam, from Donlon's first, to the last, which resulted from an action in which First Lieutenant Loren D. Hagen, 25, fought and died in a desperate firefight deep in enemy-held territory on the morning of 7 August 1971. And although, by this time, a full-strength army had taken the field, the last Army Medal of Honor action, like the first in Vietnam, was out on a distant perimeter in what might be described as an unconventional warfare environment.

The second Army Medal of Honor incident was earned in the heroic defense of a beleaguered special forces camp at Dong Xoai. The special forces detachment was led by a tough, 35-year-old professional soldier, (then) Second Lieutenant Charles Q. Williams of the 5th Special Forces Group. Among other heroic actions, he took a bazooka and maneuvered close enough to the enemy to destroy a machine gun and its crew.

During 1965 the first major Army ground combat element, the 173d Airborne Brigade, arrived in Vietnam, and three airborne troopers were named as recipients of the Medal in the early months of the brigade's deployment—Sergeant Larry S. Pierce, Private First Class Milton L. Olive, III, and (then) Specialist Sixth Class Lawrence Joel. Pierce had thrown himself on an exploding land mine to save fellow squad members; Olive, the first black soldier to be awarded the Medal in Vietnam, used his own body to cover a grenade to save four fellow soldiers; Joel, a medic, continued to tend to the wounds of fellow soldiers after he himself had suffered grave multiple wounds.

The increased number of Medal of Honor awards as the war progressed would reflect the stepped-up pace of the U.S. war effort. Following five in 1965 there would be eighteen in 1966, followed by thirty-five in 1967, and forty-three in 1968, by which time there were more than half a million Americans in Vietnam. There were thirty-one Medal of Honor actions in 1969, seventeen in 1970, and six in 1971.

By the end of the war, a total of thirteen soldiers of the 173d Airborne Brigade had received the Medal of Honor. The 1st Cavalry Division (Airmobile), which had arrived soon after the 173d Brigade, would account for twenty-six. There were twenty-two from the 25th (Tropic Lightning) Infantry Division; fifteen in the 101st Airborne Division (Airmobile); eleven in the 23d (American) Infantry Division; and ten in the 1st Infantry Division. Thirteen Medal of Honor recipients wore the green beret of Army Special Forces.

For Lyndon B. Johnson, the Medal of Honor presentations in the White House were more than a matter of tradition, they were moments of truth and reflection as to "what it was all about." On one occasion he characterized a Medal of Honor hero's act of bravery as "a patriot's gift to his country."

A more recent example of Medals being awarded for "other than war" situations occurred in October 1993, with a U.S. task force in far-off Somalia on a humanitarian mission. Members of the task force, on a seemingly routine mission, found themselves surrounded and in an unexpected

While serving as an assistant battalion advisor in the 9th Division, Republic of Vietnam Army, Captain Jack A. Jacobs made repeated forays across fire-swept rice paddies to evacuate wounded men and weapons during a fierce battle in Kien Phong Province. Jacobs's action was with complete disregard for his own safety, noted the Medal of Honor citation. (National Archives)

In action in the Fishhook, near the Cambodian border, Lieutenant Colonel Charles C. Rogers, after being seriously wounded, aggressively continued in command of a fire base being subjected to massed enemy fire. The future Army major general was commanding 1st Battalion, 5th Field Artillery, 1st Infantry Division, during the November 1968 action.

Above: *Specialist Alfred Rascon, a medic with the 173d Airborne Brigade, received his recognition —over thirty years late. His wartime buddies, stunned to learn his heroism had not been rewarded, led the search for papers to support his recommendation for the Medal. In 1999 Rascon, by then a lieutenant colonel, received the Medal from President Bill Clinton. (Pentagram)*

Right: *In a photograph taken during the 16 March 1966 battle, Specialist Rascon (center) badly wounded after sustaining shrapnel and bullet wounds while tending his buddies' wounds, actually received last rites while waiting for medical treatment. Earlier he had shielded three fellow soldiers with his body during a machine gun and grenade attack. (National Archives)*

Above: *An Army review board rescinded 911 Medal of Honor awards, mostly of Civil War vintage, in 1916. Several have since been restored. In 1977, the Medal was posthumously restored to Dr. Mary Walker, a contract surgeon in the Civil War Army. In 1982, Dr. Walker was featured on a commemorative postage stamp. She remains the only woman on the Medal of Honor Roll. (National Postal Museum, Smithsonian Institution)*

Right: *Master Sergeant Gary I. Gordon and Sergeant First Class Randall D. Shugart volunteered to be inserted into the thick of a critical firefight that threatened to take the lives of injured members of a downed Blackhawk helicopter during the ill-fated Battle of Mogadishu, Somalia, 3 October 1993. Both were awarded the Medal posthumously. (Association of the United States Army)*

and desperate shootout in the center of Mogadishu. Two extraordinary Special Forces soldiers, Master Sergeant Gary I. Gordon and Sergeant First Class Randall D. Shugart, earned the Medal of Honor that day, giving their lives in defense of wounded members of a helicopter crew.

When the Army's 1917 Board revoked 911 already awarded Medals, several were withdrawn on the basis of having been awarded to non-military personnel. In the closing decades of the twentieth century Congress provided the authority for reconsideration of some of these cases. In 1977 Congressman Les Aspin spearheaded the successful call for restoration of the Medal to Dr. Mary Walker. Walker's name was restored

to the Honor Roll of Medal recipients, and she remains to this day the only woman to have received the Medal. Similar action was initiated a few years later leading to the restoration of the Medals awarded to Buffalo Bill Cody and several other civilian scouts on 8 July 1989.

In April 1991 the Medal of Honor was presented to the surviving sister of former Private Freddie Stowers in recognition of his valor in action on 28 September 1918. This last Medal in recognition of heroism in World War I came seventy-three years after the fact and was presented by President George H. W. Bush. Recognition of Stowers's heroism in 1991 brought into focus that it was the only award of the Medal of Honor to an African-American soldier in World War I and that none had been recognized for valor in World War II. The question was soon raised as to whether racial discrimination had resulted in the failure of commanders to push aggressively for the recognition of minorities who had distinguished themselves in combat. Attention was initially focused on the fact that no black soldiers had been awarded the Medal in World War II. Another

Above, left: After hostilities ended, French officers, including the one-armed General Henri Gouraud, assisted General Pershing in the presentation of awards to wartime heroes. None of the African-American soldiers who were recommended received the Medal for service in 1917–1918 until one was awarded posthumously by President George H. W. Bush in 1991. (National Archives)

Above: Like most U.S. artillery outfits in WWI, the 167th Field Artillery brigade relied heavily on the French-made 75mm howitzer. After intensive training at La Courtine, the African-American artillerymen rejoined the 92d Division in the Oise-Aisne sector in time for the final wartime offensive under the newly formed U.S. Second Army. (National Archives)

Left: The last order before communications was lost—"hold at all costs." For two-and-a-half days, soldiers of the 28th (Keystone) Infantry Division held on without reinforcements or resupply. This bought precious time for U.S. forces in the German offensive best known as the "Battle of the Bulge." ("The Desperate Hours," Don Stivers, 112th Infantry Edition)

Page 116, top: Soldiers in the grim reality of Bastogne during the Battle of the Bulge in December 1944 fought on despite critical shortages of ammunition, weapons, winter clothing, and food. ("K-Rations," Aaron Bohrod, Army Art Collection)

THE PYRAMID OF HONOR: *To enhance the importance of the Medal, it was important that lesser decorations be created for the recognition of deeds not meeting the requirements for the Medal of Honor. An award known as the Certificate of Merit was replaced with the Distinguished Service Medal—to be awarded for exceptional non-combat service. The Congress approved this, noting ". . . if a secondary medal had been authorized in the past the award of the . . . Medal of Honor would have been more jealously guarded."*

To provide other medals for the recognition of combat heroism, an act of Congress, 9 July 1918, created the Distinguished Service Cross and the Silver Star. Other medals were added to the list in later years. The Purple Heart, which George Washington had created in 1781, was revived in 1931. The result was a so-called Pyramid of Honor.

1. **Medal of Honor.** For gallantry and intrepidity at the risk of life above and beyond the call of duty.

2. **Service Cross.** For extraordinary heroism in military operations against an armed enemy. Established 1918.

3. **Distinguished Service Medal.** For exceptionally meritorious service in a position of high responsibility. Established in 1918.

4. **Silver Star.** For gallantry in action. Established 1932.

5. **The Legion of Merit.** For exceptionally meritorious conduct in the performance of outstanding service. Like the Purple Heart, established in 1782.

6. **Distinguished Flying Cross.** For heroism and extraordinary achievement while participating in aerial flight, subsequent to 6 April 1917.

7. **Soldier's Medal.** For heroism not involving actual conflict with an enemy. Established in 1926.

8. **Star Medal.** For heroic or meritorious achievement or service against an enemy. Authorized by President F. D. Roosevelt, 4 February 1944.

9. **Air Medal.** Meritorious achievement participating in aerial flight. By Executive Order of the President, 1942.

10. **Commendation Ribbon.** For exceptional service less than that required for The Legion of Merit.

11. **Purple Heart.** For wounds received in action against an enemy of the United States. Based on 1782 Badge for Military Merit. Re-established by Congress in 1932.

12. **The Presidential Unit Citation** (formerly the Distinguished Unit Citation) is awarded to a unit, detachment, or installation (including non-U.S.) for outstanding performance of duty in action against an enemy of the United States, after 7 December 1941.

review process in 1998–1999 examined the same issue with regard to Japanese-Americans and others of Asian heritage.

The Army had, in fact, already initiated a study in September 1993, contracting Shaw University in Raleigh, North Carolina, to investigate the Medal of Honor issue as it related to black soldiers in World War II. The result was a recommendation to upgrade nine Distinguished Service Crosses and also to reexamine the case of a tenth soldier proposed for the Medal of Honor who also had been awarded the Silver Star prior to the action that resulted in his death. Of the ten names, a total of seven were destined to have their names added to the Medal of Honor Roll, by act of Congress, in the 1997 Defense Authorization Bill.

Expanded eligibility rules approved by Congress in 1996 opened the way for recognition of servicemen "native to the Pacific region" whose DSC decorations might be found worthy of upgrading to the Medal of Honor. Senator Daniel Akaka of Hawaii, a sponsor of the legislation that sparked the study, had been dismayed when he learned that the Japanese-American 442d Regimental Combat Team suffered enormous casualties, 650 killed and 8,826 wounded, but had only a single entry on the Medal of Honor roster. His legislation resulted in a review of the records of 104 combat veterans.

After extensive study the Army concluded that twenty-two Asian-Americans held DSC's that merited upgrade to the Medal of Honor. Twenty

Above: *General Mark W. Clark, Fifth Army commander, affixes unit citation streamers to guidons of companies in the 100th Battalion, 442d Regimental Combat Team. Composed of Japanese-American soldiers, the 442d fought in Italy and France and by the end of WWII, it was one of the most renowned fighting units in the entire wartime Army. (National Archives)*

Opposite, bottom: *During the Third Army's advance across France, a medium tank crew of the 761st Tank Battalion negotiates the muddy terrain near Nancy, in November 1944. The 761st, an all-black unit, is represented on the Medal of Honor Roll by the late Staff Sergeant Ruben Rivers, a heroic tank commander killed in action, 19 November 1944. (National Archives)*

Above: *Following its service in the Italian campaign, the 442d Regimental Combat Team joined the Seventh Army in the Vosges Mountains in France. It was called upon for an all-out effort to break through to a surrounded battalion of the 36th (Texas) Infantry Division. In October 1944, the Nisei warriors made it through the German defenses, relieved the Texans, and lived up to their "Go For Broke" credo. ("Go for Broke," H. Charles McBarron, Army Art Collection)*

of these brave Japanese-Americans were members of the 442d RCT. Seven of the Medals were awarded to men still living, including Hawaii's Senator Daniel Inouye, already known as a highly decorated combat hero. Inouye, whose DSC was in recognition of a firefight in which he destroyed two German machine gun nests during the Allied campaign in Italy, lost his right arm in the battle. The 442d RCT, with these new awards, is now one of the Army's most decorated infantry regiments.

In January 2001, as part of his final actions in office, President Clinton approved the award of the Medal to Lieutenant Colonel, 1st U.S. Volunteer Cavalry, and later President, Theodore Roosevelt. The award recognized his actions of 1 July 1898 in the capture of Kettle Hill and then leading a supporting attack on the Spanish forces defending San Juan Hill. This made the Roosevelts the second father-son awardees.

Because the Medal of Honor is presented "in the name of the Congress of the United States" it was frequently and popularly called the "Congressional Medal of Honor." In 1977 Congress took cognizance of this and acted to formally recognize the medal as "the Congressional Medal of Honor." Both designations are used interchangeably. Under either designation, the Medal of Honor has become the most revered and treasured of all decorations in the eye of the public and certainly in the military community.

This has probably never been better expressed than on the occasion when First Lieutenant Charles Q. Williams, a Medal of Honor recipient of the Vietnam War era, and a student of history, stood before President Lyndon B. Johnson in the White House. Looking President Johnson squarely in the eye, Williams articulated a soldier's thoughts: "As President Eisenhower said, and with all due respect to you, sir, and your duties, I would rather have the Medal of Honor than be President of the United States. These are my sentiments."

Shown here is the contemporary Medal of Honor. (Collection of Bruce Jacobs)

Opposite, bottom: A 442d RCT Medal of Honor recipient, the highly decorated Lieutenant—and later a U.S. Senator from Hawaii—Daniel Inouye.

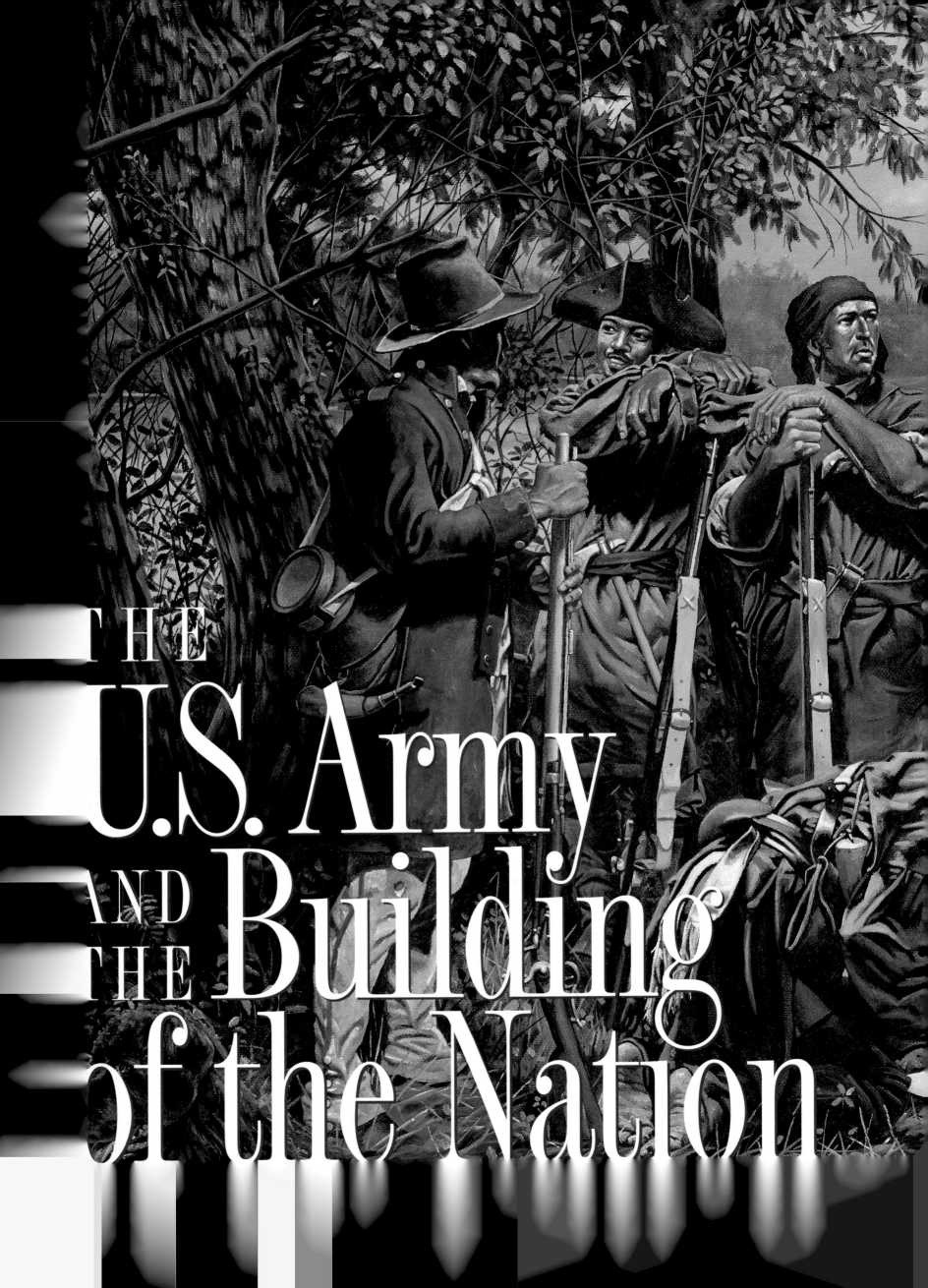

THE U.S. Army
AND THE Building
of the Nation

THE U.S. Army AND THE Building of the Nation

Soldiers Who Waged Peace and Progress

Brigadier General Harold W. Nelson, USA (Ret)

While armies exist to wreak death and destruction, most of the U.S. Army's history consists of times when its soldiers were called upon to contribute their talents and resources to positive actions when external threats did not threaten to destroy the nation's sovereignty. The Army performed a broad range of "nation building" activities since its founding. Some continue today to be an important part of the Army's mission. Others are remembered as a proud part of the Army's history. A few are the subject of continuing controversy.

Soldiers involved in nation-building toil on the frontier between democracy and disorder. Often the struggle is with natural forces; other times it is truly a fight with other men. In every case the soldiers are at risk, with little more than resourceful leaders and a spirit of selfless service to sustain them. There is a special kind of heroism in building a nation—not the flamboyant heroism of popular battlefield tales, but the resolute heroism of people who endure hardships for the sake of others. Ironically, these contributions are often overlooked or denigrated even within the Army. While cadets at the U.S. Military Academy of the nineteenth century studied French, recited details of Napoleon's campaigns, and dreamt of European-style war, their faculty included veterans of frontier battles, and exploration and engineering expeditions that still

Above: A column of the 2d U.S. Dragoons crossing the Rockies to relieve their comrades on the Utah expedition. The Dragoons, led by Lieutenant Colonel Philip St. George Cook, lost a third of their mounts during the miserable winter of 1857–1858. ("Never A Complaint," Don Stivers)

Pages 120–121: Far from home the "Corps of Discovery" led by Lewis and Clark commemorates 4 July 4 1804 on the new frontier. The explorers had by this time reached the site of present-day Atcheson, Kansas, on the Missouri River. The event was celebrated with a cannon show and an extra ration of whiskey. The Corps's keelboat and a canoe are in the background. (Rick Reeves, Collector Historical Prints, Inc.)

Opposite: A scant five years after his graduation from West Point, Lieutenant Joseph Christmas Ives led a Colorado River expedition in 1857. Travel was aboard the homemade steamboat U.S. Explorer. John J. Young based this drawing on a sketch by the German artist-writer Henrich Baldwin Mollhausen, who accompanied Ives on this and other adventures.

Above: *The Army constructed Fort Seldon in the New Mexico Territory during April–May 1865. Its first garrison consisted of two companies of the 3d U.S. Cavalry. Picket posts were established to protect the citizens of nearby towns from Mescalero Apaches. When Fort Bliss was chosen for expansion, Fort Selden's days were numbered. In 1888 the last troops left. (Peter Hurd, Army Art Collection)*

Right: *In the aftermath of the French and Indian War, frontier communities in what is now West Virginia were frequent targets for Indian bands led by French officers. Civilians who remained took refuge in fortified houses or log forts. In the spring of 1756 Captain Jeremiah Smith with twenty Virginia militiamen arrived just in time to foil a raiding party. ("...Twenty Brave Men," Jackson Walker, National Guard Heritage series)*

inspire admiration. Yet those contributions were often seen as peacetime "distractions" that took officers away from their regiments or from the proper study of war.

Taming the Frontier

Taming the frontier and taming the citizenry were much like war for those who endured that service, even if the warfare was far from Napoleonic in its grandeur. The Indian wars have been a controversial aspect of the nation's history since the first brush between colonists and Native Americans. The

new American republic of the late eighteenth century inherited strained relationships with Native American tribes. International politics, national policy, and human nature all fanned the flames of conflict throughout the first hundred years of the nation's existence.

The U.S. Army's relationship with Native Americans has not been fully explored in the many motion pictures that have touched on the subject—those movies tend to highlight the more dramatic aspects of the Army on the frontier. Much of the Army's work was in the category we tend to call "peacekeeping" today. Operating in small patrols from remote posts, soldiers helped stabilize relationships between Native Americans and ever-encroaching settlers. A majority of Indians were at peace with those settlers most of the time, but the exceptions to that generalization kept large parts of the small peacetime Army occupied for the first century of the republic's history. Rogue chieftains would break treaty agreements, prospectors would invade sacred land, Indian agents would fail to meet obligations—these and a broad array of other causes would erupt into violence, and the Army was called in to restore order.

Above, left to right: 1st Regiment, artillery officer, and infantryman in 1786; West Point artillery cadet, and an Engineer Corps private in 1805; and an engineer officer, U.S. explorer, and infantryman from 1819. ("The American Soldier," H. Charles McBarron, Army Art Collection)

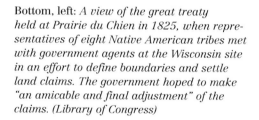

Bottom, left: A view of the great treaty held at Prairie du Chien in 1825, when representatives of eight Native American tribes met with government agents at the Wisconsin site in an effort to define boundaries and settle land claims. The government hoped to make "an amicable and final adjustment" of the claims. (Library of Congress)

Below: An Indian Scout and U.S. infantry officer. ("The American Soldier, 1839," H. Charles McBarron, Army Art Collection)

125

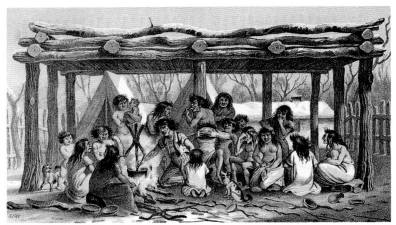

Top: *A buckskin-clad Army scout and two Indian scouts, probably Crow, fight alongside cavalrymen firing at a fast-moving circle of mounted attackers. ("Rounded-Up," Frederic Remington, Sid Richardson Collection of Western Art, Fort Worth, Texas)*

Above, left: *A keen observer and author, Captain Howard Stansbury later described the woes of Indians held prisoner at Fort Utah in the winter of 1850. Things only worsened in the "Utah Indian Disturbance" of 1852–53. Stansbury was a member of the 1st Topographical Engineers. (A. Fay, Yale University Library)*

Above, right: *A party composed of members of the U.S. Boundary Commission attacked by Apaches on 18 October 1852. Men seeking adventure coveted assignments with the various boundary commissions appointed by the government, and there was no dearth of volunteers for the available positions. (Henry Pratt, Yale University Library)*

Right: *Soldiers of the post-Civil War army played an important role in the westward expansion. In the fast-moving situations they encountered in protecting settlers from Indians, soldiers frequently found it essential to be able to improvise, as in the case of these infantrymen using their infantry rifles and equipment to carry out a mission better suited to cavalry. ("Guarding the New Frontier," Don Stivers)*

There were very few large battles, although there were many fights where the losses among the Indian tribes were excessive. As the "Indian Problem" shifted farther from the big cities of the East, many Americans treated the Army's work as routine, and it went largely unnoticed. The results were seldom directly attributed to the Army.

Nevertheless, through the Army's efforts, treaties were achieved, modified, and enforced, communications and security were improved, and immigration followed.

The Army also took the lead in a social experiment to correct what was perceived as an endemic problem. General Nelson Miles wrote in an official report in 1875:

> *The real cause [of outbreaks of Indian violence] arises from the fact that several thousand wild savages are gathered and placed on remote reservations, under no other control, restraint, or influence than that exercised by one or two individuals, beyond or on the verge of civilization, where they see only the worst features of the same, without ever having an opportunity of seeing or knowing any of the more elevating influences that govern civilized people.*

The Indian Industrial School at Carlisle Barracks appeared an obvious solution to those who saw the problem in this way. It brought young men

Above: *Nelson A. Miles, a hero of the Civil War, was destined to play an even more important role in the postwar years. Reverting from major general to colonel after the war, he regained two-star rank in 1890, and became a lieutenant general in 1900. By then he was near the end of a career that was capped with his role in helping to bring Indian resistance to an end. (Center of Military History)*

Left: *Cherokees, carrying their few possessions, are hurried along the "Trail of Tears" by soldiers given the unpleasant job of escorting them from their homelands in the east to the newly established Indian Territory in Oklahoma. Several thousand Native Americans died along the way. ("The Trail of Tears," Robert Lindneux, Woolaroc Museum, Bartlesville, Oklahoma)*

In 1888 the artist-author Frederic Remington went "vagabonding with the Tenth Horse" — his own words—and he would note, "The Tenth Cavalry never had a 'soft detail' since it was organized." Remington (wearing sun helmet, behind the commanding officer) made a number of desert marches and mountain patrols with the 10th, one of the four all-black regiments in the Regular Army. ("Buffalo Soldiers," Frederic Remington, Peter Newark's American Pictures)

127

Above: *The first government-supported school for Native Americans, not on a reservation but on an Army post, opened its doors 6 October 1879 with thirty-seven boys who made up the first class of the Carlisle Indian School, Carlisle Barracks, Pennsylvania. The school's founder was a former "Indian fighter," Lieutenant Colonel Richard Henry Pratt. The school was closed in 1918. (U.S. Army Military History Institute)*

The ghost-like Geronimo, last of the Indian chiefs to defy U.S. authority, finally surrendered in July 1886. This photograph shows soldiers relaxing near a train with Geronimo and other Apaches. In the blunt language of that era, General Miles called Geronimo, "the worst Indian who ever lived." Others said he was "a worthy foe." (U.S. Army Military History Institute)

and women from the various western Indian tribes together in an environment more typical of the settled Eastern United States, dressed them in European-style garb, instructed them in the English language, and taught them useful trades. This assimilation effort had broad support in the churches and in enlightened intellectual circles. The Army merely provided facilities, cadres, and a small amount of capital. But the experiment at Carlisle eventually died out, as automobiles, electricity, and modern schools on reservations made it unnecessary for Native American

children to travel to a distant Eastern town to receive an education that would prepare them to be productive participants in American society. Today, this nineteenth-century Army effort to transform Native Americans receives as much criticism from historians as the actions dramatized on the movie screen.

Controlling the settlers was often the larger challenge on the frontier, but U.S. marshals and other civil authorities usually could keep the lawless element under control. Soldiers played a role in taming the citizenry when

Newly promoted to brigadier general, 1st Dragoons' commander Stephen Watts Kearny led a fast-moving cavalry column to the Pacific coast in 1846–47. In defiance of Mexican complaints, he raised the American flag over the governor's palace in Santa Fe and delivered a fiery proclamation (above) at Las Vegas, declaring New Mexico a part of the U.S. and its inhabitants American citizens. (Kenneth Chapman, Courtesy Museum of New Mexico, Neg. No. 163233)

Above: *Although restrictions imposed by the posse comitatus law prohibited federal troops from being used for local law enforcement, exceptions had to be made. As was the case when President Benjamin Harrison ordered the Army to assist the U.S. marshal in the Coeur d'Alene region of Idaho. Troops are shown entering Wallace, Idaho, in 1892. (Center of Military History)*

Lawless elements were among the many hazards that existed on the roads and trails through western lands. ("The Hold Up," Frederic Remington, Peter Newark's American Pictures)

Setting off on a journey out of Hays City, Kansas, in October 1867, a stagecoach belonging to the United States Express Company welcomed the assignment of six black soldiers detailed as escorts. Stagecoaches were a favorite target of Indian bands and frontier desperados alike. (National Archives)

Left: *Immigrant Irish miners predominated the Emit Guard, volunteer militiamen in Nevada. A holiday in 1880 was the occasion for their participation in a parade through the flag-draped streets of Virginia City. (Nevada Historical Society, Reno)*

civil authorities were overwhelmed, and that role continues today. The Constitution of the United States clearly gives Congress the power to use military force to "execute the laws of the union, suppress insurrections, and repel invasions" (Article I, Section 8).

When civil authorities determine that military force must be used, there is a very precise hierarchy of responding agencies: local police call in

Above: *Sporting a flaring mustache that minimally met the Army's new regulations, the old cavalry sergeant was a cocky figure familiar in frontier towns. ("A Sergeant of the U.S. Cavalry, 1890," Frederic Remington, Peter Newark's American Pictures)*

The hard-riding 2d Cavalry garrisoned at Fort Riley, Kansas, toward the turn of the century. Troopers of Troop F turned out for this 1897 unit photo. (National Archives)

131

Army Colonel Robert E. Lee was dispatched from Washington, D.C., at the head of a raiding party composed of U.S. Marines, when the ill-fated John Brown instigated an uprising of slaves at Harper's Ferry, West Virginia. Brown was captured and subsequently put to death. But Harper's Ferry would prove to be the first spark in the tinderbox that ignited into the Civil War. ("At All Times Ready," Don Stivers)

Federal troops on escort duty in Montana during the Northern Pacific Railroad strike. At center right is the legendary Calamity Jane. (Center of Military History)

state police. The first military organizations to respond are National Guard units in state service—the direct descendants of the original colonial militias. When the situation warrants additional military resources, the state National Guard units can be called into federal service, Active Army units can be sent to the threatened area, and Army Reserve units can be called to active duty to support the operation.

The ink was scarcely dry on the Constitution when President Washington took the field in 1792 as Commander in Chief to direct a federalized force to move beyond the mountains to suppress the Whiskey Rebellion, an uprising of farmers and merchants who had taken up arms against a tax on whiskey that threatened their livelihood. While succeeding presidents have not needed to take the field, the precedent of using military force in the ways intended by the framers of the Constitution continues into the present. Most recently, in April 1992 in Los Angeles, California, the Army assisted civil authorities in regaining control of riotous elements after the verdict in the Rodney King trial.

Rebellions, riots, and strikes have been the main causes for such use of military force. There were draft riots during the Civil War requiring federal troops in much the same way that troops were called during the Vietnam War. Soldiers were used to re-establish order and guarantee civil rights in the South after the Civil War in a systematic way just as they were used in more selective applications to guarantee the enforcement of civil rights legislation

in the 1950s and 1960s. Strikes and labor disputes are seldom a major source of domestic violence in our times, but as early as 1834 a dispute on the Chesapeake and Ohio Canal project led to a call for federal forces, and the role of the Army as "strikebreaker" was an important source of alienation between workers and soldiers as late as the eve of World War II.

But the strikebreaking Army of the 1930s was also identified with a major initiative designed to curb labor unrest while improving the physical environment—the Civilian Conservation Corps. The Army was called upon

Race riots in Omaha, Nebraska, resulted in Army troops once again being ordered to assist the civil authorities from resources in the area. Federal troops with machine guns and small cannon, were soon manning positions on 29 September 1920. A fortuitous rainstorm helped cool down angry passions. (Center of Military History)

Above: *The 3rd Cavalry marches along Pennsylvania Avenue toward the Capitol, shortly after its arrival from Fort Myers on 28 July 1932, to disperse the Bonus Marchers. (National Archives)*

Left: *Racial tensions in crowded inner cities didn't take a furlough during WWII. Army units were distracted from training to find themselves on patrol in riot-ridden Detroit, Michigan, in 1943. Enemy propaganda made the most of these instances. (Center of Military History)*

Above: *California Army National Guard military police, assembling in a supermarket parking lot, were the first military forces deployed during the Los Angeles riots of 1995.*

Right: *John Charles Frémont's explorations earned him the title of "The Pathfinder." Among the Topographical Engineer officers he was one of the rare non-West Pointers. He led three important western expeditions before the Civil War, including this expedition in the Rocky Mountains. (Edward M. or Richard Kern, Henry E. Huntington Library and Art Gallery)*

After a clash with General Stephen Watts Kearny, Frémont resigned his Army commission in 1848 following a court-martial that many considered inappropriate. Appointed a major general, he returned to the colors during the Civil War, but his first command in Missouri did not live up to the success expected of the heroic former western explorer. (U.S. Army Military History Institute)

to establish the camps, induct the workers, provide some basic training for living and working together in Spartan environments, and oversee the execution of many programs. In the initial phase, the bulk of this work was performed by officers and sergeants of the Active Army, but Reserve officers soon were called into active status to take over many of the key duties, and this distribution of responsibility continued as the United States began to mobilize for World War II.

Exploration of the Continent

None of the development on the frontier would have been possible without the exploration of North America, and the Army played a central role in that aspect of nation-building. When the territory of the new republic expanded with the Louisiana Purchase in 1803, Captains Meriwether Lewis and William Clark set the precedent for many Army expeditions in

the ensuing years. They traveled over enormous distances; made numerous navigational, ethnological, biological, botanical, and geological observations; kept meticulous records; and published useful reports. Nearly a century of exploration and mapping of the continental United States followed, and Army mapping in Alaska continued into the 1940s. The justification for Army involvement in this activity, which extended throughout a vast area and long period, was best articulated by President Ulysses S. Grant in a report to Congress:

> As the country to be explored is occupied in great part by uncivilized Indians, all parties involved in the work . . . must be supplied with escorts from the Army, thus placing a large portion of the expense upon the War Department; and as the Engineer Corps of the Army is composed of scientific gentlemen, educated and practiced for just the kind of work to be done, and as they are under pay whether employed in this work or not, it would seem that [the condition that

Above: *When Meriwether Lewis and fellow scouts met with the Shoshones, Lewis laid down his rifle and walked forward carrying only an American flag. He reported that the Indians "embraced me very affectionately in their way." ("Meeting the Shoshone Indians," Charles M. Russell, Drummond Gallery, Coeur d'Alene, Idaho)*

Below, left: *Mojave Indians assisting Lieutenant Amiel Whipple's Pacific railroad party cross the Colorado River in 1853. Like many of the Army's trailblazers in the West, Whipple was a member of the Topographical Engineers. (John J. Young, Yale university Library)*

Below, right: *Isaac I. Stevens's survey party meet with Assiniboin Indians near Fort Union at the junction of the Yellowstone and Missouri rivers. Stevens was regarded among his contemporaries as "the Yankee among Yankees." A native of Massachusetts, he resigned his Army commission in 1852 when appointed governor of the new Washington Territory. (John Mix Stanley, Yale University Library)*

135

the work be done expeditiously] would be more fully complied with by employing them to do the work. There is but little doubt that they will accomplish it as promptly and as well and much more economically.

For nearly a century the Topographical Engineers attracted the top graduates from the U.S. Military Academy at West Point, and they were kept busy by a continuing succession of mapping requirements. In the early days, charting coastlines of the Atlantic, Gulf of Mexico, Great Lakes, and the Pacific was the highest priority. With the arrival of the steamboat, courses of navigable rivers had to be mapped. Simultaneously, routes to the West were explored and mapped, to be followed by settlers, the Pony Express, and telegraph lines. Later, more detailed surveys for transcontinental railroads were needed. Finally, the topographical engineers began to "fill in the blanks" as the Army took responsibility for the new national park system near the end of the nineteenth century.

When the Army took over sites such as Yellowstone National Park, soldiers were preserving wilderness and wildlife while making accessible unique environments of great natural beauty. The early travelers on horse-

back made few demands, but carriage roads had to be improved and extended when more tourists came to visit these pristine remnants of the old frontier. The Army built those roads, protected wildlife from poachers, and provided primitive interpretive services for visitors. Some Army leaders could see training value in the effort, but most saw a drain on the limited

Top, left: *Troops were sometimes detailed to prevent the stalking and killing of animals in protected areas of the Yellowstone National Park, circa 1886. ("The American Soldier" H. Charles McBarron, Army Art Collection)*

Top, right: *A sharpshooter's view of Custer's wagon train passing through the Castle Creek Valley and entering the Black Hills during the 1874 expedition. (National Archives)*

Above: *During the Black Hills expedition in 1874, General George Custer, along with fellow hunters, was photographed after killing "our first Grizzly." At the left is Bloody Knife, an Army scout who later died with Custer at the Battle of Little Big Horn. The expedition party included Colonel Fred Dent, General Ulysses Grant's oldest son. (National Archives)*

Army budget as well as a diversion of scarce military manpower. The crisis on the Mexican border allowed the Army to begin transfer of responsibility for the wilderness parks to the Department of the Interior by 1918. The Army continued to run National Parks on its old battlefields until the 1930s, when tight federal budgets, increased demands from tourists, and the pressure from the CCC camp requirement allowed the Army to transfer those parks to the Department of the Interior as well.

Communication and Infrastructure

The U.S. Army also contributed to nation-building by developing the communication infrastructure throughout the nation's history. In the early days, when mail moved by ship and stagecoach, roads and harbors were key. Army engineers built the roads and dredged the harbors. When canals and railroads became central, Army engineers selected routes and participated in construction. The arrival of electric signaling devices made the Army's contribution more complicated, because the Army fostered technological innovation while simultaneously building facilities. On the frontier in the

late nineteenth century, the Army was operating hundreds of miles of telegraph line, constructed and maintained for operational purposes but available for civilian use when capacity allowed.

While the military telegraph lines eventually passed to civilian control or were replaced by radio networks, the network effect available during the heyday of the military telegrapher resulted in a spin-off important to nation-building but often overlooked. Immediately after the Civil War, the Army's chief signal officer, Colonel Albert J. Myer, worried that his new Signal Service would disappear in the inevitable force reductions that follow America's wars. He allied himself with influential individuals who were

In the great national expansion, the United States Military Railroad system operated under the Army Quartermaster Corps. There were areas where the USMRR operated many miles of railway lines in the development of the U.S. transportation system. Shown here is one of the USMRR locomotives, the General Haupt. (National Archives)

seeking the establishment of a national weather service, and legislation fixing responsibility for the effort with the Army. By 1891, Myer produced his first "Weather Synoptic and Probabilities," and he had devised a system that transmitted key weather reports from across the continent to Washington in thirty minutes. Myer was a brilliant organizer, but he may have been even more impressive as a politician. He named his new capability the Division of Telegrams and Reports for the Benefit of Agricultural and Commercial Interests. His successors expanded coverage, improved

Right: A Signal Corps sergeant and cavalry officer stationed in New Mexico, wear the traditional post-Civil War uniform, circa 1880. This uniform, with its distinctive helmet, would soon be phased out. ("The American Soldier," H. Charles McBarron, Army Art Collection)

Far right: In 1902, Corps of Engineer officers were authorized a new full dress uniform that included the new-style cap with a visor. By the end of the year a similar full dress uniform was prescribed for all of the Army's company grade and field grade officers. (National Archives)

140

Top, left: *Chief Signal Officer Albert Myer (standing) during the Civil War Peninsula campaign. Myer was among the first to appreciate the need for quick access to accurate meteorological data, and in the postwar years his efforts were rewarded as the Army was given the mission of establishing a national weather service. (Center of Military History)*

Above: *Arctic exploration by the Army proved to be a demanding mission. Feasibility of setting up communications lines in Alaska was undertaken by a young signal corps lieutenant, William "Billy" Mitchell, in 1901. Mitchell would later make his mark as an airman and aviation visionary. (Center of Military History)*

Left: *Interior of the telegraph office, Fort Gibbon, Alaska, was the site of one of the six Signal Corps companies on duty in the Army as of November 1916. (Center of Military History)*

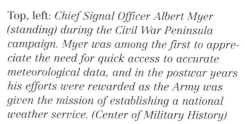

Shown is the field telephone station Number 4 near San Juan Hill, Cuba. Availability of "electrical communications" between the front lines and Washington in the war with Spain proved to be the first conflict fought by the U.S. in which electrical communications played an important role. (Center of Military History)

An aerial view of the weather observatory atop the 6,000-foot Mount Washington, New Hampshire, taken 21 February 1950. The first regular meteorological observations here were conducted by the Signal Corps personnel that maintained the station for many years. It was here, in 1934, that observers recorded a wind gust of 231 mph—still the world record for a surface station. (U.S. Army Military History Institute)

instrumentation, and developed superior forecasting techniques until 1891, when the Army transferred the division to the civilian sector, where it became the National Weather Bureau. Many reporting stations were still located on Army posts, and the military telegraph system was an important primary link in the system for many years. The Army continued to man weather stations in remote areas well into the twentieth century, and Army radio networks were an important aspect of the communication system in Alaska until the 1950s.

During the war with Spain, President McKinley had a war room set up next to his White House office. This White House communications center included a telegraphic link to the battlefront in Cuba. Army Captain Benjamin F. Montgomery (seated, left) was responsible for what was officially called "the Telegraph and Cipher Bureau" during the war with Spain. (Center of Military History)

Humanitarian Research and Development

Years of work in hazardous weather environments made the Army a natural researcher into better means and methods to preserve human life in such conditions. In the early days, all such research was empirical or borrowed from conclusions published by European armies who used boards of officers to address problems in clothing and equipping soldiers. After the Spanish-American War, when a reform movement swept through the U.S. Army, laboratories were established to conduct basic and applied research on a broad range of subjects. In fact, research conducted or subsidized by the armed forces has had tremendous impact on the American economy and the lives of the average citizen, especially regarding textiles, food preservation, immunization, sanitation, hydraulics, and metallurgy.

Top, left: *A pioneer Army surgeon, William Beaumont served from the War of 1812 through 1839. He maintained a long-term study of the progress of a gun-shot wound victim named Alexis St. Martin that led to a book on the physiology of digestion long regarded as a major contribution to the practice of medicine in the U.S. (Dean Cornwell, National Archives)*

Top, right: *Colonel John Shaw Billings served as a military surgeon in the Civil War and remained in the Army to become a pillar of the military medical community. He was called the greatest American military surgeon and the world's foremost medical bibliographer. Colonel Billings retired in 1895 as deputy surgeon general. (Cecilia Beaux, Army Medical Library)*

Bottom, left: *During the Civil War, the Army Medical Bureau built 350 hospitals and increased the number of surgeons from 113 to 9,000. This photo shows a ward in a typical "pavilion hospital" of that era—the Armory Square Hospital on the National Mall in Washington, D.C. It was demolished in 1964. (Library of Congress)*

Bottom, right: *Medical department officer, artillery private, in Cuba in 1898. ("The American Soldier," H. Charles McBarron, Army Art Collection)*

Page 144, top: *At the head of the table, chin in hand, is Major General Leonard Wood, military governor of Cuba and a former Army medical officer, with "the most famous commission in Army medical history." Behind Wood is Major Walter Reed, who served as president of the U.S. Army Yellow Fever Board. Many of the figures in the painting represent medical officers and enlisted men who volunteered as subjects in the fight to conquer Yellow Fever. (Dean Cornwell, National Archives)*

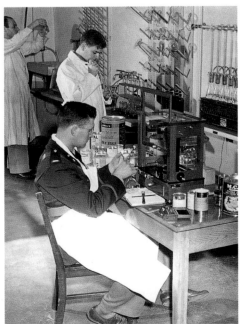

One of the best-known examples is the medical research to find the cause of yellow fever. French efforts to build a canal across the Isthmus of Panama were stymied when nearly 75 percent of their workers became casualties of the disease within a few months after arriving in the work zone. Meanwhile, U.S. Army personnel assigned to Cuba during and after the Spanish-American War were suffering similar high rates of serious illness from the disease. In 1901, a group of Army medical officers, headed by Dr. Walter Reed, determined that yellow fever is transmitted by mosquitoes. Within a few months of the discovery, Havana was cleared of a disease that had ravaged it for 150 years, and within a few years, the U.S. Army was able to begin construction on the Panama Canal.

The effort to use Army resources to improve the human condition through research matured during World War II and continued to be an important aspect of research and development investment in the U.S. economy throughout the Cold War. In the areas of communications, computers,

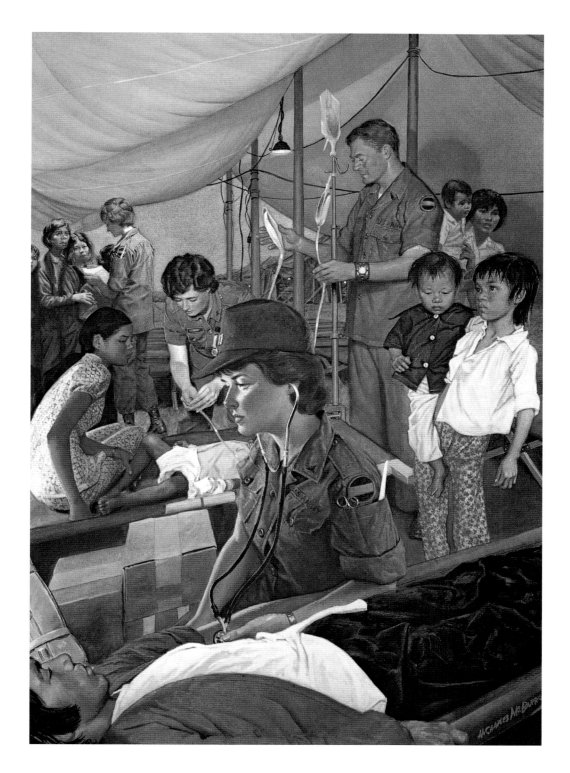

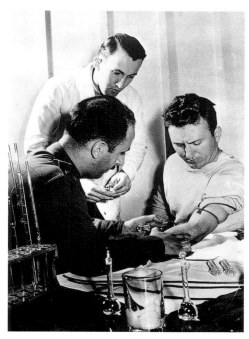

all-terrain vehicles, medicine, and camping equipment, to name a few, people's lives have been changed, and some fortunes have been made, by applying technologies discovered or developed for military application.

Public Works

The common image of the Army and its contribution to nation-building is in the realm of public works. In the United States, the Army Corps of Engineers not only helped the new republic develop infrastructure by building roads, canals, and railroads, they literally helped build the Capital. Washington, D.C., was built on a site selected for the federal government, and the Corps of Engineers became the contractor of choice to construct the Capitol building, the Library of Congress, the aqueduct and water storage system, and numerous other major projects.

Top, left: *Operation New Life provided health care to the people of Guam. ("The American Soldier, 1975," H. Charles McBarron, Army Art Collection)*

Top, right: *Components of the dry cold field uniform, circa. 1951. (U.S. Army Military History Institute)*

Above: *Important medical research has long been one of the Army's important contributions to the national interest. During WWII, blood samples were taken from soldiers participating in experimental rations tests that would yield data of significance for civilian as well as military use. (U.S. Army Military History Institute)*

Opposite, bottom: *During WWII, as the enormous deployment of forces created vast problems in providing rations for troops, Army medical lab experiments concentrated on potential for the development of dehydrated products. Some of these products found their way into use before the end of the war. (U.S. Army Military History Institute)*

Harbor dredging, river stabilization, and draining wetlands continue to be important activities for the Army Corps of Engineers. In almost all cases, they are using federal funds separate from the defense budget, and solving civil works problems by applying contract labor and equipment. The public attitude toward this work may be changing. Many environmentalists worry that draining swamps means destroying habitat, and recent decisions that will reverse earlier Corps of Engineers work in Florida may indicate that the heavy emphasis on land reclamation, transportation, and flood control may be balanced by additional considerations in this part of the Corps' public works efforts.

Disaster Relief

Floods are one of the timeless natural disasters that mobilize societies for disaster relief or nation rebuilding. Disciplined, well-equipped soldiers have long been among those who help local authorities relieve discomfort and

restore order after natural disasters. Floods, earthquakes, blizzards, tornadoes, hurricanes, forest fires, volcano eruptions—these are the events that result in an immediate call for military police, medical units, transportation companies, signal detachments, engineers, and all the other specialized capabilities an Army can bring to the disaster area and sustain there while helping others.

One of the great natural disasters early in the twentieth century was the San Francisco earthquake. The Army was there to help, and it has offered its assistance in every similar situation in ensuing years.

Top: *Army material and management played an important role in the establishment of a refugee camp in Jefferson Park, San Francisco, after the devastation of the 1906 earthquake. (U.S. Army Military History Institute)*

Above: *The extensions to the Capitol Building in Washington, D.C., consisted of two wings housing the Senate and House of Representatives. The construction, including the new dome, was almost completed by 1863, as shown in a Mathew Brady wet plate. The extensions were completed soon after the end of the Civil War. (National Archives)*

Above, left: *In southeastern Virginia, Army engineers at work dredging the Dismal Swamp canal, in 1933. (U.S. Army Military History Institute)*

Above: *A massive Army response was mounted to assist the Florida communities devastated by Hurricane Andrew in 1993. ("Dry Goods," Peter G. Varisano, Army Art Collection)*

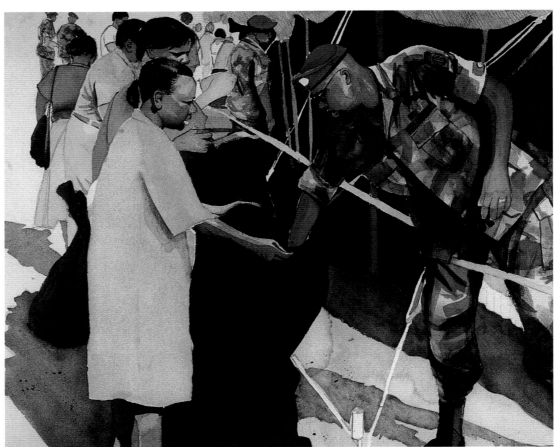

The Army was at the forefront of providing relief in many forms to the victims of Hurricane Andrew in 1993. ("Providing Food," Peter G. Varisano, Army Art Collection)

Emergency field operations center set up by the Army in Marshall Park, near City Hall, in the aftermath of the 1906 San Francisco earthquake. (U.S. Army Military History Institute)

Recently the Army has been called most often to assist in the control of forest fires. In the 1990s Hurricane Andrew required more military assistance than most other storms of that type, calling a great number of Active Army and Army Reserve units to support the heroic efforts of the National Guard, always the first line of defense when natural disaster strikes.

Many aspects of nation-building once performed by the Army are now completed or passed to other government agencies, but there are few soldiers serving today who have not been involved in an activity similar to those of soldiers serving in earlier centuries. As today's soldiers help their counterparts in other parts of the world learn how to be guardians of democracy, they draw on a proud heritage of support to domestic authorities that stretches back to the founding of our nation.

149

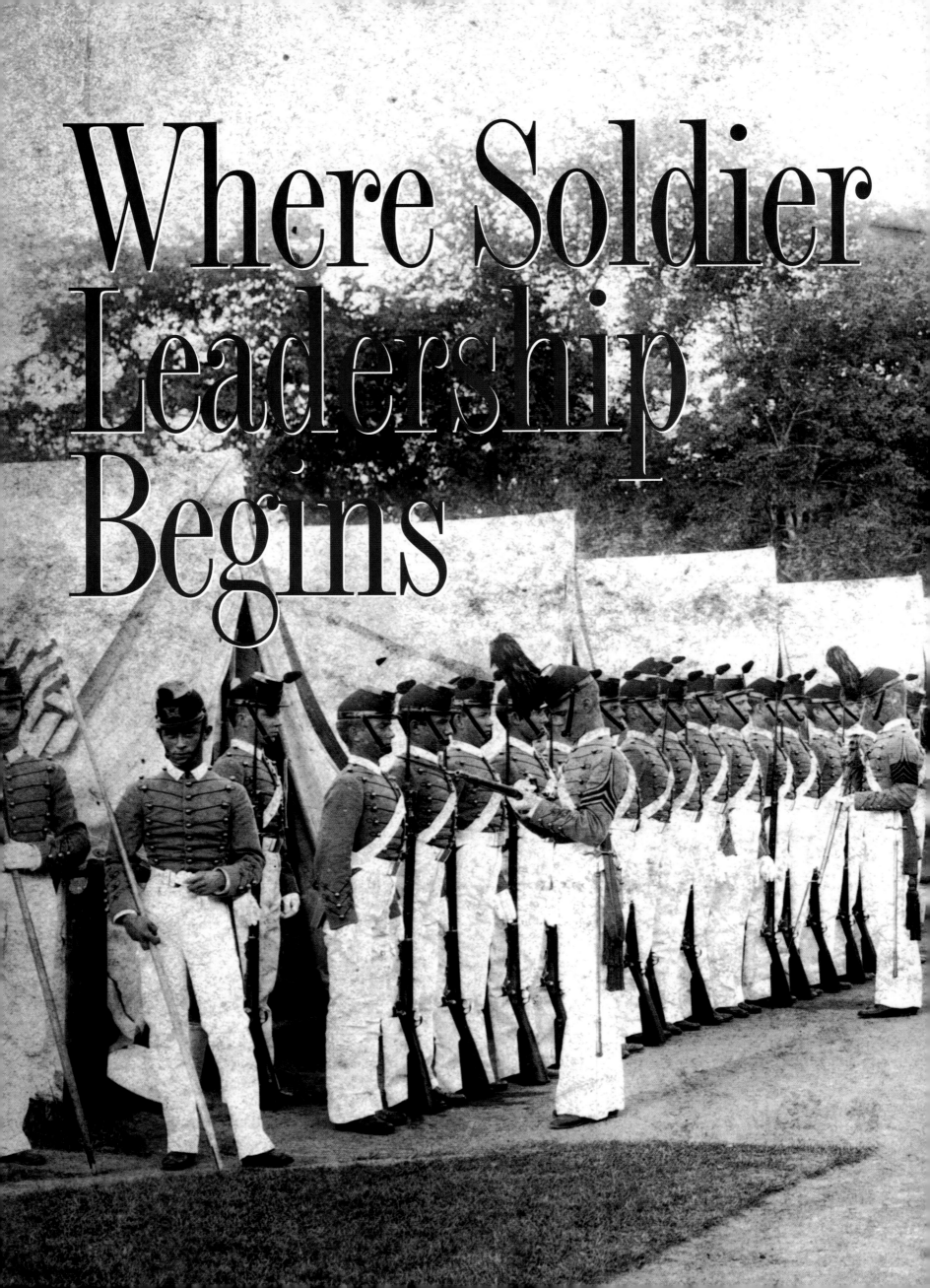

Where Soldier Leadership Begins

Where Soldier Leadership Begins
The Evolution of Army Schools and Training

General Gordon R. Sullivan, USA (Ret)

Hurrying to rendezvous with forces under Colonel Benedict Arnold for a surprise attack on Quebec on New Year's Eve 1775, Major General Richard Montgomery falls, mortally wounded, still holding his sword. The assault by Montgomery's and Arnold's forces failed. (Alonzo Chappel, Chicago Historical Society)

W henever our nation has turned to its Army, strong leaders have emerged at every level, from the tactical to the strategic and national. George Washington is the first in a long line that includes Winfield Scott, Ulysses Grant, Dwight Eisenhower, George Marshall, Creighton Abrams, and Colin Powell. In every case, these were leaders who learned the art of command at junior levels, became more accomplished as they advanced, and developed junior leaders who could contribute to achieving the objectives they set when placed in positions of national prominence.

Today's Army, like the Army of earlier centuries, recognizes the importance of investing in leader development. Whether engaged in peacetime activities or in active combat, the demands placed on units can only be met if leaders at every level have the skills, knowledge, and attributes necessary to inspire top performance from the soldiers they lead. High quality performance must be the norm because the Army simultaneously prepares for a tremendously challenging combat environment while performing important presence and peacekeeping tasks in numerous settings where soldiers can prevent violence. The Army has lived with that duality of purpose throughout its history, but it only began its consistent, focused investment in leader development in the last century.

The Founding Fathers rejected the notion that there was an aristocracy of birth, but they came close to believing in a "natural aristocracy" where military leadership was concerned. Men who had prominent positions in local society were thought to have a natural affinity for command, and in a system that depended on volunteers to fill the ranks of its Army, community leaders were key recruiters who could expect that respect in the community would translate into subordination on the battlefield. In some cases, that assumption was borne out, but more often the natural leader who sustained himself in the leadership role was one who apprenticed himself as a student of the art of war, applied himself to the requirements of drill and regulation, and committed himself to repeated arduous

Inviting the attention of the British cannoneers, Colonel William Prescott strolled the parapet of his redoubt on Breed's Hill to calm his uneasy men. On that fateful day, 17 June 1775, the colonial militiamen anxiously awaited the inevitable attack by the renowned British infantry. They continued to strengthen their earthworks under heavy bombardment from the ships in the Charles River. (F. C. Young, The Continental Insurance Company)

Daniel Morgan of Virginia led three companies of riflemen in the American force that attempted to seize Quebec on 31 December 1775. He was among the Americans taken prisoner but survived to rise to brigadier general in the Continental Army following his victory at Cowpens, South Carolina. (Library of Congress)

Pages 150–151: *Cadets drilling at West Point in the summer of 1890. "The Corps! The Corps! The Corps! The Corps, bareheaded salute it, with eyes up, thanking our God/That we of the Corps are treading where they of the Corps have trod." Herbert Shipman, chaplain at West Point, spoke these words at the time of the 1902 centennial commemoration. (United States Military Academy at West Point)*

153

Above: *Major General Nathanael Greene's masterful blending of militia and Steuben-trained Continental Army men helped to inflict appalling casualties on the British forces in the battle of Guilford Courthouse, North Carolina, on 15 March 1781. At the outset of the American Revolution Greene held the rank of brigadier general with Rhode Island militia forces. ("Nathaniel Greene at Guilford," Dale Gallon)*

Top, right: *At the age of 24, Virginian George Rogers Clark was regarded as a formidable warrior on the western frontier. He was 18 at the time his youngest brother, William, was born. William would later win fame as co-leader of the Lewis and Clark expedition. (Portrait by John Wesley Jarvis, Virginia State Library)*

Middle, left: *John Stark commanded first militia and then Continental troops during 1775 and 1776. He earned the "thanks of Congress" for the brave conduct of his New Hampshire troops and won promotion to brigadier general in the Army of the United States for his service in the battle of Bennington, Vermont. (National Park Service)*

Middle, right: *In February 1779, Clark led 172 men, nearly half of them French volunteers, through flooded countryside to surprise the British defenders of Fort Sackville. An inspirational leader, Clark encouraged his men under adverse conditions. He maneuvered them across the Wabash River and forced the surrender of the British commander. (National Park Service)*

Right: *One of the heroes of Bennington, John Stark led his New Hampshire militiamen with great exuberance. During the height of the battle he reportedly roared, "We'll beat them before night or Molly Stark will be a widow!" Stark briefly quit the Continental Army when he failed to receive an expected promotion. In September 1783 he became a brevet major general. (The Continental Insurance Company)*

Opposite, top: *After initial reverses, General Washington rallied his troops at the Battle of Monmouth Courthouse, New Jersey, on 28 June 1778. The forces were evenly matched and fought to no-decision. The British resumed their march from Philadelphia to New York and Washington and his men succeeded in occupying Philadelphia. (Emanuel Leutze, University of California, Berkeley)*

campaigns that helped him hone his skills. Men such as George Washington were exemplars of this model. His social position gave him a commission as a major in the Virginia militia when he was only twenty-one, but it was hard campaigning in the French and Indian War that made him a brigade commander five years later. An informal apprenticeship served him well because he worked hard to perfect his skills and he was exposed to demanding situations.

When faced with the challenges of leading the Continental Army, Washington built up a cadre of men like himself, but he was able to supple-

ment native American leaders with Europeans who were products of more formal systems. Baron von Steuben is recognized as first among them because he taught the Army drill and discipline at Valley Forge in 1778 when the fortunes of the Continental Army were at a low ebb. But engineers such as Thaddeus Kosciusko and artillerymen such as Philip de Coudray drew on their technical educations to show American soldiers the way to perform other tasks to European standards. While gifted American amateurs such as Rufus Putnam and Henry Knox rose to prominence as well, the Europeans set the tone.

Top, left: *Frederick von Steuben successfully added professional discipline to the individualism and initiative central to the colonial military tradition. (Charles Wilson Peale, Independence National Historical Park)*

Top, center: *At the age of nineteen and with the approval of King Louis XVI, Marie-Joseph-Paul-Yves-Roch-Gilbert du Motier, Marquis de Lafayette set off to serve with the American colonial forces. The youthful Lafayette, commissioned by Congress as a major general in the Continental Army, became a favorite of George Washington. His first son would be named George Washington Lafayette. (Charles Wilson Peale, Independence National Historical Park)*

Top, right: *Louis Le Begue de Presle Duportail, Continental Army Chief of Engineers, returned to France and rose to be Minister of War. A number of French Army engineers assisted in the organization of the Army Corps of Engineers and in the development of the engineering department at the U.S. Military Academy. (Charles Wilson Peale, Independence National Historical Park)*

Above, right: *After leading the Continental Army to victory in the War for Independence, General Washington took leave of his officers at Fraunces' Tavern in New York City on 4 December 1783. Coincidentally this was also the day that the last British troops left their posts on Staten Island and Long Island. (Alonzo Chappel, Chicago Historical Society)*

In the best of worlds a nation would have plenty of men like George Washington, willing and able to learn to lead by leading. In the worst of worlds such men would face the challenge of continuous war and conflict. The young United States found elements of both the best and the worst in the situations it faced after its successful war for independence. Frontier conflict flared up often and war with European powers threatened frequently. In these circumstances, men such as Winfield Scott could carry on the tradition begun by George Washington, but homegrown engineers were needed to replace the foreign experts. On 16 March 1802, Congress established a Corps of Engineers assigned to West Point, New York, to serve as a nucleus of a military academy. While the U.S. Military Academy's initial mission was to provide commissioned engineers for the Army, the training and education it offered soon surpassed that expectation in two important ways. First, its graduates filled junior officer positions in all branches of the young republic's Army, improving the standards of drill and discipline and setting the tone for a new professionalism. Second, the graduates filled engineering needs in a rapidly growing nation, contributing to the exploration of new territories and applying the technical skills taught at West Point to steam locomotion and new industrial production techniques.

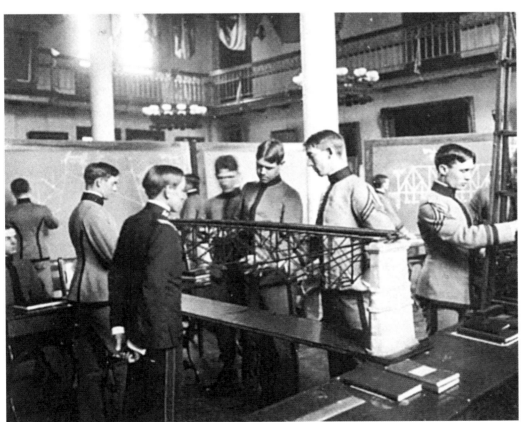

Top, left: *Cadets in 1802, the year the U.S. Military Academy was officially established on the historic grounds at West Point, New York. (H. Charles McBarron, "Military Uniforms in America Volume II: Years of Growth, 1796–1851," Presidio Press, 1977, by permission of the Company of Military Historians)*

Top, center: *A pioneer photographer in action captures West Pointers for immortality. ("U.S. Corps of Cadets, U.S.M.A., 1853–1861," Frederick T. Chapman, Company of Military Historians)*

Top, right: *U.S. Military Academy cadets shown in 1816–1817. The traditional gray uniform of the cadets was adopted in 1816 when, according to legend, the Army was short on blue cloth. In any event, "cadet gray" would come to symbolize the appearance of the Corps of Cadets. (H. Charles McBarron, "Military Uniforms in America Volume II: Years of Growth, 1796–1851," Presidio Press, 1977, by permission of the Company of Military Historians)*

Middle, left: *"Artillery, Infantry, Rifle, Dragoon, Cadet, 1813–1821." (Henry Alexander Ogden, for the U.S. Army Quartermaster General)*

Middle, right: *As West Point entered its second century, a uniform that looks familiar to this day emerged. ("Cadets of the U.S. Military Academy, 1902–1907," Henry Alexander Ogden, for the U.S. Army Quartermaster General)*

Left: *Engineering instruction at West Point in 1904. Founded as an engineering institution from the very start, West Point to this day remains dedicated to developing expertise in this field among all of its graduates. (United States Military Academy at West Point)*

Opposite, center left: *The U.S. Military Academy's coat of arms displays the Greek symbols of wisdom and military virtue, the helmet and sword of Pallas Athene, upon the American shield. "Duty, Honor, Country" is the Academy's motto. This was adopted as the Academy coat of arms on 8 October 1898.*

West Point also served as a model for other military schools, such as Norwich University, the Virginia Military Institute, and The Citadel, which drew on its curriculum, its staff, and its graduates as they developed into schools that met broad educational needs while also producing young men who were prepared to take the lead with regulars or volunteers if the need arose. The infantry, artillery, and cavalry drills they learned were all relevant to the nation's needs in wartime, and the engineering skills were in great demand in peace as well as in war. Grenville Dodge, a Norwich graduate, did as much to shape the nation through railroad construction as any graduate of any other school.

Top, left: *"General-in-Chief, Engineers, Artillery, Cadets, 1858–1861." (Henry Alexander Ogden, for the U.S. Army Quartermaster General)*

Top, right: *An offshoot of engineering studies, cadets at West Point would devote a good deal of study to the art of reading and creating maps. Here, a cartography class in session, circa 1900. (United States Military Academy at West Point)*

Above: *A contemporary sketch by George Horatio Derby, one of the top men in his West Point class (1846) and a member of the Topographical Engineers who was wounded at Cerro Gordo in 1847. In his brief lifetime he earned fame as a humorist and frequently lampooned Army life under the pen name of "John Phoenix." He was a captain when he died in 1861 at the age of 38. (United States Military Academy at West Point Library)*

Right: *Artillery training on the Plains at West Point, circa 1900. (United States Military Academy at West Point)*

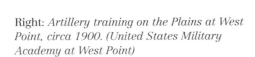

After the British fleet operated with few impediments in the Chesapeake Bay during the War of 1812, burning much of the new capital of
Washington, D.C., and disrupting trade, the United States took renewed
interest in coastal defense. One manifestation of that interest was the
Artillery School of Practice at Fort Monroe, Virginia. This school, on the
site of the Army's current Training and Doctrine Command, was the pre-
cursor of all of today's modern TRADOC schools. It was dedicated to

*On 13 September 1847 Major General Win-
field Scott's troops, including soldiers and
Marines, captured Chapultepec, a massive
hilltop fortress outside Mexico City. They then
went on to capture the capital. West Point-
trained officers in large numbers for the first
time predominated the officer corps of Scott's
Army. ("Assault on Mexico City," James Walker, West Point Museum Collection, United
States Military Academy)*

*Dismounted drill as skirmishers gave West
Point cadets the preparation for what might
later be encountered in active service. Drill
evolved into field exercises as the Army
adapted to the needs of the nation when it
became more of a participant in the world
arena after many decades of isolationism.
(Special Collections Division, United States
Military Academy at West Point Library)*

159

Above: *From its beginning in 1842, professional military instruction was provided at The Citadel. Here, Citadel cadet artillerymen as they appeared as the Civil War loomed on the horizon. ("Citadel Cadet Battery, Charleston, South Carolina, 1861," H. Charles McBarron, "Military Uniforms in America Volume III: Long Endure: The Civil War Period, 1852–1867," Presidio Press, 1982, by permission of the Company of Military Historians)*

Right: *During the United States Military Academy's centennial celebration, President Theodore Roosevelt presents Cadet Calvin P. Titus the Medal of Honor. Prior to his Academy appointment, Cadet Titus served as an enlisted soldier with the 14th Infantry during combat actions in both the Philippine War and the China Relief Expedition. It was for his heroic performance in China that he received the Medal. ("Centennial," Jeanine Mosher)*

improving the tactical and technical skills of officers, noncommissioned officers, and junior soldiers. It was heavily involved in experiments with new technologies, changes in organization, and innovations in doctrine. It helped its students master the details of "garrison life"—peacetime employment—as well as warfighting skills.

The Cavalry School of Application at Carlisle Barracks, Pennsylvania, and the Infantry School of Application at Jefferson Barracks, Missouri, eventually were added to the ranks of the Army's school system. The same broad approach to training was present in these schools, but they produced too few graduates to meet the needs of the multitude of units created for the Civil War. In 1861, both the Union and the Confederacy scrambled to find enough trained leaders to meet the demands of numerous battle fronts.

Top, left: *West Point faculty photographed in 1870. The Corps of Cadets at this time was still relatively small, about 250 young men in four classes at any given time. The class of 1870 had a total of fifty-eight graduates. (United States Military Academy at West Point Library)*

Above: *Long known as "The Military College of the South," The Citadel has produced a long line of cadets who went from the Charleston campus to distinguished careers in military service and in civilian life. (Citadel Archives)*

Middle, left: *With Major Thomas J. Jackson leading the way, the Cadet Corps from Virginia Military Institute moved to Richmond, where the cadets drilled Confederate Army recruits during April 1861. Jackson had joined the VMI faculty in 1851. He accepted a commission in the Confederate forces and left for active duty soon after the Corps arrived in Richmond. ("Road to Glory," Mort Künstler)*

Left: *The VMI Corps of Cadets fought as a unit at the Battle of New Market, Virginia, on 15 May 1864. There were 257 cadets on the field of battle formed in a battalion of four infantry companies and one section of artillery. Ten cadets were killed or died from wounds. The youngest participant was fifteen years old. The painting by a VMI alumnus of 1880 measures 18 x 23 feet and is located in Jackson Memorial Hall. ("The Charge of VMI Cadets at New Market," Benjamin West Clinedinst, Virginia Military Institute)*

Opposite, bottom: *The Virginia Military Institute was on a war footing throughout the Civil War years. The cadets were furloughed in June 1864 when Union troops under Major General David Hunter entered Lexington and set VMI afire. Academic work resumed toward the end of the year when a temporary VMI home was established at Richmond. (H. Charles McBarron, "Military Uniforms in America Volume III: Long Endure: The Civil War Period, 1852–1867," Presidio Press, 1982, by permission of the Company of Military Historians)*

The tradition of the gifted amateur once again came into play, supplemented by officers who had been exposed to formal training. While West Point graduates filled many senior positions, leaders at every level came from every walk of life and did the best they could to bring individuals and units to acceptable levels of performance. The results were often remarkable—men such as Joshua L. Chamberlain, a citizen soldier who led his 20th Maine regiment brilliantly on Little Round Top on the second day of the battle of Gettysburg and served with distinction until the end of the war, or John B. Gordon, who was equally brilliant on the Confederate side during the first day's battle and continued to serve the Confederacy well on every battlefield until the end of the war. When the war ended, these gifted "amateurs" were seasoned leaders who understood every nuance of warfare as it had been waged for four long years. As they returned to civilian life, others who stayed in the small postwar Army began reforms in training and leader development that transformed the Army.

One of the young West Point graduates who led the reforms was Emory Upton. Like Chamberlain and Gordon, he had earned promotions

Bottom, left: *Norwich University of Northfield, Vermont, dates back to 1819, when it was created by Captain Alden Partridge to link military science with a broad civil curriculum. His vision served as a model for many other U.S. military schools and colleges. Horse cavalry (shown here in 1912) was traditionally an important aspect of Norwich training, and its cadet ranks produced many officers for the Army and other services. (Norwich University Special Collections)*

Bottom, right: *An 1861 graduate of West Point, Brevet Major General Emory Upton. His famous* Military Policy for the United States *was published in the early 1900s, long after his death in 1881 at the age of 42. Upton's work was "required reading" for many years and had a profound impact upon the Army officer corps in the twentieth century. (U.S. Army War College)*

on Civil War battlefields, beginning the war as an 1861 USMA graduate and ending it as a brevet major general. He reverted to the rank of captain when the war ended, but he stayed in the service, drawing on his wartime experiences and his observations of foreign armies to bring peacetime training to new levels. In the late 1870s he transformed the curriculum at the Artillery School at Fort Monroe so that it encompassed the operation of the artillery with the other arms, especially the infantry.

Emory Upton's reforms within the Army's education system flourished because he had strong support from General William T. Sherman, the Army's Commanding General from 1869 to 1883. Sherman had no desire to see another generation of Army officers learn their professional lessons with the blood of American soldiers. In an effort to prevent earlier mistakes, he made sure that the Artillery School received the necessary resources to transform its curriculum. He also created the Engineer School of Application and the School of Application for Infantry and Cavalry at Fort Leavenworth, Kansas. New schools and old stressed the importance of learning to work together in combined arms teams. Even though the

Historical rides to Civil War battlefields were part of the Army War College curriculum from the earliest days of the institution. There were two field trips in 1909, one to the Richmond, Virginia, area; the other (above) to Gettysburg, Pennsylvania. The Gettysburg ride was led by Brigadier General William W. Wotherspoon, who dominated the college in its formative years. (Army War College)

Opposite, top: The cavalry charge of the "Cadet Rangers" from The Citadel, Charleston, South Carolina, was led by General Wade Hampton. Formed in 1862 by cadets who left the campus in favor of active duty, the youngsters fought in sixteen Civil War battles in the 6th Regiment, South Carolina Cavalry. On 11 June 1864 their timely arrival on the battlefield saved a Confederate artillery battery. ("The Charge at Trevilian Station," Mort Künstler)

The strategic military situation of Civil War campaigns provided War College classes an opportunity to develop tactical battle plans substituting contemporary tactics, weapons, and organization. This would soon prove invaluable when the U.S. entered World War I. Here, Colonel David J. Rumbough, of the 1909 class, discusses Pickett's charge during a Gettysburg tour. (Army War College)

163

Army was still scattered over numerous small posts with no opportunity for extensive or sophisticated exercises, the map problems and practical exercises in the schools allowed soldiers to develop an appreciation for the leadership requirements of modern warfare.

While Army leaders were improving their "graduate school" system, the Congress had passed legislation that dramatically improved the pool of young officers available to serve. The Morrill Act of 1862, which established land-grant colleges, also made provisions for military training of undergraduates that would prepare young men for commissions. In the

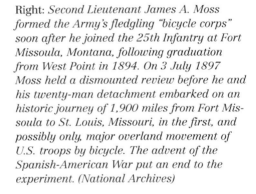

early years the Army made little use of this opportunity because the Army still had excessive numbers of Civil War veterans serving as officers at all levels. As those officers began to leave active service near the end of the century, Congress and the Army worked together to improve the training programs and make better use of graduates who were eager to serve. The Reserve Officer Training Corps (ROTC) that has been central to the procurement of new officers was finally in place as the United States emerged onto the world scene at the end of the nineteenth century.

When the United States declared war on Spain in 1898, the small cadres of trained leaders were inundated by volunteers just as they had been in earlier emergencies. The Army that deployed to Cuba, Puerto Rico, and the Philippines was reasonably well led at the regimental and brigade levels, but it had to overcome nearly insurmountable obstacles to deploy. The school system had focused on tactical problems while leaving

Below: Cavalry target practice, shown here circa 1900, could be as much a recreational pursuit as a means for honing an invaluable skill. (National Archives)

strategic and operational issues virtually untouched. The ineptitude in moving men, equipment, and supplies was a visible manifestation of this weakness. When the nation's political leaders devised solutions to the Army's problems after the crisis, another school was added. The Army War College emphasized "learning by doing" in the same way that had

proved so successful in the other schools, but the emphasis was on campaigns and strategic issues, including actual responsibility for updating the Army's war plans.

While these reforms were progressing, the Army National Guard was working hard to bring itself into the twentieth century. Beginning in 1903, the National Guard, or organized militia, was to be organized, trained, and disciplined like the Regular Army. By the time General John J. Pershing mounted his Punitive Expedition against Francisco "Pancho" Villa in 1916, the framework was in place for an orderly mobilization of trained units. Much work remained to be done before that framework had been transformed into an effective system, as subsequent events were to prove.

Eben Swift, one of the Army's premier trainers during this period, taught that armies must be able to "camp, march, and fight." In Mexico, Pershing's troops had far more opportunity to camp and to march than to fight, but he insisted on rigorous field exercises and training in marksmanship. When the United States entered World War I, he maintained his emphasis on such training. This, together with his insistence that U.S. Army troops would fight as a body under their own leaders, resulted in a balanced American Expeditionary Force (AEF). It may have been heavily dependent on other armies for some parts of its doctrine and equipment, but it fielded combined arms teams encompassing all branches and it directed those teams through a hierarchy of commanders and staffs. The AEF proved its mettle in all of the major campaigns of the war's last year. Those campaigns required leaders who could integrate the capabilities of a broad array of weapons and organizations in continuous operations. To give its leaders the necessary skills, the Army established an extensive tactical schooling system in France, including an equivalent of the Command and General Staff College.

Top, left: *Captain John J. Pershing shown in 1905. Although a member of the first class of the Army War College, Pershing did not graduate because of reassignment to the Far East. Four of the remaining class members, who went on to be the Army's first War College graduates, would command divisions under Pershing in World War I. (Army War College)*

Above: *An inspection of Engineer barracks in 1897 is a scene similar to today's activities. Meeting exacting standards and the discipline needed to make the grade are part of the foundation of an Army education. (National Archives)*

Opposite, top: *Firing for record by soldiers of Troop F, 2d Cavalry, at the National Target Range, Fort Riley, Kansas, in 1907. During these competitions, which the Regular soldiers took seriously, many national and international marksmanship records would be established. (National Archives)*

Opposite, middle: *Field exercises involving 10th Cavalry "Buffalo Soldiers" toward the end of the nineteenth century. (National Archives)*

Top, left and top, center: *The shoulder sleeve insignias worn by ROTC cadets prior to 1986. (U.S. Army Cadet Command)*

Top, right: *The Army's modern-day ROTC Command shoulder patch. (U.S. Army Cadet Command)*

Above: *Major General Samuel B.M. Young was president of the first War College Board, which served as an interim General Staff under then Secretary of War Elihu Root. General Young would soon be the Army's first Chief of Staff as Army reforms were put into practice. But the War College would continue to work on "real world" tasks assigned by the General Staff. (Army War College)*

Middle, right: *A group of Kansas State University ROTC cadets drill in formation in 1895. (U.S. Army Cadet Command)*

Right: *ROTC 75mm gun training at Purdue University in 1928. (U.S. Army Cadet Command)*

After the armistice the Army dwindled once again, shrinking to far lower levels than had been authorized in the National Defense Act of 1920. With skeletonized units and austere budgets, Army leaders once again encountered very little realistic training. But the top leaders carried on General Sherman's tradition: they funded the Army school system, and they paid attention to what happened there. Each branch school took the World War I experience as a departure point for new looks at what would be required in future war. The Command and General Staff College worked hard to evolve the necessary doctrine for combined arms operations in wars where tanks and airplanes would join the traditional branches. The War College continued its work on war plans and strategic questions while some of its former students and faculty embarked on new studies at the Industrial College, founded to fill the void in industrial mobilization and large-scale procurement encountered during the war. In every case, schools emphasized practical exercises that would portray the wartime problems as accurately as possible, but thoughtful leaders knew how hard that could be.

General George C. Marshall became Army Chief of Staff on 1 September 1939, the same day Nazi Germany invaded Poland. A nation that

had neglected its Army slowly awakened to the need for significant increases in capabilities. Marshall not only guided the mobilization but also required extensive maneuvers in 1940 and 1941 to test the condition of leadership, training, and organization in the expanding Army. Despite the "wartime" shortcomings that were evident, the maneuvers established a baseline for the tough, realistic training that the Army needed to be successful when war came.

The Army schools were relatively successful in imparting individual skills. In spite of rapid mobilization, shifting priorities, loss of equipment to Lend-Lease partners, and the surprise attack at Pearl Harbor, the schools turned out officers and noncommissioned officers who had knowledge of the technical and tactical requirements associated with a broad range of skills. The Army was less successful in combining those individuals into competent teams. There were a number of reasons for this shortcoming. One was the constant stripping of cadres from divisions that had made some progress in training in order to start the process all over again in a totally new division. Whenever it happened teams were left in disarray.

Left: *Advanced ROTC Juniors from Rutgers University class of 1944 return to campus in November 1943 after five months of basic infantry training. Like ROTC cadets elsewhere, they would now await assignments to Officer Candidate School. Around the country, many colleges and universities offered abbreviated programs, graduating classes after three years instead of the standard four, to help in the mass mobilization for World War II.*

Above: *Named for its 1867 founder, a distinguished Union Army general, Major General O. O. Howard, Howard University has long been among the traditional black colleges and universities whose graduates have served the nation in peace and war. The Army ROTC contingent proudly calls itself the "Bison Battalion" to remember the Buffalo Soldiers of the post-Civil War years. (U.S. Army)*

Above, right: *ROTC has continued, especially since post-WWII days, to prepare student soldiers for active duty. Outstanding cadets are given opportunities to compete for regular commissions. Cadets at Fort Riley, Kansas, summer camp in 1963, were destined to serve in Vietnam. (R. Bluhm Collection)*

Bottom, left: *Top-notch Army officers are selected to serve in the ROTC program. The Army's training school for ROTC instructors is the School of Cadet Command located at Fort Monroe, Virginia. (U.S. Army Cadet Command)*

Bottom, right: *All of the nation's military schools and colleges are offered the opportunity to host an Army ROTC unit to help qualify cadets for Army commissions. Here, training at the Valley Forge Military Academy at Valley Forge, Pennsylvania, in 1960. (U.S. Army Cadet Command)*

Another decision, the reorganization of the World War I "square" division into a smaller, more flexible "triangular" division, while appropriate, added to the confusion.

Veterans who were critical of the training they received might have generalized by saying that they spent a lot of valuable time learning "camp" and "march" skills while investing too little time in realistic training that would help units fight effectively. In part this was due to the fact that the Army continued to place heavy emphasis on marksmanship, using formal "known distance" firing range practice as the means to achieve that end. Live fire training using all weapons in a combined arms team was rare, usually limited to demonstration settings, and formalized by safety considerations. It was little wonder that units often performed poorly in their first encounter with the enemy. Maintaining an edge in units that had survived that first encounter was difficult, especially in the European theater, because divisions stayed in continuous contact with the enemy. Units were required to integrate replacements under extremely trying conditions, often suffering casualties among those replacements before they had any sense of the actual requirements of combat. In spite of tremendous efforts to learn the lessons of the battlefield and apply them in the training base, unit training never overcame these obstacles.

The senior officers and noncommissioned officers who built the Cold War Army tried to learn from all of these experiences. They knew the value of the Army school system, so they insisted that it continue its fine traditions. They knew the value of unit training that built on individual training, so they perfected a system of Army Training Tests that allowed units to demonstrate their proficiency. They had learned the value of major exercises, so they invested in large exercises requiring deployments of major units over great distances for realistic, umpired field training exercises. They challenged the value of formal firing ranges while insisting on

Typical of ROTC training is this depiction of cadets going through their paces during ROTC summer camp at Fort Lewis, Washington, in 1990. ("M60 Squad Tactics," Elzie Golden, Army Art Collection)

Far left: *A far cry from "R-Day," West Point cadets celebrate their graduation after completion of the demanding four-year program at the historic institution in the Hudson Valley. As new second lieutenants they proudly fall in—both men and women—at the end of "The Long Gray Line." (Soldiers Magazine)*

Left: *New cadets learn how to salute on "R-Day" in the Central Area at West Point, 2 July 1962. R-Day has been described as "a masterpiece of logistics, planned with lavish attention to detail" as new cadets start the transition from civilian life to the structured existence of fledgling candidates for membership in the Corps of Cadets. (United States Military Academy Archives)*

171

Above: *When a West Point cadet is issued his uniforms, he receives three single-spaced pages that detail all of the uniform components in his wardrobe. Most familiar to the public, the full dress uniform. (Greg Mathieson/MAI)*

Top, center: *The future United States Senator Bob Dole as photographed when he was at Fort Benning Officer Candidate School (OCS) during his WWII service. He would go on to serve as a junior officer in the Army's 10th Mountain Division, and would be seriously wounded in the Italian campaign. (U.S. Army Officer Candidate School)*

Top, right: *In a more modern era, "OCS 2000" candidates study an attack objective during field tactical training at Fort Benning, Georgia. Various branches maintained control of branch-oriented OCS programs for many years. In today's Army, all OCS training is conducted at Fort Benning, and branch training comes later in the new officer's career. (U.S. Army Officer Candidate School)*

Middle: *OCS inspection in ranks at Fort Benning in 1967. Nearly all of the graduates of this era would soon find themselves leading platoons in combat in Vietnam. (U.S. Army Officer Candidate School)*

Right: *OCS candidates on a tactical problem prepare to assault a Fort Benning "enemy" position. Both candidates wear the MILEs training system body and helmet laser detectors, and carry weapons with laser emitters. The MILEs laser system has greatly increased realism in tactical training. (U.S. Army Officer Candidate School)*

Opposite, top right: *With the pinning on of their branch insignia, OCS candidates who have been accepted into the Armor branch participate in the long awaited Branch Selection Ceremony at Fort Benning. Other successful candidates in the school pin on the "brass" of their branches in similar formations. (U.S. Army Officer Candidate School)*

high standards of marksmanship. This resulted in far more realistic training with individual and crew-served weapons, whether on "Trainfire" ranges, where targets popped up for short periods at various ranges in a random pattern, or on tank ranges, where moving tanks were required to engage a variety of targets.

Soldiers, leaders, and units that were products of this training regimen went to Vietnam. Shortsighted policies on rotation of individuals eroded much of the strength of the system, but most units continued to function well and achieve their assigned objectives in spite of the ensuing

problems. The junior leaders from World War II who became the senior leaders after Vietnam set out to correct the deficiencies, with General William E. DePuy setting the pace and direction.

General DePuy had been a young officer in the 90th Infantry Division in World War II. The 90th performed so poorly in its first few weeks in combat that General Omar Bradley considered breaking it up to provide replacements for more successful units. Instead, he relieved the division commander and assigned Major General Ray McLain to provide inspired leadership at the top while giving young officers like Captain DePuy a chance to figure out what needed to be done. Leaders like DePuy never forgot. Long before the Army went to Vietnam he had published an article entitled "Eleven Men, One Mind," describing the condition that had to be

Top, left: *Over the years the institution of formal inspection in barracks for OCS candidates is little changed from the early days of OCS. Candidates must meet exacting standards imposed by their mentors, the tactical ("tac") officers who keep them under close scrutiny. (U.S. Army Officer Candidate School)*

Top, center: *Required to master the Army's inventory of weapons, OCS candidates here assemble a .50-caliber machine gun during Fort Benning training days. (U.S. Army Officer Candidate School)*

Below: *Throughout the Army the training continues in the never-ending "school of the soldier." Here, a scene in the training area at Hohenfels, Germany, is depicted. ("Hotwash at Hohenfels," Army Art Collection)*

Above: *Soldier in Multiple Integrated Laser Engagement System (MILEs) gear is ready for participation in highly realistic combat training. (Soldiers Magazine)*

Top, right: *First appearance of the Army Officer Candidate School insignia was in 1941. The letter "O" encloses a monogram of the letters "CS." During WWII, in addition to branch OCS programs overseas, OCS schools in Europe and in the Pacific trained selected noncommissioned officers to serve as Army junior officers in combat.*

Middle, right: *Soldier in MILEs gear man a defensive position during a tactical training exercise at Warrant Officer School, Fort Rucker, Alabama. Of particular interest is the laser emitter affixed to the muzzle of the M16 rifle. (U.S. Army)*

met if an infantry squad was to be effective. He combined that focus on the fundamental team with a sophisticated understanding of the role of all elements of the combined arms team. This combination made him an extremely effective tactical leader when he commanded the 1st Infantry Division in Vietnam, but it made him even more effective when he became the first Commanding General of TRADOC.

Recognizing that a strong, capable Army could be built from the bottom up, General DePuy turned to the Army school system to develop "criterion referenced instruction." Each group of subject matter experts was required to list the tasks that soldiers in their career fields needed to be able to perform. Then the conditions under which the soldier would be expected to perform the task were defined and the standards for performance were agreed. The resulting array of individual tasks transformed the "school of the soldier" as it had been known since Von Steuben's day and provided the fundamental building blocks for objective training of individuals. The schools were then required to use the same approach to collective tasks that units might be expected to perform on future battlefields. Units could then train toward a standard, and leaders could evaluate train-

ing progress in terms of standards met. The resulting Army Training Evaluation Program was a significant departure from the pre-Vietnam Army Training Test because it assumed that training was an ongoing process with everyone involved working together to improve individual and collective performance.

Above: Here another scene from the never-ending training regimen that keeps soldiers of all levels at their best. ("Rock Drill," Army Art Collection)

Left: A platoon's mobile operations center tracks the battle on maps of an area the unit has never used for maneuvering. (Soldiers Magazine)

Rangers prepare to take cover before blowing a hole in a brick wall with explosive cutting tape, as part of an equipment test at Fort Benning, Georgia. The detonation of the explosive tape creates an instant entryway for the Rangers. Such new equipment will greatly enhance the ability of infantrymen to fight in urban terrain. (Soldiers Magazine)

Opposite, bottom: *Specialized branch training is what allows the U.S. Army to maintain its proficiency in all aspects of combat arms. ("Up and Down Range," Staff Sergeant Roger W. Price, Army Art Collection)*

Right: *A camouflaged tactical command post during field training of the 4th Infantry Division in fast-moving training at the National Training Center at Fort Irwin, California, involving more than 7,000 troops. (AUSA)*

These training initiatives would not have been possible without fundamental agreement on what units needed to do and how tasks should be performed. That fundamental agreement was the function of doctrine, and the new Training and Doctrine Command had been aptly named. General DePuy pushed hard to develop operational doctrine that would be suitable for the most challenging battlefield the Army might face—defending Central Europe against Warsaw Pact aggression. By focusing his personal attention to the capstone operations manual, FM 100-5, General DePuy set the stage for far-reaching doctrinal debates throughout the school system. The results of that debate were the doctrinal manuals that set the criteria for the broad list of tasks that individuals and units would need to perform.

As General DePuy's initiatives were being institutionalized, new technologies helped the Army carry its training to new levels of realism. By linking laser designators to computers, the Army was able to subject units to interactive field exercises that evoked the decisiveness of combat without the casualties. The National Training Center at Fort Irwin, California, was the first place where these technologies were employed, and the results were gratifying. Individuals and units could see the results of team-

work built on individual competence. The objective framework of "tasks, conditions, and standards" provided a tough but fair basis for critiques of unit and individual efforts. From the outset, "success" was critiqued just as carefully as "failure" because the name of the game was "evaluation," not "test." The critiques, called After Action Reviews, might be discomfiting, but leaders learned to overcome personal pride for the sake of improved performance.

This was the system that contributed to decisive victory in Desert Storm, and it still serves as the backbone of Army training. But with the end of the Cold War and the dawn of digitized warfare, much has changed. A threat modeled on the Warsaw Pact is dated and insufficient. The tasks that must be performed to dominate the future battlefield are different, and the Army organizations that perform the combination of new and old tasks are being transformed. Changes in doctrine encompass these innovations and direct the modifications in training. Today's "fight" may be peacekeeping in Bosnia. The units may come from "camps" in the National Guard, the Army Reserve, and U.S. Army Europe. The "march" might include self-deploying helicopters as well as strategic moves by land, sea, and air. But the Army schools and training system can prepare units and individuals for such complexity with ease. The investments of more than two centuries are paying big dividends on the "battlefields" of the twenty-first century.

Above: *A noncommissioned officer student works with an instructor on a flight control simulator during air controller training at Fort Rucker, Alabama. (U.S. Army)*

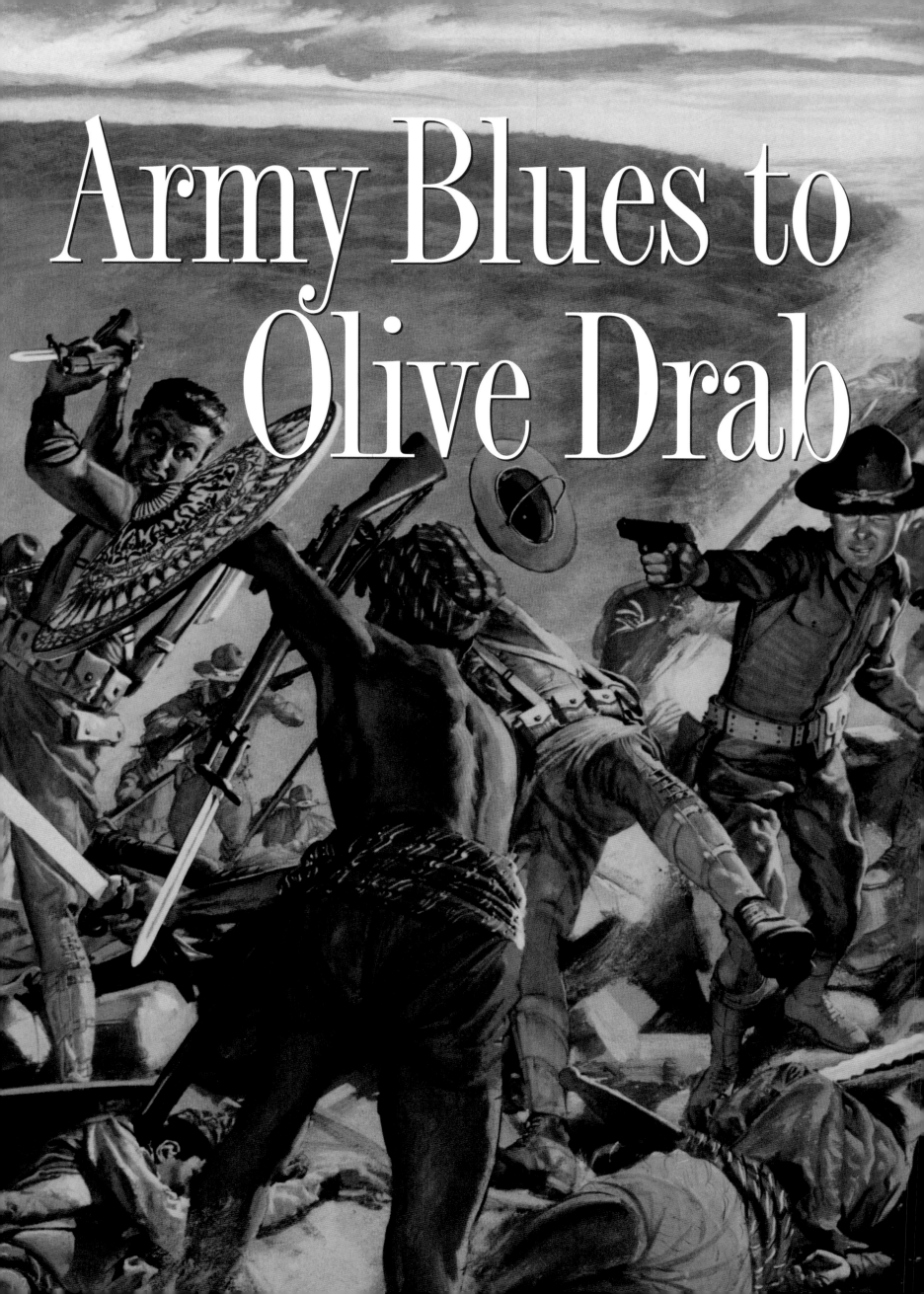

Army Blues to Olive Drab

Army Blues to Olive Drab

A Modern Fighting Force Takes the Field

Colonel Cole Kingseed, USA (Ret)

Turn of the Century 1900

Although the foundation of American military policy in 1900 remained the defense of the continental United States, the acquisition of a colonial empire as a result of the Spanish-American War signaled a new direction for the U.S. Army. During the span of five short months in 1898, the United States effectively destroyed Spain's colonial empire and began its march to global power. In addition to an army of 80,000 officers and men, two-thirds of which were deployed overseas, military governors now presided over the Philippine Islands, Cuba, and Puerto Rico. Whereas the defense of the nation's borders and the projected Canal Zone across the Panamanian isthmus presented specialized challenges, the most serious threats emerged along the western fringes of the Pacific Rim.

Having acquired the Philippines as a result of the treaty that ended the war with Spain, the United States inherited another war when Filipino insurgents, who had helped throw off the Spanish yoke, demanded joint occupation of Manila. American imperialism and Filipino nationalism immediately clashed and fighting erupted on 4 February 1899. In a conflict that bore a remarkable similarity to American intervention in South Vietnam sixty years later, the U.S. Army conducted a mixture of conventional and unconventional operations that finally suppressed the insurrection on 4 July 1902. During the interim the Filipino leader Emilio Aguinaldo gained

The drawn-out war against the Filipino insurgents led by Emilio Aguinaldo required a heavy commitment of U.S. forces in the Philippines in the years after the end of the Spanish-American War. Sometimes the cat-and-mouse game in the jungles turned into a pitched battle. ("Our Boys Against the Filipinos," B.W. Kilburn, National Archives)

Pages 178–179: Even after U.S. forces defeated the Filipino Nationalist insurrection following the end of the war with Spain, many areas fell under the influence of bandits and pirate elements. Brigadier General John J. Pershing, as commander of the Moro province, Mindanao, took to the field to defeat Moro pirates in a four-day battle in June 1913. ("Knock Out the Moros," H. Charles McBarron, Army Art Collection)

Opposite: In the spring of 1899, members of the 1st North Dakota Infantry and the 2d Oregon Infantry, detailed as scouts in advance of the main body of U.S. forces, encountered a band of 300 insurrectos near San Isidro on Luzon. When the smoke of battle cleared, the hostile force was driven out of its trenches. ("Soldiers in the Sun," Donna Neary, National Guard Heritage series)

181

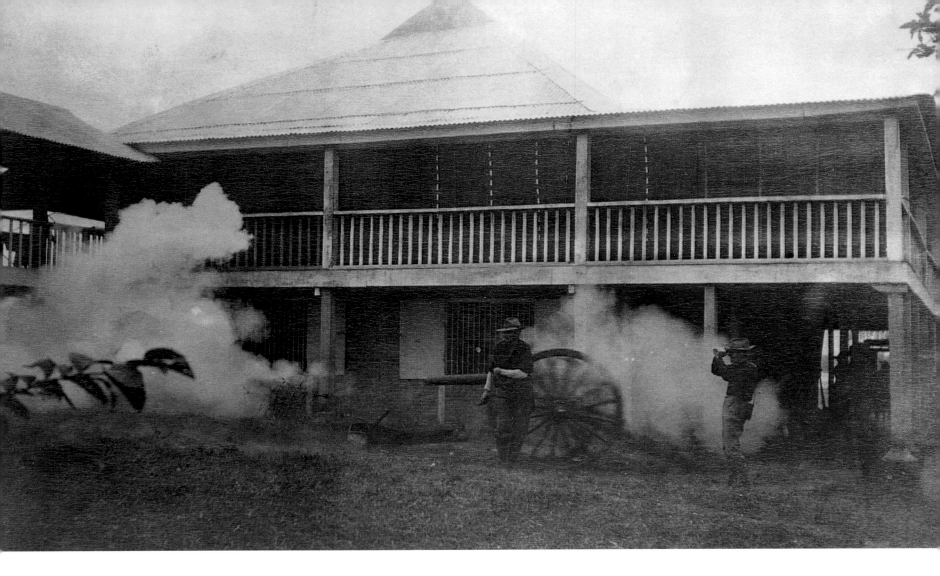

Top: *Occasionally, during the guerrilla warfare that predominated the Philippine Insurrection, U.S. forces would find an opportunity to employ artillery to overcome the natural advantage enjoyed by opponents fighting on familiar terrain. Here, U.S. artillery in action in 1899. (National Archives)*

Above: *A landmark moment in the long and grinding campaign came when Brigadier General Juan Cailles and his guerrillas surrendered to the Americans in June 1901. Cailles commanded the resistance in the Laguna province on Luzon. Americans would battle Japanese invaders in this region in 1942. (National Archives)*

Above, right: *Movement of military supplies through the difficult terrain of the Philippines forced the Army to fall back upon the ubiquitous* carabao, *the water oxen. The carabao has been described as "the best loved animal the American forces knew" in the Philippines. (National Archives)*

international notoriety for his fierce resistance to American rule. At the outset, Aguinaldo foolishly adopted a conventional strategy that was ill-suited to his resources, and the American army commanded by Elwell S. Otis and his successor, Arthur MacArthur, father of future General of the Army Douglas MacArthur, soon defeated him. In a daring gamble, a group of American Army officers and allied Filipino scouts, led by Colonel Frederick Funston, posed as POWs to penetrate Aguinaldo's base and capture the elusive rebel on 23 March 1901. Rather than ending the war, Aguinaldo's capture merely signaled the end of the conventional phase. The next year witnessed tenacious guerrilla fighting on the southern archipelago, and the war dragged on until the last surviving Filipino leader surrendered, and President Theodore Roosevelt proclaimed victory in July 1902.

By most standards, the Philippine Insurrection was the most successful counterinsurgency in the nation's history. By U.S. Army estimates, troop strength averaged 40,000 and actually peaked at 70,000 in December

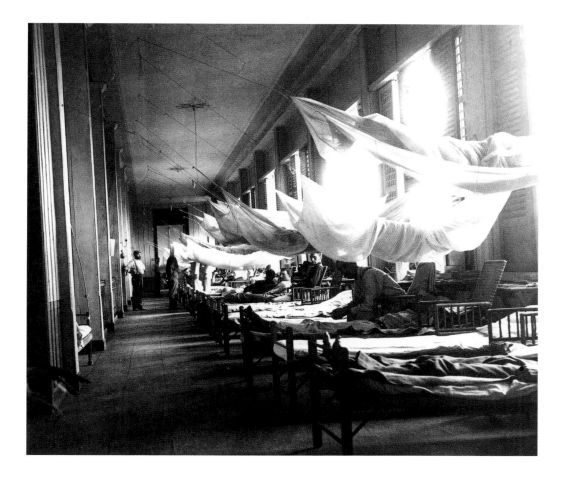

1900. Over the course of the conflict, more than 125,000 soldiers saw service, of whom 4,200 died in action or from disease. Combining military operations by American troops and Filipino auxiliaries with a sustained effort of pacification and social reform produced the ultimate American triumph. What gave the American military forces the edge was not their numbers, but their effectiveness. Superior weaponry, organization, and leadership at the senior officer and field commander level proved a lethal combination that the insurgents were unable to match.

In the midst of the Philippine War, the U.S. Army also participated in a multinational relief expedition to rescue the beleaguered American legation in Peking, China. Besieged by a group of anti-Christian and anti-foreign nationalists known as the Boxers, the garrison was successfully relieved by a coalition of American, European, Russian, and Japanese forces in August 1900. Commanding the task American force of infantry, cavalry, and artillery was Adna R. Chaffee, who later succeeded MacArthur

Above: *Brigadier General James Harrison Wilson, an old Civil War cavalry hero, returned to the Army in 1898. Sent to China in 1900, he commanded U.S. troops in and around Peking (now Beijing) during the intervention of allied forces in the Boxer Rebellion. Wilson, foreground, established his headquarters (in background) at the Temple of Agriculture. (National Archives)*

Above, right: *With the impressive Great Wall of China looming in the background, an artillery detachment opens fire near Peking—now Beijing—as part of the China Relief Expedition in 1900. Some of the Americans came from the Philippines while others were sent from the United States. With the exception of brief interludes, the U.S. would keep a military presence in China until 1938. (National Archives)*

Above: *On the route to the Ming Tombs, troopers from a detachment of the 6th U.S. Cavalry pass the Avenue of Statues. The cavalry, along with three U.S. Infantry Regiments, field artillery elements, and Marines, made up the U.S. contribution to a joint allied force organized to enter China's Forbidden City to rescue western hostages. (National Archives)*

Above, right: *Officers of the 6th Cavalry pose for a portrait en route to assist in the China Relief Expedition in 1900. A full assortment of uniform styles are visible, including the khaki blouse with standing collar as adopted by the Army in 1898. (National Archives)*

as commanding general in the Philippines and was himself a future Army chief of staff. Though short-lived, the Boxer Rebellion heralded a new era for the Army in which expeditionary operations became the norm for the next several decades. The western frontier constabulary of the nineteenth century was rapidly transitioning to an army for empire, a military force designed to protect American political and economic interests overseas.

The administration of this force, coupled with evolving roles and missions, dictated massive reforms of the antiquated War Department, whose supervision of the Spanish War was shoddy at best. On 1 April 1899, President William McKinley appointed a brilliant New York lawyer, with the unlikely name of Elihu Root, to supervise the reforms. Root initially demurred, but McKinley persisted, telling Root that he needed a lawyer to administer the colonial territories acquired in the recent war with Spain. Root accepted, giving up his position as "the acknowledged leader of the American bar" to tackle the persistent problems in the War Department.

Root's first annual report in December 1899 addressed itself to the fundamental tenet of military professionalism that "the real object of having an army is to provide for war." Quickly marshaling congressional support, Root embarked on a series of reforms that profoundly affected the Army long after Root's tenure as Secretary of War, reforming the Army's command structure, its reserve force, and its contingency planning.

Modern Army Emerges

Root's initial proposal called for the establishment of an Army war college to devise plans and to advise the Secretary of War and the Commander-in-Chief. Established 27 November 1901, the War College Board immediately began studying several proposals aimed at creating a general staff that Root hoped would serve as a unified "brains of the Army." Emory Upton, a military intellectual who traveled extensively to study foreign military establishments following the Civil War, undoubtedly influenced Root. He proposed a greater reliance on regular forces, a general staff organized along the lines of the Prussian model, and a revamped system of institutionalized professional education. Politically astute enough to realize that Upton's proposals would attract powerful political and military enemies, Root moved cautiously. His efforts came to fruition in the 1901 legislation that marked the most substantial military reforms since the days of Secretary of War John C. Calhoun.

Two years later Congress passed the General Staff Act of 1903, which created the General Staff and replaced the Commanding General of the Army with a Chief of Staff answerable directly to the Secretary of War. No longer tied to military seniority, the Secretary could appoint any officer in whom he had confidence. The change of title from commanding general to chief of staff also reinforced civil control over the military. In his own words, Root stated, "The titles denote and imply in the officers bearing them the existence of widely different kinds of authority." The Army Chief would serve a tenure of four years and supervise a staff of forty-five officers, many of whom would themselves rotate between Washington and the Army's geographic departments. For the first Chief of Staff, Root nominated Major General Samuel B. M. Young, the same officer who had chaired the War College Board. Congress did not go as far as Root intended and granted the General Staff only "supervisory and coordinating" authority over the War Department and its powerful bureaus. Still it was a beginning, and Root next moved to expand the Regular Army.

Convinced that the United States' colonial responsibilities dictated a permanent military expansion, Secretary Root successfully lobbied Congress to enlarge the Regular Army to 3,820 officers and 84,799 men to meet the challenges of the new century. In February 1901 Congress increased the twenty-five Regular infantry regiments to thirty and the ten regiments of cavalry to fifteen. Equally important was the formation of an artillery "corps" consisting of thirty batteries of field artillery and 129 companies of coast artillery. Congress also authorized three battalions of

Top: *Selected as Secretary of War at a critical time for the Army, the Honorable Elihu Root of New York proved to be exactly the right man. With the Army ripe for reform following a myriad of mobilization and deployment problems in 1898, Root supported a modern General Staff, installed the first Army Chief of Staff, and advocated militia reform. It is said that he brought the Army into the twentieth century. (Center of Military History)*

Above: *The reforms sweeping the Army after the war with Spain included uniforms as well. The uniform for infantrymen in the Philippines in 1903 is based upon the khaki tropical service dress with bronze buttons first adopted in 1898. The campaign hat, distinctively American, became the official headdress and was the headgear best-liked by U.S. soldiers. (H. Charles McBarron, The American Soldier series, Army Art Collection)*

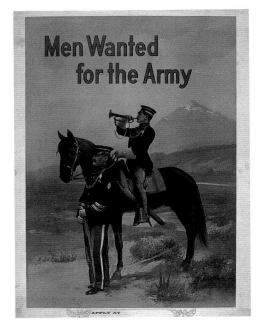

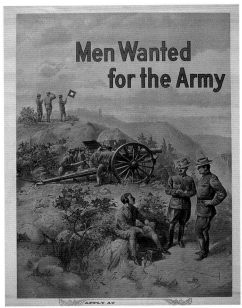

engineers. Though Congress failed to appropriate sufficient funds to field a force this large, Root sought a clearer delineation of the nation's reserve forces to augment the Regulars in time of war.

The improved reserve system found its expression in the Militia Act of 21 January 1903, usually called the Dick Act after its principal congressional sponsor, Representative Charles W. Dick of Ohio. Under the Dick Act, the National Guard became the Organized Militia and evolved into the nation's first-line reserve force, gradually replacing the historic state militia. The legislation and its modification in 1908 provided federal equipment and training standards to the National Guard companies, increased the time for which the president could call the Guard into federal service, authorized inspections by Regular Army officers, and improved joint maneuvers between the Guard and Regular units. Most importantly the 1908 legislation directed that the president call forth the National Guard before asking for any additional volunteers and removed the geographic restrictions under which the old state militia had previously operated. In effect, Congress recognized that the president could summon the Organized Militia into federal service "either within or without the Territory of the United States."

Root's most far-reaching reforms and the ones that enjoyed immediate success, however, lay in the field of professional military education. With the passage of the General Staff Act, the War College Board dissolved and gave way to the Army War College, which then as now, constituted the pinnacle of an Army officer's education. Root also directed that every military post of significant size establish a program of professional education. Within a decade, these schools emerged as the Army School of the Line, the various branch-specific schools, and the birth of the Staff College at Fort Leavenworth, Kansas.

By the time Root relinquished his office in 1904, he could view his reforms with justifiable pride. His achievements included: a permanent increase in the Army's strength; creation of a General Staff; rotation of officers between staff and line; reduced dependency upon seniority; joint planning by the Army and Navy; an improved reserve program with special attention to the National Guard; and reorganization of the Army school

system. The American Army was now posed to play an important role on the international stage.

National leaders were not reluctant to use the Army to assist in domestic disasters or disturbance as well as to support American diplomatic interests abroad. In 1906, the Army established order and directed rescue and disaster relief operations following the great San Francisco earthquake. Later, in 1912, soldiers were used to restore order during a series of labor strikes and demonstrations in several cities. President Roosevelt and President William Howard Taft called on the Army's Corps of Engineers to build a canal across the Isthmus of Panama. Two officers, chief engineer Brigadier General George W. Goethals and the Medical Department's Colonel William C. Gorgas, directed the construction and conquered yellow fever in the process.

Above: *The ongoing education and training of the Army's officer corps took advantage of opportunities to study the terrain where important engagements had taken place during the Civil War years. ("The Staff Ride," Don Stivers, CGSC Edition)*

Opposite: *Prints depict (left) members of the 7th Regiment, New York National Guard, in fatigue and field service uniforms, circa 1900–1905; (center) a private, field officer, and company officer of the New York 69th Regiment, in summer full dress, 1869–1884; and (right) members of 5th Battalion (Colored) —corporal, captain (full dress), 1st sergeant (overcoat), private (fatigue uniform). (Company of Military Historians)*

Above: *Civil disaster on a large scale in the San Francisco earthquake of 1906 brought a quick response by the Army. Troops from the Presidio and other western locations raced to the scene of the disaster to establish law and order and to set up needed relief services. ("Thank God for the Soldiers," H. Charles McBarron, The American Soldier series, Army Art Collection)*

Above, right: *Work under the direction of the Army Corps of Engineers was critical to the success of building the Panama Canal across the Isthmus of Panama. Ultimately, the canal, which was opened to shipping traffic in 1914, was hailed as one the engineering marvels of the twentieth century. ("The Heavenly Hoist," Jonas Lie, West Point Museum Collection, United States Military Academy)*

Right: *The extraordinary "dig" started with the excavation at the Culebra Cut, a ten-mile stretch through the highest and rockiest region of the proposed canal route. Manpower, heavy engineer equipment, and 19 million pounds of explosives would move 96 million cubic yards of dirt from the Cut. ("Steam Shovel in the Culebra Cut," William Pretyman, West Point Museum Collection, United States Military Academy)*

Opposite, bottom left: *Troopers of the 13th Cavalry view the body of a Mexican intruder, a casualty during the raid by Pancho Villa on Columbus, New Mexico, on 9 March 1916. (Army Art Collection)*

Three years after the Panama Canal officially opened in 1914, the Army assumed responsibility for its defense.

In addition to assisting American gunboat diplomacy throughout the Caribbean, the Army also dispatched the Fifth Brigade under Brigadier General Frederick Funston from Texas in support of the occupation of Vera Cruz, Mexico, in 1914. The occupation did little but topple the Mexican government and exacerbate growing anti-American feeling throughout Mexico. A future Army chief of staff also faced enemy fire for the first time at Vera Cruz when then Captain Douglas MacArthur, operating as a personal representative of the War Department, conducted an unauthorized reconnaissance into the interior. A member of MacArthur's party recom-

mended the young officer for the Medal of Honor for his actions under fire, but the recommendation was subsequently denied due to the covert nature of MacArthur's foray. MacArthur remained in Mexico for four months before returning to duty with the General Staff in Washington.

Tensions between the United States and Mexico temporarily eased, but in March 1916, Francisco "Pancho" Villa crossed into the United States and raided Columbus, New Mexico, killing fifteen Americans. Within a week the War Department organized a punitive expedition under Brigadier General John J. Pershing to capture the elusive Mexican bandit. Ramrod straight and a strict disciplinarian, Pershing was widely recognized within the Army as one of its foremost fighters. Cadet First Captain of his class at West Point, he had served with highest distinction in Cuba, where one superior labeled him "the calmest man he had ever seen under fire." Additional combat against the Philippine Moros added national luster to his star. In 1906 President Roosevelt, on the recommendation of Pershing's father-in-law, Senator Francis E. Warren, who coincidentally was chairman of the Senate Military Affairs Committee, nominated Pershing for the next vacancy that occurred in the grade of brigadier general, promoting Captain Pershing over hundreds of senior officers in the process.

Above, left: Pioneering research and methodical on-the-ground isolation of mosquito breeding places under Colonel William Crawford Gorgas resulted in the near elimination of yellow fever and malaria in Panama and played an important role in the successful construction of the Panama Canal. The Alabama-born Gorgas joined the Army as an assistant surgeon in 1880. (National Archives)

Above: The military was needed in the early part of 1912 as a result of violence in the streets of Lawrence, Massachusetts, during a strike of 30,000 textile workers. Nearly all of the Massachusetts militia was called out before it became necessary for the governor to ask for the commitment of Army troops.

Captain Douglas MacArthur, in a uniform design to his own liking, shown while serving on a special War Department mission during U.S. operations at Vera Cruz, Mexico, in 1914. (MacArthur Memorial)

Pershing opened his headquarters on 14 March. His force was designated as the Punitive Expedition, U.S. Army, and was organized as a provisional division consisting of three brigades. With little fanfare Pershing invaded Mexico at the head of 5,000 Regulars. Accompanying Pershing was First Lieutenant George S. Patton, who served as one of the general's aides-de-camp. When Mexican president Venustiano Carranza threatened war unless the United States withdrew the invading force, Wilson federalized the National Guard under the provisions of the newly passed National Defense Act of 1916 and sent approximately 110,000 Guardsmen to the Texas-Mexico border. Neither side wanted war, and aside from two major skirmishes with the Carranzistas, Pershing returned north across the international border in January 1917. Although he failed to accomplish his mission, Pershing gained a great deal of experience with respect to mobilization and sustainment of a large field force.

Though he did not capture his quarry, the Punitive Expedition was hardly an abject failure. Pershing's force was the largest American force to enter Mexico since the Mexican War of 1846–47. Defeating Villa's bands at every encounter, Pershing was successful in dispersing his adversary to the point that they were largely ineffective. Of far greater significance was the training laboratory that prepared numerous officers for World War I. Pershing had not only employed motor transportation, but he had also experimented with airplanes for reconnaissance. Moreover the experience also led to changes in armament, not the least of which was an increase in

Left: *An artistic depiction of a mounted charge by the 11th U.S. Cavalry soldiers against the forces of Pancho Villa in Mexico commemorates an era that was about to come to an end. Although horse cavalry would remain on the Army's rolls for another twenty-five years, the curtain was starting to come down and horse cavalry played only a minor role in WWI. ("The Last Charge," Don Stivers)*

Opposite, top: *During the summer of 1916, much of the National Guard was mobilized and ordered to the Mexican Border. The training the Guardsmen received would stand them in good stead in 1918 when most of them would see service in France with the American Expeditionary Force. Connecticut infantrymen featured in this painting served at Nogales, Arizona. ("On the Border," Donna Neary, National Guard Heritage series)*

the number of machine guns assigned to a division. Additionally, the mobilization of the National Guard for an extended period produced lessons that served the Army well when the war tocsin sounded the following April.

Equally important for the U.S. Army was the emergence of several officers who gained valuable operational experience over unfamiliar and rugged terrain. First and foremost was Pershing himself, who became a logical choice when President Wilson and Secretary of War Newton Baker selected a commander for the American Expeditionary Force (AEF) once the country entered World War I. Second only to the commander of the expedition was Major John L. Hines, Pershing's Adjutant General, who would later command a division and corps in France and succeed Pershing as Army chief of staff in 1924. Another rising star in Pershing's eyes was his young aide, George Patton, for whom destiny beckoned on distant battlefields of a later conflict.

Pershing's return to U.S. soil was undoubtedly hastened by the growing crisis with Germany. With Europe engulfed in war since August 1914, President Wilson had carefully maintained American neutrality for nearly three years. During the years preceding America's own entry into the war, the Army struggled to establish a coherent military policy. Led by former

Below, left: *The commander of the Punitive Expedition against the Mexican rebel force under Pancho Villa was the 36-year-old Pershing. Here he leads members of his staff across the Santa Maria River on an inspection tour of U.S. forces chasing an elusive enemy. (National Archives)*

Below: *Army airplane No. 75, a Curtiss R-2 model, at Camp El Valle, Mexico, where a flying field was established by the 1st Aero Squadron, Army Signal Corps, during its service on the Mexican Border. In the hot, dry climate, propellers frequently shattered. Soldier in photo is a 16th Infantry private. The squadron was under the command of Captain (later brigadier general) Benjamin D. Foulois. (National Archives)*

During the months when Pershing's forces were scattered between Columbus, New Mexico, and El Valle, Mexico—with Pershing himself at Colonia Dublan—the Curtiss R-2 airplanes of the 1st Aero Squadron took over the task of maintaining communications along the 140-mile route. Occasional scouting missions added a new dimension to reconnaissance. ("Blackjacks' New Scouts," James Dietz)

Army chief of staff Leonard Wood, the Army became an active participant in the war preparedness movement. As chief of staff, Wood had sponsored the "Plattsburg idea" and organized summer camps at which college students, and later professional men, received rudimentary military training. The concept spread and soon thousands of volunteers flocked to Wood's camps. During the summer of 1916, nearly 10,000 volunteers attended the various camps across the nation. Naturally the preparedness movement assumed political overtones when Wood's ideas mirrored those of influential Republicans, one of whom was Theodore Roosevelt.

Gathering momentum with news from the Western Front and German atrocities on the high seas, Wood's preparedness movement next pressed for universal military service. Although Wilson signaled his administration's opposition to conscription, the President toyed with several proposals regarding the nation's reserve forces before placing his support behind increased federal responsibility for the National Guard. In addition he supported a bill that increased the Regular Army to 140,000 officers

The Army's artillery largely depended upon horses for its mobility on the Mexican border, and for a long time thereafter. Although motor trucks would soon come into the Army inventory, artillery continued to be largely "horse-powered" almost up to the eve of U.S. entry into World War II. ("Field Artillery on the Move," Michael Whelan, Army Art Collection)

192

and men. Under Wilson's compromise, the federal government would strengthen the federal standards in training in return for the Guardsmen agreeing to swear an oath to respond with their entire units to federal calls for service anywhere.

Congress then stepped in and drafted new legislation that resulted in the most comprehensive military legislation in a century. The National Defense Act of 1916, under whose authority Wilson soon federalized the National Guard for service on the Mexican border, increased the authorized strength of the Regular Army to 175,000 and designated the National Guard as the Army's first-line reserve force.

Despite the passage of the National Defense Act, the country and the Army in particular were woefully unprepared for the approaching European war. It would be up to Pershing, the former commander of the Punitive Expedition, to weld his expeditionary army into a world-class fighting force.

Above, left: A 16th Infantry soldier at El Valle, Mexico, during the Punitive Expedition, on 8 July 1916. His bayonet is mounted on his new Model 1903 Springfield Rifle. The bandana, although practical in the summer heat of Mexico, was strictly non-regulation. (National Archives)

Above: One of the Army's four traditional black regiments for many years, the 25th U.S. Infantry on parade in Honolulu, prior to World War I. The regiment's gallant service in Cuba was recognized by the El Caney block-house on its distinctive regimental insignia. (National Archives)

"Over There"

When Congress declared war against Germany on 6 April 1917, to "make the world safe for democracy," the U.S. Army had a combat strength of slightly over 200,000 men, ranking seventeenth in the world. It had not conducted major operations above division level since the Civil War. Though the preparedness movement had prepared the country for potential mobilization, the American Army was still in the throes of its transition from a constabulary to an expeditionary force.

On 2 May 1917, Major General John J. Pershing, commanding the Southern Department of the Army at Fort Sam Houston, Texas, received "for your eyes only" orders to select five regiments to form the core of the first division for service abroad. Pershing selected the 16th, 18th, 26th, and 28th Infantry Regiments and the 6th Field Artillery. With two other artillery regiments, these units formed the famous 1st Division, known by war's end as the "Big Red One." The division's operations officer was Captain George C. Marshall, who would subsequently earn

In the ongoing evolution of the uniforms of the Army: (left to right) corporal in dress uniform; first lieutenant wearing summer field dress; and sergeant in summer field dress, circa 1916. (Company of Military Historians)

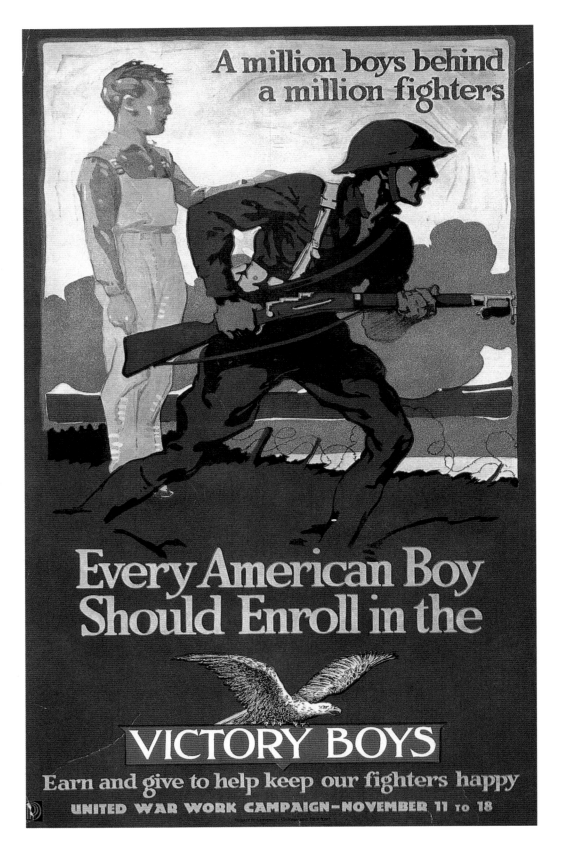

Top: *General John J. Pershing as commander of the WWI American Expeditionary Force (AEF) in France. Pershing wears the Sam Browne belt that was mandatory for all officers serving under him in France, but banned by the War Department when AEF officers returned to the U.S. (National Archives)*

Above: *During a lull following the St. Mihiel campaign in France during September 1918, Douglas MacArthur, by then a brigade commander in the 42d (Rainbow) Division, was photographed in the chair vacated by the owner of this St. Benoit Château. (National Archives)*

Right: *Recruiting poster encourages American youth to serve in the "Victory Boys" and to join the depleted workforce on the home front. The recruiting campaign was planned to kick off 11 November 1917. One year later— to the date—the war would end with an Allied victory over Germany. (National Archives)*

his reputation as the Army's most brilliant staff officer. When President Wilson inquired through his Secretary of War as to the best manner for employment of the National Guard, Major Douglas MacArthur, serving on the War Department's General Staff, suggested they take units from the different states. This idea resulted in the formation of the 42nd "Rainbow" Division, with newly promoted Colonel MacArthur as its chief of staff. In October 1917, the division sailed for France.

To command the AEF, Secretary of War Baker selected John J. "Black Jack" Pershing. Pershing was not the senior officer in the Army, but his performance during the Punitive Expedition had earned him the respect of President Wilson and Baker.

Never had an American commander received such broad powers as did Pershing. Secretary Baker issued Pershing his orders personally. Designated the commanding general of all the land forces of the United States operating in continental Europe and in the United Kingdom, Pershing was directed to cooperate with the Allied forces, but to remember that "the forces of the United States are a separate and distinct component of the combined forces, the identity of which must be preserved." Equally important, Baker directed Pershing to "communicate his recommendations freely and *directly* to the Department."

Pershing's expeditionary army consisted of America's citizen soldiers, drawn by conscription from the towns and cities across the United States. In response to Wilson's urging, Congress passed the Selective Service Act on 18 May 1917. Unlike previous drafts, 4,648 local draft boards, headed by civilians, were responsible for registration. Eventually, 24 million men registered for the draft, and it was from this pool that the wartime army was raised. Unlike its Civil War counterpart, the World War I draft worked reasonably well, funneling in excess of 2,700,000 to the armed forces and thousands into war industries in the United States.

As the nation geared its industrial and manpower strength to fight the Great War, Pershing set sail from New York with the General Headquarters (GHQ) AEF aboard the White Star Line's SS *Baltic* on 28 May. Following a brief stop in England to confer with Great Britain's political

Above, left: *Arduous training routines helped convert civilians to soldiers at military bases throughout the U.S. Here, new soldiers scale an obstacle at Camp Wadsworth, South Carolina, in 1918. (National Archives)*

Top, right: *A New York Guardsman of the 71st Infantry Regiment, 27th Division, says goodbye to his sweetheart on departure for training at Camp Wadsworth, South Carolina. A few months earlier the New York division returned from training and service on the Mexican border. It would soon be in the trenches as part of the American Expeditionary Force. (National Archives)*

Above: *A scene that took on a familiar look—draftees fresh from civilian life reporting for active duty. In all, 24 million American men were enrolled in the draft and a somewhat cumbersome procedure was established to determine who would actually be called. About 2,800,000 men were actually called into service. (National Archives)*

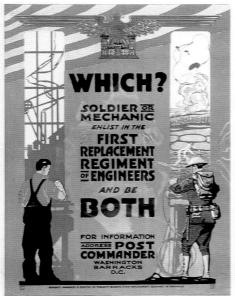

Above: *Colorful recruiting posters sought to help the Army obtain not only raw recruits, but men with civilian skills needed in military units. Army engineer regiments, in particular, needed men who already had proficiency in handling a wide variety of heavy equipment. (National Archives)*

Top, right: *Immediately upon arrival in France, U.S. troops were given additional training to prepare them for the rigors of trench warfare on the front lines. Here, a simulated night attack with phosphorous bombs during a maneuver conducted by the I Corps School at Gondrecourt. (National Archives)*

Right: *Intensive stateside training was conducted, frequently with the assistance of officers and NCOs back from front line service. New soldiers with gas masks in place, but without helmets, prepare to go "over the top" during a training exercise at the Presidio, San Francisco, in June 1918. (National Archives)*

and military leaders, Pershing and his party arrived in France. On 4 July 1917 Pershing traveled to Picpus Cemetery to honor the Marquis de Lafayette. During the ceremony, Pershing made a few casual remarks and then turned to Colonel C. E. Stanton, his chief disbursing officer. Speaking for the United States and the U.S. Army, Stanton pledged his country's support with the dramatic last line, "Lafayette, we are here!"

Pershing's principal chore now became the training of American divisions for combat. Clearly understanding that training required time, he now insisted that the standards for the American army would "be those of West Point." To the AEF commander, "the rigid attention, the upright bearing, attention to detail, uncomplaining obedience to instruction required of the cadet will be required of every officer and soldier in our armies in France."

Establishing GHQ at Chaumont, Pershing busied himself with countless inspections, war councils, and routine staff duties. Ever present was Allied pressure to amalgamate American doughboys into British and French divisions. Pershing stood steadfast against amalgamation, determined to maintain the integrity of the AEF until he deemed it fit for combat in its own sector. By November 1917, 87,000 doughboys had arrived in France, with thousands more arriving every month. By year's end, troop strength

Above: *Pitted against the last great German offensive of the war, the 30th and 38th Infantry Regiments, 3d Division, stoutly defended the Marne River line in July 1918 and helped save Paris. The battle earned the 3d Division its long-lasting nickname, "Rock of the Marne." ("The Rock of the Marne," H. Charles McBarron, Army Art Collection)*

stood at 9,804 officers and 165,080 men. By spring 1918, the AEF was ready to fight.

The Germans struck first. On 21 March 1918, the enemy launched its spring offensives, a series of five concentrated attacks designed to force a final decision on the Western Front before the bulk of the AEF could disrupt the balance of power. The German High Command under Field Marshal Paul von Hindenburg and General Erich Ludendorff hit the British hard on the Somme and then launched a supporting attack in Flanders. With their backs to the wall, the British Expeditionary Force commander, Sir Douglas Haig, pleaded for American reinforcements. Casting aside amalgamation, Pershing offered the entire AEF to the war effort. American troops were rushed to the front, just in time to meet another German

Below: *A column of doughboys packing full field gear marches along a roadway in France to the beat of military music provided by a British army band. (National Archives)*

Left: *Early during the fighting on the Lorraine front, Battery C, 6th Field Artillery, shown in action at Beaumont, France, 12 September 1918. A spent shell casing can be seen in the air as a new shell goes into the breech. (National Archives)*

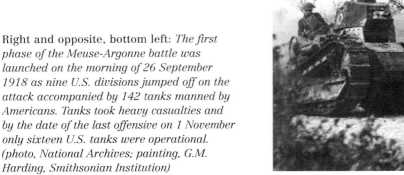
assault, this time against the French near Reims. Holding the line at Chateau-Thierry aside the Marne River, just forty miles from Paris, were the U.S. 2d and 3d Divisions. The 2d Division launched its own counterattack to seize Belleau Wood and the 3d prevented a determined German attack from crossing the Marne. In the process the 3d Division earned its sobriquet "the Rock of the Marne."

In the interim between the second and third German attacks, the 1st Division earned its battle spurs by recapturing Cantigny on 28 May, the first American victory of the war. Though events along the Chemin des Dames region where Ludendorff launched another attack quickly overshadowed the battle of Cantigny, the U.S. Army demonstrated that it could plan and execute an independent operation. The success enhanced the AEF's self-confidence and earned the respect of friend and foe alike.

By mid-summer the Germans had shot their bolt and Marshal
Ferdinand Foch, the Allied Supreme Commander, prepared to launch his
own counteroffensives. By now doughboys were arriving in France at a
rate of 250,000 per month, reaching a peak of 306,302 in July. On 24
July, Pershing created the U.S. First Army, effective 10 August. By the
time First Army opened its St. Mihiel attack on 12 September, it consisted
of three American corps of fourteen divisions, a total of 550,000 American
troops, plus 110,000 French soldiers. With the stream of American
arrivals unchecked, Pershing organized the Second Army on 10 October.

In the war's final campaigns, the U.S. Army attained its full maturity.
In September First Army, under direct command of Pershing, launched the
St. Mihiel offensive. The objective was a salient of some 200 square miles
along the Meuse River. Four French and eight and one-half American

Top and above: *An artist's view of a WWI
battlefield and a recruiting poster for the
newly created "U.S. Army Tank Corps"
promoted the theme, "Treat 'em Rough . . .
Join the Tanks." The élan associated with
tank units would be elevated to a high note
by the pioneer tankers who served under
Colonel George S. Patton in the 304th Tank
Brigade. (painting, "Storming Machine Gun,"
George Harding, Army Art Collection; poster,
National Archives)*

A gun crew from Regimental Headquarters Company, 23d Infantry Regiment, 2d Division, fires a 37mm gun during an advance against German entrenched positions. The 23d would earn battle streamers for six campaigns in France and would be cited by the French and Belgians for valor. (National Archives)

divisions participated in the attack. The battle was Pershing's first real test as an army commander, and First Army achieved a stunning success. The Americans eliminated the salient in two days, helped in part because the enemy had already begun a tactical withdrawal on the eve of the attack. Despite high casualties, the limited offensive validated Pershing's contention that the AEF had come of age.

Shortly after the doughboys earned their chief his greatest victory to date, Pershing massed his forces for the Meuse-Argonne campaign, destined to be the AEF's largest and most costly battle of the war. Designing the movement order of 600,000 men and 3,900 guns was none other than Colonel George C. Marshall, now working at GHQ. This campaign was the culmination of Foch's great counteroffensive to break the Hindenburg Line. The American objective in the Meuse-Argonne attack was the German's main line of communication through Metz, Sedan, and Mezieres. To achieve that goal, the AEF had to penetrate three lines of German defenses. The terrain heavily favored the defender, but on 26 September, the AEF attacked.

Unlike St. Mihiel, the Germans bitterly contested every inch of territory. Pershing and his subordinate commanders envisaged open tactics, but the enemy fought with a ferocity that inflicted massive casualties on the Americans. After four days of intense combat, the line advanced only eight miles. The attack soon stalled and First Army regrouped. The general pause did not affect all the divisions on line. On 2 October 1918, the 77th Division pushed a battalion forward that quickly got cut off from its parent organization. As the Germans swarmed around the beleaguered remnants, the "Lost Battalion," actually elements of three battalions, fought for its survival. Commanded by Major Charles W. Whittlesey, the battalion repulsed several enemy attacks before being relieved on 7 October. Only 194 Doughboys of an initial contingent of 554 officers and men walked from the pocket under their own power. The relief of the "Lost Battalion" quickly achieved epic proportions and the AEF had its first legend. Whittlesey and his second-in-command, Major George McMurtry, were awarded the Medal of Honor.

The second phase of the Argonne offensive began on 4 October, and this time it took the Armistice to halt the American advance. Fighting was intense and casualties appalling, particularly among junior officers and

Above: *American soldiers on the Piave front shower Austrians with hand grenades near Varage, Italy, on 16 September 1918. The U.S. 332d Infantry, from the 83d Division, was deployed to the Italian front in July 1918 in response to urgent requests from the Italian government. Other than medical and support units it was the only U.S. unit in Italy in WWI. (National Archives)*

In action near Breteuil, France, in May 1918, soldiers of the 26th Infantry, 1st Division, take cover as a French tank maneuvers nearby. (National Archives)

Above: *During a training "stand to" in the trenches near the maneuver area at Gondrecourt, France—soldiers of the 28th Infantry, 1st Division, ready themselves for combat, 15 October 1917. (National Archives)*

Right: *Baptism of fire for the 28th Division, Pennsylvania National Guard, came on 15 July 1918 at Courthieze, France. Two infantry companies of the 109th Infantry Regiment stood fast in the face of heavy enemy fire and fought a delaying action against the veteran German 36th Division. An enemy report referred to them as "Men of Iron." ("Men of Iron," Don Troiani, National Guard Heritage series)*

Opposite, top left: *Near Essey, France, Lieutenant Colonel R. D. Garrett, chief signal officer, 42d (Rainbow) Division, tests a telephone left behind by the Germans in their hasty retreat from the St. Mihiel salient, on 19 September 1918. (National Archives)*

Opposite, top right: *Snipers from the 166th Infantry Regiment, (formerly 4th Ohio Infantry, Ohio National Guard) picking off Germans on the outskirts of Villers sur Fere, 30 July 1918, during an attack carried out by troops of the 42d (Rainbow) Division. (National Archives)*

noncommissioned officers. Two small unit leaders earned the renown of the entire AEF in the first week of the renewed offensive. On 8 October, Corporal Alvin C. York, from Company G, 328th Infantry Regiment, 82d Division, single-handedly destroyed thirty-five enemy machine gun nests, killed twenty-eight Germans, and captured 132 prisoners in one of the war's most dramatic actions. What made York's achievement even more spectacular was the fact that he was not only a draftee, but also a consci-

entious objector to boot. York quickly became the 82d "All American" Division's greatest hero.

If York emerged from the war as America's most recognized doughboy, Pershing selected First Lieutenant Samuel A. Woodfill, a company commander in the 5th Division, as the "outstanding figure in the AEF." Pershing admired the hardcore NCO of the old Army, and Woodfill wore six hash marks on his sleeve before he accepted a battle-

Above: *Captain Samuel Woodfill, an Old Army Regular, wore six hash marks on his sleeve before he accepted a commission. (Center of Military History)*

Above: *Early aviation was a dangerous pursuit. Adding aerial combat to that could be a daunting experience. Yet the exhilaration of flight attracted many young Americans. ("Red, White & Blue," James Dietz)*

Right: *Lieutenant Eddie Rickenbacker (left), a former race car driver who became America's greatest air ace in WWI; Lieutenant Douglas Campbell (center), the first American air ace; and Captain Kenneth Marr (right), were all members of Army Air Service's 94th Aero Squadron serving at the front in France. They fought the air war flying British and French airplanes. (National Archives)*

Opposite, top: *First Lieutenant Reed M. Chambers, flying a Spad with the 94th Aero Squadron, shot down two Fokker D-7s to become an ace on 22 October 1918. The Tennessee aviator earned the Distinguished Service Cross with an oak leaf cluster for heroism in aerial combat. ("Two Down to Glory," William S. Phillips, National Guard Heritage series)*

Opposite, bottom right: *A recruiting poster issued soon after the end of WWI depicts the colorful array of shoulder sleeve insignia approved for members of U.S. divisions that fought in the war. Most divisions did not obtain insignia until after the war ended. Poster includes insignia for several units that were still in training camps in the U.S. when the Armistice was signed on 11 November 1918. (National Archives)*

Below: *Artillery fire was often directed by a ground telephone line connection from the baskets of observation balloons. Once airborne, the observers—usually a crew of two— became prime targets for German airplanes, enemy machine guns, and even artillery fire. (National Archives)*

field commission. With his company pinned down by enemy fire, Woodfill systematically destroyed five German machine gun nests in a single action. Armed with his Springfield rifle and a pistol, he killed twenty-five Germans, the last two with a pickax when his rifle jammed. Laurence Stallings, a doughboy who later wrote the story of the AEF, called Woodfill the eternal sergeant of Black Jack Pershing's esteem, the Doughboy of Doughboys.

In the air Captain Eddie Rickenbacker became America's ace of aces with twenty-six confirmed kills. A nationally known racing driver before the war, Rickenbacker had come to France as a chauffeur with GHQ before transferring to the aviation section. Joining the 94th Squadron, he shot down his first enemy plane on 29 April 1918 and later commanded the squadron during the Meuse-Argonne offensive. As with York and Woodfill, Rickenbacker earned the Medal of Honor.

Another flyer, Colonel Billy Mitchell, became Chief of the Air Service of the First Army and soon commanded all American air combat units. During the St. Mihiel attack, Mitchell commanded 1,481 airplanes and maintained air superiority during the AEF's final offensive. Mitchell later claimed he survived on only three hours of sleep a night during the last six months of the war. In his fitness report, his superior noted that Mitchell "thinks rapidly and acts quickly, sometimes a little too hastily."

The official end of hostilities found the AEF bloodied, but still full of fight. Over the course of the forty-seven-day Meuse-Argonne campaign, the American Army lost 120,000 killed, wounded, and missing. In return they had cracked the vaunted Hindenburg Line, liberated 150 villages, freed 16,059 prisoners, and had driven forty-seven German divisions back thirty-two miles. At war's end, the forward elements of the AEF were overlooking the vital German railhead at Sedan. With revolution at home and defeat on the Western Front, Germany requested an armistice, which went into effect on 11 November 1918. The war was over.

Although Allied leaders rejected Pershing's demand for unconditional surrender, all were ecstatic that the slaughter was finally over. In 200 days of combat, the AEF had proved the catalyst for victory, and the infusion of American manpower had tilted the balance on the battlefield in favor of the Allies.

The American doughboys had attacked with an élan and a ferocity that had not been seen since 1914. One German general summed up the AEF thus: "The American soldier showed himself full of courage, even if he lacked experience. Fresh, well-fed, and with strong nerves that had known

Left: *American forces throughout France in 1918 took part in activities in honor of July Fourth. Troops stationed in the Paris area celebrated U.S. Independence Day with a parade through the city. (National Archives)*

Above: *The 332d Infantry Regiment fought with the Italian Army at Vittorio Veneto. The colors carry a streamer that reads: "Donated by the Young Italy Inc., of New York." (National Archives)*

Above, right: *St. Mihiel American Cemetery occupies a 40.5-acre site at the west edge of Thiaucourt, France. It contains the graves of 4,153 American soldiers, most of whom died in the offensive that reduced the St. Mihiel salient. In the background is Soldier Monument and Chapel as it appeared circa 1925. (American Battle Monument Commission)*

Right: *President Warren G. Harding places a floral wreath on the casket of the Unknown Soldier in the Rotunda of the Capitol, 9 November 1921. Interment at the Arlington National Cemetery took place on 11 November 1921, and to this day it remains a focal point of visitors to the cemetery. (National Archives)*

Gleeful soldiers were mustered out of wartime military service at Camp Dix, New Jersey, after return from France. Many believed— and a nation hoped—that it had indeed been "the war to end all wars." (National Archives)

no strain, he advanced against the German Army . . . and in the great numerical re-enforcements which the Americans brought to our opponents at the decisive moment lies the importance of the American intervention." All in all it was a resounding performance.

The war also changed the American Army. During World War I, the U.S. Army increased from 133,111 Regulars, augmented by 185,000 National Guardsmen, in April 1917, to 3,685,458 on 11 November 1918. Fully 2,000,000 soldiers answered Wilson's call and joined the Allies in France. AEF casualties included 50,475 battle deaths and another 193,611 wounded. The influenza epidemic in 1918 claimed another 57,000 soldiers, for a grand total of 120,139 dead at home and overseas. At war's end, fully 2,057,675 military personnel were serving in the AEF, whose combat strength was 1,078,222 in the front-line divisions.

Without a doubt the United States emerged from the war as a major military power.

Interwar Years: Preserving an Army

The cessation of hostilities heralded the rapid demobilization of America's armed forces. Despite a commitment to support two expeditionary forces still fighting in Russia, and an occupation force along the Rhine in Germany, by 1 January 1920, only 130,000, mostly Regulars, remained under arms from a force that once numbered over four million officers and men at the peak of the war. Republican nominee Warren G. Harding campaigned on a platform calling for a "return to normalcy," and his victory in the November election confirmed that the military was embarking upon lean times.

For the U.S. Army, the primary emphasis reverted to continental defense and the relationship between the Regular Army and its reserve forces. Army chief of staff Major General Peyton March immediately proposed an expansion of the Regular force to 500,000 officers and men, and universal military service that would then provide a reservoir of 500,000 conscripted reservists for wartime. Under this plan, the National Guard reverted to third string.

Congress disagreed, and in the resulting National Defense Act of 1920, limited the Regular Army to 280,000 men and rejected a call for universal military training. Congress also ordered the Army to train its civilian components and reconfirmed the National Guard as the Army's primary land reserve. It also called for an Organized Reserve, whose officers would be drawn from an expanded Reserve Officers Training Corps (ROTC).

Above, left: American troops in the expeditionary force sent to Siberia in August 1918 consisted of two regiments sent from the Philippines, the 27th Infantry and 31st Infantry. They were photographed on parade in Vladivostok soon after arrival as Japanese marines stood at attention. The Siberia force was withdrawn from the region in February 1920—the last deployed American soldiers of the WWI era. (National Archives)

Above: A need for increased Army strength occurred in 1914 as the Army mounted an expedition to Vera Cruz, Mexico. In this recruiting poster, the evolution toward the WWI era uniform can be seen—the campaign hat with infantry blue cord, load-carrying web equipment, and sturdy, brown shoes. (National Archives).

Bottom left, and below: An Army task force from the 85th Division, augmented by Army railway companies, mounted an effort to keep stores and supplies at Archangel in Northern Russia from falling into the hands of the Bolsheviks. Russian counter-revolutionary action failed to materialize. American soldiers rounded up Bolshevik prisoners before leaving Russia in August 1919. (National Archives)

The passage of the National Defense Act of 1920 also initiated two decades of meager budgets as the Army groped with both mobilization and modernization. Despite budgetary constraints and forced reductions in manpower, the Army made significant improvements, especially with the Army Air Service. The 1920 legislation confirmed the separation of the Air Service from the Signal Corps and its status as a separate combat arm. With Billy Mitchell as its chief spokesman, the air service quickly captured the public imagination in the 1920s. In a series of highly publicized tests in 1921 designed to demonstrate the effectiveness of aerial bombardment, Mitchell's bombers sank the former German battleship *Ostfriesland*. While the Navy fumed, Mitchell achieved a public relations coup. The reluctance by the service chiefs to accept his far-sighted programs and the death of a close friend in an aerial mishap led Mitchell to release a public statement, in which he accused the Navy and War Department of "incompetence, criminal negligence, and the almost treasonable negligence of our national defense."

This led to his court-martial in 1925 for "insubordination and conduct prejudicial to the service." The court found Mitchell guilty of all charges and specifications, and he resigned. He lost his battle, but he won his campaign. In 1926 Congress passed the Air Corps Act, changing the Air Service to the Air Corps, giving it equal access to the Army chief of staff, and increasing the numbers of officers and men assigned.

In 1920 Congress also placed tanks under the control of the chief of infantry, but advocates fought for a separate tank corps. Two young officers, Major Dwight D. Eisenhower and Major George S. Patton, argued that the proper role of armor was penetration of enemy lines and subsequent exploitation. They were immediately chastised by the chiefs of infantry and cavalry and directed to keep such heretical ideas to themselves, but the General Staff took up the study of mechanization. In 1928 an Experimental Mechanized Force was established at Camp Meade, Maryland, and overall it demonstrated the potential of an armor service. A mechanized force was formed, but soon disbanded in 1931 by the new chief of staff, Douglas MacArthur, who directed all branches mechanize. The Cavalry branch converted the 1st Cavalry Regiment to a mechanized regiment and in 1936, the 13th Cavalry joined it at Fort Knox, Kentucky, to form the 7th Cavalry Brigade (Mechanized). Enthusiast Adna R. Chaffee became brigade commander, and was a leader in the Army's mechanization.

The greatest success story in the interwar Army, however, was in the field of institutionalized professional education. Virtually every senior Army commander in World War II was a product of Leavenworth's staff

Top, left: *In this impressive show of contemporary technology, the Army shows off some of its latest "combat cars." Cavalrymen were attracted to armored cars and tanks and were encouraged to "think mounted." (National Archives)*

Top, right: *In a 1938 scene, a cavalry sergeant accompanies Major General Adna Chaffee, the "father" of the modern armored force. Chaffee was instrumental in formation of the Cavalry Brigade (Mechanized), which was a major step in establishing a requirement for an armored combat entity independent of the infantry branch. (H. Charles McBarron, The American Soldier series, Army Art Collection)*

Above: *Captain Dwight D. Eisenhower poses beside an M1917 light tank at Camp Meade, Maryland, in 1920. Eisenhower authored a thoughtful essay on utilization of tanks that appeared in* Infantry Journal. *For this he was reprimanded by the chief of infantry who directed him to keep his unconventional views to himself. Through most of the interwar years, tanks would remain under infantry control. (National Archives)*

Left: *Company E, 31st Infantry, "shows the flag" on the march through a Chinese city. Two soldiers in front rank wear the three-pocket magazine bandolier of a BAR man. Japanese Army troops posted nearby took a lively interest in the equipment issued to U.S. infantrymen. (National Archives)*

Opposite, top: *A poignant moment in history when Army troops took part in eviction of WWI Bonus Marchers who had come to lobby, in the dark days of the Depression, for early payment of a proposed bonus for wartime duty. On 28 July 1932 tear gas was used to rout the veterans from the Anacostia flats in Washington, D.C., where they had set up a crude campsite. (National Archives)*

Right: *Army signalmen in the 1930s used a reel mounted on the rear of a Chevrolet truck to lay wire during an exercise to test communications capabilities. (National Archives)*

Below: *The spit-and-polish 15th Infantry Regiment, one of the Boxer Rebellion units, again returned to China in 1912 when the internecine warfare between the warlords became a threat to regional stability. The 15th would remain a familiar sight in Tientsin until 1938 when it was withdrawn on the eve of the pre-WWII Army buildup. (National Archives)*

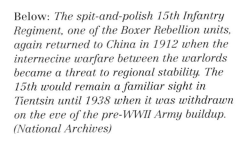

Opposite, bottom left: *After President Franklin D. Roosevelt created the Civilian Conservation Corps (CCC) in the 1930s, Army officers and NCOs were called upon to run the camps. As the program grew in size and scope, the Army relied upon reserve officers to help provide leadership and management of CCC camps and projects. (National Archives)*

college and the senior service school. Dwight D. Eisenhower, for example, graduated first in his Leavenworth class in 1926 and attended both the Army War College and the Industrial War College.

Planning for war was not the only mission given the Army in the 1930s. The 15th Infantry Regiment remained stationed in Tientsin, China, and the 31st Infantry deployed from its base in the Phillippines in 1932 to restore order in Shanghai's international settlement. Douglas MacArthur became the Army's youngest chief of staff at the age of fifty in 1930. The most poignant episode during his tenure was the Bonus March of 1932. At the height of the Great Depression, thousands of World War I veterans gathered in Washington to petition Congress to grant an immediate cash bonus that had been promised. Violence soon erupted, and on 28 July, MacArthur received instructions to proceed to the scene of disorder and to cooperate fully with the District of Columbia police force and to restore order. Bedecked in his uniform, MacArthur was at the forefront of the Regulars, who quickly pushed the Bonus Marchers back to their camp across the Anacostia River. Ignoring instructions from his civilian superiors,

MacArthur ordered his men to cross the river, at which time the marchers' shantytown caught fire. Several marchers were injured, including an eleven-year-old boy who accompanied the veterans.

Once he became president, Franklin D. Roosevelt called upon the Army to assist in the administration of the Civilian Conservation Corps (CCC). While such a task detracted from the Army's primary mission of preparing for war, the benefits and the good publicity generated by the Army's cooperation created a more positive image in the eyes of the American public. The CCC was a federal initiative to employ thousands of

Above: *General Douglas MacArthur, Army chief of staff, issues orders to Perry L. Miles, commander of the 16th Infantry Brigade, following President Herbert Hoover's order for the Army to intervene in the matter of the Bonus Marchers. (Center of Military History)*

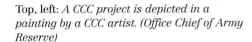

Top, left: *A CCC project is depicted in a painting by a CCC artist. (Office Chief of Army Reserve)*

Top, right: *The full Citizens Military Training Camps (CMTC) course committed young men to one month of training each year, for four years. CMTC candidates wearing WWI-style "tin pot" helmets, fire machine guns near Monterey Bay during 1925 training at Camp Del Monte, California. Many CMTC graduates qualified for reserve commissions and many would be called for WWII service. (National Archives)*

Above: *The CMTC were established in the 1920s to provide a taste of military life to young men. CMTC lasted until the few months before U.S. preparations for possible entry into WWII began. Above, CMTC candidates, circa 1930, hone their combat skills working as a machine gun team. (National Archives)*

Below: *In keeping with the tradition that anything beats walking, CMTC candidates at Camp Knox, Kentucky, pose for this 1923 photo in a dramatically overloaded truck of World War I vintage. (Donald M. Kington collection)*

idle young men in conservation projects. The Army's role was to be limited to enrolling the men and transporting them to Army stations for organization. The Army soon assumed a more important role—that of organizing and operating the work camps.

From 1921 through 1940, the Army sponsored the Citizens Military Training Camps (CMTC), a program designed to turn out minimally trained officers for the Army Reserve after attendance at four summer camps. While no replacement for an expanded Regular force, or for a universal military training program, the little known CMTC did provide a service of officers to help meet the manpower demands of the approaching world war. It introduced a number of men destined for future national prominence, including two presidents, to the Army.

In 1938 Congress appropriated sufficient funds to field an army of 165,000, but the mood of the country remained decidedly noninterventionist. Of the nine infantry divisions in existence in 1939, only three maintained any semblance of a divisional structure, and all were woefully unprepared for modern war. With a keen eye on the rise of Asian and European dictators, the Army General Staff began developing manpower mobilization plans for an expanded field force.

World War II: "The Great Crusade"

The story of improved military readiness on the eve of Pearl Harbor is essentially the story of General George Catlett Marshall. A graduate of the Virginia Military Institute, Marshall had served with highest distinction during the Great War and ended the war as Pershing's aide-de-camp. He continued in the same capacity when the president elevated Pershing to chief of staff, following his mentor to Washington in 1919. From executive officer of the 15th Infantry Regiment based in China, Marshall migrated to Fort Benning, Georgia, where he served as assistant commandant of the Infantry School. At Benning, Marshall renovated the academic program, constantly emphasizing simplistic tactical orders and fast-moving offensives reminiscent of Pershing's open tactics of World War I. No matter relating to warfighting escaped Marshall's scrutiny, and by the time he departed Fort Benning in 1932, he had imbued a generation of officers with his own brand of battlefield leadership. Virtually every infantry commander who advanced to senior level command in World War II bore the mark of Marshall's influence. All told, over 200 future general officers passed through the Infantry School during Marshall's tenure as assistant commandant. To be known as one of "Marshall's men" became a badge of distinction. When it came time to appoint division and corps commanders for deployment overseas, Marshall had scores of officers whom he knew intimately from his tour at Fort Benning.

General Marshall succeeded Malin Craig as Chief of Staff on 1 September 1939, the very day that Germany attacked Poland. The Regular Army Marshall inherited in 1939 ranked nineteenth in the world, just ahead of Bulgaria and next to Portugal. Marshall worked feverishly to build a modern army, and devoted his efforts toward establishing control over

Top: *Readiness training throughout the Army was well underway on the eve of Pearl Harbor. Soldier holding a 45-cal. Thompson submachine gun is posed before an array of contemporary (circa 1940) infantry weapons including a British anti-tank gun, a .30-cal. machine gun, a Browning automatic rifle, and (far right) an 81mm mortar. (National Archives)*

Above: *Army Air Corps P-12C pursuit aircraft fly over Oahu during routine training in the 1930s. From humble beginnings, the air corps program for defense of the Hawaiian Islands was regarded as "relatively imposing"—until 7 December 1941. (U.S. Army Museum of Hawaii)*

Opposite, bottom right: *A WWI field artillery battery commander and a former Missouri Guardsman, Colonel Harry Truman kept his reserve commission after the war. In 1933 he did a tour as CMTC commander at Camp Pike, Arkansas. In this 1926 photo Truman (right) was on annual active duty at Fort Riley, Kansas. (The Harry S. Truman Library)*

the promotion and retirement of Regular Army officers. He lobbied Congress to increase the size of the Regular and reserve components; to promote officers on merit instead of seniority; placed renewed emphasis on service schools and the cadre system; and battled the budgetary constraints. He was successful in each endeavor.

Marshall served as the Army's principal spokesman in congressional hearings on reinstating compulsory military service, and he was instrumental in the passage of the Selective Service and Training Act of 1940, the nation's first peacetime draft. Three months before Pearl Harbor, the Army mustered 1.2 million men, now designated the Army of the United States.

As the United States drifted toward war in late summer 1941, Marshall and his Navy counterpart, Admiral Harold Stark, drafted a plan that outlined what was needed to defeat Germany. Dubbed the Victory Program, it was officially titled the "Joint Board Estimate of the United States Over-all Production Requirements." It proved one of the most prescient documents in the annals of military history, correctly anticipating a two-front war against Nazi Germany and Imperial Japan.

To train the new force Marshall directed large-scale maneuvers of corps and armies. The most famous maneuvers pitted Second Army against Third Army in the fall of 1941 across Texas and Louisiana. During these war games, Colonel Dwight D. Eisenhower rose to national prominence, and another officer, George S. Patton, confirmed his reputation as one of the Army's most dashing leaders.

Marshall then turned his attention toward the General Staff. What Marshall envisioned was a Washington command post, from which he could train the field force and supervise military operations. In June 1940 a new Army regulation created the U.S. Army Air Force, with General Henry "Hap" Arnold subsequently designated its chief. GHQ Air Force was subordinated to GHQ, and the Army's training function was allocated to Army Ground Forces under Lieutenant General Lesley McNair. Lieutenant General Brehon B. Somervell was elevated to chief of the Services of Supply. With strategic planning reverting to the General Staff, Marshall created the Operations Division (OPD). As head of OPD, Marshall selected Brigadier General Eisenhower.

Thus the U.S. Army entered World War II far stronger than its predecessor had done in 1917. Nevertheless, glaring deficiencies were still obvious, both in lack of training and outdated equipment. None of the combat divisions were fully prepared for war, but significant strides had been made. Balancing these shortcomings were concrete manpower and industrial mobilization plans. The real question was whether Marshall and the GHQ had time to prepare the Army before the United States entered the war. The Imperial Japanese Navy answered that question on 7 December 1941, when it attacked Pearl Harbor. With one masterful stroke, the enemy

Top, left: *Traversing a training challenge known as an "infiltration course," trainees got "realistic experience" in a 75-yard crawl that gave them a taste of moving around emplaced demolitions and under live machine-gun fire overhead. (National Archives)*

Top, right: *Training continued even as units left stateside camps and started toward the combat area. Troops near Harmon Field, Newfoundland, found themselves "advancing toward the enemy" through enemy artillery fire simulated by demolition devices during realistic training in 1943. (National Archives)*

Above: *The conditioning necessary to build strong bodies would start at the beginning of the Army buildup and would continue through all of the war years. Calisthenics and exercises became a normal part of the process of conditioning men to be soldiers. (National Archives)*

Opposite, bottom right: *World War II soldiers, soon to earn the nickname of "GIs," began to be seen regularly in the nation's newspapers and magazines as the Army went to work to take the young men fresh from civilian life and to condition them for the possible rigors of war. Up until the eve of Pearl Harbor, the new soldiers took this in stride as a mere one-year interruption of their lives. (National Archives)*

Above: A burned-out B-17C aircraft amid the destruction wreaked by Japanese aircraft at Hickam Field, Oahu, during the attack on Pearl Harbor, 7 December 1941. The attack occurred almost concurrently with the arrival of B-17s coming in from the U.S. west coast. (National Archives)

Right: Throughout the course of the four years of war, civilians and soldiers alike would be encouraged to buy war bonds. This wartime poster promoted a motion picture tribute to the infantry and at the same time advocated buying bonds to help support the war effort. (National Archives)

I WANT YOU

for the U.S.ARMY

UNITED STATES ARMY RECRUITING SERVICE

Above: To spur the recruiting effort, the most famous poster of WWI was reprised, as James Montgomery Flagg's famed "Uncle Sam Wants You!" illustration was brought out of moth-balls and returned to active duty. The Army used poster advertising throughout the war as many famous artists and illustrators rallied to the war effort. (National Archives)

Right: Following the fall of Bataan, many U.S. prisoners of the Japanese perished in the infamous "Death March." The route of the death march was from the Bataan peninsula to the hastily designated prison camp at Cabantuan, north of Manila. (National Archives)

Opposite, bottom: General Douglas MacArthur at the front on Bataan with Major General Jonathan Wainwright. When ordered by President Roosevelt to leave the Philippines to build up Army forces in Australia, MacArthur turned his army over to Wainwright. It was left to Wainwright to suffer the ignominy of surrendering his battered command to the Japanese. (MacArthur Memorial)

had crippled the only threat to its strategic designs in the western Pacific. The next day, Japan also attacked the Philippine Islands, now under the command of General Douglas MacArthur, whom President Roosevelt had recalled to active duty the preceding July.

In Washington, Roosevelt quickly resolved any debate as to who would direct America's war effort. With the possible exception of Lincoln, Roosevelt proved to be the most active commander in chief in the nation's history. The president personally made all major decisions regarding grand strategy, including the fundamental proposition that Germany must be defeated first. As head of the Army, Marshall became the president's most trusted advisor and served as his principal conduit for issuing orders to the Army's theater commanders.

On the battlefront, neither MacArthur nor America's armed forces could stem the steady tide of Japanese conquest during the first six months of the war. In May, the Philippines had fallen and Lieutenant

General Jonathan Wainwright and the "battling bastards of Bataan" were imprisoned in dozens of Japanese camps. That same month Japan had established an outer defensive perimeter and waited for the inevitable onslaught by the United States. The turning point in the Pacific war occurred in June 1942 with the decisive Battle of Midway. The Army's staging base for the counteroffensive ran through the Hawaiian Islands to Australia, where MacArthur galvanized a nation with his promise to return and to liberate the Philippines.

On the heels of the Japanese attack on Pearl Harbor, Nazi Germany declared war on the United States, forcing the country into a two front war. Given Roosevelt's "Europe First" strategy, the Army's immediate priority was to transport experienced divisions to England, where Marshall and his protégé, Eisenhower, hoped to launch a cross-channel attack aimed at the heartland of Germany. The buildup in England, code-named Bolero, took form in mid-1942. Army planners at OPD envisaged two possible scenarios for the cross channel assault: Sledgehammer, an invasion in late 1942 in the event of a Soviet collapse, and Roundup, an assault in 1943 aimed at the destruction of the German *Wehrmacht* in western Europe. To command this force, Marshall nominated Eisenhower, who assumed command of

Above: When the Japanese attacked Clark Field in the Philippines on 8 December 1941, they were quickly fired upon by gunners of the 200th Coast Artillery. The New Mexico National Guard unit had been rushed to the Philippines just a few weeks earlier. It was soon forced to Bataan and its survivors marched into Japanese prison camps. ("First to Fire," Don Stivers, ADAA edition)

Above: *England was soon teeming with U.S. units of all types in training for the eventual invasion of Europe. This photo depicts a squad of U.S. Rangers, armed with Thompson submachine guns, taking a break from serious training to have a picture taken. (National Archives)*

Right: *Troops of the 34th (Red Bull) Division, Guardsmen from Iowa, Minnesota, North Dakota, and South Dakota, march past local civilians in Northern Ireland on their way to training locations. Still wearing old-style helmets, they were the first Army troops to reach European soil. The first contingents reached Belfast on 26 January 1942, less than two months after Pearl Harbor. (National Archives)*

Opposite, top: *On 3 May 1942, the Japanese moved a task force of light carriers and supporting ships into position 165 miles from Dutch Harbor, Alaska, in the Aleutian Islands where the U.S. was starting a base buildup. The Japanese aviators launched a surprise attack that was countered by the 206th Coast Artillery Regiment (AA) equipped with obsolete 3-inch guns and 50-cal. water-cooled machine guns. ("Defense of the Aleutians," Domenick D'Andrea, National Guard Heritage series)*

U.S. Army, European Theater of Operations, on 25 June 1942. Eisenhower correctly predicted that the command in the European theater "will be the biggest American job of the war."

The decision as to when and where to commit the American Army in 1942 was Roosevelt's, not Marshall's, and the president considered it to be of "the highest importance that the U.S. ground troops be brought into

action against the enemy in 1942." Though Marshall and Eisenhower favored a cross-channel attack by the summer of 1943, Roosevelt accepted British Prime Minister Winston Churchill's recommendation for a peripheral attack in North Africa. Determined to commit American forces against Japan and Germany prior to the November congressional elections, Roosevelt also hoped to strengthen Allied solidarity by opening a second front in Europe to prevent public sentiment from abandoning the Europe First strategy. Inclement weather delayed the invasion a week, but on 8 November 1942, U.S. Army units landed on the African coast as part of Operation Torch. Simultaneously in the Pacific, MacArthur launched a limited attack to seize Buna Mission on the island of New Guinea, beginning his long trek to the Philippines.

In the war against Germany, the American Army fought in two principal theaters: the Mediterranean and the European theaters of operation. From 1942 through 1943, Eisenhower served as commanding general in the Mediterranean region and commanded the combined forces of the United States and the United Kingdom from Operation Torch through the initial invasion of Italy (Avalanche) in September 1943. Eisenhower then departed to assume command of the invasion of western Europe, and command in the Mediterranean shifted to the British.

The high degree of Allied cooperation that characterized the European theater did not exist in the Pacific. Lieutenant General "Vinegar Joe" Stilwell exercised virtually no influence on Generalissimo Chiang Kai-shek or Admiral Lord Louis Mountbatten in the China-Burma-India (CBI) theater,

A new recruiting theme appeared in September 1943 as the Women's Army Corps became an official component of the Army of the United States. Many former WAAC members (Women's Auxiliary Army Corps) made the transition but far more were needed in the war effort. At the high-water mark in April 1945, there were 99,288 women in the WWII Army, exclusive of nurses. (National Archives)

Above: *The difficulties in moving supplies to where they were needed was a problem that haunted Lieutenant General Joseph Stilwell's meager forces in China during the war with Japan. ("Pack Train in China," Howard Baer, Army Art Collection)*

Above, right: *Lieutenant General Joseph Stilwell, the senior United States Army officer in the China-Burma-India theater for three wartime years, explains the situation in Burma to Lieutenant General Barry M. Giles (center), Chief of the U.S. Air Staff, and Major General Howard C. Davidson, commander of the 10th U.S. Air Force, based in northern India. (National Archives)*

Opposite, top left: *U.S. M3 light tanks equipped with 37mm guns maneuver into position near Duropa Plantation, New Guinea, on 21 December 1942. Tanks arrived by boat a few days after Buna village was captured by U.S. infantrymen. Japanese pockets of resistance continued to hold out until 2 January 1943. (Center of Military History)*

Right: *In the Army's first major offensive in the Pacific, U.S. and Australian forces were sent against heavily fortified Japanese positions at Buna on the southeast coast of New Guinea during November 1942. It proved to be a protracted and difficult campaign in unfamiliar, steamy jungle terrain. The 32d Division (Wisconsin and Michigan) suffered high casualties. ("Red Arrow at War: The 32d Infantry Division at Buna," Michael Gnatek, Jr., National Guard Heritage series)*

and the British and the Australians had only a minor role in MacArthur's Southwest Pacific area. The most successful coalition commander in the U.S. Army during World War II was Eisenhower, whose headquarters served as a model for Allied cooperation and solidarity.

By 1943, the Army was engaged in a multitude of theaters across the globe. In January, Major General Robert Eichelberger restored the fighting spirit of the 32d Infantry Division and led it to victory at Buna on the northern coast of New Guinea. With Buna secure and Stilwell rallying American troops in the CBI theater, Major General Alexander Patch directed XIV Corps to relieve the Marines on Guadalcanal. In a series of swift offensives, he eliminated Japanese resistance and cabled Admiral William "Bull" Halsey on 9 February: "Total and complete defeat of Japanese forces on Guadalcanal effected today… Am happy to report…Tokyo Express no longer has terminus on Guadalcanal."

The way was now clear for MacArthur to conduct his "leapfrogging" campaign to isolate the Japanese garrison at Rabaul on New Britain island and to begin his northwest advance up the coast of New Guinea. In the ensuing campaign, MacArthur employed Eichelberger and Alamo Force commander Walter Krueger with consummate skill. The campaign displayed MacArthur at his bold, audacious, and visionary best. By mid-1944, New Guinea was in American hands, and MacArthur successfully lobbied Roosevelt in July 1944 for a direct assault on the Philippines.

Half a world away, the United States continued its buildup of forces in England, while Eisenhower's Anglo-American force drove the Germans toward Tunisia. An enemy counterattack inflicted severe losses on the American army at Kasserine Pass in February 1943, resulting in Eisenhower's appointing Major General George Patton to command II Corps. Patton revitalized II Corps, won the first significant American victory against German forces at El Guettar, and drove eastward, linking up with British General Bernard Law Montgomery's Eighth Army. The days of Field Marshal Erwin Rommel's *Afrika Korps* were numbered. In May 1943, 240,000 German and Italian soldiers surrendered.

At the Casablanca conference in January, Roosevelt and Churchill had already decided the next step. Deferring the cross-channel attack to 1944, the Allied leaders expanded operations in the Mediterranean and initiated the Combined Bomber Offensive against German industrial and civic centers. Roosevelt also enunciated the clearest political objective of the war— the total and complete unconditional surrender of the totalitarian states.

Top: *During the Buna campaign in New Guinea, the 37mm gun was used to good effect for firing into enemy positions at close range. (Center of Military History)*

Middle: *In a brief but intensive Central Pacific campaign, soldiers of the 165th Infantry (formerly the "69th Fighting Irish") went ashore at Butaritari, Makin Atoll, Gilbert Islands, on 20 November 1943. The regiment fought in the Pacific as an element of the 27th Infantry Division from New York. (National Archives)*

Above: *U.S. troops scramble down the rope ladders of a Coast Guard-manned troop transport to get into the landing barges for the trip to the beachhead. The landing site was Empress Augusta Bay in early November 1943. (National Archives)*

Above: *A U.S. medium tank in the Kasserine Pass, Tunisia, area. Nearly half of the tanks of the U.S. 1st Armored Division would be lost to the veteran 21st Panzer Division in a devastating battle on 14 February 1943. (National Archives)*

Above, right: *Elements of the 16th U.S. Infantry, 1st Infantry Division, march over a mine-cleared road through Kasserine Pass en route to regroup at Farriana in Tunisia on 26 February 1943. (National Archives)*

Right: *In one of the epic aerial battles of WWII, B-24s under 9th Air Force command, set off from desert bases in North Africa to strike a blow at the enemy oil refineries at Ploesti, Romania. The low-level attack would be a bloody and costly affair. Later nine of the Army airmen would be awarded the Medal of Honor. ("Fire Over Ploesti," Roy Grinnell, National Guard Heritage series)*

Below: *Lieutenant Colonel Lyle W. Bernard briefs Lieutenant General George S. Patton on the results of a daring amphibious landing behind enemy lines on Sicily's north coast in 1943. A 1933 West Point graduate, Bernard commanded the 2d Battalion, 30th Infantry, 3d Infantry Division. Road sign points to Messina, a major objective of Patton's Seventh Army. (National Archives)*

As the Allies mopped up enemy resistance in North Africa, Eisenhower had already initiated planning for the conquest of Sicily. Operation Husky began on 10 July 1943, with Patton commanding the U.S. Seventh Army and Montgomery commanding the British Eighth Army. Fighting was bitterly contested across the island, but by mid-August the Allies had emerged victorious. The campaign was far from perfect. Not only had the majority of German defenders escaped across the Straits of Messina to the Italian peninsula, but inter-Allied bickering between Patton and Montgomery resulted in two separate campaigns instead of a well-coordinated advance.

Operation Husky also served additional purposes that boded well for future campaigning. The battle-hardened 1st Infantry Division and the 82d Airborne Division gained additional combat experience that paid huge dividends in the invasion of Normandy the following spring. The campaign also portrayed Patton at his best. Displaying a characteristic dash and

genius for pursuit, Patton conducted a series of amphibious operations that captured Palermo and Messina, demonstrating that he possessed a more acute sense of operational insight than any Allied commander in the Mediterranean theater.

Omar Bradley, Eisenhower's classmate at West Point and Patton's deputy commander in North Africa, also emerged from the campaign with additional luster, when he skillfully commanded II Corps in the advance up the center of Sicily. Marshall and Eisenhower were so impressed with Bradley's command style that they appointed him to command American ground forces for the upcoming invasion of France. Last but certainly not least, the American Army came of age in Sicily. Patton's operational success and the fighting ability of the American G.I. finally earned the respect of the British Tommy and the British high command. In North Africa, the U.S. Army had been mauled and the command structure was rudimentary at best. In Sicily, the Seventh Army had beaten the strongest German divisions and closed the campaign with the impressive seizure of the principal objective on the island.

In September, the Allies invaded Italy in an attempt to knock her from the war and to attack Germany through what Churchill termed "the soft underbelly of Europe." As Montgomery invaded the toe of the Italian

Top: *The era of modern military medical treatment on the battlefield became a reality in WWII. After being wounded by shrapnel in Sicily an infantry private was quickly given an infusion of blood plasma by field medic Harvey White, on 9 August 1943. (National Archives)*

Above: *A soldier cautiously removes a German "S" Mine during the slow and agonizing campaign to dislodge the German defenders after the Salerno landing in November 1943. This particularly effective weapon was called "Bouncing Betty" by U.S. GIs because it took an upward jump into the air before exploding. (Center of Military History)*

Top: *The amphibious landing at Anzio turned into a drawn-out struggle—first to protect the tenuous hold on the beachhead, and then to launch a break-out to enable Anzio forces to link up with other Allied troops in Italy. Bitter fighting was waged at close quarters. ("Battle of the Caves," Robert Benney, Army Art Collection)*

Above: *Fighting in Italy lasted from the initial landings in November 1943 until the waning days of the war in Europe. ("Bailey's Bridge," Tom Craig, Army Art Collection)*

Right: *A soldier who has suffered facial wounds during fighting in Italy waits patiently to be evacuated from the battle area. ("High Visibility Wrap," Joseph Hirsch, Army Art Collection)*

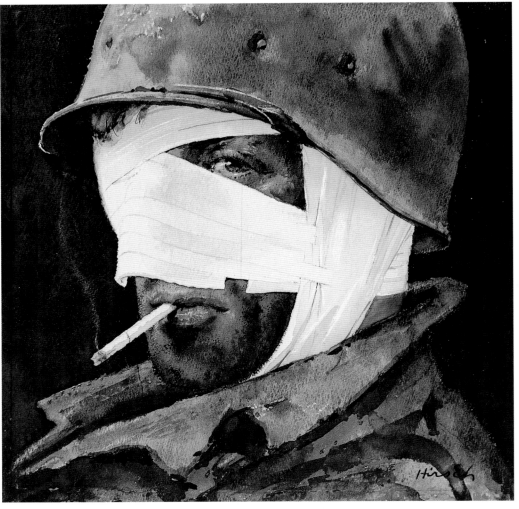

boot, Lieutenant General Mark Clark's Fifth Army assaulted the beaches of Salerno in Operation Avalanche. After two months of intense fighting, the Allied armies had only advanced to the Gustav Line, an entrenched series of fortifications 100 miles south of Rome. Fighting on the Italian peninsula soon devolved into a slugfest in which the Allies could not obtain operational mobility. Allied operations were also hampered by terrain ideally suited for defense and the lack of imagination of their own commanders.

In an attempt to outflank the *Gustav* Line, Clark ordered VI Corps commander Major General John Lucas to conduct an amphibious assault at Anzio. Without adequate support and with little tactical imagination from either Clark or Lucas, that attack bogged down and a siege followed that needlessly cost hundreds of American lives. Not until spring 1944 did the Fifth Army relieve the beleaguered defenders of the Anzio beachhead. As Lucas battled at Anzio, Clark tried a more direct approach against the German defenses. In January, he twice threw the badly depleted U.S. 36th Infantry Division against German strongpoints along the Rapido River, which anchored the Gustav Line. The enemy repulsed both attacks with such ease that their after-action reports reflected they had only encountered a diversionary attack. The 36th suffered 1,600 casualties as the Rapido ran red with American blood. Rome finally capitulated on 4 June, with the defenders simply withdrawing to new defensive works dubbed the Gothic Line in front of the Po River valley.

Mark Clark had a penchant for glory seeking and an inability to conduct sustained operations, but he also faced difficulties that were endemic to his theater alone. The Italian campaign never received top priority with respect to leadership and resources. The Allied effort was also complicated by the presence of soldiers from twenty-two Allied nations, who often were unfamiliar with Anglo-American operations. Still the cost had been excessively high. From September 1943 to May 1945 when the Germans capitulated at the base of the Alps, the Allies suffered 312,000 casualties, while inflicting 435,000 on their adversaries. It had proven to be a useful diversion of German troops from northwest Europe where the two-million-strong Allied Expeditionary Force was set to embark on a great crusade to liberate western Europe.

Of all the risks taken by General Marshall in World War II, none was bolder than the decision in midwar to maintain the Army's ground combat strength at ninety divisions. During the course of the war, the Army actually mobilized ninety-one divisions, of which eighty-nine engaged in combat. In the campaign in western Europe alone, the 2d and the 90th Infantry Divisions remained in combat in excess of 300 days. The turnover in the 4th Infantry Division that landed at Utah Beach on D-Day was 252.3 percent before the end of the war. To replenish losses that often exceeded 100–200 percent in the front line regiments, the Army relied on a controversial individual replacement system. The replacements paid the cost. Frequently, only half spent more than three days on the line before becoming casualties.

The central debate between the western Allies since the United States entered the war was the timing of the cross-channel attack. The British won the initial round with Roosevelt's agreement to commit American troops to the Mediterranean. By late 1943, however, the American preponderance of Allied military resources dictated that U.S. strategic decisions would dominate the deliberations in the Anglo-American alliance. In November 1943, Roosevelt named Dwight D. Eisenhower as Supreme Commander to command the cross-channel

All Army supplies, equipment, and rations had to be transported thousands of miles from U.S. production facilities to the front lines. Posters were frequently used to beam important messages directly to the troops. In this take-off on a more-familiar Uncle Sam poster, soldiers are reminded of the need to take care of equipment. (National Archives)

At home, civilians were learning to live and work more efficiently as more and more resources were dedicated to the war effort. Posters such as this were used to inspire the American workforce. (National Archives)

Combat paintings illustrate the drama and confusion of the most epic assault in world history. The Allied invasion of Europe on D-Day, 6 June 1944. (Above, "Rangers Lead the Way, Omaha Beach," and right, "Overlord, Utah Beach," both by James Dietz)

Opposite, top: The Army Air Force promised ground commanders air superiority on D-Day, 6 June 1944, and they came through. In preparation for the invasion, the 107th Tactical Reconnaissance Squadron, flying the F-6A, the reconnaissance version of the P-51 Mustang, flew missions over Normandy beaches. They would later be the first recon unit to operate from French soil to support the U.S. First Army. ("Mission Over Normandy," William S. Phillips, National Guard Heritage series)

invasion. Eisenhower's selection was a bitter pill for Marshall, who had hoped to command the invasion himself. Within weeks, Eisenhower arrived in England to prepare for Operation Overlord, scheduled for May 1944.

The first five months of 1944 witnessed the largest concentration of military power in history as Eisenhower prepared for the invasion. As Supreme Commander, Allied Expeditionary Force, he organized his headquarters and appointed his commanders with the approval of their national governments. Serving as ground forces commander was General Montgomery, with British Admiral Sir Bertram Ramsey and Air Marshal Tafford Leigh-Mallory commanding the maritime and air components. Commanding the First U.S. Army was Omar Bradley. As soon as the lodgment area was secured, Eisenhower intended to elevate Bradley to command 12th Army Group with Lieutenant Generals Courtney Hodges and George Patton assuming command of First and Third U.S. Armies, respectively.

In the months preceding the invasion, Eisenhower made three critical decisions that assured the success of the invasion. Against the recommendation of his Army Air Forces commanders, Ike diverted strategic air assets from bombing German industrial and oil centers to destroying the French transportation network behind the invasion beaches. Next he approved

Below: *A famous WWII photo depicts U.S. troops leaving landing craft to splash ashore at Omaha Beach on 6 June 1944. The most complex amphibious assault of all time was the first step on the long road that would be taken to overcome entrenched Axis forces and achieve the liberation of western Europe. (National Archives)*

Above: A depiction of the fierce action on the Normandy coast by an artist who was himself a World War I veteran and a one-time art student in France. ("Omaha Beach," Joseph Gary Sheahan, Army Art Collection)

Right: Shown are among the first Army nurses to arrive on Okinawa, on 3 May 1945. These experienced medical professionals were already veterans of fourteen months of service in Africa and Italy. (National Archives)

Below: On their way to St.-Lô, soldiers of the 35th Infantry Division found themselves fighting the enemy and the bocage— hedgerows—as they neared the tiny village of Saint Georges Montcocq. A bitter fight took place at Hill 192 before the 134th Infantry from Nebraska swept into the battered French city. ("From Cornrow to Hedgerow: the 134th Infantry," Keith Rocco, National Guard Heritage series)

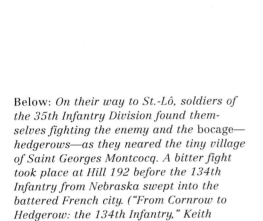

In response to the urging of French General de Gaulle, a U.S. victory parade was staged in Paris on 29 August 1944, a few days after the liberation of the French capital. Loath to spare troops needed at the front, General Eisenhower directed the 28th (Keystone) Infantry Division to march down the Champs Elysées and then move directly to join the fighting northeast of the city. (National Archives)

Bradley's recommendation for the employment of two airborne divisions, Major General Matthew Ridgway's 82d and Major General Maxwell Taylor's 101st, to secure the exits from Utah Beach. Finally, Eisenhower made the decision that he was born to make—to launch the invasion itself. Following a two-week delay to assemble additional landing craft, Ike set the date of the invasion for 5 June 1944. Inclement weather delayed the invasion an additional day, but on D-Day, 6 June 1944, the combined forces of the Allied Expeditionary Force waded ashore on the beaches of Normandy. By evening 135,000 Allies were on the continent of Europe. Allied casualties exceeded 10,000, with the majority being inflicted on "bloody Omaha," where the 1st and 29th Infantry Divisions penetrated the strongest German defenses in Normandy.

Normandy proved a killing ground for the U.S. Army, but after two months of intense and bloody combat, the Allies penetrated the German defenses in Normandy. Paris fell on 25 August, and both Bradley and

American howitzers continued to pound at the enemy retreating in Normandy. This gun crew were members of a battery in action near Carentan, France, on 11 July 1944. (National Archives)

Montgomery raced toward the Rhine. Eisenhower assumed command of all ground operations on 1 September and directed his army group commanders to advance across a broad front toward the German border. In mid-August, a third army group commanded by Lieutenant General Jacob Devers landed in southern France and joined Patton's army on 15 September, at which time Eisenhower assumed command of all Allied forces in France.

The performance of the U.S. Army in the drive to the Rhine is an epic of courage and resolve. The Allied advance slowed somewhat in September due to logistical shortfalls. The respite, along with Montgomery's failure to bridge the lower Rhine at Arnhem (Operation Market Garden), allowed the enemy to regroup. During Market Garden, Taylor's 101st Airborne Division and Brigadier General James Gavin's 82d Airborne Division fought with conspicuous gallantry. Winter found the Allies on the German frontier where they waited to recuperate from the autumn battles and to garner their strength for the final offensive.

The Germans struck first, flinging two *panzer* armies against Hodges' First Army in an attempt to seize the logistical center at Antwerp. The ensuing Battle of the Bulge was the largest battle the U.S. Army fought in World War II. From 16 December 1944 to 25 January 1945, every asset at Eisenhower's disposal was thrown into the fray. With the Allies' strategic reserves

Medics come to the aid of an injured soldier during action in France in 1944. (National Archives)

already committed and foxhole strength at dangerously low levels due to the "90-Division gamble," the American G.I. hung on by his fingernails at St.Vith and other isolated garrisons. Finally Patton's Third Army relieved the defenders of Bastogne the day after Christmas. The fighting did not cease there as it took an additional three weeks to eradicate German resistance in the Bulge. The American Army suffered in excess of 70,000 casualties in the month-long ordeal.

Having expended their last reserves in the Ardennes offensive, the Third Reich was powerless to halt the Anglo-American advance. With Soviet forces inside the German border in the east, Eisenhower launched his final offensive in the west in early spring. Hodges' 1st Army was first across the

Top, left: Parachutes fill the sky as far as the eye can see as waves of airborne troops land in Holland during Operation Market Garden. Two U.S. airborne divisions, the 82d and 101st, took part in air assault as part of the First Allied Airborne Army under the command of U.S. Lieutenant General Lewis H. Brereton. (National Archives)

Top, right: Brigadier General Anthony C. McAuliffe, then artillery commander, 101st Airborne Division, issued last-minute instructions to glider pilots before the launch of Market Garden, initiated on 17 September 1944—a daylight airborne assault designed to secure routes of advance for British armored columns. (National Archives)

Above: During the battle and long afterwards, Army medics brought casualties out of the lines under trying and hazardous conditions. ("Night Shift," Joseph Hirsch, Army Art Collection)

Left: The newly arrived 75th Division was rushed to the front as the Battle of the Bulge reached a climax. They relieved the 82d Airborne Division near the Salm River, Belgium, during the first week of January 1945. Men of the 290th Infantry Regiment found themselves dealing with a fresh snowfall as they took up positions and readied to go on the offensive. (National Archives)

Opposite: Supply personnel of a U.S. infantry unit pitch in to unload desperately needed rations and re-supply of ammunition in the rear of a front-line unit. Truck columns earned fame as the "Red Ball Express," a name that became familiar to combat troops at the end of the supply line. ("The Red Ball Express," H. Charles McBarron, The American Soldier series, Army Art Collection)

Above: *On 13 January 1945, the 87th Infantry Division, on the attack after the Battle of the Bulge, reached the Ourthe river. Before pressing on into Luxembourg, members of the 347th Infantry Regiment paused briefly for rations before continuing on to La Roche. (National Archives)*

Below: *The long-anticipated crossing of the Rhine River came about unexpectedly on 7 March 1945, the result of aggressive reconnaissance by infantrymen of the 9th Armored Division who elatedly reported they found a bridge intact—the Ludendorff Bridge at Remagen. U.S. troops seized it and used it to good advantage until it finally collapsed. (H. Charles McBarron, Army in Action series, Army Art Collection)*

Rhine in early March, quickly followed by the remainder of Bradley's army group and Montgomery's 21st Army Group in the north. Now in the exploitative phase, the Allies bagged 300,000 German prisoners in the Ruhr pocket and organized resistance came to a swift end. On 7 May, the Third Reich ceased to exist as the German High Command surrendered unconditionally to the members of the Grand Alliance. The war in Europe was over.

In the Pacific, World War II continued with unabated intensity. As Nimitz drove across the central Pacific in accordance with War Plan

Orange, MacArthur prepared to fulfill his pledge to the Philippines. Having secured the southward passages to the islands, MacArthur landed at Leyte in October 1944. The Japanese defenders fought with a frenzy not yet seen in the Pacific war. The Imperial Japanese Navy marshaled its remaining battlefleet and was obliterated in the Battle of Leyte Gulf. Meanwhile the strategic bombing campaign wrought destruction against the Japanese home islands as the XXI Bomber Command took advantage of bases in the Marianas to launch continuous attacks against Japanese cities.

Following the conquest of Leyte, MacArthur launched his main attack against Luzon on 9 January 1945 with Krueger's Sixth Army,

Top: Eerily reminiscent of scenes in France at the end of WWI, badly damaged German towns were awaiting the arrival of victorious U.S. forces in the early spring of 1945. An anonymous Army medic noted: "All [the] wreckage around us was little enough compensation for the human wreckage we hauled back and forth." (National Archives)

Opposite, bottom right: Battered and besieged Bastogne became a symbol of determination as encircled U.S. forces held the town in spite of intense efforts by the Germans to take it. Here, the 4th Armored Division moves to relieve the American forces at Bastogne on 27 December 1944. (National Archives)

Left: As Eisenhower's forces rebounded after the Bulge, advancing First Army troops seized the vital German communications center at St. Vith, Belgium, in late January 1945. Soon U.S. troops would be crossing into Germany and taking the battle to the enemy, who would fight the remainder of the war on their own soil. (National Archives)

along with Eichelberger's Eighth Army as a follow-on force. Krueger secured Manila on 27 February, but the Philippine capital lay in ruins. An estimated 100,000 Filipino civilians died in the rubble. The campaign on Luzon continued to the end of the war, although MacArthur declared the archipelago secure on 4 July 1945. American casualties during six months of combat on Luzon numbered 8,140 killed and 29,557 wounded, with non-battle casualties proportionately higher. In turn the U.S. Army inflicted losses of 173,563 dead and 7,297 wounded on its enemy.

As the Philippine campaign reached its end, the United States launched its final offensive of the Pacific war. On 1 April 1945, American land, sea, and air forces under the overall command of Admiral Raymond

A. Spruance invaded Okinawa, only 350 miles from the Japanese home islands. Lieutenant General Simon Bolivar Buckner, commander of the U.S. Tenth Army, commanded the ground forces, which included seven combat-experienced divisions in two combat corps, the all-Marine III Amphibious

Above: In one of the critical Central Pacific campaigns where Army men fought under Admiral Chester Nimitz, infantrymen of the 7th Infantry Division employed flamethrowers to smoke out Japanese manning a block house. Riflemen readied themselves to engage enemy soldiers who might emerge. Action was during the U.S. assault on Kwajalein in the Marshall Islands. (National Archives)

Left: In the spring of 1945, even after the fall of Manila, U.S. forces continued in pursuit of determined Japanese defenders on the island of Luzon. The veteran 158th Regimental Combat Team, an Arizona National Guard unit, withstood a number of Banzai counter-attacks and overcame the enemy's resistance in the late spring of 1945. (Army in Action series/National Guard Heritage series)

Opposite, top: In a moment that captures the classic infantry leader's command, the colorful Colonel Aubrey S. "Red" Newman moves off the Leyte, Philippines, beachhead with his regiment, the 34th Infantry of the Army's 24th Infantry Division, on 20 October 1944. Newman was a 1925 graduate from West Point an Olympic athlete in 1928. ("Follow Me!" H. Charles McBarron, Army in Action series, Army Art Collection)

Top: *Four days before the official end of the Okinawa campaign, Lieutenant General Simon B. Buckner, commander of the U.S. Tenth Army, was killed by enemy shellfire. He was observing an attack at a forward observation post of the Sixth Marine Division. Buckner was killed a few moments after this picture was taken. (National Archives)*

Top, right: *A difficult moment during the fighting on Leyte, and a scene repeated many times in many different places as an American GI comes to the aid of a wounded child. ("Soldier Carrying Wounded Child," Paul Sample, Army Art Collection)*

Above: *Men of the 77th Infantry Division prepare to advance, with the assistance of armored battalions, against the heavily defended Escarpment near Kakazu Ridge during the battle for Okinawa in the spring of 1945. By this time troops had learned of President Roosevelt's death but knew little about their new commander-in-chief, former Vice President Harry Truman. (National Archives)*

Above, right: *As casualties mounted on Okinawa, the campaign was further impeded by flooding and mud. Conditions during this period can be seen in this photo of 77th Infantry Division soldiers trudging toward the front past bogged-down, mud-clogged tanks. (National Archives)*

Opposite, top: *An Army nurse makes a lonely round of her ward in a Pacific location where patients slumbered under mosquito netting to ward off rampant dangers of malaria and dengue fever. ("Night Duty," Franklin Boggs, Army Art Collection)*

Corps, and the XXIV Army Corps of four divisions under Major General John R. Hodge. Landing without opposition, Buckner hoped for an easy victory. Once ashore, Tenth Army encountered the most elaborate defense the Japanese had devised during the entire war. Okinawa witnessed war in its most hellish form. To clear caves, the attackers used what Buckner described as his "blowtorch and corkscrew" method. Tank-infantry teams drilled holes in cave roofs and then used phosphorus grenades to ignite gasoline or napalm poured through the crevices.

Okinawa was the only Pacific campaign that took the lives of both opposing commanding officers. While visiting a forward observation post on 18 June, Buckner was killed by a shell fragment. His adversary, Lieutenant General Mitsuru Ushijima, committed ritual suicide, *seppuku*, as the Americans approached his command bunker. Okinawa was finally secured on 22 June after eighty-three days of combat. Total American casualties were enormous, including 12,500 dead or missing and 36,631 wounded. Of the total, Tenth Army endured 4,582 killed, 93 missing, and 18,099 wounded. Considering the high casualties on both Iwo Jima and Okinawa, it was no wonder that President Harry Truman considered an alternative to invading the home islands.

Above: *On 15 August 1945 General Douglas MacArthur was appointed Supreme Commander for Allied Powers. In this capacity he orchestrated the details of the Japanese surrender in formal ceremonies on board the* USS Missouri *in Tokyo Bay on 2 September 1945. At attention behind MacArthur, Lieutenant Generals Jonathan Wainwright (U.S.) and A.E. Percival (British), who spent war years as prisoners of Japan. (National Archives)*

Left: *Raising the U.S. flag during a field ceremony on Corregidor in 1945 symbolized "the end of organized resistance." After intensive "mopping up," on Okinawa, the campaign in the Ryukyus was declared over on 2 July 1945. The price for Okinawa was high—total battle casualties were the highest of any Pacific battle—49,151—of which 12,520 were killed or missing and 36,661 wounded. There were over 25,000 non-battle casualties. It was later reported that President Truman, in reviewing plans for the invasion of Japan, told military leaders he did not want "another Okinawa." (National Archives)*

The alternative took the shape of the greatest technological discovery in the twentieth century, the harnessing of atomic power. Since the beginning of the war, American scientists under the supervision of J. Robert Oppenheimer and Army Brigadier General Leslie Groves worked on the Manhattan Project. On 16 July 1945, the team exploded a prototype atomic device at Alamogordo, New Mexico. The test was successful and Truman made the decision to use the atomic bomb against Japan at first opportunity. The task fell to Colonel Paul Tibbetts, commander of the 509th Bombardment Group (Composite). On the morning of 6 August, Tibbetts piloted the *Enola Gay* and delivered the atomic bomb to Hiroshima. Three days later, Major Charles Sweeney, piloting *Bock's Car*, dropped a second atomic weapon on Nagasaki. On 14 August, Japan accepted the Potsdam Declaration, thereby ending the Pacific war. General of the Army Douglas MacArthur received the Japanese surrender aboard the *USS Missouri* in Tokyo Bay on 2 September 1945. The most devastating war in history was over.

At the close of the war, the United States Army was the most powerful it had ever been. Its numbers had risen to 8,250,000 and its members had defeated skilled adversaries with far more combat experience. Much of the credit belonged to Marshall, whom Winston Churchill named the "true organizer of victory." But it is not only Marshall who must receive credit for the ultimate victory. With few exceptions, the Army's commanders displayed a tenacity most thought impossible had one observed the field force on the eve of the war. The United States emerged victorious because of its citizen soldier, airman, and sailor. Born in the immediate aftermath of World War I, they survived the Great Depression and answered their country's summons when totalitarianism and fascism threatened the world. Although Marshall was writing to Eisenhower, he could have just as easily been describing the American G.I. when he stated: "You have made history, great history for the good of mankind." For the soldier in the trenches and the jungles, Marshall's words became their final bequest.

Opposite: The potential of "another Okinawa"—in terms of casualties—was rendered moot with President Truman's decision to order the Army Air Forces to proceed with the delivery of the atomic bombs—the first at Hiroshima and the second (photo) at Nagasaki on 6 and 9 August 1945. Soon after, the Japanese government agreed to unconditional surrender. The war in the Pacific—indeed World War II—was over. (National Archives)

Following the safe arrival in Japan of troops flown in from Okinawa and the Philippines by air transport, additional divisions and support for Occupation forces poured into the Japanese homeland aboard naval vessels. U.S. and Japanese photographers were waiting to record the unopposed landing of the 81st Infantry Division at Aomori, Honshu, where the scene might have been very different. (National Archives)

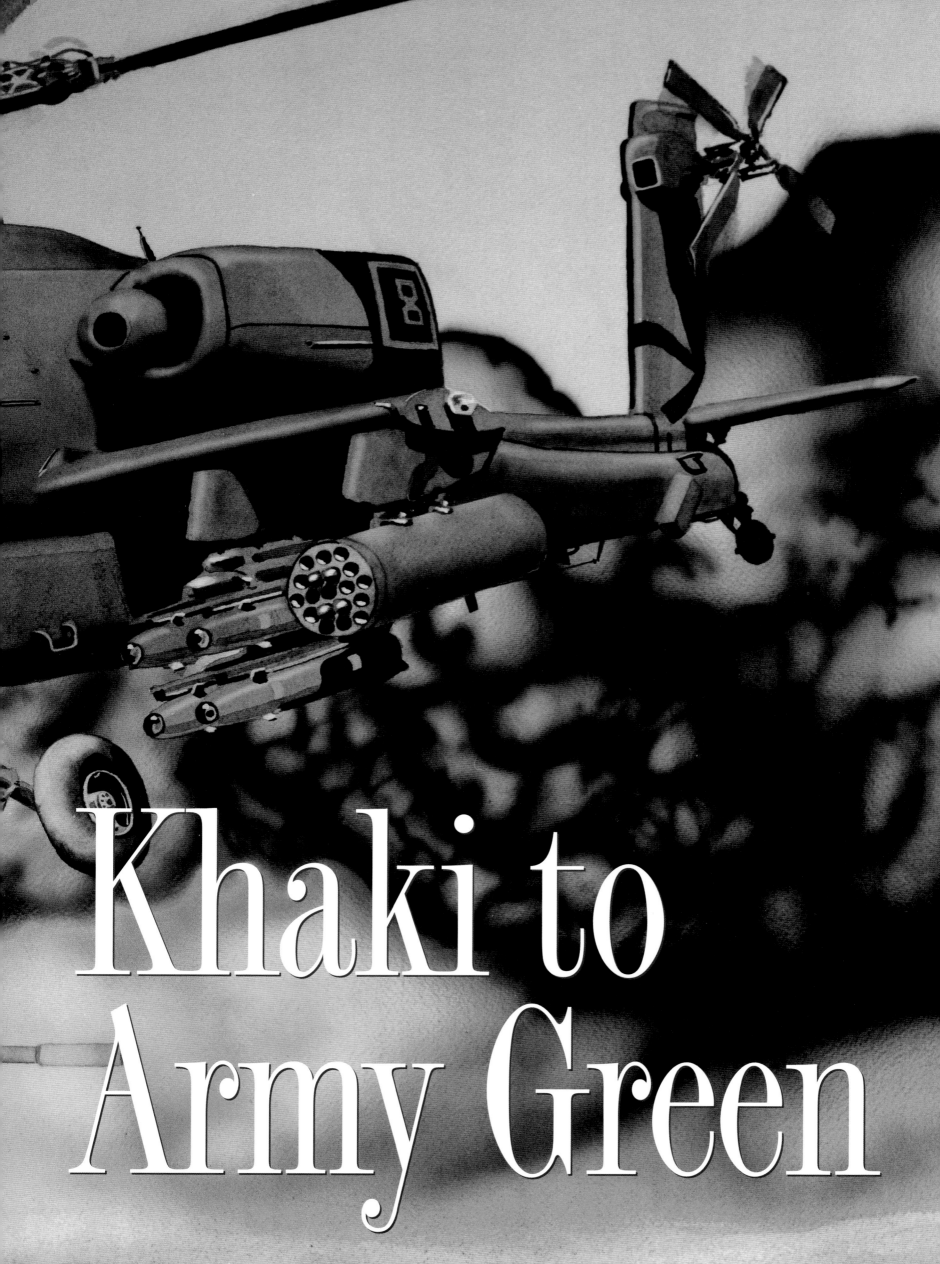

Khaki to Army Green

ACEVEDO 91

Khaki to Army Green

Lewis Sorley

The Cold War Context

The respite from military concerns following World War II proved brief. Challenges to the security of western Europe from the Soviet Union and states under its domination became apparent even before hostilities ceased, and in 1949 a new defensive alliance designated the North Atlantic Treaty Organization (NATO) was formed to counter that threat.

Initially comprising fifteen nations, including the United States, it soon began to put in place a deterrent military force along the eastern frontier of occupied West Germany. Thus began a long period of tension and danger, extending nearly an incredible half-century, known as the Cold War.

From the beginning, elements of the United States Army occupied a central role. The U.S. army of occupation stationed in Germany was the basis on which the American contribution to NATO military forces was built, and as early as 1949 the 1st Infantry Division was more concerned with the deterrence mission than with occupation duties.

243

Top: *Americans were proud of their Cold War armed forces, many of them famous veteran outfits such as the 18th Infantry Regiment, which traced its lineage to the outbreak of the American Civil War. Renowned artists such as cartoonist Milton Caniff, creator of "Terry and the Pirates," lent their talents to portraying the soldiers. ("Colors and Drums," Milton Caniff, The Company of Military Historians)*

Top, right: *The Cold War "Iron Curtain" brought down by the Soviets across Europe was dramatically apparent along West Germany's borders with East Germany and Czechoslovakia. At points where armed patrols from each side came in contact, tensions sometimes came to a head, as was the case on 27 October 1961. ("Standoff at Checkpoint Charlie," Don Stivers)*

Opposite, top: *Two cultures met in the Republic of Korea, where U.S. soldiers have been stationed from the end of World War II to the present day, advising the South Koreans, fighting alongside them during the Korean War (1950–1953), and cooperating in the common defense thereafter. ("Seoul Street Scene," Steven R. Kidd, Army Art Collection)*

Opposite, bottom: *U.S. troops arriving by rail at points in Korea early in the war often moved directly into combat. U.S. divisions brought from Japan that had been organized at two-thirds strength, were augmented by provisional units formed virtually on the march and shipped from the United States. (U.S. Army Center of Military History)*

Right: *The 4th Armored Division, a lead element of General Patton's Third Army during World War II in Europe, subsequently formed part of the U.S. Army's Cold War forces stationed in Germany. Troops manning self-propelled artillery pieces, tanks, and armored personnel carriers were familiar sights on Germany's cobblestone streets for half a century. (U.S. Army Military History Institute)*

Army elements stationed in Germany, backed by support units and facilities throughout western Europe, grew to a powerful and modern force consisting of an army of two corps and four armored and mechanized divisions, . During the years 1945–1995 the Army provided the bulk of the sixteen million troops, civilian employees, and families who were at one time or another stationed with the U.S. forces in Germany.

The Army, along with the other services, underwent a significant change in status with enactment of the National Security Act of 1949. That measure created the Department of Defense and subordinated to it the separate departments of the Army, Navy, and Air Force which had previously been executive departments in their own right. In addition, the position of Chairman of the Joint Chiefs of Staff was created separate from the heads of the individual services who served as members of the Joint Chiefs of Staff. The Army and the other services lost substantial autonomy.

The Korean War: 1950-1953

On 25 June 1950 war erupted not in Europe, but in Korea. Six divisions of the North Korean People's Army, aided by surprise, and robust in artillery, supported by Russian-built combat aircraft, and led by T-34 tanks, swept across the 38th parallel, the military demarcation line between North and South Korea established at the end of World War II, and drove south. South Korea, unprepared and surprised by this onslaught, found its lightly armed forces reeling backward in confusion and disarray.

Above: *Despite being understrength, inadequately trained, and equipped with obsolete and poorly maintained equipment, American forces rushed to South Korea from Japan and the United States conducted a stubborn defense in the Pusan perimeter. Concluded historian Russell Weigley, "In establishing the Pusan perimeter General Walton Walker exhibited generalship of the highest order." As the forces built up, they went over to the offensive and, in coordination with the daring landings at Inchon, drove North Korea's forces from the south. ("The American Soldier, 1950," Charles H. McBarron, Army Art Collection)*

245

Having driven across the 38th parallel and north to the Yalu River, U.N. forces were forced to fall back in late 1950 after large numbers of Chinese troops entered the war. These American soldiers used Korean A-frames to carry loads during withdrawal from P'yongyang in December. (U.S. Army Center of Military History)

Opposite: *In Korea's rugged terrain and harsh weather, troop movements were often difficult. These soldiers used tanks and a cow converted to pack duty as they moved through Waegwan in 1950. The Sherman M4A3 tank of World War II vintage again saw service in Korea. (U.S. Army Center of Military History)*

Right: *An artillery battery provides support to infantry positioned forward in the Korean hills. Even under such strenuous conditions, heavy winter dress is needed against the brutal Korean winters. (U.S. Army Reserve painting)*

President Harry S. Truman stood up to be counted. In the wake of a United Nations resolution condemning North Korea's aggression and authorizing a U.N. force to help South Korea defend itself, Truman ordered U.S. forces to Korea. The Army bore the brunt of this intervention. And, it also turned out, it was not prepared. The first forces dispatched were Army troops from Japan, where under the overall command of General Douglas MacArthur they had been allowed to reach a low state of readiness, in large measure due to budget restrictions.

The U.S. Eighth Army, MacArthur's principal ground force, consisted of four understrength divisions. Regiments normally authorized three battalions had only two, and overall units were at less than 70 percent of full strength. The weaponry in the hands of these troops was mostly left over from World War II. In some instances these weapons were already obsolete and in other instances unserviceable due to maintenance deficiencies. Insufficient training left these formations far from combat ready.

Nevertheless these forces were hastily thrown into battle on the Korean peninsula, going into position initially in a rapidly shrinking perimeter above Pusan in the southeastern corner of South Korea. On 2 July, only a week after the invasion began, elements of the 24th Infantry Division arrived in Korea. The lead element, a reinforced company of the 21st Infantry designated Task Force Smith, went forward to make contact with the enemy. It was slammed into by an entire enemy division with some thirty tanks. Hanging on doggedly in spite of the odds, T. F. Smith delayed the enemy advance for several hours before being overwhelmed by superior numbers and weaponry.

In short order the 25th Infantry Division reached Korea, followed by the 1st Cavalry Division. The Eighth Army commander, Lieutenant General Walton H. Walker, had three understrength American divisions and five ROK divisions to maneuver, and the situation began to stabilize. In early August more U.S. forces, including the 2d Infantry Division, the 1st Marine Brigade, and the 5th Regimental Combat Team, augmented the

Above: *Troops of the 31st Regimental Combat Team, 7th Infantry Division, employ a 75mm recoilless rifle in fighting near Oet'ook-tong, Korea, in June 1951. While the war of large-scale thrusts and counterthrusts died down after the first year of the war, troops still faced hard fighting in thousands of local actions. (U.S. Army Military History Institute)*

U.N. forces. So desperate was the equipment situation that in the United States armored vehicles on display were taken down and reconditioned, after which these "monument tanks" were rushed to the battlefield.

By September the United Nations forces had established the Pusan perimeter, a defensive position at the southern end of the Korean peninsula. Walker was able to stem the enemy's advances and build up manpower and logistical strength while planning a counteroffensive. His forces made

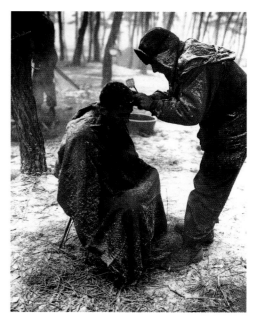

a spectacular breakout, in tandem with a daring U.N. amphibious landing at Inchon, west of Seoul, on 15 September.

Thrusting his units ashore, MacArthur drove a wedge into the flank of the enemy positions, far to their rear, unhinging and quickly routing the North Korean forces. Almost simultaneously the forces massed at Pusan drove northward. Within a matter of days the entire tactical situation reversed, with U.N. forces liberating Seoul and driving northward across the 38th parallel.

At this point the United States decided on a fateful change in objectives. Rather than settle for having restored the northern border of the Republic of Korea, President Truman authorized continuation of the advance into North Korea. General MacArthur had assured the president that Communist China would not enter the war, and that if the Chinese did become involved he would destroy their forces with air power. By late October U.N. forces had decimated North Korean forces, occupied their capital city of Pyongyang and, in bitter weather, driven farther north toward the Yalu River border with China.

249

Above: *The intensity and destructiveness of the fighting in Korea were apparent as men and tanks of the 17th Regimental Combat Team, 7th Infantry Division, moved through the streets of Hyesanjin near the Manchurian border in November 1950. (U.S. Army Military History Institute)*

Right: *A U.S. soldier, his caliber .30 M1 rifle at hand, eases his tired feet in a helmet footbath while catching up on his reading. (U.S. Army Center of Military History)*

Below: *Lieutenant General Matthew B. Ridgway took command of a dispirited Eighth Army in December 1950, and by force of personality and hard-driving personal example, restored its fighting spirit. Here Ridgway inspects front-line operations of the 27th Infantry Regiment in March 1951. (U.S. Army Military History Institute)*

250

MacArthur was wrong in both his predictions. On the night of 25 November, eighteen previously hidden Communist Chinese divisions struck the U.N. forces "a stunning blow," forcing withdrawals all along the line.

Bitter rearguard actions were fought in harsh winter conditions at such places as the Kunu-ri and and the Chosin Reservoir. Endless columns of civilian refugees streamed south, perhaps two million in all, further complicating military operations. Eventually General Walker managed to hold defensive positions south of the 38th parallel. On 23 December, however, General Walker was killed in a traffic accident. Lieutenant General Matthew B. Ridgway replaced him as commander of Eighth Army.

Ridgway's impact on his new command, symbolized by the names of the offensive operations he quickly mounted—Thunderbolt, Killer, Ripper— was dramatic. Leading from the front, he set about restructuring the outlook of his subordinates, beginning with his own staff. "There will be no more discussion of retreat," he ordered. "We're going back!" Harold K. Johnson, a regimental commander who later became Army Chief of Staff,

Top, left: *U.S. troops move through mountain terrain typical of Korea's ruggedness and desolation. (U.S. Army Center of Military History)*

Above: *Harsh weather conditions, including snow and sub-zero temperatures, compounded the misery experienced by the Korean War soldiers. (National Archives)*

Above, right: *Airborne soldiers, who made some of the most dramatic history of World War II, continued in service during the Korean War, where the 187th Airborne Regimental Combat Team deployed, and beyond. (U.S. Army Center of Military History)*

recalled Ridgway spoke to leaders down through company commander. "The sheer force of his own personality turned the situation in Korea. A retreating, despondent, defeated army was turned around by the power of the personality of its commander." Eighth Army forced the Chinese back north above the 38th parallel and then, as resistance stiffened, set up defensive lines.

Right: *The artist described these Korean War soldiers, who in isolated squads of the lead platoon had fought their way to the summit under small-arms fire, as depicted in silhouette as they aimed their rifles down the other side. ("From the Crest of Hill 233," Howard Brodie, "Drawing Fire: A Combat Artist at War")*

Above: *Enemy forces invading South Korea included T-34 tanks. As U.N. forces built up for the counteroffensive, U.S. tanks provided striking power and shock effect. In the drive north from the Pusan perimeter the 70th Tank Battalion led the 1st Cavalry Division, covering 106 miles in 11 hours to a link-up north of Osan. Such successes led Russell Weigley to observe: "I think we exaggerated the extent to which the mountainous terrain militated against the use of armor." ("Korea," T. H. Jackson, Army Art Collection)*

MacArthur had argued for taking the war to China in public statements and correspondence despite President Truman's having ruled that out. There came a point at which Truman could no longer tolerate such insubordination, and in mid-April 1951, MacArthur was relieved of his command, brought home, and retired. Ridgway was elevated to Commander in Chief, Far East, and General James A. Van Fleet took command of

Left: *An artist's depiction of operations on 14 February 1951 reveals the intensity of fighting as dug-in U.S. units, supported by armor, struggle to repulse successive "human wave" attacks by enemy forces. ("First Victory," James Dietz)*

253

Right: *Multiple rocket launchers in action in the 40th Infantry Division sector, Korea, 26 November 1951. (National Archives)*

Above: *Troopers of the 187th Airborne Regimental Combat Team make a practice jump from C-119 "Flying Boxcars." (U.S. Army Center of Military History)*

Above: *A Korean War helicopter ambulance with two patients aboard lifts off from a 7th Infantry Division collecting station in August 1952. (U.S. Army Military History Institute)*

Right: *North Korean prisoners, clad in their distinctive padded uniforms, are brought in by U.S. soldiers. (U.S. Army Center of Military History)*

Opposite, bottom left: *Members of the 24th Infantry Regiment's Intelligence & Reconnaissance Platoon proudly display their Combat Infantryman Badges, Korea, May 1951. (U.S. Army Military History Institute)*

Opposite, bottom right: *Soldiers of the 351st Infantry Regiment, part of the force garrisoning what was then the Free Territory of Trieste, model uniforms they wore in 1951. (The Company of Military Historians)*

Eighth Army. Secretary of State Dean Acheson remarked in his memoirs, "While General MacArthur was fighting the Pentagon, General Ridgway was fighting the enemy."

Over the next two years, while negotiations for a peace settlement dragged on without resolution, the fighting continued, characterized by a long series of limited but intense and bloody battles. Losses were even heavier during this phase than during the first year of mobile warfare. An armistice was finally signed on 27 July 1953.

Reserve forces made an important contribution during this conflict, with eight National Guard divisions called into active service, two of which, the 40th and 45th, deployed to fight in the front lines in Korea. Many individuals were also called up for service, including nearly a quarter million from the Army Reserve.

Technologically, the helicopter came into battlefield prominence for the first time during the Korean War. Rapid casualty evacuation enabled many more wounded men to quickly reach field hospitals and get the emergency care that enabled them to survive. Better antitank weapons also entered the inventory during these years.

Racial integration of the Army took place during the Korean War, first as a combat necessity and then more generally in response to President Truman's directive. Subsequently the Army led the way in American society in providing opportunities to move up on the basis of demonstrated ability and commitment, a work environment that attracted many ambitious young men and women of whatever race.

Top: *Cannoneers of the 300th Armored Field Artillery Battalion, Wyoming Army National Guard, fire in support of the 2d Infantry Division in a fierce seven-day battle against attacking Chinese forces in May 1951, an action for which the battalion was awarded a Presidential Unit Citation. ("Cowboy Artillery at Soyang," Mort Künstler, National Guard Heritage series)*

Above: *The battlefield potential of helicopters first began to be realized during the Korean War, when medical evacuation flights greatly reduced the time needed to get casualties to treatment facilities, with consequent saving of lives. Early versions carried litter patients in externally mounted pods. (U.S. Army Center of Military History)*

255

Above: *Corporal Edward Reynolds, a radio operator with the 7th Infantry Regiment, is depicted pinned down by enemy fire during combat in Korea, in 1951. ("300 Radio Operator," Howard Brodie, "Drawing Fire: A Combat Artist at War")*

Right: *The loader protects his ears as his gunner fires a 57mm recoilless rifle at an enemy position in Korea. (U.S. Army Center of Military History)*

On Hill 233 in Korea four GIs retrieve the body of their platoon leader, shot in fighting two days earlier. ("Bringing Back the Dead," Howard Brodie, "Drawing Fire: A Combat Artist at Work")

In this difficult, protracted conflict in miserable weather and rugged terrain, the Army suffered the majority of the nearly 37,000 American dead. That sacrifice was honored in the motto adopted for Korean War commemoration a half-century later: "Freedom Is Not Free."

Post-Korean War Drawdown

General of the Army Dwight D. Eisenhower campaigned for president on a promise to end the war in Korea. Soon after his inauguration in January 1953 he moved to do so, and in July of that year, concluding two years of negotiations, a peace agreement was signed. Army forces, including the 1st Cavalry and 7th Infantry Divisions, remained in the Republic of Korea as insurance against renewed hostilities, a commitment that would endure for decades to come.

However, contrary to the expectations of the Army from which he had come, Eisenhower proved to be a president under whom life was very hard for the soldier. Early on Eisenhower committed his administration to a nuclear-based deterrence strategy giving prominence to those services primarily equipped to deliver nuclear weapons, the Air Force and the Navy. "More bang for the buck" was the catch phrase for this approach, and it left the Army scrambling for a mission and the resources to carry it out.

General Maxwell D. Taylor, Army Chief of Staff during 1955–1959, retired to write an influential book, *The Uncertain Trumpet*, detailing the problems he perceived with such an approach. Setting forth a proposed alternative, Taylor wrote that "the national military program of flexible response should contain at the outset an unqualified renunciation of reliance on the strategy of massive retaliation." In the succeeding administration of President John F. Kennedy, Taylor was recalled to serve in a series of key assignments, while his views influenced Kennedy and Secretary of Defense Robert S. McNamara to give renewed prominence to modern and effective ground forces.

A Forward-Deployed Army, Deterrence and New Ideas

During the 1950s and 1960s the Army evolved into a globally deployed force. New and greatly improved tanks and armored personnel carriers were among the new combat systems fielded during these years. The Army's conventional weaponry was also augmented by a range of tactical nuclear weapons, including cannon artillery and rockets, along with atomic demolitions.

President John F. Kennedy, accompanied by General James K. Polk, reviews troops of the 1st Infantry Division stationed in Germany. (U.S. Army Military History Institute)

Troops of the 40th Infantry Division pack up in preparation for withdrawal from Heartbreak Ridge, Korea. (U.S. Army Center of Military History)

Besides a residual force of two reinforced divisions securing a demilitarized zone in the Republic of Korea, the forces committed to NATO in Europe grew to five divisions with a robust supporting infrastructure. Annual exercises—called "REFORGER," signifying "Return of Forces to Germany"—demonstrated the capability of U.S.-based elements to deploy rapidly to Europe, take up prepositioned equipment, and move out to augment the forces already in place. Additional troops were positioned in many other overseas locations, to include Japan, Okinawa, and Panama. In a radical departure from pre-World War II practice, the United States was maintaining in "peacetime" a large standing army. The threat of communist expansion was the precipitating factor.

Experimentation with new divisional structures, development of atomic artillery, early versions of air cavalry concepts, and other innovations meant that the Army that would fight in Vietnam was beginning to take shape during these years.

Top, left: Specially selected military policemen performed postwar duty in Korea, in 1970. ("Six Foot Minimum," William H. Steel, Army Art Collection)

Top, center: Warrant officer pilots were an important part of Army aviation units deployed in Korea, here in 1992. ("Awaiting Clearance," Brian Fairchild, Army Art Collection)

Top, right: Scout dogs and their handlers augmented security in the 2d Infantry Division, Korea, in 1970. ("Alert," David Grinstein, Army Art Collection)

Stockpiled M113 armored personnel carriers await shipment to Europe for the winter 1986 version of REFORGER, a periodic exercise demonstrating the capability for rapid reinforcement of U.S. forces in Germany. (U.S. Army Military History Institute)

Above: *A historic occasion as the Army fired the first atomic artillery shell at Frenchman's Flat, Nevada, on 23 May 1953. (U.S. Army Center of Military History)*

Above: *During the 1950s the Army developed new weaponry, especially in the field of missiles and rockets, and experimented with futuristic devices. Here an Honest John free-flight artillery rocket is loaded onto its launching platform. (U.S. Army Center of Military History)*

Right: *An experimental one-man helicopter is flight tested in 1957. (U.S. Army Center of Military History)*

Below: *First firing test of the Lance ballistic missile. (U.S. Army Center of Military History)*

Civil Rights Duty: 1957 and After

In the United States, Army forces—both active and those of the National Guard—found themselves frequently deployed to keep the peace, or restore it, during a series of civil rights crises. In September 1957 President Eisenhower sent the 101st Airborne Division to Little Rock, Arkansas, to maintain order during racial integration of the city's public school system. Army troops performed similar duties at the University of Mississippi when that institution was integrated in 1962, assisting federal marshals overwhelmed by unruly crowds. When widespread urban rioting erupted during these turbulent years, active Army and Army National Guard troops restored calm in the streets of Washington, Newark, Detroit, Baltimore, Chicago, and other major cities.

At the same time, the "Space Age" was in its infancy, with the Army playing an important role right from the start. The first U.S. Satellite, *Explorer I*, launched in 1958, was designed and developed by the U.S. Army.

Early Vietnam Commitments

Army involvement in perhaps the most traumatic major event of the century, the war in Vietnam, also began in the 1950s with the assignment to South Vietnam of American advisors and other specialists. In 1955, when the United States took over from the French responsibility for training and mentoring South Vietnam's Army, a Military Assistance Advisory Group was established. The modest initial commitment of advisors grew dramatically, especially after President John F. Kennedy took office in 1961.

Kennedy named Robert S. McNamara as Secretary of Defense, and General Maxwell D. Taylor as Military Representative of the President. In short order steps were being taken to restore the balance between conventional and nuclear forces about which Taylor had written, along with a new emphasis on "special warfare" or unconventional forces as represented by the Army's Green Berets.

During 1964 the situation in South Vietnam became increasingly difficult, with the prospect that defeat was probable without significant reinforcement of the Republic of Vietnam Armed Forces (RVNAF).

In May 1965 the Army's 173d Airborne Brigade deployed to Vietnam. Then, on 28 July, President Lyndon Johnson announced deployment

Below: *President John F. Kennedy strongly advocated development of increased unconventional warfare and counterinsurgency capabilities. In October 1961 he conferred with Brigadier General William P. Yarborough at the U.S. Army's Special Warfare Center, Fort Bragg, North Carolina. (U.S. Army Center of Military History)*

Bottom: *The helicopter came into its own during the Vietnam War, performing roles as gunship, troop carrier, aerial artillery, ambulance, command post, flying crane, resupply vehicle, communications relay, among many others. (U.S. Army Center of Military History)*

Top: *A combat artist's portrayal captures the feel of a solitary soldier in the jungle terrain so typical of much of South Vietnam. ("Machine Gunner in the Afternoon," Roger Blum, Army Art Collection)*

Above: *Patrolling riflemen of the 173d Airborne Brigade, armed with the M16 rifle developed for the Vietnam War, advance through a clearing in the jungle. In May 1965 the 173d was the first major Army ground unit deployed to Vietnam. (U.S. Army Center of Military History)*

of 50,000 more troops to Vietnam, for a total of 125,000, and indicated that in the future more might be needed. Thus began a process that, when it reached the high water mark in April 1969, would see U.S. forces in Vietnam peak at 543,400 men.

Dominican Republic Intervention

Even as these events were unfolding, another Army commitment, this one closer to home, was underway. In late April 1965, concerned that a revolution in the Dominican Republic endangered U.S. citizens there, and more broadly that it might bring to power a hostile communist government, President Lyndon Johnson ordered U.S. forces to intervene. Lieutenant General Bruce Palmer, Jr., was given command of a force composed primarily of the 82d Airborne Division. In the Dominican Republic Palmer, who would subsequently serve in Vietnam and then as Army Vice Chief of Staff, formed a close professional relationship with Ambassador Ellsworth Bunker, the U.S. representative to the Organization of American States. Together the two engineered a remarkable feat, a peaceful settlement of a civil war.

Reserve Call-Up Denied

When President Johnson revealed that he had ordered deployment of significant U.S. ground forces to Vietnam, it was anticipated within the armed forces that he would also announce a call-up of reserve forces. Instead, contrary to all expectations, Johnson declined to do so. This was a real bombshell, since all contingency plans for operations of this magnitude had been premised on access to the Army Reserve and the Army National Guard. And, since the Office of the Secretary of Defense had approved all those plans, availability of reserves was not even thought to be in question.

Instead of being able to draw on the experience and capabilities of the long-nurtured reserve forces, the active Army had to make up out of whole cloth many of the types of units required for Vietnam. Deprived of the resources in leadership, manpower, and equipment of its reserve forces, the Army saw greatly increased turbulence and a progressive decrease in the experience and maturity of its leadership, especially among sergeants and junior officers. Despite renewed pleas from the Joint Chiefs of Staff over a period of years that he authorize calling up reserve forces for Vietnam

Top, left: These soldiers are part of an American force, including the 82d Airborne Division, dispatched to the Dominican Republic in April 1965 to prevent takeover by a communist regime. (National Archives)

Above: Fire Support Base Colorado, manned by elements of the 25th Infantry Division in Tay Ninh Province, was typical of the large number of temporary and semi-permanent installations providing support to maneuver elements during the fighting in Vietnam. (U.S. Army Center of Military History)

Below: The crew of an M48A3 tank from the 11th Armored Cavalry Regiment observes the effects of a F-4 Phantom's air strike. This regiment, three tank battalions, and ten mechanized infantry battalions demonstrated that armor could operate effectively even in South Vietnam's difficult terrain. (National Archives)

Left: A "tunnel rat" of the U.S. Army's Americal Division emerges from an underground complex near Chu Lai. Detection and seizure of such enemy facilities and prepositioned supplies was key to General Creighton Abrams's determination to cut off the enemy's logistics "nose." (U.S. Army Center of Military History)

service, President Johnson would never agree to do so to any significant degree. Only in the wake of the USS *Pueblo* crisis and the Tet Offensive of early 1968 did he reluctantly agree to two small call-ups.

Airmobile Operations and Battle of the Ia Drang

Top: *Patrolling was essential to finding the often elusive enemy in Vietnam's jungle terrain. The one-year tour provided every soldier an established date for completion of his arduous service. ("Indiana Rangers: The Army Guard in Vietnam," Mort Künstler, National Guard Heritage series)*

Above: *Convoy security was an important mission, especially in parts of Vietnam where enemy mines and ambushes were a constant threat. Even with the swarms of helicopters deployed, most cargo still moved by truck. (U.S. Army Reserve painting)*

Greatly increased emphasis on Army aviation had led to experiments that soon produced a new type of division called "airmobile." Heavily equipped with some four hundred helicopters for both troop lift and combat, including for the first time armed helicopters, the 1st Cavalry Division (Airmobile) was deployed to Vietnam in July 1965 as part of the first major commitment of U.S. ground forces to the war.

This new kind of division would provide the archetype for the way U.S. forces fought the Vietnam War, particularly during the early years. The division had evolved from a long series of innovative tests and maneuvers. It capitalized on the mature capabilities of Army aviation, and particularly the helicopter, to form a unit whose maneuver elements could rapidly deploy by air, provide close-in fire support by air, and resupply by air.

Top, left: *1st Infantry Division engineers rappel into the jungle from a CH-47 Chinook helicopter. Carrying chain saws and explosives, they are prepared to clear a helicopter landing zone for resupply of troops during Operation Cedar Falls. (U.S. Army Center of Military History)*

Left: *A CH-54 Flying Crane prepares to lift a 155mm howitzer from an artillery fire base in Vietnam. Quipped one ground soldier, "No bird with a belly wound that bad should still be able to fly." (U.S. Army Center of Military History)*

Above: *A CH-53 resupply ship brings supplies to a remote fire base. Cargo-carrying heavy lift helicopters were essential to establishing such bases and keeping them stocked with ammunition and other necessities. (National Archives)*

Left: *Troops of the 1st Cavalry Division (Airmobile) engage enemy forces during the battle of the Ia Drang in November 1965. This fierce fight against North Vietnamese Army elements in South Vietnam's Central Highlands was the first major combat test of the Army's newly developed airmobile division. (National Archives)*

Army aviation support in Vietnam was not confined to the airmobile division, however, but it permeated virtually every aspect of combat operations and support countrywide. The workhorse of the aerial fleet was the UH-1, nicknamed the "Huey," which was fielded in a range of configurations for troop lift, fire support, medical evacuation, and command and control. Later in the war a newly designed gunship version, the AH-1 Huey Cobra, was deployed with great success. Heavy lift cargo helicopters, the CH-47 Chinook and the CH-54 Flying Crane, also played an essential role. Army aviation came into its own during this extended conflict.

Very soon after closing in Vietnam and establishing a base camp at An Khe in the Central Highlands, elements of the 1st Cavalry Division became engaged with large North Vietnamese Army (NVA) forces in an area close to the Cambodian border known as the Ia Drang Valley. There, in a series of battles extending over more than a month, troopers of the 1st Cavalry Division inflicted heavy casualties on the NVA, but also suffered significant friendly losses.

Lieutenant General Harold G. Moore, who as a lieutenant colonel had commanded the 1st Battalion, 7th Cavalry, in the thick of this fighting, later

Top, left: *The early years of American involvement in Vietnam, with General William C. Westmoreland in command, featured large "search and destroy" sweeps. These troops of the 1st Cavalry Division (Air Mobile) move across a rice paddy in search of Viet Cong in the Bong Sun District during Operation Masher in January 1966. (National Archives)*

Above: *Helicopter door gunners performed crucial functions in protecting their ships during low-level operations in Vietnam. (A. J. Alexander)*

Left: *The Army's fleet of helicopters, and its number of qualified aviators, expanded manyfold during the years in Vietnam. ("Paddy Patrol," Stephen H. Sheldon, Army Art Collection)*

Below: *Development of an extensive and modern infrastructure, and the logistical buildup thus enabled, were impressive parts of the Army's performance in Vietnam. One of the most extensive facilities was this complex at Cam Ranh Bay featuring a deepwater port, jet capable airfield, and huge depot. (U.S. Army Center of Military History)*

wrote that the Ia Drang campaign was "a dress rehearsal" for how General Westmoreland would conduct the war for the next several years.

The outcome of these fierce clashes was indeed viewed by General William C. Westmoreland, Commander of the U.S. Military Assistance Command, Vietnam, as highly satisfactory, with a "kill ratio" of twelve enemy to one friendly, confirming him in his preferred approach to conduct of the war, what he termed a "war of attrition."

As the build-up of U.S. forces continued, an extensive infrastructure was developed to accommodate the deployed troops and the logistical

Above: *The pace and magnitude of the buildup and operations in Vietnam are apparent in this representation of the Saigon docks. Eventually "Newport," an entirely new Saigon port facility, was constructed to ease the crunch. ("Saigon Docks," William Linzee Prescott, Army Art Collection)*

bases needed to sustain them. At places such as Cam Ranh Bay, and Newport near Saigon, seven deep-draft port facilities were constructed, while a network of jet-capable airfields and smaller tactical airstrips was built all across the land. Major base camps for American forces became semi-permanent facilities where every aspect of military operations could

Oppoosite, top: *One of the best-known battles of the war took place at Ap Bia Mountain, nicknamed "Hamburger Hill" by a journalist, where this "dustoff" medical evacuation was underway in May 1969. In an eleven-day battle a brigade of the 101st Airborne Division and five South Vietnamese battalions drove out enemy forces and reestablished control of the A Shau Valley. (U.S. Army Center of Military History)*

Right: *This November 1969 aerial view of a fire base near Ben Het shows howitzers positioned to fire in multiple directions and nearby ammunition stocks sandbagged to provide overhead protection. (National Archives)*

be supported. Vast areas of storage space were put in place, roads and bridges constructed or upgraded, and petroleum pipelines laid. Westmoreland deemed that "surely one of the more remarkable accomplishments of American forces in Vietnam."

One of the most significant such developments was installation of a comprehensive modern communications network benefiting both U.S. and Vietnamese users. The Army's 1st Signal Brigade in Vietnam eventually became larger in strength than a division. Lieutenant General Thomas M. Rienzi, who commanded the brigade for nearly two years, concluded that "the magnitude of Army communications in the war in Vietnam…exceeded the scale of their employment in any previous war in history."

Perhaps the most famous support element was the "dustoff" emergency medical evacuation helicopter, manned by fearless crews who had the admiration and gratitude of every combat soldier. Nearly half a million dustoff missions were flown during the course of the war, with some 900,000 patients "airlifted from battlefields, rice paddies, destroyed villages, and triple-canopy jungles, at all hours of the night or day, under all weather conditions, in the face of intense enemy fire."

Above: *An extensive communications network was essential to U.S. operations in Vietnam, as illustrated by this forest of antennas at the 1st Cavalry Division's Hon Cong Mountain site near An Khe. (U.S. Army Center of Military History)*

Top, left: *An artist captures the drama and heroism of combat medics treating casualties in Vietnam. (A. J. Alexander)*

Top, right: *The pilots and crews who conducted medical evacuation missions, universally known as "dustoffs" in Vietnam, were considered the bravest of the brave by those whose lives they saved. ("Bringing Them In," John Wheat, Army Art Collection)*

Above: *Medical Service Corps Major Patrick H. Brady, later a major general, was the only Medical Department officer to win the Medal of Honor during the Vietnam War. Brady, an Army aviator, was awarded the decoration for his January 1968 evacuation of fifty-one casualties, using three helicopters, in a series of extremely hazardous missions in mountainous terrain and difficult weather near Chu Lai. (U.S. Army Center of Military History)*

The medical facilities where the wounded and injured were taken were the best the Army had ever fielded, eventually numbering twenty-three hospitals and countless other treatment facilities. Army civic action teams visiting South Vietnamese hamlets and villages invariably featured on-the-spot medical treatment as a very popular part of their repertoire.

While all the various functions were important to the functioning of the forces deployed, both U.S. and South Vietnamese, perhaps intelligence activities held pride of place. The capabilities deployed included everything from battlefield monitoring and intercept of enemy communications, aerial reconnaissance and photography, and radio direction-finding, to exploitation of captured documents, prisoner of war interrogation, enemy order of battle assessment, and comprehensive intelligence estimates. Intelligence information relating to enemy infiltration down the Ho Chi Minh Trail from North Vietnam into Laos and Cambodia was especially important in developing counters to planned enemy offensives in South Vietnam.

In addition to the conduct of military operations and the requisite logistical and other support for them, of course, Army forces in Vietnam had the critically important mission of providing advice and assistance to their Vietnamese counterparts. Indeed, in the early days, that had been the primary U.S. role in the conflict. While this function may have been somewhat neglected during the years of the U.S. troop buildup, it would subsequently again become the primary American role, especially after general mobilization in South Vietnam and the consequent substantial expansion of the RVNAF.

In the years immediately following deployment of large numbers of ground forces to Vietnam, the U.S. Army also developed a family of advanced weaponry and equipment. Best known, probably, is the M16 5.56mm rifle, a lightweight, automatic weapon with a high rate of fire. The M60 machine gun, M79 grenade launcher, and the Light Anti-Tank Weapon (LAW) were other important new weapons, while the

Top, left: *Millions of leaflets scattered across South Vietnam encouraged enemy soldiers to "chieu hoi," or rally to the government side. Tens of thousands of them did, more than 47,000 in 1969 alone, the equivalent of several enemy divisions. ("Chieu Hoi or Die," Michael R. Crook, Army Art Collection)*

Left: *Captain Elizabeth Finn, a staff nurse at the 93d Evacuation Hospital, watches two small girls do a native dance at the Bien Hoa orphanage in June 1967. During the Vietnam War eight female nurses lost their lives, one due to hostile action. The heroic service of Army nurses has been commemorated by a statue placed near the Vietnam Veterans Memorial. (National Archives)*

Above: *Viet Cong suspects are held for interrogation. During the war's latter stages, the Phoenix program, devised by William E. Colby, drove out the enemy's clandestine infrastructure that had used terrorist tactics to dominate the rural populace. ("Viet Cong Suspects," Ronald A. Wilson, Army Art Collection)*

Troops of the 173d Airborne Brigade conduct an assault on Hill 875, near Dak To, in November 1967. (National Archives)

Above: *1st Cavalry's (Air Mobile) baptism by fire took place in the elephant grass at Landing Zone X-Ray in the Ia Drang Valley. Here, a similar insertion is made on a rocky parapet, sacrificing cover for high ground. (National Archives)*

Above, right: *An innovative approach to conduct of the war in the watery Mekong Delta was the mobile riverine force, Army troops and weaponry embarked on shallow draft Navy vessels. Here an assaulting force scrambles ashore along the My Tho River in September 1967. (National Archives)*

Below, left: *Elements of the 9th Infantry Division embarked in U.S. Navy boats move along a canal in Dinh Tuong Province during mobile riverine force operations in early 1968. (U.S. Army Center of Military History)*

Below, right: *Rome plows were used extensively in Vietnam to clear areas around base camps and along major roadways, thus denying concealment to enemy forces. (U.S. Army Center of Military History)*

AN/PRC25 radio provided superior tactical communications. "Rome plows," new heavy mechanized equipment, were also introduced to cut into the dense jungle.

Unique operations designated "riverine" were conducted in the Mekong Delta region of South Vietnam by a brigade of the Army's 9th Infantry Division and supporting naval elements. Deploying on armored troop carriers and supported by armored gunboats in the delta's extensive system of rivers and canals, ground assault forces lived afloat on barracks ships and barges, conducting extensive operations to disrupt and interdict enemy movement on waterways and protect vital civilian commercial traffic.

Westmoreland continued in command of U.S. forces in Vietnam until June 1968. During his tenure repeated requests for additional U.S. forces resulted in deployment of a force of well over half a million troops, including seven Army and two Marine divisions. These were the forces in place

Top, left: *The mobile riverine forces packed their own indirect fire support, including these M102 105mm howitzers able to fire from their floating barges. (U.S. Army Center of Military History)*

Top, right: *Barracks ships provided billets for mobile riverine force soldiers and sailors, as well as a helicopter landing pad and facilities for smaller craft to moor alongside. (National Archives)*

Center, left: *9th Infantry Division soldiers operating in the Mekong Delta, crisscrossed by a network of streams and canals, often faced deep water. (National Archives)*

Above: *The long years of war impacted heavily on the people of South Vietnam's rural hamlets and villages, for they were the real target of the enemy. ("Street Scene," Kenneth J. Scowcroft, Army Art Collection)*

when, at the end of January 1968, the enemy launched what came to be known as the Tet Offensive. Coinciding with South Vietnam's traditional celebration of the lunar new year, enemy attacks struck almost simultaneously at many points across the country, including thirty-six of the forty-four provincial capitals and all but one of the autonomous cities.

In fierce fighting over the next few days, South Vietnamese forces, backed by those of the U.S. and other allies, repelled and soundly defeated

The primitive state of South Vietnam's existing infrastructure is illustrated by this view of a main thoroughfare, here being swept for mines by U.S. Army engineers of the 28th Infantry operating in Lai Khe in 1969. (U.S. Army Center of Military History)

273

Artillery fire support was provided by U.S. Army cannoneers to both their own maneuver elements and those of ARVN, the Army of the Republic of Vietnam. The system of mutually supporting fire bases, often emplaced, resupplied, and later extracted by helicopter, was a distinctive innovation of the Vietnam War. (A. J. Alexander)

the attackers at almost every point. Only in Saigon, where the fight continued for a week or more, and in Hue, where it took a month to dislodge the invaders, did the offensive last longer. U.S. forces, especially those with the mobility of gunships, tanks, armored cavalry, and mechanized infantry, made important contributions to defeating the enemy.

During January and February alone the enemy lost some 45,000 killed and another 5,800 captured, and over the first half of 1968 enemy

losses totaled an estimated 120,000 men. In the United States, however, the Tet Offensive had a powerful negative psychological effect, leading to further erosion of support for continuation of the war. The following year, under the successor administration of President Richard Nixon, progressive withdrawal of U.S. forces from Vietnam would commence.

In the aftermath of the Tet Offensive some troops of the Army's 23d Infantry Division, nicknamed the American Division, committed a despicable massacre of innocent South Vietnamese civilians at a place called My Lai. Lieutenant General William R. Peers, who headed a subsequent investigation of the massacre's cover-up, found that "failures [of leadership] occurred at every level within the chain of command, from individual non-commisioned-officer squad leaders to the command group of the division." Lieutenant William Calley, convicted and sentenced to life imprisonment, was paroled after serving only about three years following intervention by President Nixon.

Top: *Colonel Arthur D. "Bull" Simons led a daring raid on Son Tay prisoner of war camp and later described it using this scale model. While the camp was found to be empty and no prisoners were rescued, treatment of Americans held elsewhere in North Vietnam improved soon after the raid. (U.S. Army Center of Military History)*

Above: *Members of the Son Tay raiding force are shown aboard a helicopter inbound for the North Vietnamese POW compound not far from Hanoi. They had rehearsed the operation for months beforehand. (John F. Kennedy Special Warfare Museum)*

On 21 November 1970, a group of Special Forces volunteers led by Colonel Arthur "Bull" Simons made a night raid by helicopter deep into North Vietnam. Their mission was the rescue of U.S. prisoners of war said to be held in a compound near Son Tay. The raiders successfully landed but found the prison empty. After engaging a nearby enemy force, the raiders withdrew without losing a man.

Change of Command and Approach

In late June 1968 General Westmoreland was assigned as Army Chief of Staff. In the field, General Creighton Abrams was appointed Commander, U.S. Military Assistance Command, Vietnam, an appointment that precipitated fundamental changes in concept of the nature of the war and of how it should be prosecuted. "The tactics changed within fifteen minutes of Abrams's taking command," recalled General Fred Weyand.

Abrams viewed the essential task as providing security for the population of South Vietnam's hamlets and villages, not killing enemy soldiers per se. Thus the strategy of attrition was replaced by a strategy of population security. "Search and destroy" operations gave way to "clear and hold," with the multi-battalion sweeps replaced by thousands of small unit actions, day and night, especially patrols and ambushes.

Abrams discerned the enemy's reliance on a logistics "nose," the technique of pushing the wherewithal needed to fight a battle out in front of the troops rather than, as traditional armies would do it, supplying them from the rear by means of a logistical "tail." In this approach, necessitated by lack of transport and secure lines of communication, Abrams had identified a major enemy vulnerability. Exploiting it tended to preempt or lessen the severity of planned enemy offensives.

Above: *General William C. Westmoreland commanded U.S. forces in Vietnam during 1964–68. His strategy was built around waging a war of attrition to inflict heavy personnel losses on the enemy. This required large unit operations in the deep jungle regions of South Vietnam. His repeated requests for additional forces resulted in U.S. deployments peaking at 543,000 U.S. troops. (National Archives)*

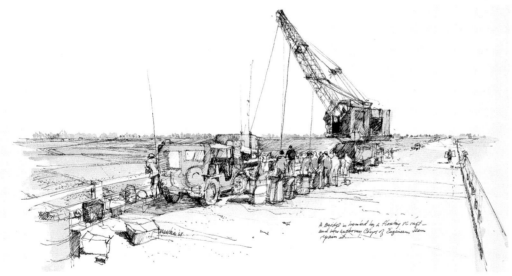

Top, left: *An American soldier shares some of his provisions with a South Vietnamese family. After spending a year in Vietnam, veterans said in a later survey, the overwhelming majority developed a greater appreciation for the blessings they enjoyed at home. (U.S. Army Center of Military History)*

Top, right: *Tubes pointing in every direction at this remote artillery fire base underscore the reality that there were no front lines, and hence no secure rear areas, in the war in Vietnam. (National Archives)*

Above: *Unprecedented battlefield mobility for the Army's artillery, even in the steep mountainous terrain of the Annamite Chain, was provided by such heavy lift helicopters as this Sikorsky CH-54. (National Archives)*

Left: *Road and bridge installation, repair, and upgrade were major missions for Army engineers and supporting contractors throughout South Vietnam. By the latter years of the war a much improved infrastructure, plus gains in security, had upgraded the rural economy and the farmer's quality of life. ("Bridge Repair," Stephen Matthias, Army Art Collection)*

Whereas in the earlier years pacification had largely been left to the South Vietnamese forces, American units now became deeply involved in helping produce the climate of local security in which local government, farming and transport of crops and goods to market, and other aspects of normal life could proceed.

A key objective of the pacification program was neutralization of the covert enemy infrastructure in the villages that had for so many years used intimidation, threats, and terrorism to keep the rural population under its domination.

Opposite, bottom right: *General Creighton W. Abrams (center), commander of U.S. forces in Vietnam during 1968–1972, confers with the 1st Cavalry Division's commanding general, Major General George Forsythe (right). Abrams completely changed conduct of the war, shifting from emphasis on body count to protection of the rural populace, and with far better results. (National Archives)*

Above: *American advisors played a key role in the Vietnam War from start to finish. General Abrams considered them the "glue" that held everything else together. Here a U.S. advisor listens in during a class at South Vietnam's signal school in Vung Tau. (U.S. Army Center of Military History)*

Above, right: *Lieutenant Colonel John Paul Vann (left), senior advisor to the South Vietnamese 7th Division, confers in the field. Later, as a civilian, Vann became the senior pacification advisor in the Central Highlands and played a key role in bringing about security gains before his death in a helicopter crash during the 1972 Easter offensive. (U.S. Army Center of Military History)*

American advisors, both those with South Vietnamese forces in the field and those in every major Vietnamese headquarters, were immensely important to the improvements during these critical years. General Abrams called them the "glue" that held the whole thing together, and shifted some of what he called his "blue chip" talent from U.S. units to the advisory effort to beef it up even more.

Drawdown

In July and August 1969 President Nixon ordered withdrawal of the first increment of U.S. forces, 25,000 in all. This was the first step in a process that continued until nearly the entire force was redeployed by the time of the cease-fire agreement in early 1973. As units that had fought in Vietnam, some for years, stood down and prepared to redeploy, Abrams went to tell them goodbye and to thank them for what they had accomplished.

Right: *An American advisor brings in a helicopter to extract a "Mike" Force (Mobile Strike Force) of Montagnard troops after a sixteen-day sweep near Bet Het in November 1969. These indigenous forces were very effective in conducting reconnaissance and combat operations. (National Archives)*

Opposite, top: *Mechanized forces and helicopters operating together formed a potent combination. (A. J. Alexander)*

Opposite, bottom: *General William B. Rossen, Deputy Commanding Officer, MACV, examines a cache site on the Minot Plantation, discovered during "Operation Shoemaker." This search and clear mission was carried out by the 2d Battalion, 47th Mechanized Infantry, attached to the 1st Cavalry (Air Mobile) in the Sprok Menut and Cha Lang districts of Cambodia, in May 1970. (National Archives)*

Cambodian Incursion

American commanders had long urged denying the enemy the sanctuaries he made such good use of across the Vietnamese border in Laos and Cambodia. At the end of April 1970 General Abrams was allowed, in cooperation with South Vietnamese elements, to mount what amounted to a large raid into Cambodia. Abrams employed elements of the 1st Cavalry Division (Airmobile), the 4th and 25th Infantry Divisions, the 101st Airborne Division, and the 11th Armored Cavalry Regiment.

Limited to sixty days of operations and a depth of penetration not exceeding eighteen kilometers, the incursion was, in its own terms, quite successful. The take included 9,300 tons of weapons, ammunition, and supplies seized, plus 7,000 tons of rice, constituting altogether enemy

Top: *During an assault on Hill 875, fifteen miles southwest of Dak To, members of the 173d Airborne Brigade guard the perimeter before the final push forward on 22 November 1967. (National Archives)*

Above: *Troops of the 25th Infantry Division, supported by tanks of the 34th Armor, prepare to move out during the 1970 incursion into Cambodia. (National Archives)*

Above, right: *Members of the 25th Infantry take inventory during the incursion into Cambodia. While limited in both duration and depth of penetration, this action resulted in seizure of enormous quantities of enemy arms, ammunition, and supplies. (National Archives)*

requirements for at least six months of operations. Another important result was the capture of huge treasure troves of intelligence, more than a million pages of documents and thirty-two cases of cryptographic material in just the first three weeks. Gratifyingly, these materials confirmed the reliability of MACV intelligence on enemy infiltration.

Armor in Vietnam

During the early years of General Westmoreland's tenure in Vietnam, the outlook had been that the terrain and weather there were inhospitable to employment of armored forces. Early deploying U.S. divisions had, in fact, been stripped of their mechanized infantry, and Major General Fred

Weyand had had to fight to bring the tank battalion when his 25th Infantry Division moved to Vietnam. This was despite the fact that South Vietnamese forces had been effectively employing armor for a number of years.

Subsequently, though, and especially after General Abrams, a renowned tank commander under General George S. Patton in World War II, came on the scene, the effectiveness of armor was appreciated and utilized. Eventually three tank battalions, an armored cavalry regiment, and ten mechanized infantry battalions were deployed to Vietnam. Some of those mechanized infantry battalions that had originally been dismounted were even re-mechanized in the war zone. The armored personnel carrier proved to be the workhorse of the armored fleet, fielded in dozens of different configurations from troop carrier to command post vehicle, mortar carrier, ambulance, bridge launcher, and cargo hauler. Modified in ways

281

An armored convoy comes under heavy assault. ("Find the Bastards," James Dietz)

pioneered by the South Vietnamese, including the addition of more armor-protected machine guns and supplemental body armor, the APC was transformed into the ACAV, or armored cavalry assault vehicle, equivalent almost to a light tank.

When the drawdown began, planners followed Abrams's guidance to strip armored units—tanks, mechanized infantry, air and armored cavalry—out of departing units and hold them in country, where Abrams valued their ability to provide the most firepower per man of any units. This constituted a complete reversal of fortune. "The armor units," said General Donn Starry, who as a colonel had commanded the 11th Armored Cavalry Regiment during the Cambodian operation, "specifically excluded from the buildup until late 1966, would anchor the withdrawal of American combat units from Vietnam."

U.S. Army aviation elements provided massive support during Lam Son 719, South Vietnam's February 1971 incursion into Laos. Troop lift, resupply, and gunships, such as these AH-1G Cobras, flew an incredible 353,287 sorties at the cost of 107 helicopters lost to hostile action. (U.S. Army Center of Military History)

Last Years of the War

By early 1971 congressionally-imposed restrictions on the use of U.S. troops in Southeast Asia meant that they could play only a supporting role when South Vietnamese troops mounted Lam Son 719, a raid into Laos to cut the Ho Chi Minh Trail and seize stockpiles of enemy supplies and equipment. That supporting role, however, was key to the operation, especially when it came to Army aviation support. U.S. ground forces, including advisors, were prohibited from crossing the border into Laos, but aviation elements were permitted to do so.

During an operation that lasted some six weeks, U.S. Army aviation elements committed some 600 helicopters to the battle on a daily basis. Overall, 107 helicopters were lost to hostile action, with many more dam-

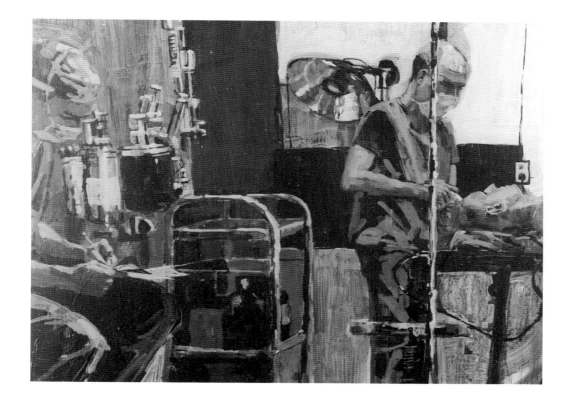

aged but repaired. Those losses occurred during an incredible total of 353,287 sorties and 134,861 flying hours.

By 27 January 1973 a perilous cease-fire agreement had been negotiated in Paris, one that left North Vietnamese forces intact inside South Vietnam while requiring withdrawal of the last elements of U.S. forces. The U.S. troop strength as a result of unilateral withdrawals was down to only about 27,000. Those few, the last representatives of some 2,600,000 Americans in all the services who had served in Vietnam at one time or another during the war, and 700,000 more who participated in the war from stations elsewhere in Southeast Asia, were all withdrawn by the end of March 1973.

North Vietnam immediately commenced massive violations of the terms of the agreement, building up its forces for renewed aggression against the South. When the United States Congress blocked fulfillment of

Top, left: An artist's rendition dramatically portrays Army doctors and the tools of their trade at a field hospital in Vietnam. ("Field Hospital," Paul Rickert, Army Art Collection)

Above: Army Special Forces were substantially expanded during the war in Vietnam, where the 5th Special Forces Group, headquartered at Nha Trang, controlled detachments at many locations throughout the country. Meanwhile other Special Forces groups were stationed in Okinawa, Germany, and at Fort Bragg. (The Company of Military Historians)

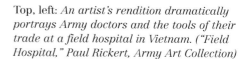

President Nixon began unilateral withdrawal of U.S. forces from Vietnam in July-August 1969. As successive units departed, they handed over their facilities, and often their equipment as well, to the South Vietnamese. Here men of the 101st Airborne Division transfer Fire Support Base Tomahawk to the ARVN in November 1971. By that time U.S. forces in Vietnam, which had peaked at 543,400 in April 1969, were down to 184,000. (National Archives)

American guarantees to South Vietnam, and North Vietnam's sponsors intensified their logistical support, the eventual outcome was no longer in doubt. On 30 April 1975 Saigon fell to the invading North Vietnamese and all of Vietnam was forcibly united under Communist rule.

American armed forces suffered over 58,000 dead in the Vietnam War, some 47,000 of them due to hostile action. Altogether nearly eleven million men and women served in the American armed forces during the Vietnam War years. Contrary to popular belief, nearly four-fifths of them were volunteers rather than draftees, including two-thirds of those who served in Vietnam itself.

Rebuilding the Army

The war in Vietnam took a toll on the Army and its resources worldwide. In the autumn of 1972 General Creighton Abrams, newly assigned as Army Chief of Staff, began rebuilding the force. His own example of principled leadership and commitment to service set the tone. His emphasis was on the care and well-being of soldiers and on combat readiness, tasks made more challenging by termination of the military draft. "Soldiers are not *in* the Army," Abrams emphasized, "soldiers *are* the Army."

Abrams also stressed development of future combat systems, largely neglected during the decade of preoccupation with Vietnam. Concentrating on what he termed the "Big Five," he put in place programs for a new main battle tank, an infantry fighting vehicle, cargo and attack helicopters, and a field army air defense system. These initiatives all proved to be successful in the later Gulf war, including a superb tank by then fittingly designated the "Abrams." Realistic and intensive training was conducted at the Army's new National Training Center at Fort Irwin in the California desert, where on a high-tech instrumented mock battlefield units could maneuver force-on-force, then review in objective detail how they had performed. Abrams died after only two years in office, but the legacy he left the Army was rich.

The course of rebuilding was, however, long and difficult. A core of dedicated officers and noncommissioned officers, determined to rebuild the Army to a standard of excellence, persevered over long years to achieve that admirable goal.

Meanwhile there were catastrophic failures in such places as the Iranian desert, where an Army-led task force sent to rescue Americans held hostage in Iran failed and was forced to turn back after a series of mishaps and a fatal collision between two of its aircraft. Clearly there was still much rebuilding to be done.

Above: Following the Vietnam War the Army had a lot of rebuilding to do. General Creighton Abrams, brought home from Vietnam to become Chief of Staff, got the process moving with insistence on the twin imperatives of combat readiness and taking care of the soldier. A "training revolution" included institution of training to standards and new instrumented facilities, in particular a new National Training Center established at Fort Irwin, California. There units on a "rotation" maneuvered in force-on-force engagements against the resident OPFOR (opposing force) in a series of engagements that were closely monitored by sensors, then played back and critiqued to extract the "lessons learned." The great success of the endeavor, which stressed training rather than testing, was demonstrated by the performance of Army units in the Gulf war. ("OPFOR Briefing," Patrick Farrell, Army Art Collection)

Opposite, top: Men of the 101st Airborne Division arrive home from Vietnam. By March 1972, when the division's last elements returned to Fort Campbell, the 101st had served in Vietnam for more than four years. (National Archives)

285

Above: *Throughout the long years of the war in Vietnam, U.S. units continued their defense of western Europe as part of NATO forces, but the war took a toll in diminished readiness and maturity of the force. The Army's post-war rebuilding effort included these forces and was so successful that many of the units deployed to Saudi Arabia for Desert Shield and Desert Storm were shipped from Germany. ("End of the Day," Gary Lewis, Army Art Collection)*

Opposite, top: *During Operation Just Cause in Panama, begun 20 December 1989, Army Rangers parachuted in to seize and hold key objectives and stabilize the situation. The incursion, intended to protect U.S. citizens and restore democracy in Panama, as well as seize Panamanian President General Manuel Noriega and bring him to trial in the United States on charges of drug trafficking, ended in fifteen days with Noriega surrendering himself to U.S. authorities. ("Energetically We Lead the Way," James Dietz)*

All-Volunteer Force

Late in the Vietnam era President Richard Nixon decreed an end to military conscription, with the last draftees being inducted during December 1972. Thereafter the armed forces, and in particular the Army, faced a major challenge in attracting large numbers of qualified enlistees to fill the ranks of even a much reduced force structure. Initially the approach taken was economically based, but that proved less than fully effective. Under the leadership of then Major General Maxwell R. Thurman, Army recruiting was recast with the now famous theme "Be All You Can Be." An Army College Fund was established by congressional action, so that young soldiers could qualify for major college tuition benefits while maturing and gaining skills during an initial enlistment. Soon both the quality of recruits and the quality of their service improved dramatically.

Reserve Components Policy

An extremely traumatic aspect of the Vietnam War had been President Lyndon Johnson's persistent refusal to call up reserve forces. General Abrams had been determined that this not happen again in any conflict as

large and significant as Vietnam. "They're not taking us to war again without calling up the reserves," he told the staff. Abrams and his successors then built into the Army's structure a reliance on reserves, and hence the Army could not be deployed without calling them up. This served to ensure that in future conflicts the Army would benefit from the public support that customarily follows involvement of reserve forces. This would have major impact on the Army in the years and decades to come.

Berlin Wall Comes Down and End of the Cold War: 1989

In 1989 the Cold War Soviet threat evaporated when the Berlin Wall came down and the Soviet Union dissolved. In ensuing years the United States Army was reduced by over 500,000 soldiers, nuclear and chemical weapons were stripped from the force, and hundreds of bases around the world were closed.

Below: *Armored and mechanized forces were powerful elements of U.S. forces in Germany. They remained still vigilant after half a century when the Berlin Wall came down in 1989, followed closely by dissolution of the Warsaw Pact and then the Soviet Union itself, dramatically bringing the Cold War to a close. ("On Line," Roger W. Price, Army Art Collection)*

Airborne, heliborne, and mechanized forces took part in Operation Just Cause, the U.S. intervention in Panama. ("Jump into Night, Torrijos Airport," (above); "Attack on the Commandancia," (bottom, left); and "Night Gunner," Al Sprague, (bottom, right) (Army Art Collection)

Panama Invasion: 1989

In late December 1989 the United States deployed some 14,000 troops to Panama in Operation Just Cause, an intervention designed to arrest Panamanian President Manuel Noriega and arraign him on charges of narcotics trafficking. The fairly complicated operation was brought off with considerable skill and effective coordination among the several services. Composed primarily of Army forces, "Just Cause integrated

armored, light, air, amphibious, and special operations forces in airborne forcible-entry, air assault, and urban combat operations at night." Noriega was captured and returned to the U.S. for trial.

The Gulf War: 1990-1991

A more serious threat next appeared in the Middle East. On 2 August 1990 military forces of Iraq's President Saddam Hussein invaded Kuwait, seizing its valuable oilfields. This triggered a coalition response, led by the United States, that eventually involved a multinational force. Following the arrival of 82d Airborne Division quick reaction units, U.S. and coalition forces were built up, intensively trained, and provided upgraded equipment. As a preparatory air campaign weakened the Iraqis, the allies moved into position.

The armored forces assembled for the ground war in Kuwait were awesome. One tank, for example, carried as much small arms ammunition as an entire Iraqi Republican Guard infantry company. When the U.S. Third Army launched its attack under Lieutenant General John Yeosock, he had under his command 1,870 such tanks. Stunningly underscoring the end of the Cold War, the U.S. Army rented Soviet ships (leased roll-on/roll-off vessels) to take its tanks to Saudi Arabia.

Above: *A heavily loaded trooper of the 82d Airborne Division deploying to Saudi Arabia. (U.S. Army)*

Above: *Weapons and equipment moved by ship to supply U.S. forces in Operation Desert Shield are unloaded at a Saudi port. (U.S. Army)*

Left: *Troops of the 101st Airborne Division (Air Assault) deploy to Saudi Arabia in Operation Desert Shield. (U.S. Army)*

Top, left: *Troops deployed to Saudi Arabia for Operation Desert Shield lived under austere conditions, but benefited from uninterrupted opportunities for some great training. ("Building an Outhouse in the Field," Sieger Hartgers, Army Art Collection)*

Top, right: *Extensive medical facilities and staffs deployed for the Gulf war were fortunately little utilized, due to unexpectedly light casualties. ("Nurse, 5th MASH," Sieger Hartgers, Army Art Collection)*

The armored striking forces, complemented by arms and services of both active and reserve components, provided a heartening example of well-led, well-trained, and well-equipped troops at their best. Troop E (Eagle) of the 2d Armored Cavalry Regiment was VII Corps' screening force in the big left hook around the Iraqi flank. In the initial meeting engagement with the Iraqi Republican Guard, the troop's Abrams tanks and Bradley cavalry fighting vehicles took only 23 minutes to destroy an enemy brigade with no friendly casualties. That set the tone. The M1A1 tank's ability to reach out and hit the target at ranges up to 4,000 meters, concluded an after-action report, "was almost binary—one round, one hit,

FRANK M. THOMAS 92

one kill." In a desert swept by 50- to 60-knot winds, smoke from burning oil wells, and blowing sand, that capability seemed near miraculous. Commented one observer after this overwhelming victory, "An armored division is like a tuxedo. When you need one, there is no substitute."

Lieutenant General Fred Franks commanded VII Corps. With its four armored divisions, a mechanized infantry division, and an armored cavalry regiment, it was the largest armored corps ever fielded. This force executed the big swing around the Iraqi flank, making good on what Chairman of the Joint Chiefs of Staff General Colin Powell had said was going to be done to the Iraqis in Kuwait: "Our strategy for dealing with this army is very simple. First we're going to cut it off, and then we're going to kill it."

The ground war was over in just a hundred hours. Iraq lost about 3,800 of its 4,550 tanks, while some 71,000 Iraqis became prisoners of war. Of 42 Iraqi divisions in the Kuwaiti theater of operations, at least 29 were judged to have been rendered "completely ineffective." Iraq went from the fourth-largest army in the world to the second-largest army in Iraq in one hundred hours. By 28 February 1991 it was all over.

In addition to this impressive combat performance, Gulf War operations constituted a superb logistical feat. The U.S. Transportation Command's ships and aircraft had delivered one billion pounds of weapons, ammunition, and other supplies. Said General H. Norman Schwarzkopf, overall commander of American forces in the Gulf, "We'd moved more

Above: *Elements of the 158th Field Artillery, Oklahoma Army National Guard, support the allied ground offensive into Kuwait with the MLRS (multiple-launch rocket system). National Guard and Army Reserve personnel played an indispensable role in the Gulf war, both as individuals and as mobilized units. ("Steel Rain," Frank M. Thomas, National Guard Heritage series)*

Opposite, bottom left: *A machine gunner and his assistant, wearing night vision goggles, pour fire into Iraq during Operation Desert Storm. ("Night Run," Frank M. Thomas, Army Art Collection)*

Opposite, bottom right: *Intelligence warned that Iraq might resort to chemical warfare, so U.S. troops were equipped with full chemical protective gear. (U.S. Army)*

Above: *Tanks fitted with barrier breaching equipment were put to use during extensive training under desert combat conditions. (U.S. Army)*

Left: *M1 tanks of advancing American forces roll past destroyed Iraqi tanks as the advance into Kuwait continues during darkness. ("Night Attack," Mario Acevedo, Army Art Collection)*

forces farther and faster than ever before in history." Army Reserve and Army National Guard forces were indispensable to this and subsequent sustainment of the deployed forces. Their attitude was summed up by one reservist who was asked by a reporter what he did in real life. "This is real life!" the soldier retorted.

Opposite, top: *Troops preparing for Desert Storm trained at Tire City, a simulated Iraqi defense complex, in the Eastern Province of Saudi Arabia. (U.S. Army)*

Opposite, bottom: *Soldiers practice breaking through barbed wire barriers during Desert Storm training in Saudi Arabia. (U.S. Army)*

Conclusion

While serving as Chief of Staff as the Army entered the twenty-first century General Dennis Reimer often stated that "soldiers are our credentials." He derived that observation from a World War II incident in which Brigadier General Charles Canham, then assistant division commander of the 8th Infantry Division, was about to receive the surrender of a German unit. "I'm here to receive your surrender," he told the three-star German commander, who replied, "I won't surrender until I see your credentials." Canham gestured to the infantry soldiers accompanying him: "These are my credentials." Reimer understood the profound significance of that response. With such soldiers the Army is ready to meet its global challenges of the future with the same spirit of dedicated service as it had met those of the 225 years of its illustrious past.

Writing about World War II, Lieutenant General Theodore Stroup observed that in that conflict "the troops of America's Army, citizen-soldiers in every sense of the word, saved the world." Such an accolade was earned again in the Cold War, when a half century of vigilance and

Above: *As Commanding General, Third U.S. Army, Lieutenant General John Yeosock headed Army ground forces committed to Desert Shield and Desert Storm. Here he is portrayed in the New York City homecoming parade honoring Gulf war veterans. ("Desert Storm NYC Homecoming Parade," Peter Varisano, Army Art Collection)*

deterrence by forward-deployed Army forces, and those of their sister services, kept tyranny in check until it collapsed from within. General Gordon Sullivan concluded that when the Berlin Wall came down in 1989 it was "the most significant event of our lifetime." British historian Sir Michael Howard described the global stability thus achieved as greater than at any time in the past hundred years. We had, he observed, navigated our way through "the most terrible century" in history to relatively calm waters. The Army's contribution to that historic victory for freedom, democracy, and the rule of law was immense.

Above: *Following the collapse of the U.S.S.R., the U.S. Army began a major reduction and realignment of its forces in Europe. As a part of the change, the 1st Infantry Division, formerly at Fort Riley, Kansas, returned to Germany after a lengthy absence. It replaced the 3rd Infantry Division that was reassigned to Fort Stewart, Georgia. On a rainy April evening in 1996 the symbolic exchange of unit colors took place in front of the historic Wurtzburg Residenz, Wurzburg, Germany. V Corps commander Lieutenant General John Abrams is shown here handing the 1st Infantry Division color to Major General Montgomery Meigs, the new 1st Infantry Division commander. The division headquarters and two brigades are in Germany today as a part of the Army's forward deployed forces. One brigade is at Fort Riley. ("The Legacy Continues," James Dietz)*

Left: *American soldiers of Task Force Eagle move carefully on patrol through a damaged village near Tuzla, Bosnia-Herzegovina, following the NATO-imposed cease fire and the subsequent Dayton Peace Accords. Working as a part of a multinational force, Task Force Eagle provides a security and stabilizing force separating the potentially hostile ethnic factions living in the area, and bringing peace to the war ravaged countryside. Peacekeeping and enforcement operations have long been a part of the Army's mission around the world, from the early American frontier to the Korean DMZ to the Balkans. ("Duty First—Keeping the Peace," James Dietz)*

Opposite, top: *Ground forces and the delivery of their supplies were well served by such refueling units. (Army Reserve Historical Painting)*

Patriots All of the Time

Patriots All of the Time

The Guard and Reserve: Only in America

Major General Bruce Jacobs, AUS (Ret)

> *They are*
> *Citizens most of the time,*
> *Soldiers some of the time,*
> *Patriots all of the time.*
>
> —JAMES A. DRAIN, 1922

Many years after the first militiamen entered the pages of history, the fruition of their efforts would come full circle with the emergence in World War II of combat leaders of the first order. They would put to rest for all time the notion that soldiers from civilian life could not aspire to command American troops in battle.

They and the soldiers they led were there—and ready—because of events that evolved over nearly 200 years, starting on the trails and byways of colonial America and in the daunting events that pushed the frontier ever westward. All this time, as the country itself matured, volunteer defenders and fighters helped to define the role they would play over the many decades when the country could not afford a standing army of a size sufficient to its ever growing responsibilities.

These citizen-soldier leaders were the brand of men like James A. Drain, Raymond McLain, and Robert Beightler. James Drain (1870–1943) was a most unusual citizen-soldier and World War I veteran. In his lifetime, Drain put his imprint upon three major organizations with whom he enjoyed close connections over a period of many years—the National Rifle Association, the National Guard Association, and the American Legion.

In 1938, at the National Guard annual meeting in San Francisco, Drain talked about the wisdom of U.S. military policy, which encouraged reliance upon the availability of part-time soldiers to be ready to rally to the colors when the country needed them, stating "they are citizens most of the time, soldiers some of the time, patriots all of the time."

Born on a farm in Illinois, Drain was the epitome of a late-nineteenth-century "self-made man." He quit school at sixteen to work as a laborer in the railroad yards. He later worked in a bank, became an

accountant, and finally, a lawyer. He moved to Spokane, Washington, where he was admitted to the bar, and joined the National Guard.

In 1898 Drain organized a militia company at Spokane. The unit was not mobilized at the time of the Spanish-American War but the young company commander caught the eye of his superiors. In 1900 he lost his right arm in a hunting accident, but he continued to play a leading role in the state's marksmanship program. In 1908 he captained the United States Olympic rifle team. Still an excellent shot, he didn't actually shoot during the games but coached his men.

Drain rose to become adjutant general of Washington. He volunteered for active duty in World War I and was commissioned a major in Ordnance, becoming the first assigned ordnance officer of the 1st Division after wrangling his way out of a War Department staff post. He was pulled out of the 1st Division to assume important ordnance-related duties in the AEF during the war and had a great deal to do with the development of weaponry for tanks.

General James A. Drain was a man to remember for his wisdom and for his words. He was but one of the many thousands who came voluntarily from civilian life to be soldiers in their country's service.

The less-than-efficient mobilization for the Spanish-American War in 1898 made an indelible impression on many Americans. From its humblest citizens to those in power in the nation's capitol, it was clear that the

United States had been fortunate in its success after blithely plunging into a war in the Caribbean and Asia against a third-rate military power.

The nation was fortunate that in those early moments of the twentieth century a number of factors converged to initiate a great body of reform that would lead to the evolution of a modern defense system in the United States. Two important results of the reform were the emergence of the National Guard in its role as a key element of the nation's armed forces, and the creation of a federal military reserve.

A critical juncture came in 1901 as a new chief executive sat in the White House following the assassination of President William McKinley. Scarcely three years earlier, the relatively short "splendid little war" had been brought to its successful conclusion, but many of its citizen soldiers remained disgruntled. For his part, President Theodore Roosevelt was not pleased either. Roosevelt wrote to his close friend Henry Cabot Lodge regarding the National Guard: "They were really not very good soldiers and are sore and angry and mortified about the hardships they have encountered." When this was made public it did not endear "T. R." to his militia troops. The Guard's bad temper was also due to the fact that its regiments were not called up. Instead, members of its regiments were forced to join newly created "volunteer" regiments if they wanted to go to war. These regiments were given state designations but were classified as U.S. Volunteers.

A studio portrait typical of the 1870–1890 period shows an officer of the 71st New York Infantry of whom little else is known. The photograph is from a Gettysburg, Pennsylvania, studio, which suggests the officer was there to attend one of the post-Civil War reunion encampments. (Bruce Jacobs collection)

Above: During tense times in the emergence of the civil rights movement, Georgia National Guardsmen were called into state service to help protect marchers during protest demonstrations. (Army National Guard)

Above, right: Called upon by the governor to assist state authorities in maintaining law and order, Ohio National Guard members were "at the ready" outside the perimeter of the Southern Ohio Correctional Facility in Lucasville in April 1993. During the riot, guards found it necessary to move 400 inmates from a cellblock after eight had already been killed by other prisoners. (Army National Guard)

Troops moving around the city in military vehicles became a common sight on the streets of Miami, Florida, during riots in 1980. Up to 3,800 National Guardsmen provided support for the Miami Dade County police. (Army National Guard)

Against this background many angry words were uttered. But cooler heads prevailed and the National Guard, aided by a friendly secretary of war, Elihu Root, set about to deal with the problems that hampered the mobilization as well as the problems that had given rise to doubts about the ability of the Guard to produce effective units. In fact, it was but the continuation of an old fight. Since post-Civil War days the Guard had been seeking to replace the obsolete Militia Act of 1792.

In the wake of the strikes that swept over the nation in 1877 and in the enforcement of the laws in the occupied South, it had become necessary to deploy federal troops on a large scale. Members of Congress took the lead in declaiming opposition to having federal troops in the nation's streets. It passed the *posse comitatus* law, which forbade federal troops the jurisdiction of local law enforcement officials. In the future it would turn to the state militia, or as it was rapidly becoming known, the National Guard, for such duties.

The leadership of the Guard recognized that as noble as the purpose of *posse comitatus* might be, it was unlikely to work unless the militia was more closely aligned with the Army. It needed to meet the federal (Army) standards for training, method of organization, and, most importantly, to be equipped with weapons similar to those used by the Regular Army. A survey in the 1890s told the astonishing story that over fifty different models of shoulder weapons were used in the militia. To upgrade, the Guard would require far more than the $2 million annually provided by Congress.

By the waning years of the nineteenth century the advocate for the National Guard, the National Guard Association of the United States, had languished and idled into obscurity. General William B. Bend of Minnesota declared in 1892: "There is an association [NGAUS] which is conspicuous for what it doesn't do. We accomplished nothing about as thoroughly as anything you ever saw in your life." Not content, a number of the militia leaders took action. The call went out for a meeting of "persons interested in the National Guards of the United States." Ten states sent representatives to a meeting at the old Planters Hotel in St. Louis, Missouri, 7–8 December 1897. They founded a new entity known as The Interstate National Guard Association (ISNGA). Interest grew, and their second annual meeting attracted attendees from seventeen states.

Left: *The victory of the Americans under command of "Old Hickory," Major General Andrew Jackson, brought militia troops into close combat with crack British regulars. ("Battle of New Orleans," James Dietz)*

Above: *Portrait of Andrew Jackson, a militia hero of the War of 1812 and a future president of the United States. (Anne S. K. Brown Military Collection, Brown University Library)*

The old NGAUS had its final meeting in Tampa, Florida, in 1899 and named a commission to negotiate amalgamation with the upstart ISNGA organization. Their common purpose would be to obtain legislation to create an efficient militia and to replace the Militia Act of 1792. The leader in this effort was General Charles Dick of Ohio, a member of Congress who was also recognized as the titular head of the National Guard. Dick commanded a regiment in the Spanish-American War, and was rewarded with promotion to major general in command of the "Ohio Division" after the war. He was a powerfully connected Republican whose links to Mark Hanna and William McKinley endowed him with "insider" credentials of the highest order.

Wily Secretary of War Root had set about the creation of a militia committee in each house of Congress and he had a hand in getting Dick appointed as chairman of the House committee. The strategy was successful and after much time given over to research and legislative drafting in 1900 and 1901, followed by considerable internal debate in 1902, the ISNGA agreed upon a proposed bill that was delivered to Secretary Root and, with his blessing, to the Congress.

The bill was largely ignored, and there was little congressional debate on the legislation for many months. It took the combined efforts of Dick, President Roosevelt, and Secretary Root to energize passage of the "Dick Act" by Congress, but early in 1903 it became the law of the land. The act officially bestowed the name National Guard upon the old militia and provided federal support that would lead to the emergence of the "well-regulated" militia envisioned by George Washington and others in the infancy of the Republic.

The act also brought the National Guard family together. The old NGAUS was absorbed into the ISNGA and its members were welcomed by the leadership of the newer organization. By 1910, two years after the sec-

The streets of Boston in the War of 1812 were patrolled by volunteer militia whose uniforms were said to be patterned after those worn by Napolean's Régiment de Chasseurs à Cheval— Boston Hussars, Massachusetts Volunteer Militia, 1810–1817. (H. Charles McBarron, "Military Uniforms in America, Volume II: Years of Growth, 1796–1851," Presidio Press, 1977, by permission of the Company of Military Historians)

Top: *When Major General William Harrison engaged British troops 75 miles east of Detroit, his command included the colorful Regiment of Kentucky Mounted Riflemen. These select militia volunteers were picked for their prowess with long Kentucky rifles and tomahawks. Their successful battle at Moraviantown, Upper Canada, on 5 October 1813 was revenge for an earlier massacre of Kentucky militia on the River Raisin. ("Remember the River Raisin!" Kenneth Riley, National Guard Heritage series)*

Above: *Action in battle during the War of 1812. (H. Charles McBarron, Army Art Collection)*

ond Dick Act, all of the states were in the ISNGA fold. The following year the new organization formally adopted National Guard Association of the United States as its name.

After the 1903 Dick Act became law, Secretary Root spoke about the role of the militia under the Constitution and added, "I congratulate the National Guard upon being now, probably for the first time, unquestionably a constitutional force." He referred to the eighth section of the first article of the Constitution, which succinctly defines the federal authority by providing for "the authority of training the militia according to the discipline prescribed by Congress."

One of the consequences of the Dick Act was the requirement for the remaining states that still used a militia designation to be redesignated National Guard. The last state to comply was Virginia.

The National Guard and the nation now had its new militia law, one that recognized the status of the Guard and which provided a basis for a federal support under which the state military forces could improve combat efficiency. In addition, the groundwork was clearly established for the creation of a federal reserve force. The Guard wasted little time in developing close working relations with the Regular Army and it soon became a routine matter for the Guard to conduct its annual "summer camp" on Army installations where it could work closely with its Army counterparts.

At a meeting of militia officers in Buffalo, New York, in 1911, the members of the National Guard Field Artillery Committee presented a series of papers in support of a proposed bill to encourage adding more artillery batteries to the units of the Organized Militia. Clearly many of the states did not relish the fact that they might have to foot the bill for an increase in field artillery. One officer pointed out that even if the cost of equipment for a battery (estimated to be $80,000 per 3-inch gun battery) was fully funded by the federal government there would still be the cost of horses, maintenance, and caretakers.

This prompted the chairman to call upon Major John F. O'Ryan of New York, a very junior member of the Artillery Committee. "I wish he would tell us a little about how he handles his battery in New York City," said the chairman by way of introduction. O'Ryan, whose innovative notions were well known in his home state, explained that his battery had been expanded to three batteries and that with state assistance he employed twenty Guardsmen on a full-time basis. These were either ex-Field Artillery Regulars or men picked from his old battery. They were paid $21 a week. After daily drill from 7:30 to 9:00 each morning they took care of the horses, guns, gun carriages, and instruments.

O'Ryan went on to explain how he met the cost and upkeep of the horses by a program he confessed that he deeply deplored, but one on which he remained dependent. On Sundays the artillery horses were hired out to the public. "We hire them out at a dollar an hour. Depending upon the season and the weather this takes in about $400 a month." O'Ryan used this fund to purchase additional horses, and he noted that the program had started two years earlier with one $80 horse. He now had thirty-six horses and four mules, "all pretty good stock."

In 1913 the name of a most interesting student appeared on the roster of the new class enrolled in the U.S. Army War College, then located in Washington, D.C.—Major General John F. O'Ryan, now commanding general of the National Guard's New York Division. O'Ryan was the first National Guard officer to attend the War College. With special permission from President Woodrow Wilson he was admitted to the class of 1914. In 1916 O'Ryan led his command to the Mexican border; in 1918 he took it (redesignated the 27th Division) to France. He was, at forty-three, the youngest division commander in the American Expeditionary Force and

Top: *A prominent ceremonial unit in the early nineteenth century, the Governor's Guard Battalion included the Band, Governor's Guard Battalion, New York State Artillery, whose public appearances drew a good deal of attention. (H. Charles McBarron, "Military Uniforms in America, Volume II: Years of Growth, 1796–1851," Presidio Press, 1977, by permission of the Company of Military Historians)*

Above: *A onetime Maryland semi-pro baseball player who joined the National Guard as a youth, Milton A. Reckord rose to command the 115th Infantry (former 5th Maryland Regiment) in WWI. During the years between the world wars he served as adjutant general of Maryland and commander of the 29th Division. He helped draft legislation that gave the Guard dual state and federal status.*

Far left: *Major General John Francis O'Ryan was the first militia officer to attend the Army War College (class of 1914). He was the only National Guard officer to command a division in combat (27th Division) in World War I. He was prominent as the New York City police commissioner after the war. (Army War College, Carlisle Barracks, Pennsylvania)*

Left: *James C. Dozier from Rock Hill, South Carolina, earned a lieutenant's bar in WWI with the 30th Division and won the Medal of Honor. After the war, he served as the adjutant general of his home state and commanded the National Guard throughout his long and distinguished career until his retirement after WWII.*

Above: *Abraham Lincoln served as an infantry captain in the Illinois militia after a reappearance of Chief Black Hawk in April 1832 caused widespread panic and citizens demanded military intervention in the so-called Black Hawk War. (H. Charles McBarron, "Military Uniforms in America Volume II: Years of Growth, 1796–1851," Presidio Press, 1977, by permission of the Company of Military Historians)*

Above, right: *When Florida became part of the U.S., the forced removal of Seminole Indians was undertaken, but Indians who failed to move were soon confronted with militia called into federal service to assist the Regulars. Part of Georgia's commitment to the force was the Macon Volunteers, who served under General Winfield Scott in Citrus County, Florida, in April 1836. After several skirmishes on the edge of swamplands, the Georgians returned home, although the Seminole War continued for another six years. ("The Macon Volunteers," Jackson Walker, National Guard Heritage series)*

Above: *One of the "fathers" of the modern United States Army Reserve, Colonel Ralph Davenport Mershon, earned acclaim as an engineer, inventor, and professor at Ohio State University. Foreseeing the need for expansion of the Corps of Engineers in wartime, Mershon pushed to have civilian engineers commissioned as reserve officers prior to U.S. entry into WWI. He qualified for a commission and rose to colonel in the reserves. (Ohio State University Archives)*

was later recognized as one of the most successful commanders under Pershing. When he died in 1961, a New York newspaper noted in its obituary: "He revolutionized matters to such an extent that many old-line men protested, but he refused to deviate from his purpose—to create an efficient military organization."

In several of the early versions of the Dick Act, the Army included provisions that called for "a volunteer force of trained men [to] be ready for immediate service whenever called for." This was the first sign of the support that was building for a "federal militia"—an army reserve similar to the National Guard, but entirely separate from any state control.

The case for the appointment of specialists from civilian life as federally commissioned reserve officers ready to come on active duty when

needed began to gain impetus. One of the most influential men in promoting this cause was an unusual and brilliant professor at Ohio State University, Dr. Ralph Davenport Mershon. Mershon, who was a mechanical engineer and an inventor who held many important patents, was also on his way to becoming one of the richest men in Ohio.

In the drafting of the forthcoming national defense legislation he urged fellow engineers to join him to lobby the government for a place in the Army for "engineer reserves." Others made the case for "medical reserves." The War Department was not blind to the fact that in the event of a mobilization both specialties would be urgently needed. Mershon and his colleagues found many allies on Capitol Hill.

Mershon also pushed for the colleges and universities, even beyond the traditional land-grant colleges, to form student training organizations. He was, to a very great extent, the father of the legislation that produced the Reserve Officers Training Corps (ROTC). This action, which was taken before World War I, had an enormous impact upon the Army and its ability to mobilize leadership for World War II. Mershon himself was among the first to receive a commission in the engineer reserves and he served as a captain in World War I. He stayed active in the Army Reserve after the war and rose to the rank of colonel.

The National Defense Act of 1916 was a far-reaching and comprehensive statement that provided an increase in strength for the Regular Army, enlarged and validated the role of the National Guard, authorized a reserve force and a Volunteer Army. It provided for the establishment of ROTC as a means of providing officers for the newly created Reserve Officers' Corps. In the fall of 1916, ROTC units were formed at thirty-seven mostly land-grant colleges. An initial enrollment of 40,000 was reported.

The passage of the 1916 legislation virtually coincided with the events on the Mexican border that brought U.S. forces into conflict with

Columns of General William J. Worth's 1st Division pursued the retreating Mexican garrison of San Antonio toward Mexico City. Heavy fighting ensued when American troops reached the well-fortified Churubusco on 20 August 1847. Regulars deployed in the Mexican War were reinforced by 73,260 volunteers in 58 state regiments. ("Battle of Churubusco," Carl Nebel, Anne S.K. Brown Military Collection, Brown University Library)

On a hot summer morning the Union Army met Confederate forces in Northern Virginia. As a gap in the Confederate lines opened up it was defended by the Fourth Alabama, which stalled the Union attack and gave the Confederate forces the time needed to regroup and snatch victory from defeat in the Battle of First Manassas, 21 July 1861. ("The Fourth Alabama," National Guard Heritage series)

Opposite, bottom: The battle raged near Buena Vista, Mexico, on 23 February 1847. As the Mexican army made its attack, Colonel Jefferson Davis, in command of the Mississippi Rifles regiment, bellowed, "Stand Fast, Mississippians!" The regiment, ancestor of the modern day 155th Infantry, stood firm, then attacked with drawn Bowie knives. ("The Mississippi Rifles," Kenneth Riley, National Guard Heritage series)

Above: *A motorized "truck train" hauls troops of the 4th South Dakota Infantry on Mexican border patrol in 1916 following the raid by Pancho Villa's men at Columbus, New Mexico. Mexican border duty provided valuable training to mobilized National Guardsmen who would find themselves in France with the AEF the next year. (National Archives)*

Right: *In the closing days of the Civil War gunners from the famed Washington Artillery of Louisiana found themselves in action at Fort Gregg, Virginia, near the Appomattox River. The Union Army struck on 2 April 1865. A soldier storming the parapets warned an artilleryman not to pull the lanyard or he would fire. The tenacious response—a moment before the cannon roared—created a regimental legend. ("Shoot and Be Damned!" Keith Rocco, National Guard Heritage series)*

Above: *After starting his wartime service as a mobilized Missouri Guardsmen on a battalion staff, Captain Harry S Truman took command of Battery D, 129th Field Artillery, 35th Division, in combat in France. Much to the amazement of his fellow officers, Truman brought order and efficiency to a unit that had a reputation for boisterous and unruly conduct. ("Truman's Battery," National Guard Heritage series)*

Mexican rebels under the leadership of Pancho Villa. In 1916 most of the National Guard was mobilized for service under Brigadier General John J. Pershing on the Mexican border. The Guardsmen saw little action, but trained hard and gained invaluable experience for what was to come in 1917–1918.

Scarcely had the Guard units returned from the Mexican border when they were alerted to the call-up to serve with the expeditionary force that would soon be dispatched to France. The procedure took a good deal longer than expected. There was an acute shortage of training sites where divisions could be assembled, there was not nearly enough shipping available, and training areas had to be negotiated with the French for U.S. troops to continue and complete training in order to get ready to enter the trenches.

The National Guard's sixteen divisions were called up concurrently with the activation of the first increment of National Army divisions, eighteen in number with more on the drawing board that would never be needed. A seventeenth National Guard division, the 42d ("Rainbow") Division, was assembled with elements from twenty-six different states. Eight

Regular Army divisions would also compete for the assignment of officers to bring their units up to strength and then maintain the strength as casualties mounted. The officer corps of the AEF was built around the resources of the small Regular Army. In addition to the Regular officers, many NCOs earned commissions as officers. Beyond the officers in the small Regular Army and those brought into service with mobilized National Guard, many more would be needed. In all, 120,000 wartime officers would be commissioned, nearly all of them reserve or temporary officers.

After war was declared, the War Department suspended ROTC in favor of the Students' Army Training Corps (SATC). This provided training for enlisted men for special assignments but not necessarily for commissions. At its zenith there were 170,000 young men in the SATC. This program came to an end after the armistice and ROTC was soon resumed in the nation's colleges and universities.

Top, left: *The National Guard divisions and new divisions composed of draftees needed to be toughened up through training before they could be sent into the rigors of trench warfare in WWI. Obstacles courses were set up at training installations throughout the U.S. (National Archives)*

Top, right: *National Guardsmen on parade to attract new recruits needed to fill the ranks after the United States entered World War I in April 1917. The call-up of the Guard brought fourteen divisions into active service, but many more would be needed and soon the nation's male population would be subject to the first national "draft" in the country's history. (National Archives)*

Above: *Major General Donald W. McGowan of New Jersey was a career National Guardsman who served as a First Sergeant in France in WWI, commanded a field artillery regiment, and then led a mechanized cavalry group ashore at Omaha Beach. He later rose to two-star rank, commanded a National Guard armored division, and served in the Pentagon as Chief of the National Guard Bureau.*

Above, right: *Over 29,000 medical reserve officers served with units of the AEF in France, initiating a tradition that continues today. (Army Reserve Historical Painting)*

The Army quickly drew on the graduates of the prewar citizens training camps that had been established at the urging of ex-President Theodore Roosevelt and Major General Leonard Wood, a former Army Chief of Staff. These camps provided a cadre of officers for quickly formed wartime divisions put together for service in France.

Soon after the U.S. entered the war in April 1917, officer training schools were set up at a number of locations around the country, and General Pershing eventually formed an officer candidate school in France to facilitate the flow of officer replacements into the AEF. The seeds were thus sown for the training, and retaining, of men who had proven themselves in wartime. This would mark the emergence of the Organized Reserve Corps, which in time would become the United States Army Reserve.

The vast majority of junior and middle grade officers for the wartime Army came from civilian life—the National Guard, the training camps and schools, and the ranks of the AEF. This would be the first time since the Civil War that non-Regular officers would predominate the officer corps. Many of these junior and even youthful field grade officers would be men who would in time rise to prominence.

Harry Truman, National Guard artilleryman from Missouri, gave up a job on the battalion staff and took command of the most cantankerous

battery in the old 1st Missouri Artillery (now the 129th Field Artillery in the 35th Division). He commanded the battery throughout the campaigns in France. He would never shake the soubriquet "Captain Harry," even after he rose to full colonel in the reserves. He continued to be known as Captain Harry to the old timers of Battery D, even after he became President and Commander in Chief.

Harry's cousin and friendly rival for family military honors, Ralph Truman, commanded a rifle company in the 140th Infantry Regiment of the same division and was designated his regiment's intelligence officer. He had become close friends with Major Edward Beau, a French officer assigned to the regiment as an interpreter. Frequently Ralph, accompanied by Beau and his scouts, moved out ahead of the regiment looking for Germans and gun emplacements and trying to find the best routes for the troops to advance.

On one of these scouting trips he entered the little town of Corbie, France, and was walking down the main street of the town when the Germans fired one of their "Big Berthas" right into the middle of the town. It hit a pool hall and one of the cue balls came rolling down the street and stopped right in front of Ralph. He picked the cue ball up, put it in his knapsack, carried it with him the rest of the war, and then brought it home with him. When his youngest son was born in 1923 he named him Corbie after this little town. Corbie used the cue ball to cut his teeth, and he kept it all his life. Harry would be a U.S. Senator when Ralph, as a major general, brought the 35th Division back into federal service when it was called up in December 1940.

Julius Ochs Adler was a graduate of the Plattsburg training camp program. He would go on to command a company in the 77th Division in the AEF. While rising to prominence with *The New York Times,* he stayed active in the Reserves, helped train Citizen Military Training Camp (CMTC) cadets, and was a full colonel in 1940. He was quickly assigned to command a regiment and was soon a brigadier general assigned as an assistant division commander with a division in the Pacific theater.

Top, left: *Near Neufchateau, France, in January 1918, officers of 26th (Yankee) Division led a movement of troops in preparation for taking over a sector of the front lines. The 26th won the race with the 42d (Rainbow) Division in the competition to be the first National Guard division to reach France. (National Archives)*

Above: *A soldier of the 15th New York Infantry in World War I with full field equipment. After reaching France the regiment, assigned to combat under French command, received War Department orders redesignating it the 369th U.S. Infantry Regiment. ("Full Study of Corporal, 15th N.Y. Infantry," Raymond Desvarraus, Army Art Collection)*

Below: *In the 1920s and 1930s the Kansas National Guard fielded two all American Indian units composed of students from the Haskell Indian Institute. The three Indian troopers here belonged to Troop C (later Troop I), 114th Cavalry Regiment. Many of the Haskell cavalrymen were converted to field artillery when the unit was mobilized for WWII. (Kansas Historical Society)*

Top: *Near Binarville, France, on 6 October 1918, French soldiers found the site of a crash that claimed the lives of Army aviators searching for the "Lost Battalion" of the 77th Division. The pilot, Lieutenant Harold Goettler, had been an all-American basketball player at the University of Illinois before he entered officer's training. ("The Highest Possible Courage," John D. Shaw, National Guard Heritage series)*

Above: *Prior to WWII the National Guard's eighteen aviation units were organized as elements of infantry divisions allocated to the individual states. The 103d Observation Squadron, equipped with North American O-47 aircraft, took part in 1937 maneuvers with its parent 28th (Keystone) Division. (National Archives)*

Butler B. Miltonberger had enlisted as a private for Mexican border service with the 1st Nebraska, and by the time he got to France, he was a first sergeant in the 4th Division during the war. Back in civilian life he rejoined the Guard and was commissioned from the ranks as a first lieutenant in 1923. This was the first step in his climb toward regimental command, and by the brink of World War II, he had earned command of the 134th Infantry Regiment in the 35th Division. He was one of the rare wartime colonels (non-Regular) to be promoted to brigadier general on the field of battle. After World War II he would be hand-picked by President Harry Truman to lead the postwar reorganization of the National Guard.

Miller G. White was the sergeant major of a machine gun battalion. He returned home to Macon, Georgia, after his Army assignment, joined the local police force and was appointed a captain in the Georgia National Guard. In 1931 he was promoted to major. He graduated from the 1934 National Guard officers class at the Command and Staff School and was urged to put in for one of the prized General Staff tours available to exceptional non-Regular officers. During his peacetime tour of duty in the War Department, he caught the eye of General George C. Marshall. When war came—White was by then back with his 30th Division unit in Georgia—Marshall brought him back to Washington, and within a few months, he was the Army's G-1, responsible for all personnel matters for the wartime Army. He would remain at Marshall's side until he successfully lobbied for an overseas assignment in the last months of the war.

Hanford MacNider, a lawyer from Iowa, fought in the campaigns of the 2d Division in France. He was also a member of the select group of AEF officers—Theodore Roosevelt, Jr., among them—who founded the American Legion at a soldiers' caucus in Paris in 1919. A classic citizen soldier reservist in the interwar years, MacNider also attained prominence as an assistant secretary of war (1925–1928). In early 1942, he took command of the 158th Regimental Combat Team from Arizona. As a brigadier general he led the 158th RCT in a series of Pacific campaigns.

Theodore Roosevelt, Jr., a reserve officer, earned the Distinguished Service Cross and rose to the command of a battalion in the 1st (Big Red One) Division in World War I. He returned to his old outfit when the U.S. began preparing for World War II. He was assistant division commander when the 1st Infantry Division fought in North Africa and Sicily. He later served with the 4th Infantry Division. and was slated for a second star when he suffered a heart attack on 12 July 1944, nearly six weeks after taking part in the D-Day operations on the Normandy coast. He was posthumously awarded the Medal of Honor.

Milton Atchison Reckord of Maryland commanded the 175th Infantry and served in a brigade under the renowned John MacAuley Palmer. Palmer was a Regular Army officer who would be called upon by Generals Pershing and later Marshall to author plans for inclusion of the National Guard and Reserve in the Army's mobilization. Reckord, one of the future "rocks" of the National Guard hierarchy, would bring his beloved 29th

Above: *Destined to attain the highest rank of any citizen-soldier in WWII, then Major General Raymond S. McLain (left) confers with General Dwight D. Eisenhower, after his XIX Corps seized Julich, Germany. By war's end the former Oklahoma banker and 45th Infantry Division Artillery commander would be wearing the three stars of a lieutenant general. In postwar years he would serve as the first Army comptroller. (U.S. Army/TimePix)*

The trooper is a member of the 102d Cavalry Regiment, the Essex Troop of New Jersey. The 102d would be mustered into service as a horse regiment in February 1941, but it was a mechanized cavalry group when it landed at Omaha Beach on D-plus-1 in June 1944. (Harry C. Larter, Company of Military Historians)

Division to active duty in 1941 and would later serve as the provost marshal general in the ETO.

An exuberant and youthful first sergeant in MacAuley Palmer's brigade was a New Jersey National Guardsman, Donald Wilson McGowan. McGowan would return from France with an appointment to West Point. After one year he left the USMA and returned to the Guard, where he joined the horse-drawn field artillery. Transferred to fill a vacancy, he took command of the 102d (Essex Troop) Cavalry, which he led ashore at Omaha Beach on D-plus-1. After World War II he reached two-star rank and served as Chief of the National Guard Bureau, the last Guard chief who was also a veteran of World War I.

The post-World-War-I Army was provided with an infusion of experienced officers as a substantial number of men mobilized with the Guard, or who earned wartime reserve commissions, opted to remain in the Army and make it a career. The World War I generation of battle-hardened sergeants and wartime officers from the battlefields of France would provide a cornerstone around which the officer corps of the future would be built as the U.S. had to create the largest army in its history.

For the first time in its existence the Army offered reserve commissions to wartime officers with the stipulation that these would have to be renewed every five years. Additionally, changes to the law in 1932 provided for National Guard officers appointed by their respective governors to be granted "federal recognition," which was tantamount to saying they were concurrently federal "reserve" officers while maintaining their assignments in their state's National Guard.

In the years following World War I, the Army maintained its hold on the wartime officers by appropriating funds for occasional tours of active duty, for extension courses to help them qualify for advancement, and for

opportunities to serve short tours of duty with active Army units. This pool of reserve officers would grow to a significant force with the entry of new officers from ROTC and with the advent, starting in 1921, of the CMTC, which also offered opportunities for high-quality and dedicated young men to earn reserve commissions. The Army goal of keeping its reserve officers "connected" was given substantial help by the advent soon after World War I of the Reserve Officers Association (ROA). Among the World War I officers who stayed active in the Reserve and helped to make ROA a powerful spokesman for the reservists was Harry Truman, who rose to the rank of colonel in the field artillery reserve. He offered to leave the Senate to go back on active duty in 1941, but General George C. Marshall declined the offer and said the Army needed him in the Senate.

The result of this was that when war clouds loomed for the U.S. in 1940–1941, the Army was able to start drawing upon this pool of commissioned officers as it grew in size. The demand for junior officers in particular was almost insatiable.

Top: *For many, the return to the Philippines and the liberation of Manila was a mission of the highest importance in restoring confidence in America. Following the 9 January 1945 landings at Lingayen Gulf, U.S. divisions turned toward Manila. The Japanese defenders fought with great tenacity, but by 4 February troops of the 37th (Ohio) Infantry Division entered the ravaged city. ("Manila Would Do," Keith Rocco, National Guard Heritage series)*

Above: *As mobilized units of the National Guard and Army Reserve received orders for duty in the Korean War, they provided essential reinforcement for the Army. Photo shows Arkansas 937th Field Artillery Battalion in action. Equipped with its versatile 155mm M40 guns, it would soon light up the Korean night when the "Long Toms" pounded enemy positions. (U.S. Army Military History Institute)*

By June 1941 approximately 118,000 ROTC graduates had been commissioned, not counting some 7,000 who had used Army ROTC to obtain commissions in the Regular Army, National Guard, and Marine Corps. For example, General David Shoup, a Marine Corps recipient of the Medal of Honor at Tarawa in World War II, entered the Marines from Army ROTC.

The Guard and Reserve provided the nation with an extraordinary source of leadership manpower. Starting in the earliest days of the build-up, 50,000 reserve officers were quickly called to active duty. It would not take long before another 68,000 were added to the rolls. When the Guard was mobilized, with its eighteen infantry divisions and hundreds of nondivisional units, it brought 6,000 federally recognized officers to active duty. In addition, nearly 80,000 mobilized National Guard enlisted men earned commissions after entering active duty.

In the critical weeks and months of 1940–1941, before the U.S. actually entered the war, the mobilized National Guard and the influx of reserve officers provided a platform on which the Army would be able to build an officer corps for what would become the largest army in U.S. history. Without them it is likely that even with the forthcoming induction of millions of drafted men, the nation's ability to undertake a response to the events of Pearl Harbor would have been seriously hampered.

Three in particular who illustrate the quality of the wartime leadership that the mobilization brought to the active duty Army are worthy of closer examination: Raymond S. McLain, a banker from Oklahoma; James Earl Rudder, a college football coach from Texas; and Robert S. Beightler, a

state highway engineer from Ohio. Their accomplishments are worthy of attention not only for the rank and fame they would attain, but for the kind of men they were and how their leadership would impact on others.

More than 100,000 college graduates earned reserve commissions via ROTC between the wars, among them Jim Rudder from Eden, Texas. Rudder graduated from Texas A&M in 1932 as a second lieutenant in the infantry. He soon became a teacher and football coach at Brady High School in Brady, Texas. By 1938 he had moved along to the head coach's job at Tarleton Agricultural College, where he had spent two undergraduate years in 1928–1929. He and his wife Margaret started their family and would eventually raise five children.

He was called to active duty in 1941 and was a captain stationed at Fort Sam Houston, Texas, when the U.S. found itself at war on 7 December. By the spring of 1943, and by then a major, he was at Camp Forrest, Tennessee, with a challenging assignment—orders to form the 2d Ranger Battalion. The 1st Ranger Battalion was already in action under the famed William O. (Bill) Darby.

The exploits of Darby's Rangers in North Africa had attracted volunteers for the new battalion. Rudder's most serious personnel task was to weed out the misfits, those who were too old and those who could not reach the tough physical standards required of Rangers. The training program occupied the 2d Rangers through the remainder of 1943 and into early 1944. Having reached England in December 1943, Lieutenant Colonel Rudder soon learned of the mission his Rangers would be assigned in the invasion. In preparation for the storming of Pointe du Hoc on D-Day, Rudder worked the Rangers hard, concentrating on cliff climbing, weapons training, night land navigation, and physical endurance. He ignored the staff officers who looked at the maps and reconnaissance photos of Pointe du Hoc and concluded, "It can't be done."

Rudder and his Rangers did it on 6 June 1944. The battalion took heavy casualties and Rudder himself was wounded twice during the assault, but the Rangers seized this critical objective at the far west end of Omaha Beach. Rudder lobbied vociferously following Pointe du Hoc to keep his lightly armed battalion from being given conventional infantry assignments, but he was consistently overruled. The 2d Rangers fought on as ordered, frequently being outgunned but never outfought.

Above, left: A pre-patrol briefing is held before moving out on a mission on 21 June 1952, in the sector manned by the 160th Infantry, 40th Infantry Division. The 40th, originally from the California National Guard, entered combat in Korea early in 1952.

Above: It didn't take long after reaching South Korea for Puerto Rico's 65th Infantry Regiment to reach the battlefront. During its service in Korea, the regiment, composed of soldiers from Puerto Rico, earned four Distinguished Service Crosses and 125 Silver Stars. In post-Korea years, the 65th was absorbed into the Puerto Rico National Guard. ("The Borinqueneers," J. Andrea, National Guard Heritage series)

An inspirational leader even before he was called to active duty as a reserve officer, Lieutenant Colonel James E. Rudder, a future major general, led the 2d Ranger Battalion at Pointe du Hoc, Normandy, on 6 June 1944. Not long after he was promoted to colonel and placed in command of one of the infantry regiments of the 28th Infantry Division. (Cushing Memorial Library, Texas A&M University)

Top, left: *A Sherman M4 tank, 179th Infantry, 45th Infantry Division, fires its 76mm gun on an enemy bunker, west of Chorwon, Korea, on 2 January 1952. The Oklahoma Thunderbird division had a defensive mission in Hokkaido, Northern Japan, before being moved to Korea in December 1951, to relieve the 1st Cavalry Division.*

Top, right: *The only National Guard officer to retain division command throughout WWII, Major General Robert S. Beightler directs a 37th Infantry Division tank-infantry attack on Bougainville on 17 March 1944. A civil engineer for the State of Ohio prior to mobilization, Beightler took command of the Buckeye 37th Infantry Division on 12 October 1940, and led it through training and Pacific combat. His National Guard service started in 1911 and included WWI combat. (National Archives)*

When Rudder was promoted to colonel he left his beloved Rangers to take command of the 109th Infantry Regiment, 28th Infantry Division. He joined his new outfit in time to lead it in the Battle of the Bulge. By the end of the war, he was one of the best-known as well as most decorated officers in the Army. Rudder would not only go on to a distinguished career in civilian life leading to his appointment as president of Texas A&M, but he would also attain the rank of major general in the U.S. Army Reserve, in command of the 90th Infantry Division. In 1967 President Lyndon B. Johnson called him to Washington for yet another medal for distinguished service to the nation. His name would go into the history books as a great American soldier and a great citizen.

Robert S. "Bob" Beightler, born in Marysville, Ohio, in 1892, was a classic citizen soldier who joined the Ohio National Guard somewhat inadvertently, but he stayed with it for a career. He was probably the only division commander in World War II who organized his division, trained it, took it overseas, and led it in combat. He was also the only National Guard officer to retain command of his division throughout the war.

Beightler was a crack marksman. In his youth he accompanied the National Guard unit in his hometown to Camp Perry, Ohio, for marksmanship competition, and did remarkably well. In fact, he did too well. He came to the attention of the range officer, who recognized that Beightler was there under false pretenses, using the name of a fellow Ohio State student, John Paul Sellers, who was unable to make the trip. The C.O. kept a straight face and told Beightler he could enlist officially or "face the music."

Right: *An 81mm mortar platoon, 180th Infantry Regiment, 45th Infantry Division, prepares for a fire mission 4 January 1952. (National Archives)*

Far right: *A Guardsman who earned a battlefield promotion to one-star rank, Colonel Butler B. Miltonberger from North Platte, Nebraska, led the 134th Infantry Regiment, 35th Infantry Division, in liberation of St.-Lô, France, in July 1944. He was promoted to major general in 1946 and served as the first post-WWII chief of the National Guard Bureau at the Pentagon. Miltonberger worked for the state highway department prior to mobilization for WWII. (Nebraska National Guard)*

318

Beightler, in 1911, signed the enlistment papers to become a private in Company E, 4th Ohio Infantry.

In 1914 he was elected, as was the practice for many years in the Guard, to be a second lieutenant. During his service on the Mexican border in 1916, the Army selected him to attend a Regular Army training course at Fort Bliss, Texas. He was offered a commission in the Regulars and given orders to Fort Thomas, Kentucky. But he thought it over and decided to stay with his Guard outfit, soon to be designated the 166th U.S. Infantry and deployed to France as part of famed 42d Division.

Beightler returned from France a captain and was soon working for the State Highway Department as an engineer. Later he would strike out on his own. But he was also deeply committed to his military service and he jumped at the opportunity to take a six-month active duty tour with the War Plans Division of the War Department as "an additional member of the War Department General Staff." The six months turned into four years.

Beightler was determined to improve his military skills. He graduated at the top his class in the 1926 National Guard Officers' Course at Command and General Staff School at Fort Leavenworth. He graduated from the Army G-2 Course given by the Army War College, and his active duty in the War Plans Division from 1932–1936, working on plans for a proposed interstate highway system, provided him with exposure not readily available to most officers from the reserve components.

He returned to Ohio in 1937 and was soon in command of the 74th Infantry Brigade. In 1940 Governor John Bricker named him to command the all-Ohio 37th Infantry Division, and he retained this command until after V-J Day, when the division was returned to state control after forty-three months in the Pacific. Beightler was asked to stay on duty, and he served in the Regular Army until his retirement in 1953.

Raymond Stallings (Ray) McLain was an Oklahoma City banker when he was mobilized in the fall of 1940 with the 45th (Thunderbird) Infantry Division. He was then a one-star in command of the division artillery. An Army inspector reported to his boss that McLain should be wearing two

Above: Alongside a Korean mountainside, a hot meal is served to infantrymen of the Thunderbird Division holding a position. Within a few hours, they would be fighting to maintain it.

With Fort McCoy, Wisconsin, an important Army Reserve training site, as its background, a tribute to the many unsung heroes of the Army Chaplains Corps. ("The Chaplain," Peter G. Varisano, Army Art Collection)

Top and opposite, top left: *The National Guard and Army Reserve have made important contributions to the Army's ability to carry out its peacekeeping responsibilities in places like Bosnia. For Bosnia missions, Guardsmen and Reservists have been called upon for far more than the traditional two weeks, frequently for six months at a time or more. (Army National Guard)*

Above: *During its tour of duty in Vietnam, the 3d Battalion, 197th Field Artillery, New Hampshire National Guard, operated a medical assistance program for Vietnamese in villages in the battalion's operations area. In one stretch, three Army doctors treated 465 villagers in seven hours, assisted by battalion personnel. Here Specialist Fourth Class David L. Burditt tends an apprehensive young patient. (Bruce Jacobs collection)*

stars and he should be commanding the division. But McLain had no ambition to be promoted over the heads of his contemporaries and he preferred to wait his turn.

As an artillery commander in the Sicily and Italian campaigns he was frequently to be found in the front lines, satisfying himself that his artillery was providing support to the infantry. His frequent and dangerous forays were the cause of great dismay to many, including his jeep driver. McLain was moved to the 30th Infantry Division during the early days of the campaign in France but was there only a brief time when the Army again turned to him to take over a command in need of help. The 90th Infantry Division had faltered after taking part in the D-Day landing at Utah Beach. Its commander was relieved and General Eisenhower initially considered disbanding it. Instead, he decided to turn the division over to McLain. It wasn't too long before the ETO high command was boasting about how well the 90th was doing.

McLain would relish the story of the events that ensued in the winter of 1944 as the campaign in France progressed. Ordered to his corps commander's command post, the corps commander told him, "You will be relieved tonight by General Van Fleet. He will take over the command immediately." That seemed little sense to him. McLain knew that Patton, Bradley, Eisenhower, and others had given him credit for improving the 90th Infantry Division after Normandy. Then the corps commander grinned at him and said, "They're going to give you a corps!" McLain soon learned he would command the XIX Corps in Patton's Third Army. He would now lead a force of 90,000 men in the drive into Germany. He was still a major general and would command three division commanders, all senior to him in two-star rank. The Army later would promote him to lieu-

tenant general in June 1945, making him the only officer of National Guard origins to reach three-star rank in wartime. He stayed on in the Army for a number of years to lend his expertise to the creation of the newly created position of Comptroller of the Army. For the soldier whose military career started when he joined the Oklahoma National Guard as an infantry private in 1912, Ray McLain had come a long way.

McLain, Rudder, and Beightler are the validation of how America raises, leads, and commands an army of citizen soldiers. Their stories attest to something innate in the American character. It speaks for the way this nation goes to war and how, at its best, the system allows its citizens to share in the heavy burdens and responsibilities of leadership, which, in other countries, are reserved largely for a much narrower segment of its society. Only in America.

Above: Keeping the peace. A Guardsman on the street is a familiar sight when civil authorities need reinforcement during troubled times. In the latter part of the last century Guardsmen came on duty to enforce law and order in cities including Los Angeles, Detroit, Newark, Chicago, Cleveland, Washington, D.C., and Miami. This is regarded by men and women of the Guard as "tough duty" that goes with the territory. (Army National Guard)

Below: In its state support mission, the National Guard is always ready to answer a governor's call when help is needed as natural disasters strike. Most frequently the call for help goes out when winter and spring floods inundate surrounding countryside. (Army National Guard)

America's Army Tomorrow

America's Army Tomorrow
Technology to Win the Land Battles of the Future

Lieutenant Colonel Clayton R. Newell, USA (Ret)

merica has the finest army in the world. It has faithfully served
the nation for more than 225 years, and it is working hard today to
meet the challenges of tomorrow. Since the end of the Cold War in
1989, the world has changed dramatically, but America's Army has
successfully accomplished every mission that it has been assigned. Armed
with a decade's experience of adapting to change, the Army is poised to
transform itself into a force that will remain on point for the nation as it
moves into the twenty-first century.

Since the end of the Cold War, the Army has become extraordinarily
adept at coping with uncertainty. After forty years of preparing to face a
well-defined enemy, the Soviet army, and the Warsaw Pact, America's
Army saw the world turned upside down during the 1990s. The war
in the Persian Gulf saw the advent of astonishing new techniques and
systems, a hint of the technology to come in the twenty-first century.

Technology has always had an influence on warfare, but today the
rate of change is faster than at any time in history. As a result, the distinc-
tions between the tactical, operational, and strategic levels of war are
rapidly fading. The tactical level of war was once the almost exclusive
domain of the soldier who wages battles to attain specific objectives such
as capturing a piece of ground or destroying an enemy force. At the

Above: *The modern Army and its objectives
demand a sophisticated set of skills from
its soldiers—both on and off the battlefield.
(U.S. Army)*

Opposite: *An updated depiction of an old
classic—the Centennial of Armor—captures
the spirit and essence of the evolution of
battlefield mobility, from the cavalry of
yesterday, through the appearance of
primitive tanks on the WWI battlefield,
to the appearance of armor as "an arm of
decision" in WWII, and continuing to today.
("Spearhead," Jody Harmon, U.S. Armor
Association)*

Pages 322–323: *The view through new Army
night vision equipment offers an eerie view of
troops crawling across open ground under the
cover of darkness during an attack exercise
at the Army's basic training site at Fort
Jackson, South Carolina, in May 2001. But
the night is no longer an ally, since the advent
of night-vision technology in the Vietnam
War and its coming-of-age in Desert Storm.
(Greg Mathieson/MAI)*

Top: *The Global Command and Control System-Army (GCCS-A) provides an integral element of the Army's new digital information system. The GCCS-A provides readiness, planning, mobilization, and deployment capability information for commanders with theater and strategic responsibilities. There is no known foreign counterpart to GCCS-A. (U.S. Army)*

Above: *An artist's conceptual sketch of a future armored combat system. In this particular configuration, which the Army has under study, wheels replace tank treads and the armament consists of a missile launcher rather than a conventional tank gun. (U.S. Army)*

Right: *The Advanced Field Artillery Tactical Data System (AFATDS) will provide an automated command, control, and communications system for fire support. It will enable the commander to plan and execute attacks on the appropriate target, at the correct time, with the best weapon system, and with the employment of the most appropriate munitions. (U.S. Army)*

operational level, senior military commanders plan and execute campaigns consisting of a series of battles that culminate in a strategic goal. The strategic level coordinates the military and political objectives of war. Within the Army, the command structure paralleled the three levels of war. Units from squad to corps level focused on the tactical level, headquarters above the corps were concerned with the operational level, and the highest levels of national command addressed questions of strategy.

The levels of command were separated doctrinally and, until recently, the limits of technology contributed to that separation. Radios and other means of communications operated within narrow communications bands. In World War II, for example, artillery and infantry radios operated on different frequencies. Command radio nets only communicated one or two echelons up or down the chain of command. The system was partly a legacy of the past and partly a limitation of technology. For centuries the only means of communications on the battlefield was word of mouth or handwritten notes. At the lowest tactical levels, flags and sound signals such as drums or bugles passed instructions to soldiers. With the introduction of the telegraph, the telephone, and the radio, communications became faster and wider, but the organization remained the same. Plans and orders passed from one level to the next, with each layer making modifications as necessary. But the changing nature of war now demands a new vision for the Army.

Above: Deployed signal units can use the Integrated System Control (ISYSCON) as a centralized network that provides an automated, theater-wide network. This enables such signal units to efficiently manage multiple tactical communication systems and networks in support of battlefield operations. As shown, the system can be made mobile. (U.S. Army)

The Army Vision

The Army's vision of the future includes a lighter, more lethal force less dependent on the massive logistics needed for Desert Storm. During Operation Desert Shield, the buildup of forces for the Persian Gulf War,

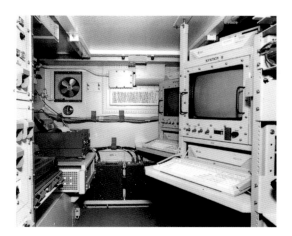

Bottom, left: During an intensive field training exercise in California, a soldier of the 4th Infantry Division fights his war at a work station of the new Army digital command and control system. The 4th Division, with many years of history as a traditional infantry command, is currently the Army's prototype unit for conversion to a digitized force and is playing an important role in the Army transformation initiatives. (U.S. Army)

Bottom, right: An interior view of the high mobility vehicle shown in the photograph above. It contains four high-tech work stations to be manned by soldiers assigned to operate ISYSCON, which is expected to increase the ability of the signal command to sustain tactical communications networks. (U.S. Army)

Above: *The Army Tactical Missile System (ATACMS) consists of ground-launched missile systems featuring surface-to-surface guided missiles that can hurl an anti-personnel/ anti-materiel (APAM) warhead deep into an enemy's territory. The ATACMS with APAM can strike at soft targets at extended ranges, providing surface-to-surface fire support under almost all weather conditions. (U.S. Army)*

Top, right: *The Line-of-Sight Anti-Tank (LOSAT) weapon system provides accurate missile fire against heavy armor and field fortifications at ranges exceeding current tank main gun range. This is expected to result in significant casualty reductions for light infantry when opposing heavy armor. The LOSAT can be deployed by helicopter sling load or by C-130 air drop. (U.S. Army)*

Right: *The RAH-66 Comanche is the Army's next generation helicopter, designed to expand the Army's ability to conduct reconnaissance and attack operations in all battlefield environments, day or night, and in adverse weather conditions. Eventually the Comanche will replace three current types of helicopters in the Army Aviation fleet—AH-1, OH-58, and OH-6—that now perform armed reconnaissance missions. (U.S. Army)*

the Army moved two light and three heavy divisions, along with various support elements, to Saudi Arabia. Tomorrow's Army will be able to deploy rapidly from multiple locations around the world, reacting quickly to emerging crises. It will have the versatility to sustain fast-paced operations, defeat an opponent with minimum losses, and quickly reposition and prepare for the next mission. It will be able to deploy one brigade within ninety-six hours, one division within 120 hours, and five divisions within thirty days from the United States to anywhere in the world.

The first step toward that objective is developing combat-ready, air-transportable brigade combat teams equipped with medium-armored vehicles known as MAVs. The MAV will be significantly smaller than an Abrams tank and transportable in a C-130 aircraft, making the brigade capable of rapid deployment to remote areas. The MAV will move rapidly with a sustained speed of 40 miles an hour with a cruising range of 300 miles. Variations will include an infantry carrier, a mobile gun system with a direct fire capability, and a 155mm self-propelled howitzer for indirect fire support. While new vehicles and weapons will give tomorrow's Army greater lethality and mobility, success on the battlefield will depend, as it always has, on individual soldiers.

Above: *An artist's concept of the Medium Extended Air Defense System (MEADS). This is a response to the need to provide air and missile defense to land forces. It offers a 360-degree defense against surface-to-surface missiles as well as rotary and fixed-wing aircraft. It will be able to ensure a seamless interface with the next generation of battle-field management systems. (U.S. Army)*

Left: *Designated as the Army's IAV, this is expected to become the basic battle resource of the future Brigade Combat Team (BCT). With its Mobile Gun System it will enable the BCT to carry out a broad range of combat missions, and it will be deliverable to the scene of battle by C-130 aircraft if needed. ("Flashpoint," Jody Harmon, U.S. Armor Association)*

Tomorrow's Soldier

On future battlefields the infantryman will be equipped with the new Land Warrior System (LWS), an integrated and imaginative combination of five high-tech subsystems: an individual weapon, an integrated helmet assembly, protective clothing and individual equipment, a computer and radio, and software.

The weapon is a modular carbine that includes electrical optical components to provide accurate targeting information. It includes a thermal sight, a multifunctional laser sight, and a daylight video sight, allowing infantrymen to operate in all types of weather and at night.

The integrated helmet assembly provides ballistic protection at less weight than the current helmet. A helmet-mounted computer and sensor display connects the soldier to the other LWS subsystems and many sources of information. Through the helmet-mounted display, the soldier views computer-generated data, digital maps, intelligence information, troop locations, and imagery from his weapon-mounted thermal sight and video camera.

The LWS protective clothing and individual equipment consists of a backpack frame design based on automotive racing technology that bends with the soldier's natural body movements. The cables for the computer and radio connections are integrated into the frame. The lightweight body armor, like the helmet, provides improved ballistic protection at a reduced weight. The modular body armor can stop small-arms rounds fired at point-blank range.

Top, left: *Tomorrow's soldier will be armed with the Objective Individual Combat weapon (OICW), which is destined to replace both the M16 rifle and M4 carbine as the infantryman's individual weapon. Through the use of high explosive airburst ammunition the OICW will dramatically increase lethality, range, and capability of the infantryman and double his stand-off range to 1,000 meters. (U.S. Army)*

Top, center and top, right: *The Land Warrior System (LWS) is an integrated fighting system for infantry soldiers that incorporates an assortment of technologies to improve a soldiers ability to perform effectively, and survive, on the battlefield. It will also heighten the effectiveness of training exercises in the soldier's ongoing task of preparation for battle. The LWS here is being used by members of the 82d Airborne Division. (U.S. Army)*

Left: *The Objective Crew Served Weapon (OCSW) ATD will provide a new and highly lethal heavy machine gun capability to the Army's fighting units. It is under development as a lightweight, two-man portable, crew-served weapon. The OCSW will defeat armor-protected enemy personnel at a maximum range of 2 kilometers. (U.S. Army)*

The LWS computer contains a radio and a Global Positioning System (GPS) locator. The unit leaders' version has two radios and a flat panel display and keyboard. A hand grip wired to the pack and attached to the soldier's chest acts as a computer mouse and allows him to select screens, change radio frequencies, and transmit digital information. The weapon-mounted camera, for example, can be used to send video images to squad or platoon leaders. The LWS software includes tactical and mission support

331

The Lightweight Laser Designator Rangefinder (LLDR) is a portable, target location and designation system. LLDR is designed to provide Army and Marine Corps forward observers with the capability to detect, recognize, locate, and designate targets at a range of 5 kilometers. It weighs less than thirty-five pounds and is easily transported by a two-person team. (U.S. Army)

information, maps and tactical overlays, and the capability to record and display video images. The software allows the soldier to tailor the display, menus, and functional operation to mission needs and personal preferences. When combined with the training, dedication, and ingenuity of the American soldier, the Land Warrior System brings a formidable capability to the battlefield of the twenty-first century.

Digitizing the Army

In Operation Desert Storm, the U.S. Army clearly demonstrated that it was the most flexible and powerful land force in the world. But the ten years that followed the Persian Gulf War brought widespread reductions for the Army. But, as it began to do more with less, the Army took full advantage

of the latest technological advances for fighting and winning the land battles in order to meet its many and varied post-Cold War challenges.

The Army identified digitization, defined as "taking advantage of revolutions in electronics and information technologies to make dramatic gains in all battlefield operating systems," as a key element of its modernization effort. The Army began to develop the concept in 1992 with the modern Louisiana Maneuvers, "a laboratory to practice roles and missions, to develop and explore options, and assess and direct progress." By 1994, the Army Digitization Office was formed and had assumed the task of digitizing the Army.

Above: *The Guardrail/Common Sensor (GR/CS) is a fixed-wing airborne signals intelligence (SIGINT) RC-12 aircraft designed to provide signal intercept and accurate location of enemy electronic emitters. A standard system consists of six to twelve of the aircraft flying operational missions in sets of two to three. The aircraft are expected to operate at corps level, using the fixed-wing aircraft to enable precision target locations. (U.S. Army)*

Right: *The Tactical Unmanned Aerial Vehicle (TUAV) is intended for use in areas where real-time information is needed, but where manned aircraft are unavailable or the risk is too great to use piloted aircraft. The TUAV provides reconnaissance, surveillance, and target acquisition at a range of 50 kilometers, day or night, with an extended range of 200 kilometers now being planned. (U.S. Army)*

Opposite, top: *The Joint Land Attack Cruise Missile Defense Elevated Netted Sensor System (JLENS) provides the Army with over-the-horizon cruise missile defense and detection. The JLENS also extends the ranges of missile fire support. Components include surveillance radar as well as precision track and illumination radar (PTIR). (U.S. Army)*

The Army now has multiple initiatives underway to harness the power of the microprocessor and information technology. Digital technology will be used to acquire, exchange, and employ timely information throughout the battle space to provide a common operating picture of friendly and enemy forces to commanders at all levels. The objective is seamless digital command and control throughout the fighting force.

Command and Control

During the Gulf war the Army fielded the most technologically advanced land forces the world had ever seen. But with all the high-tech gear it deployed to the desert, the Army planned and conducted the land campaign pretty much the way it had in World War II. In 1991, as in World War II, it was difficult for a single command post, or CP, to develop an accurate, real time picture of the battlefield, much less for multiple CPs to share a common operating picture.

In contrast to those in the Gulf war, the Army's twenty-first-century command posts will look more like mobile television production studios. Walls of video screens will display a variety of real and near real time information. The multiple screens will be able to show live video from unmanned aerial vehicles; enemy movements being tracked by the Joint Surveillance Target Attack System, which detects both moving and fixed

targets on the ground; and maps showing friendly locations down to individual vehicles. There will even be a CNN news feed. The Army's future command posts will be able to share this information and maintain a common operating picture of the battlefield by way of the tactical internet, an innovative network of digital computers and communications.

Above: *The M120/M121 120mm mortar system is a conventional mortar system enhanced with the Mortar Fire Control System (MFCS). The MFCS integrates a fire control computer with an inertial navigation and pointing system that enables mortar crews to fire in less than one minute, instead of the current eight-to-ten minute standard. (U.S. Army)*

Left: *The Crusader 15mm self-propelled howitzer is the cornerstone of modernizing fire support systems. The Crusader will increase field artillery survivability, lethality, and mobility. Its reduced weight and smaller size mean that two howitzers are transportable in the C-17 aircraft. (U.S. Army)*

Infantry units need to be able to call on a weapon capable of knocking out armored vehicles at extended ranges. This is the mission for the TOW (tube-launched, optically tracked, wire-guided) missile. The battalion-level Improved Target Acquisition System (ITAS) guided missile system is regarded as the successor to the current TOW 2. (U.S. Army)

Modernization of the Stinger, a fire-and-forget infrared/ultraviolet (IR/UV) missile system, is critical to future Army operations. As the principal air defense weapon in the forward area, the Stinger has been developed into a short-range air defense system for brigade, division, and corps area combat units to meet the threat of cruise missiles and low-flying aircraft. (U.S. Army)

The Tactical Internet

Integrating command and control systems requires a horizontally and vertically integrated digital information network with reliable, seamless, and secure communications. This integrated tactical internet will provide a common operating picture of the battlefield to all commanders. At brigade and below, the tactical internet will extend the Army's command and control systems to individual soldier, vehicles, and weapons platforms. It will provide tactical, mobile, simultaneous multi-band, multi-mode, voice, data, and video communications as well as routing and network services to the soldiers and commanders using the system.

One of the first systems to use the tactical internet is the Army's Force XXI Battle Command Brigade and Below initiative known as FBCB2. It uses computer systems mounted on weapons platforms and vehicles at brigade and lower echelons that integrate hardware, installation kits, software, logistics support, and training packages. In 2000 the Army fielded prototypes of the FBCB2 systems in the Balkans, where the system provides patrols and their headquarters with a real time common operating picture of the area. The Balkan system uses computers installed on armored Humvees, with a satellite transponder that receives and reports information. The system software places the vehicle and other friendly vehicles on the same electronic map display. To overcome the communications problems posed by the difficult Balkan terrain, the system uses

Top, left: The soldier on the ground will utilize new technology like the Target Location and Observation System (TLOS) to enable him to obtain direct view and electro-optic targets. The TLOS is a lightweight, image-intensified day/night weapon sight that employs a near-infrared low-energy laser. (U.S. Army)

Top, right: Useful to soldiers in a broad spectrum of missions, the night vision goggle (AN/PVS-7D) is based upon a proven design. It is, however, lighter in weight and is expected to enable troops to operate more efficiently under difficult battlefield conditions. (U.S. Army)

Above: The aviator's night vision imaging system (ANVIS/HUD) provides image intensification for helicopter crews in the conduct of night missions under minimal ambient light conditions. It is powered by aircraft power or a helmet-mounted battery pack. (U.S. Army)

Top, left: *The Striker, affixed to the M1025A2 Humvee, locates and designates targets for laser-guided ordnance. In addition, it provides surveillance and fire support mission execution in heavy and light divisions. It is designed to operate as an integral part of the combat brigade reconnaissance team and can move on the road at 55 m.p.h. (U.S. Army)*

Top, right: *To have the ability to conduct deep precision strikes, or to provide armed reconnaissance and security day or night, the Apache Longbow developmental helicopter is expected to add important capabilities to the Army Aviation fleet. With a maximum speed of 167 m.p.h. and coordinated rapid-fire capability, it can service sixteen targets within one minute. (U.S. Army)*

Above and right: *An entire eleven-man, fully equipped infantry squad can be carried in a single Black Hawk (UH-60) helicopter for transport to landing zones faster than ever before. Model shown at right is configured for the aero medical evacuation mission. The Black Hawk replaces the ubiquitous UH-1 Huey. (U.S. Army)*

space-based communications to send signals via satellite to an earth station in Germany that relays data back to Bosnia.

By fielding and using its emerging digital capabilities in an operational environment today, the Army is gaining invaluable experience and information for tomorrow's battles. But, unlike yesterday's Cold War environment, it is not at all clear when or where tomorrow's battles will be fought. The tactics, doctrine, organization, and equipment of tomorrow's hostile forces are uncertain, making it imperative for the Army to quickly deploy tactical forces ready to fight with the most current intelligence, logistics, fire support, and air defense status and capabilities.

The Future is Now

Digital command and control systems are in use now, and the future promises a much more comprehensive capability. The Army is developing digitized systems that will integrate information in five different functional areas: fire support, intelligence, air defense, combined arms maneuver, and logistics and personnel support.

Above: *Army mobility is dramatically enhanced with the Black Hawk in the rotary wing inventory. With a range of 320 nautical miles, it can manage an external load of 8,000–9,000 pounds. Its airframe is designed to progressively crush on impact to protect the crew and passengers. In a single lift the L model can reposition a 105mm howitzer, its crew of six, and thirty rounds of ammunition. (U.S. Army)*

Left: *Named for one of the great armor commanders of WWII, the Abrams tank has become the primary weapon in the armor arsenal. The modernization strategy standardizes the Abrams (M1A2 SEP) with its 120mm main gun, special armor, and a 1,500 horsepower turbine engine capable of speeds of 42 m.p.h. Improvements include technology changes that permit use of Army common command and control software to enable rapid transfer of digital situational data and overlays. (U.S. Army)*

Omar N. Bradley was regarded as "the infantryman's general" in WWII, and it is fitting that the Army's premier armored personnel vehicle bears his name. The Bradleys, in slightly differing configurations, are infantry and cavalry fighting vehicles with digital command and control capabilities. Two forward-looking infrared and commanders independent sight, combined with the 25mm cannon and TOW missile system, provide its "hunter-killer" capability. (U.S. Army)

Top, left: *The OH-58 Kiowa Warrior is the Army's rapidly deployable, lightly armed reconnaissance helicopter. The Kiowa includes advanced visionics, navigation, communications, weapons, and cockpit integration systems, and is fully operational within minutes of deployment. The armament systems combine to provide anti-armor, anti-personnel, and anti-aircraft capabilities at standoff ranges. (U.S. Army)*

Top, right: *The AN/PRD-13(v) two man-pack signal intelligence system brings network systems to the field with ground personnel. (U.S. Army)*

Below *While new technologies continue to increase the capabilities and the efficiency of the modern Army, intelligent, well-trained, physically fit men and women provide the foundation on which the future Army will be built. Here, new recruits receive traditional introduction to Army life during basic training at Fort Jackson, South Carolina. (Greg Mathieson/MAI)*

The advanced field artillery tactical data system, known as AFATDS, processes fire mission and other related information to coordinate fire support weapons with air support and naval gunfire, providing an appropriate mix of firing platforms and munitions to defeat enemy targets. The all source analysis system, or ASAS, gathers, correlates, and processes large amounts of intelligence data, permitting the intelligence community to process and fuse hundreds of reports an hour. This system provides a clearer, more accurate, up-to-date view of the enemy. Commanders from corps through brigade receive intelligence support from ASAS. The forward area air defense system is designed to counter the low-altitude air threat over and beyond a division's area of operations. It will alert air defense artillery and protected units, cue fire units, and exchange air defense command information.

The maneuver control system, or MCS, distributes tactical information on friendly and enemy forces in both text and graphic formats using data obtained from other command and control systems. Commanders can transmit critical mission information, courses of action, schemes of

maneuver, warning and operations orders, and changes in priorities. MCS will exchange information between command posts from battalion through corps to give commanders a common operating picture for making decisions. The combat service support control system consolidates and collates the vast quantities of data for logistics and personnel support, providing tactical commanders timely, critical information on ammunition, supplies, personnel, transportation, maintenance, and other field services.

These five functional systems will be linked together through the Army tactical command and control system. This digital integration will provide a horizontal and vertical digital information network to support the Army's war-fighting systems. By networking sensors, command posts, processors, and weapons, commanders at each level of command will see a simultaneous, common picture of the battlefield, fostering a better understanding of what both friendly and enemy forces are doing on the battlefield.

Tomorrow's Doctrine

The AirLand Battle doctrine developed by the Army in the late 1970s was a major factor in the Army's success in the Persian Gulf War. New technologies offer an opportunity for a new doctrine that will exploit every possible advantage on future battlefields. Traditional doctrine for ground combat is to make physical contact with the enemy, to develop

In the Army of the future—even on the high-tech battlefield—some things are unlikely to change. There will be moments when the lives of individual infantrymen and the success of their missions will be determined by their proficiency in time-tested combat skills. This will continue to require learning the skills that a soldier starts to acquire during basic training. (Greg Mathieson/MAI)

Soldiers train to be prepared for action in circumstances that are unpredictable. Reminiscent of scenes in Saudi Arabia when troops "suited up" when Scud attacks were launched by Iraq during the Gulf war, recruits in basic training experience the rigors of chemical/biological (CB) weapons training. (Greg Mathieson/MAI)

Above: Army units train for a wide variety of possible battlefields in future conflicts, from low-intensity and anti-terrorist scenarios to all-out major conflicts. They may encounter extremes ranging from desert to arctic conditions. The 10th Mountain Division, which has deployed elements to such diverse hot spots as Somalia and Haiti, undergoes winter training at its Fort Drum home in northern New York. (Greg Mathieson/ MAI)

Right: Space Shuttle Columbia *launches from John F. Kennedy Space Center on 12 April 1981. Going back to the pioneering work by the Army team led by Werner Von Braun at Missile Command in Huntsville, Alabama, the Army has played a significant role in the development of propulsion technology. ("Launch of Space Shuttle* Columbia," *Mort Künstler)*

the situation to ascertain enemy strength and capabilities, and finally maneuver to close with and destroy the enemy. With the common operating picture offered by a fully digitized fighting force, tomorrow's Army will be able to develop the situation before making physical contact with the enemy. With complete knowledge of the size, location, and capabilities of the enemy force facing them, and the ability to share that knowledge with virtually every soldier in the force, commanders will be able to maneuver into advantageous positions that will make the initial contact with the enemy lethal and decisive.

Such a future doctrine will require almost flawless communications, navigation, and timing; access to real time information about weather, terrain, and the environment; and accurate intelligence and missile warning. That kind of detailed and timely information depends on space-based systems, and tomorrow's Army must be able to use space capabilities and technologies effectively.

The Army in Space

The Army activated the 1st Space Battalion in December 1999. Located at Peterson Air Force Base, Colorado, the battalion will help institutionalize the Army's use of space and enable the Army to field its fighting force of the future. Mobile technology teams will keep up with rapidly advancing space technologies and ensure those capabilities and products are readily available to the rest of the Army.

The Army's use of space is not new. It used space capabilities to great advantage in the Persian Gulf War. The Global Positioning System, for example, provided real time, accurate ground locations to forces moving across the desert. That capability has been integrated into the Army's digital command and control systems. Systems under development that promise to be of great value to the Army include a more effective distribution of intelligence and weather information to commanders on the battlefield. The tactical exploitation system allows forces on the ground to receive intelligence information from space-based sources through laptop computers, eliminating the need for large vans and other

An Army astronaut proudly shows his colors. Colonel William S. (Bill) McArthur, Jr., a North Carolina native, was ranked fourth in the West Point graduating class of 1973. He went from Armor to Army Aviation before joining NASA in 1987. He was designated an astronaut in 1990 and flew on space shuttle missions in 1993 and 1995. In this photograph he is shown, amid mementos of his West Point days, on board the Space Shuttle Discovery. He has twice been awarded the NASA Space Flight Medal. (National Aeronautics and Space Administration)

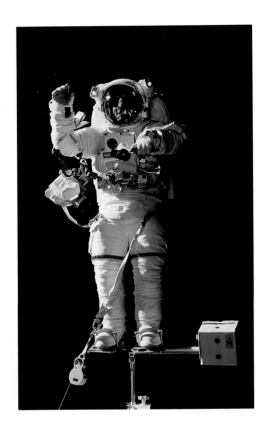

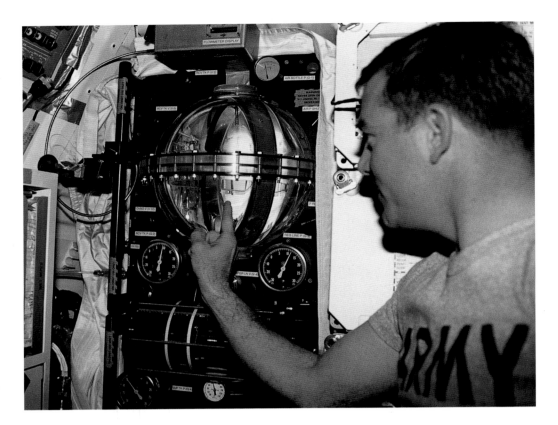

Above: *Bill McArthur, an Army astronaut since 1990, takes a space walk during one of several space shuttle missions since his assignment to NASA. (National Aeronautics and Space Administration)*

Top, right: *Astronaut James S. Voss, mission specialist, monitors flight equipment onboard Space Shuttle* Discovery *in December 1992. Voss's working clothes include an Army T-shirt. (National Aeronautics and Space Administration)*

Below: *Army Astronaut Nancy J. Currie is pictured on Space Shuttle* Discovery's *flight deck during a July 1995 mission. (National Aeronautics and Space Administration)*

equipment. The integrated meteorological system will provide digital overlays of weather information integrated into the common operating picture shared by all commanders.

Tomorrow's Total Army

America's Army includes the active duty forces, the U.S. Army Reserve, and the Army National Guard, all working together as a Total Army team. In Vietnam the nation mobilized only a fraction of the Army's reserve components from the Guard and Reserve. Since then, more effectively than ever before, the Army has integrated the National Guard and Army Reserve with the active force in a Total Force policy. Desert Storm, in contrast to Vietnam, was a Total Force effort. Of the 306,730 American soldiers deployed to the Persian Gulf during the war some 78,000 were reservists and guardsmen. A total of more than 1,040 Reserve and National Guard units with more than 140,000 personnel mobilized to support the Army's deployment effort during the war.

Four years later, during the Army's deployment of forces to the Balkans in 1995, for example, almost 12,000 Army Reserve and Army National Guard soldiers were mobilized to support the operation. Since then Army National Guard division headquarters have mobilized, deployed to the Balkans, and commanded operations there. America's twenty-first-century Total Army will continue to take advantage of the capabilities provided by the reserve components as they all continue to serve the nation.

The Army of the twenty-first century will be responsive to crises all over the globe; it will be capable of deploying forces rapidly; it will be able to sustain itself with a manageable logistical tail; it will have flexible forces that can be quickly tailored to meet specific threats; and it will continue to

Top, left and top, right: *An Army non-commissioned officer, Sergeant Joe Patterson, at the Soldier Systems Center, Natick, Massachusetts, wears the Army's Future Warrior mock-up uniform. At left he hefts model of a pod system weapon that weighs five pounds. This "under-development" advanced infantry system features a uniform that changes color, and head protection that incorporates a zoom lens built into the visor. (U.S. Army Soldier Systems Center)*

be the most deadly ground force in the world. To do all this, the Army will take advantage of everything technology can offer. But it takes more than technology. Competent, dedicated, disciplined soldiers who understand the value of teamwork and believe in the equipment are the key to the success of tomorrow's Army. For over two centuries, America's soldiers have been on point for the nation, and they will be there tomorrow, leading the way into the future.

Below: *The soldiers of America's Army of Tomorrow will wear battle gear that is a far cry from today's—or yesterday's—"GI issue." The soldier of the future will be proficient with an array of individual and crew-served weaponry. But in personal and traditional terms, the "Future Warrior" will bring the same values to the Army that have marked those who have manned the ramparts since the infancy of the republic. (Army Reserve Historical series)*

Suggested Reading

The Army Historical Foundation Website at **www.armyhistoryfnd.org** provides information on recent publications as well as links to U.S. Army sites such as the U.S. Army Center of Military History, which provides a list of its official histories, monographs, and miscellaneous publications.

The Army Chief of Staff has published a reading list that addresses Army Heritage and Military History. It includes books that go beyond the Army story, but it is nearly perfect as a suggested list for the general reader. Those who seek a general history of the Army to supplement the essays in this volume might consult Russell F. Weigley, History of the United States Army. Bloomington: Indiana University, 1984.

The Chief of Staff of the Army's Recommended Reading List

ARMY HERITAGE AND MILITARY HISTORY
(FOR CADETS, SOLDIERS, AND JUNIOR NCOS)

Stephen E. Ambrose. *Band of Brothers: E Company, 506th Regiment, 101st Airborne from Normandy to Hitler's Eagle's Nest.* New York: Simon and Schuster, 1992.

Rick Atkinson. *The Long Gray Line.* New York: Owl Books, 1999.

Tom Brokaw. *The Greatest Generation.* New York: Random House, 1998.

T.R. Fehrenbach. *This Kind of War: A Study in Unpreparedness.* New York: Brassey's, 1994.

Charles E. Heller and William A Stofft, editors. *America's First Battles: 1776-1965.* Lawrence: University Press of Kansas, 1986.

David W. Hogan, Jr. *225 Years of Service: The U.S. Army, 1775-2000.* Washington, D.C.: CMH, 2000.

John Keegan, *The Face of Battle.* New York: Vintage Books, 1977.

Harold G. Moore and Joseph L. Galloway, *We Were Soldiers Once, and Young.* New York: Random House, 1992.

Anton Myrer. *Once an Eagle.* Carlisle Barracks: USAWC Foundation Press, 1995.

Michael Shaara, *The Killer Angels,* New York, Ballantine Books, 1974.

(FOR COMPANY GRADE OFFICERS, WO-CW3 AND COMPANY CADRE NCOS)

Stephen Ambrose. *Citizen Soldiers.* New York: Simon and Schuster, 1997.

Edward M. Coffman. *The War to End All Wars: The American Military Experience in World War I.* New York: Oxford University Press, 1968.

Samuel P. Huntington. *Soldier and the State.* Cambridge: Belknap Press of Harvard University, 1957.

Gerald F. Linderman. *Embattled courage: The Experience of Combat in the American Civil War.* New York: The Free Press, 1987.

Charles. B. McDonald. *Company Commander.* Springfield, NJ: Burford Books, 1999.

S.L.A. Marshall. *Men Against Fire: The Problem of Battle Command in Future War.* Gloucester, MA: Peter Smith, 1978.

Alan R. Millett and Peter Maslowski. *For the Common Defense: A Military History of the United States.* New York: The Free Press, 1984.

Robert H. Scales, Jr. *Certain Victory.* Ft. Leavenworth: USACGSC Press, 1994.

Mark A. Stoler. *George Marshall: Soldier-Statesman of the American Century.* Boston: Twayne Publishers, 1989.

Tom Willard. Buffalo Soldiers (Black Saber Chronicles). Forge Press, 1996.

(FOR FIELD GRADE OFFICERS, CW-4-CW-5, AND SENIOR NCOS)

Roy E. Appleman. *East of Chosin: Entrapment and Breakout in Korea, 1950.* College Station: Texas A&M Press, 1987.

Graham A. Cosmas. *An Army for Empire: The United States Army and the Spanish American War.* Second Edition. Shippensburg, PA: White Mane Press, 1994.

Robert A. Doughty. *The Evolution of U.S. Army Tactical Doctrine, 1946-1976.* Ft. Leavenworth: Combat Studies Institute, 1979.

Antoine Henri Jomini. *Jomini and His Summary of the Art of War.* Harrisburg: Stackpole Publishers, 1965.

Charles B. MacDonald and Sidney Matthews. *Three Battles: Arnaville, Altuzzo and Schmidt.* Washington, D.C.: Center of Military History, 1991.

James M. McPherson. *Battle Cry of Freedom: The Civil War Era.* New York: Oxford, 1988.

Roger H. Nye. *The Challenge of Command.* Wayne, NJ: Avery Publishing Group, 1986.

Dave R. Palmer. *Summons of the Trumpet: U.S.-Vietnam in Perspective.* San Rafael, CA: Presidio, 1978.

Martin Van Creveld. *Supplying War: Logistics from Wallenstein to Patton.* New York: Cambridge University Press, 1977.

Russell F. Weigley. *The American Way of War: A History of U.S. Military Strategy and Policy.* Bloomington: Indiana University Press, 1977.

(FOR SENIOR LEADERS ABOVE BRIGADE)

Carl von Clausewitz. *On War.* Princeton: Princeton University Press, 1984.

Kent Roberts Greenfield, editor. *Command Decisions.* Washington, D.C.: Center of Military History, 1960.

Michael Howard. *War in European History.* Oxford: Oxford University Press, 1976.

Paul Kennedy. *The Rise and Fall of the Great Powers.* New York: Random House, 1987.

Henry Kissinger. *Diplomacy.* New York: Simon and Schuster, 1994.

Williamson Murray and Alan R. Millett, editors. *Military Innovation in the Interwar Period.* New York: Cambridge University Press, 1996.

Richard E. Neustadt and Ernest R. May. *Thinking in Time.* New York: The Free Press, 1986.

Peter Paret, editor. *Makers of Modern Strategy from Machiavelli to the Nuclear Age.* Princeton: Princeton University Press, 1986.

William B. Skelton. *An American Profession of Arms: The Army Officer Corps, 1784-1861.* Lawrence: University Press of Kansas, 1992.

Harry Summers. *On Strategy.* Novato, CA: Presidio Press, 1982.

Thicydides. *The Peloponnesian War.* Baltimore: Penguin Books, 1972.

Editors and Authors

EDITOR
BRIGADIER GENERAL HAROLD W. NELSON (USA RET.)
(This We'll Defend, The U.S. Army and the Building of the Nation)
was commissioned in the Army in June 1963 upon graduation from the U.S. Military Academy. He retired in 1995 after 32 years in uniform, including combat in Vietnam and service in Korea, Germany, and Belgium. He taught history at the Military Academy, the Command and General Staff College, and the Army War College. He served as the Army's Chief of Military History for five years. He helped establish the Army Historical Foundation as its president, 1995-2001. He has written or contributed to numerous books, published many articles and reviews, and lectured and conducted battlefield staff rides around the world.

MANAGING EDITOR
MAJOR GENERAL BRUCE JACOBS (AUS RET)
(Brotherhood of the Brave, Patriots All of the Time)
was commissioned in the Army Reserve following enlisted service in WWII. He was detailed as a combat historian in the Marianas, Iwo Jima and Okinawa. He transferred to the Army National Guard in 1957. He served with U.S. Army Vietnam, 1968-69 and after a detail to the White House, 1970, was appointed Chief of Public Affairs, National Guard Bureau, 1971-1974. He was Secretary of the Army Reserve Forces Policy Committee, 1975-1979. He joined the staff of the National Guard Association of the U.S. in 1979 and was Chief Historian when he retired in 1995. He is the author of books and articles on military topics. He earned an M.A. in diplomatic history at Georgetown University. He became an adviser to the Army Historical Foundation in 1983, joined the Board of Governors in 1995 and has served two terms as Secretary.

GRAPHICS EDITOR
COLONEL RAYMOND K. BLUHM, JR. (USA, RET)
(Selected Milestones in the History of America's Army)
received his Army commission from the University of Illinois ROTC Program in July 1963. After thirty years of service as an Infantry officer, he retired in October 1993. His varied service included two tours in Korea, eighteen months in combat in Vietnam, two tours in Europe, senior positions on both the Army and Secretary of Defense staffs, and Defense and Army Attaché to Belgium. His final position was as a division chief with the Center of Military History. He has led battlefield tours in Europe, co-authored a book on the Army and contributed to several historical articles and reviews. After retirement he served six years as the first Executive Director of the Army Historical Foundation (1994-2000), and continues today as an officer of the foundation.

AUTHORS
COMMAND SERGEANT MAJOR SCOTT GARRETT (USAR)
(Top Soldiers)
He enlisted in the U.S. Army Reserve in 1978. Serving primarily in Armor, he held every enlisted leadership position from squad leader through battalion CSM, and was awarded the Soldier's Medal.

Garrett is a 1995 graduate of the Sergeants Major Academy and has a Ph.D. in history. He is Associate Professor of History at Paducah Community College in Kentucky; a director of the Institute of Military Heraldry in Scottsdale, Arizona; and currently assigned to the U.S. Army Center of Military History, Fort McNair, DC.

COLONEL COLE C. KINGSEED (USA RET)
(Army Blues to Olive Drab)
was commissioned in the Army in April 1971 upon graduation from the University of Dayton ROTC Program. He earned his MA and Ph.D. from Ohio State University and is a graduate of the U.S. Naval War College. After thirty years of service as an Infantry officer, he retired in May 2001. His varied service included tours in Hawaii, Fort Riley, the Pentagon, and the U.S. Military Academy at West Point. His final position was Chief of Military History, Department of History, West Point. He has written or contributed to numerous books, published thirty seven articles on combat leadership, written one hundred seventy-five book reviews and lectured and conducted battlefield staff rides in Normandy and American Civil War sites. After retirement from the Army, he is currently a consultant, specializing in leadership and military professionalism. He is the author of "Eisenhower and the Suez Crisis of 1956".

LIEUTENANT COLONEL CLAYTON R. NEWELL (USA RET)
(America's Army Tomorrow)
retired in 1992 after 27 years of active duty which included tours in Germany and Vietnam. While on the faculty of the Army War College he held the John J. Pershing Chair of Military Planning and Operations. He frequently contributes to the analysis of Army operations in the Balkans, is a research fellow of the Institute for Land Warfare, and has served on the Army Historical Foundation board of directors since 1994. His books include *Lee vs. McClellan: The First Campaign* (Regnery, 1996), a History Book Club selection, and *The Historical Dictionary of the Persian Gulf War* (Scarecrow Press, 1999). He has written articles for the *Encyclopedia of the American Military* (Charles Scribner's Sons, 1994), *The D-Day Encyclopedia* (Simon and Schuster, 1994), the *Reference Guide to the United States Military* (Facts on File, 1995), and numerous professional journals.

SAMUEL J. NEWLAND, PH.D. (COLONEL, ARNG, RET)
(Legends)
has taught history on virtually every educational level since his graduation from college and holds Doctorate in European history from the University of Kansas. He began his military career with attendance in the Kansas OCS and was commissioned in the Kansas National Guard in 1980. He retired From the Pennsylvania Army National Guard in 2000, with over twenty years service in both the Kansas and Pennsylvania Army National Guards and on active duty. During his military career he commanded two Military History Detachments and was Assistant G-2 of the 28th Infantry Division (M). Dr. Newland first served the active duty army as an analyst at the Army's Strategic Studies Institute and since 1989 has been a faculty member at the U.S. Army War College. He is currently Professor of Military Education at the Army War College and holds the Henry L. Stimson Chair of Military

Studies. He has written numerous books, monographs and articles on German and U.S. Military history and is a staff ride Guide for the War College. His published works include "Cossacks in the German Army" , "The Pennsylvania Militia: The Early Years")

GENERAL ERIC K. SHINSEKI
(No Substitute for Victory)
became Chief of Staff of the Army in 1999 after serving as the Army's vice chief of staff and commanding general, U.S. Army Europe and Seventh Army. General Shinseki graduated from the Military Academy in 1965. He served two combat tours in Vietnam and held numerous staff and command positions in the United States and Germany, including command of the First Cavalry Division. He earned a Master's Degree at Duke University and taught at the Military Academy. His military education includes the Army Command and General Staff College and the National War College.

DR. LEWIS SORLEY
(Khaki to Army Green)
graduated from the U.S. Military Academy in June 1956 and was commissioned in Armor. His Army service included leadership of tank and armored cavalry units in Germany, Vietnam and the United States, as well as staff positions in the offices of the Secretary of Defense and the Army Chief of Staff. He also served on the faculties at West Point and the Army War College. Following retirement from the Army he was a senior civilian official of the Central Intelligence Agency. He holds a Ph.D. degree from the Johns Hopkins University and is the author of four books on military history, biography, and international affairs; is a Director of the Army Historical Foundation; and is Executive Director of the Association of Military Colleges and Schools of the United States.

GENERAL GORDON R. SULLIVAN
(Where Soldier Leadership Begins)
is the president of the Association of the United States Army. He retired as the Chief of Staff of the Army in 1995. He was commissioned upon graduation from Norwich University in 1959. He served two combat tours in Vietnam and held numerous staff and command positions in the United States and Germany, including command of the First Infantry Division. He earned a Master's Degree at the University of New Hampshire. His military education includes the Army Command and General Staff College and the Army War College. Upon his retirement from the Army he published, Hope is Not a Method: What Business Leaders can Learn From America's Army. He has contributed to several other books and has published numerous journal articles.

Acknowledgments

The editors are grateful for assistance provided by many organizations, agencies, universities, museums, and individuals both in and outside the United States Army community. The generous access to the Army Center of Military History in Washington, D.C., has been of utmost importance, especially the availability of wise advice and counsel provided by the curators of the Army Art Collection. The support of the Association of the United States Army (AUSA) has been of substantial significance. The staff of the Army Historical Foundation provided invaluable backup and administrative support. Among the agencies of the Army that have provided valuable contributions to this effort are the History Office, National Guard Bureau; the Historian, United States Army Reserve; Soldiers Magazine (U.S. Army); West Point Library, United States Military Academy; and the Military History Institute at the Army War College, Carlisle Barracks, Pennsylvania. Acknowledgment must be made of the resources of the National Archives, and the many unnamed Army, Navy, and Marine Corps photographers whose efforts remain for posterity in the National Archives holdings.

Among the many individuals who have been especially helpful, Brigadier General Creighton Abrams, Jr., USA, Ret., Mr. Matthew Seelinger (AHF), Mr. Kevin Hymel (AUSA), Renée Klish (CMH), and Debby Zindell and Charles Schoenfeld at Levin Associates; artists Al Alexander, James Dietz, Dale Gallon, Jody Harmon, Mort Künstler, Jeanine Mosher, Rick Reeves, Jim Ryan, Don Stivers, Steve Smith, and Don Troiani.

Also Lenore Bane, Curt Biderdorf, Walter Bradford, Adrian Combs, Sandra Daugherty, Deborah Dawson, Jana Drvota, George Ehling, LT Jason Edwards, MSG Troy Fadardeau, MSG Robert Haskell, Vincent Hawkins, Lori Johnston, LTC Robert Jones, Paul Kotakis, John Lapman, Thomas Mani, Robert Melhorn, Greg Mathieson, Captain Les' Melnyk, Ned Reader, MAJ Scott Ross, James O'Donnell, Vivian Oerth, GEN Colin Powell, MAJ Herbert Ramsey, David Reel, Janet Riggs, Maggie Reynolds, GEN Norman Schwartzkopf, Albert Shwartz, Chester Simpson, CSM Jimmie Spencer, Kelly Spinks, James Stratford, John Sterne, Bob Stevenson, David Sullivan of the Company of Military Historians, Sarah Underhill, Donald Vogus, Courtney Welton, and Janet Wray.

Index